W9-CTW-482

SOMETHING ABOUT THE AUTHOR

AUTOBIOGRAPHY SERIES

ISSN 0885-6842

SOMETHING ABOUT THE AUTHOR

AUTOBIOGRAPHY SERIES

Gerard J. Senick
Editor

VOLUME **22**

GALE

STAFF

Gerard J. Senick, *Editor*

Linda R. Andres, Motoko Fujishiro Huthwaite, Thomas F. McMahon, and Diane Telgen, *Associate Editors*
Marilyn O'Connell Allen, Joanna Brod, and Sheryl Ciccarelli, *Assistant Editors*
Heidi J. Hagen, Carolyn C. March, Cynthia M. Pease, and Lori J. Sawicki, *Contributing Copyeditors*

Victoria B. Cariappa, *Research Manager*

Hal May, *Publisher*
Joyce Nakamura, *Managing Editor, Children's and Young Adult Authors and Their Works*

Mary Beth Trimper, *Production Director*
Deborah Milliken, *Production Assistant*

Barbara J. Yarrow, *Graphic Services Manager*
C. J. Jonik, *Desktop Publisher*
Randy A. Bassett, *Imaging Supervisor*
Robert Duncan, *Imaging Specialist*

Theresa Rocklin, *Manager, Technical Support Services*

Gale Research
835 Penobscot Building
645 Griswold Street
Detroit, MI 48226-4094

Library of Congress Catalog Card Number 86-641293
ISBN 0-8103-9332-8
ISSN 0885-6842

Printed in the United States of America

10   9   8   7   6   5   4   3   2   1

Contents

Preface

A Unique Collection of Essays

Each volume in the *Something about the Author Autobiography Series* (*SAAS*) presents an original collection of autobiographical essays written especially for the series by prominent authors and illustrators of books for children and young adults.

SAAS is designed as a place where young readers, students of children's and YA literature, teachers, librarians, and parents can meet their favorite authors and illustrators "in person" and make the first acquaintance of many others. In *SAAS*, readers can find the answers to an endless list of questions about these creative individuals: What people and events influenced their early lives? How did they begin their careers? What prompted them to write or illustrate particular books? What advice would they give to aspiring writers and illustrators? And so much more.

SAAS provides an opportunity for writers and artists who may never write a full-length autobiography to let their readers know how they see themselves and their work, what brought them to this time and place, and what they envision for the future. Individually, the essays in this series can enhance the reader's understanding of a writer's or artist's work; collectively, they are lessons in the creative process and in the discovery of its roots.

Even for those individuals who have already published full-length autobiographies, *SAAS* allows these writers to bring their readers up-to-date or perhaps to take a different approach in the essay format. In some instances, previously published material may be reprinted or expanded upon; this fact is always noted at the end of such an essay.

SAAS makes no attempt to give a comprehensive overview of authors or illustrators and their works. This outlook is already well represented in biographies, reviews, and critiques published in a wide variety of sources. Instead, *SAAS* complements that perspective and presents what no other ongoing reference source does: the view of writers and illustrators that is shaped by their own choice of materials and their own manner of storytelling.

Who Is Covered?

Like its parent series *Something about the Author,* the *Something about the Author Autobiography Series* sets out to meet the needs and interests of a wide range of readers from upper elementary school through junior and senior high school. Each volume includes essays by international writers and artists whose work has special appeal for young readers. We consider it extraordinary that so many busy authors and illustrators from throughout the world are able to interrupt their existing writing, drawing, teaching, speaking, traveling, and other schedules to converge on a given deadline for any one volume. So it is not always possible that all genres can be equally and uniformly represented from volume to volume, although we strive to include individuals working in a variety of categories, including fiction, nonfiction, picture books, and poetry. These categories, however, do not begin to suggest the diversity of the works of the authors and illustrators represented in the series. Many of the contributors to this volume have also written fiction and nonfiction for adults and have worked in movies, television, and radio as well as for newspapers and journals.

What Each Essay Includes

Authors who contribute to *SAAS* are invited to write a "mini-autobiography" of approximately 10,000 words. In order to give the writer's imagination free rein, we suggest no guidelines or pattern for the essay. We ask only that each writer tell his or her story in the manner and to the extent that feels most natural and appropriate. In addition, writers are asked to supply a selection of personal photographs showing themselves at various ages, as well as important people and special moments in their lives. Our contributors have responded generously, sharing with us some of their most treasured mementos. Illustrators also provide a small representative selection of their published work. The result is a special blend of text, photographs, and illustrations that provides a wealth of distinctive information in a format that will attract even the casual browser.

Other Features

- A **Bibliography** at the end of each essay lists book-length works in chronological order of publication. Each bibliography in this volume was compiled by members of the *SAAS* editorial staff and submitted to the author or illustrator for review.

- A **Cumulative Index** in each volume cites all the essayists in the series as well as the subjects presented in the essays: personal names, titles of works, geographical names, schools of writing, etc. In order to ensure ease of use for these cumulating references, the name of the essayist is given before the volume and page number(s) for every reference that appears *in more than one essay*. In the following example, the entry in the index allows the user to identify the essay writers by name:

> Andersen, Hans Christian
>   Aiken **1**:24
>   Beatty **4**:41
>   Cavanna **4**:113
>   etc.

For references that appear *in only one essay*, the volume and page number(s) are given but the name of the essayist is omitted. For example:

> Butterflies **4**:330

SAAS is something more than the sum of its individual essays. At many points the essays touch common ground, and from these intersections emerge new patterns of information and impressions. The index is an important guide to these interconnections.

For Additional Information

For detailed information on awards, adaptations of works, critical reviews, and more, readers are encouraged to consult Gale's *Contemporary Authors* cumulative index for listings in other Gale sources. These include, among others, *Something about the Author, Contemporary Authors, Contemporary Authors New Revision Series, Dictionary of Literary Biography, Children's Literature Review,* and *Authors and Artists for Young Adults.*

Special Thanks

We wish to acknowledge our special gratitude to each of the authors and illustrators in this volume. They all have been most kind and cooperative in contributing not only their talents but their enthusiasm and encouragement to this project.

Contact the Editor

Please tell us if we can make *SAAS* even more helpful to you or if you have suggestions for prospective essayists and additional features. Give your comments and suggestions to the editor:

BY MAIL: Gerard J. Senick, *Something about the Author Autobiography Series,* Gale Research, 835 Penobscot Bldg., 645 Griswold St., Detroit, MI 48226-4094.

BY TELEPHONE: (800) 347-GALE, extension 1424

BY FAX: (313) 961-6599

BY E-MAIL: CYA@Gale.com@Galesmtp

A Brief Sampler

Each essay in *SAAS* has a special character and point of view that sets it apart from its companions. A small sampler of anecdotes and musings from the essays in this volume hints at the unique perspective of these life stories.

Piers Anthony, remembering his childhood: "I had an active imagination, and it didn't stop with corpses. By day I saw monsters. They followed me as I walked home from school through the forest alone, and hid behind the trees when I turned to look. They lurked under my bed, ready to grab my ankles if I was careless enough to put them in reach. They were everywhere. I had to have a night-light, for light was the only thing that kept them at bay. Today I put those monsters into my fiction, and I love them. But fantasy monsters don't chase adults, only children. So the dominant emotion of my later childhood was fear. Fear of bigger kids at school, of a monster in the forest, and fear of the corpse. Fear, really, of life. I hated being alone, but others neither understood nor cared, so I was alone a lot. That is, often physically, and almost always emotionally. Today when I get a letter from a reader who feels almost utterly alone, I understand, because I remember."

Patricia Coombs, recalling her decision to become an author of children's books: "I wrote every morning, doodling, drawing characters, finding their names. Waterford had a big new library, with a well-stocked children's section. Several times a week, I sat there on the floor and read my way along the shelves, getting a feel for the vocabulary for six- to nine-year-olds. Know your market, that was Noel's valuable advice. The stories I read had boys as heroes; all the action, the adventure, was for them. The girls were the audience. Well, my feelings on that score had simmered a long, long time. Whatever I wrote, it would be for girls who did things."

Penelope Farmer, explaining the havoc her birth caused after her twin sister was born: "The first my mother knew about me was twenty-five minutes or so after my sister's birth, when at my urgent signs of wanting to follow her into the world the doctor cried, 'My God, there's another one!' And out I came, leaving my mother doubly exhausted. The nurse ran quickly for brandy to revive her and came back with the only bottle she could find, in the sideboard in the dining room, more than three quarters empty. She emptied all of it into a large glass. Because of the brandy my father, too, suffered a double shock. Not only did he have two daughters where he'd expected one, the bottle contained a rare and vintage brandy that he was saving for a special occasion. In the circumstances, I doubt if he would have objected to my mother being given such an expensive sip. But the nurse's emptying the remainder of the glassful—most of it—down the sink was another matter."

Ken Mochizuki, describing the discrimination he encountered growing up in Seattle, Washington: "My lessons in justice, prejudice, and doing what is right go back as far as I can remember, even back to the first grade. The teacher, a devoutly religious woman, led her class in morning prayer at the same time we recited the Pledge of Allegiance. We also prayed before having our midday snack of milk and graham crackers. I remember one day, my first-grade teacher told us about all the food and beverages we should not partake in. One of the forbidden beverages was tea. My grandparents, immigrants from Japan who had lived in America for over fifty years by that time, always drank tea. When I told my teacher they drank tea, she replied, 'That's because they're not Christian.' They were. I grew up in a Methodist church in Seattle, and my grandparents attended the same church. But my teacher assumed that, since they were of Japanese ancestry, they couldn't be Christian. During that same school year, the class wrote letters to relatives, inviting them to come to the 1962 Seattle World's Fair. I tried to tell my teacher that the name of my uncle living in Chicago was 'Ayao,' a Japanese first name. She kept repeating, 'Who?' and finally told me to call him 'Uncle Al.' Being six years old, I didn't realize my first grade teacher was trying to stamp my Japanese heritage out of me. My real, legal first name is 'Ken,' but other teachers later on insisted that it must be 'Kenneth.' Incidents such as those shaped the rest of my life: I would often have to struggle against others who thought I was somehow 'different' or not American like them, just because of my last name or because of the way I look."

Colby Rodowsky, explaining what being a writer means to her: "I look on whatever ability to write I have as a kind of gift, and my responsibility to that gift is to use it as well, as faithfully as I can. And so I take the words that have been given to me—words that I must sometimes fight for, and struggle for, through occasional sleepless nights and many cups of tea, days spent filing my nails and straightening my desk. And with these words I weave my stories—hesitantly, tentatively, always sure that when a book or a story is finished I'll never think of another one. But they are woven with joy, and much love."

William Jay Smith, discussing a poetry competition in Barcelona: "After the poems have been read aloud, the judges award the prizes in a most unusual fashion. The author of the third best poem receives a rose made of silver, the author of the second best, a rose made of gold, and the author of the best—the most enduring and most original—a real rose. One might think of these awards as a metaphor for the making of poems. What is given the poet—that phrase, that image, that scrap that circles around for months in his head, that God-given inspiration—is of silver. The second stage, that of composition and revision, when the poet must work constantly over every syllable, never at the same time losing sight of the whole, and when anything earned seems more precious than anything received— that stage is of gold. The third and final stage when the poem is released and belongs to the reader and to the world, if the poet has succeeded and has been true to his vision, that final stage is the *natural* one, when the finished work may take its place; organically whole, beside the great work of life itself."

These brief examples only suggest what lies ahead in this volume. The essays will speak differently to different readers; but they are certain to speak best, and most eloquently, for themselves.

Acknowledgments

Grateful acknowledgment is made to those publishers, photographers, and artists whose works appear with the essays by the authors in this volume.

Photographs

Piers Anthony: pp. 1, 9, 12, 16, C. M. Jacob

Eth Clifford: p. 34, Lewis G. Hall, Jr.

Penelope Farmer: p. 78, © Bassano Ltd.

Dennis Hamley: pp. 85, 87, 91, 97, John Cotton; p. 100, Hertfordshire Mercury.

X. J. Kennedy: p. 105, Dorothy M. Kennedy; p. 117, Christopher Longyear; p. 118, Hinton/*Los Angeles Times Book Review;* p. 121, © The Martin Studio.

Constance Levy: pp. 125, 135, 136, 139, Monroe D. Levy.

John Marsden: p. 176, Courtesy of the *Geelong Advertiser.*

Ken Mochizuki: p. 196, Bessie Loo Agency.

Colby Rodowsky: p. 229, Rettberg Brothers; p. 237, © 1994 R. W. Rochfort.

J.otto Seibold: p. 246, Leslie Flores; p. 251, Ann Dodge.

William Jay Smith: p. 253, Robert Turney; p. 268, Jon Allen; p. 271, B. Kopotkopuko.

Illustrations/Art

Patricia Coombs: Illustration from *Dorrie and the Blue Witch,* written and illustrated by Patricia Coombs. Lothrop, 1964. Copyright © 1964 by Patricia Coombs. Illustration from *Lisa and the Grompet,* written and illustrated by Patricia Coombs. Lothrop, 1970. Copyright © 1970 by Patricia Coombs. All reprinted with permission of the author.

Leslie H. Morrill: sketches used by permission of the author.

William Jay Smith: Illustration from *Typewriter Town,* written and illustrated by William Jay Smith. Dutton, 1960. Copyright © 1960 by William Jay Smith. Reprinted with permission of the author.

Text

X. J. Kennedy: Poem "King Tut," from *One Winter Night in August.* Reprinted with permission of the author.

SOMETHING ABOUT THE AUTHOR

AUTOBIOGRAPHY SERIES

Piers Anthony

1934-

Piers Anthony, 1995

My American grandfather was known as the Mushroom King; he had started growing edible mushrooms in his cellar, and built it into a business that made him a millionaire. He didn't have much formal education, but was a savvy businessman; two weeks before the great stock market crash of 1929 he sold the business. I believe that about half of the mushrooms produced in the United States still come from the region around West Chester, Pennsylvania, where he started it, though now it is split between a number of companies. He married, and his wife died of cancer; he remarried, and she also died. He married a third time, Caroline, and she survived him, living to the age of ninety-nine.

My father, Alfred, was the opposite of rich; he was intellectual. His mother, my grandfather's first wife, was in the hospital, and he visited her there. She asked him to go out and read the words at the entry to her ward, and he did. They were in Latin, and he didn't understand them, but he described them to her as well as he could. She thanked him. Next day she was dead. She seemed to have given up the struggle to live. He always felt guilty, because the words he had conveyed to her identified the ward: it was for incurables. He had given his mother the news that destroyed her hope. He went to England to continue his education, where they took it more seriously than they did in America. He was to graduate

1

from Oxford University, but that isn't my immediate concern. He met a British girl, Joyce, and really liked her. But when summer passed, and a new semester started, she wasn't there. She had caught a fever, maybe typhoid fever, maybe from polluted water when she went camping, and died. He was never to get over that. Again he had been cursed by death. Indeed, I know of only one person who ponders death as much as I do: my father. Later he met another British girl, Norma, who graduated from Oxford with top honors, and she was the one he married. He sent my grandfather a newspaper clipping reporting the marriage: that was the extent of his announcement. Later they both went on to earn Ph.D.'s. The relationship didn't work out, but in the course of their marriage my sister and I were born. I arrived in AwGhost 1934, and Teresa in OctOgre 1935. Bear with me on the oddly spelled months; I was later to make my fortune in funny fantasy, and I renamed the months accordingly. There are oddities about me that I will try to explain here; I'm not normal, and I relate well to other abnormals. For now it is enough to know that everyone in my immediate family was academically gifted except me. I was the dunce who made up for it all, pulling the average down.

I think we children were something of an afterthought, because our parents did not seem to be unduly interested in us. Instead they went to Spain to do relief work with the British Friends Service Committee, feeding starving children. They were members of the Religious Society of Friends, more popularly known as Quakers, and the Quakers are known for silent meetings for worship, good business practice, integrity, and good works. This was among the latter. In 1936 the Spanish civil war started, a kind of prelude to World War II, wherein Spain's own military fought to take over the country from the civilians. In three years it was successful, but it was hell on the children. So my parents were helping to keep those devastated children alive, by importing food and milk and feeding them on a regular basis. It was worthy work, and I don't fault it, but there was a personal cost.

The family at Treasure Island Beach, 1970–71

It was not safe for my sister and me during the Spanish war, so we remained in England, cared for by our British grandparents and a nanny. I loved that nanny, whom I thought of as my mother. I remember when she took us to the park in London, and there was a bird hopping on the ground. We feared it was injured, so we told the keeper. He picked up the bird and stretched out its wings, to ascertain whether they were broken. He concluded that the bird was all right, and set it down again. I was amazed; it seemed that there was no bird there, just folded wings. I wondered whether it would be possible to make another bird by folding paper cleverly enough. Would it come alive?

I also remember going to the hospital at age four. For years I said I went there to be born, until my mother corrected me: I had been born earlier. She was in a position to know, though she did not acquaint me with the details. So this visit was actually for a tonsillectomy, an operation thought necessary at the time for all children.

In 1939 we joined our parents in Spain, for the war there was then over. This was my first real crisis of identity, because my parents seemed like acquaintances rather than close kin. The nanny was the one I really knew, but she wasn't going. I think of it in retrospect as root pruning: it may be necessary to transplant the young tree, and the tree looks complete, but it isn't. It is hurting where it doesn't show. I had abruptly lost what I valued most, and it was the beginning of a downward spiral that was to leave me depressive even decades later. I never saw the nanny again. I understand she was a Scottish girl, perhaps one of two similar sisters, very good with children. Surely so, for I remember no evil of her; I remember only happiness of a kind I was never to achieve again.

Spain was interesting in new ways. My sister had a nice little Spanish dress. I remember waking alone in my bedroom in Barcelona and seeing moving patterns on the wall. It was the morning sunlight outlining a neighboring palm tree, casting shadows through my window. To me it was like a show; as the wind blew the fronds, the shadows moved back and forth, sometimes almost all the way off the wall. I loved to watch it. Later I got to see a real movie: a cartoon of the three little pigs and the big bad wolf. Absolutely fascinating! Also

my first experience with an elevator. Here was this little room we went into, and suddenly it moved, and when the door opened again, everything outside had changed. It was like magic, and for years thereafter I imagined magical rooms that could take me anywhere I wanted to go.

And my first ice cream cone. The funny thing was, the ice cream was square, not round. I think that supplies must have been limited, so that they lacked the tubs and scoops, and had to use packaged ice cream. The man crammed it into a cone, and I ate it and loved it. By the time I reached the bottom of the cone, the ice cream there was melting. But it was a great experience. And we got a pair of sandals made from string; the soles were this mass of coiled string, actually hemp. I don't think they lasted long, because the string tended to unravel, but they were nice.

There was also the old man who told me stories and played a trick on me: he gave me a candy, and ate one himself, then took back the wrappers and balled them and wrapped them in another wrapper so cunningly that it looked just like a real candy. Then my sister arrived, and he gave it to her. I could hardly contain myself, waiting to see her dismay as it turned out to be empty. But she unwrapped one, two, three wrappers—and there was a candy inside. The joke had been on me.

At one point we went to a hotel in a nearby town, Tossa, about forty miles up the Mediterranean coast from Barcelona, on top of a steep hill; we thought no car could get up that hill, but a man in a motorcycle zoomed right up it, amazing us. I remember swimming in the warm Mediterranean sea. Actually I couldn't swim; I was floating on an inflated raft. It banged into another, and I fell off, sinking under the salty water. I was quickly rescued—it was only about two feet deep—but it was a memorable experience. I remember the big cigar-shaped balloons that moved silently over the beach: military blimps, I think.

Another time I was walking with my family when I realized that I had somehow gotten lost; I was with strangers. I didn't know what to do, so I just kept going. They seemed to accept me; the woman even gave me roasted peanuts. Later my mother came to recover me. It must have been a baby-sitting device; my mother had slipped away unseen so that I wouldn't make a fuss. But that had left me without moorings, uncertain of my fate. I had discovered that my mother could disappear without warning. I never did that to my own children.

Another time my father was playing with us, showing us magic blocks. He was really better at games and stories than my mother was. He put a coin on one, and covered it with a block-shaped shell, then removed the shell—and the coin was gone. Where could it be? We looked all over. It occurred to me that it might be hidden under the block, so I picked it up— and another shell came off, with the coin under it. My father departed in a huff; I had spoiled the trick. I really hadn't meant to.

And I remember Easter: I was given a huge wooden egg. It opened, and inside was a model of a sailing ship and a number of chocolates. Thereafter I loved Easter, though I think none since has been as great. But I also remember my sister and I standing in the garden with tape stuck across our mouths, evidently our punishment for talking out of turn. I don't approve of that sort of punishment, and don't know whether our parents knew of it. Another time we were with a woman doing laundry in the cellar, which was a converted jail cell, and a young man came and locked the gate, shutting us in. The woman screeched at him so violently that he had to return to let us out. He was Jorge, pronounced "Hor-Hee," and was always fun.

It was in Spain that my sister Teresa and I suffered a shock that was to mark us in separate ways for life. I will tell it first as I saw it. I was in a room, alone, when I heard my sister protesting something. So I followed the sound, going to see what was the matter. I saw her on a counter of some sort, with a group of adults clustered around her. She was trying to get away, but couldn't. Then her screams became piercing; they were torturing her. I saw her little feet pounding the counter as she cried to run away, but could not. They were doing something to her face; I think I saw a splash of water. Then, when they had hurt her enough, they let her go, and turned to see me standing there. "He saw!" one said. At that point my terrible memory fades out. It was to remain for fifty years as a disconnected scene I couldn't explain, until at last it clicked into place, like a piece of a puzzle: that was when my sister had her tonsillectomy. The full story I had learned before, but never connected to my horrible vision. When it was time for

her operation, my mother inquired of the local medical facilities, and was told they had no safe anesthetic. The war had devastated Spain, and many supplies were low or gone. So they would have to do it without any pain killer. "Not on *my* child!" my mother said. So they agreed: they would find something. She brought the child in to the clinic, telling me to stay in the waiting room, and took Teresa on in. Whereupon the nurses snatched the child away from her, took her to the counter, propped her mouth open, and cut out her tonsils while she screamed. That was the way it was done in Spain at the time.

I don't think my mother knew that I had seen it happen. I never spoke of it. It was my private horror. I knew then that doctors existed to make children hurt. That was confirmed when I was ill in Spain; a doctor came, checked me over, then asked for a spoon. He turned it over and poked it deep into my mouth until I vomited on the bed. Satisfied, he departed; he had made me hurt enough. Later experiences with horrible needles added to it; I remember one needle being stuck slanting under the skin, and a fluid injected so that the skin swelled up in an excruciating blister while I was held down, screaming. Vaccination, they called it. By whatever name, its point was obvious; no doctor could let a child go without hurting it. My parents, strangely, never protested.

Our departure from Spain was another ugly matter. My father liked Spain, and wanted to remain there. I have mixed feelings about that; I liked Spain too, but I am not at all sure I would have had a worthwhile life there. But fate took the decision out of our hands. As I understand it, Adolf Hitler of Nazi Germany was trying to get Generalissimo Franco of Spain to join the Axis, and a meeting between them was scheduled. Security was tight. And there was my father, with a lot of money, near the border. He was there to buy food to feed a trainful of Jews being deported from Germany. So they "disappeared" him: they arrested him and dumped him in prison, uncharged. For three days my mother desperately tried to find out what had happened to him. The Spanish authorities denied knowing anything about it. Meanwhile he was confined with other men in a dungeon cell, whose sanitary facility was a trench. There were female prisoners too, in another cell, only theirs had no trench; periodically they were herded to the male cell to do their business, while the men stood around and watched, seeing whatever they could see. One prisoner was allowed a visitor, who brought a hot drink to him in a thermos; Alfred got them to put a postcard of his into the empty thermos, to be taken out and mailed. My mother received the card, and so learned of what had happened. Armed with that, and with the forceful assistance of a wealthy Quaker of influence who could have cost Spain a lot of needed monetary assistance, she was able to get them to admit that they did after all have a prisoner of that name. But dictatorships don't admit mistakes, so they agreed to let him go only on condition that he depart the country. The relief mission of that area was shut down, and thereafter the children had to survive as well as they could without that food. I like to think that some people are alive today because of what my parents did in Spain. I was later to write a novel, *Volk,* relating to Spain and Germany and World War II, but have not as yet found a publisher for it, because it is controversial.

So it was that we left Spain. I remember traveling from Barcelona to Madrid, the capital city, where we toured the big earthworks around the city: its former defenses. Then we went on to Lisbon, Portugal, to catch the ship to America. I remember stopping high in a mountain pass to go touch the spongy bark of a cork tree, and driving way up on a high hill where there was a kind of amusement park. There were many small stands with toy trains. My mother put in a coin, and the little train buzzed around and around its little mountain on its little tracks. Finally it disappeared into a tunnel and didn't come out: the show was over. In Lisbon we took a taxi, and the cabby unfolded a child seat from the floor or somewhere, a novelty. We also got to ride in paddleboats; foot pedals made the paddles go around, and the boats moved forward. So it was fun. But not without its cautions. I remember seeing my mother naked for the first and only time, there, and being amazed to see that she had hair on her crotch. It had never occurred to me that adults were different from children. But what appalled my mother was the fact that the hotel room was overrun with roaches.

Even our voyage on the ship to America was unusual. I did not know it at the time, but the former King Edward VIII of England was on that ship with us. He had gotten interested in an American divorcée, and had a difficult choice: the crown or the woman. Romance had won, and he gave up his throne and married her. They happened to be in Portugal at this time. The Nazis thought he was sympathetic to their cause, and hoped to abduct him and talk him into supporting them politically. But they fouled up, and didn't get him, and he boarded the ship, going to Bermuda. That was the *Excalibur,* the same ship and the same voyage we were on, the last trip out before the war shut off such travel. No, I don't believe I ever saw the erstwhile king, but I do remember seeing his car unloaded in Bermuda: it dangled from a crane line dropped into the hold, and was swung out onto the dock. I had my sixth birthday on the ship, where I had a cake made of sawdust because they lacked provisions for a real one; they brought it to us with the candles burning, and then we couldn't eat it. Later my own children were to be jealous: *they* never got a cake made of sawdust. I was given a harmonica, and I loved it, and played it endlessly as I walked around the deck. I still wonder whether the former king of England was gritting his teeth somewhere, wishing that kid would cut out the noise. And I had my first bout with seasickness; I remember my father holding me up so I could vomit over the rail, seeing it fall down into the distant water. There was also a swimming pool set up on the deck; the canvas had a leak in one corner, and I got to play in that jet of water. I think my elder daughter inherited that delight; she was hyperactive, but could play endlessly in flowing water.

The trip took ten days, and we made it safely to New York. I think I remember seeing the Statue of Liberty, without understanding its significance. I was an immigrant, a subject of the Queen; that statue welcomed folk like me. We docked, and my American grandparents—yea, the Mushroom King, and his third wife, Caroline—met us and drove us to Pennsylvania, the Quaker State. My mother was uncertain of her reception by my father's folks, for she was not even American, and might be considered an intruder, but Caroline, similarly new to the family, welcomed her, and that started a friendship that was to last fifty years, until they died just a month apart.

My memories of that time are scattered, but some do stand out. My grandfather Edward's house was at the end of a street in West Chester, Pencil Vania (well, I warned you about my funny fantasy), with a fish pond behind and a rolling meadow leading down to the highway and a golf course beyond it. It was like a slice of heaven. The house was large, and even had a maid's quarters with a separate little winding stairway for her. Fascinating! Grandfather was hard of hearing, so at meals had a hearing aid that looked like a toaster; my father joked about putting bread in it. Grandfather's wife was known as Aunt Caroline, carried across from the way she was known in her own family. Later I liked to refer to her as my wife's step-grandmother-in-law. She was a great person, competent and diplomatic and very much a Quaker, speaking with "thee" in the manner of the elder generation. So, as I became acquainted with my American relatives, I liked them.

We spent a while at Grandfather's cabin in Seaside Park, New Jersey (no parody for that state; I already have a mental picture of a freshly purchased garment). That was on the Atlantic beach, and was sheer delight. There was a boardwalk that extended endlessly north and south. There was the white sand and the constant washing sea. There was a telescope on the front porch that seemed magical. Once I saw a tiny dot on the horizon, but when the telescope focused in it, it became a yacht with girls running around its decks and jumping into the water. I never had a city apartment, but can appreciate the lure of a high rise telescope; who knows what sights one might see. There was an amusement park, with little machines that you looked into, and turned a crank on the side, and they flipped the pages of picture books, making them become animated cartoons. I loved that. Today's more sophisticated animation is far superior, yet I loved those magic moving pictures.

Another time I was ill, and had to be quarantined. Was it German measles? I don't know. I was at a house somewhere else, and only my mother was there with me. I spent the long hours drawing things on a sketch pad. I remember the bread she brought: huge slices that were incredibly delicious with butter. So this illness was a pleasant experience.

We moved to a place called Pendle Hill. It was a kind of Quaker school for adult studies.

We had a little apartment squeezed in the rear of one of the buildings. I was given a scooter, and I loved it; I scooted constantly. Years later I learned the penalty: my right leg became an inch longer than the left leg, because I had always pushed with it. That wasn't discovered until a chiropractor looked at me; at a glance he saw my uneven stance, and put me on two scales, one foot to each. I weighed 100 pounds, divided 60-40. I had to wear a corrective shoe to force my stance to change, enabling my legs to grow back to the same length.

It wasn't all fun. A neighbor boy invited me over, but he wasn't necessarily as friendly as he seemed. He had a big dog, which he would encourage a stranger to pet; after a moment the dog would leap up, growling, scaring the child, and the boy would laugh. Another time some of his other friends were there, so he told me to go home. Realizing that I was being dissed, I balked. When he threatened to push me, I threatened to kick him. He stepped in and punched me in the face. Completely defeated, in tears, I fled. I didn't tell, but I remembered. Today when someone tries to push me around, I am apt to find a way to make him regret it. I don't like bullies. When my second daughter was treated exactly the same way, I went immediately to the scene and got it straightened out. Another time, when three boys beat up my two girls, I went and virtually challenged the eldest boy's father; had he not departed quickly, I might have tried to do to him what his boy had done to my girls, and take him down and grind his face in the dirt. As it was, I merely called the police and sent them to the errant household. At any rate, I did make my point; his boy never touched my girls again. When my elder daughter's college treated her contemptuously, I wrote a sharp letter to the college president, to similar effect; their unfair action was instantly reversed. I am not small any more, and I saw to it that my children did not suffer as I had. I don't claim to be always nice, but there's always justice in my cases, and I have taken down many bullies, in my fashion, though the arena is no longer physical. Few have cared to tangle with me a second time.

I started school. Somehow what I did was never satisfactory to the teacher. She showed me another student's paper, which was much neater than mine, but I couldn't do it the way the teacher wanted. In fact it took me

The author with wife Carol, daughters Cheryl and Penny, and Canute, "visiting Aunt Caroline's house at Bayside Drive, winter 1970 71"

three years and five schools to make it through first grade, because I couldn't learn to read and write. My sister, in contrast, had no trouble at all. She had the good fortune to catch tuberculosis and spent six months in bed, so our mother taught her to read. She entered first grade with a sixth-grade reading skill. People would come up to me and say "Aren't you thrilled to have a smart sister like her?" Somehow I didn't see it that way; maybe I was too dull to appreciate such a blessing. In my day things like learning disabilities or dyslexia didn't exist, just stupid or careless children. It wasn't until I saw the trouble my daughter had in school that I realized what must have been my problem. Actually it was more complicated than that, and I may still not understand the whole of it, slow learner that I am. Theoretically intelligence doesn't change through life, but tests showed me to be subnormal early, and normal later, and superior later yet, and my success in school and life varied accordingly. So the kid who couldn't read later became an English

teacher, and a highly successful writer. How could I have been so dull before, and so smart after, if IQ is fixed?

Well, it's possible. First, I may indeed have had a problem in seeing and learning writing. Eyes do not mature immediately, and some studies have shown that many children suffer measurable ocular damage from the close work demanded in school. That's one reason that so many adults, myself included, need glasses for reading. We protected our dyslexic daughter by having her wear special glasses in first grade, so that her eyes would not be damaged, and as an adult she didn't need glasses. But most children are not that fortunate. I may also have had something like dyslexia, and it took me time to learn to compensate. It was as if I had an analog mind in a digital world. When I did learn to handle it, I started forging ahead, and in adult life few have ever thought me stupid, and some of those who have, have been surprised when they learned more of me. In fact I think it may be that only those who are not as smart as I am ever think me to be dull. I have an analogy I like: suppose a sports car races with a locomotive. At the starting line, the car races ahead. If the finish line is a hundred yards away, there's no contest. But if the finish line is three thousand miles away, the locomotive will win, because once it gets up steam it proceeds at a very high rate of speed without pausing. So I was a loser as a child, but not as an adult; my locomotive had finally gotten up speed, and it left most others behind. There is one more thing: I was always slow. I was slow to learn to walk, and to speak. I am still slow to catch on to new things. I was slow to grow, and slow to reach maturity. I am still slow to eat, and still read slowly. That is not a euphemism for stupid; I just take my time, but I get there in the end. Like the locomotive. Give me a timed test and I will not be a high scorer, but I can compete on an open-ended basis. School is timed, but life is an open-ended experience.

So school was difficult for me. It didn't help having to learn a new school, with its different grounds, teachers, students, and rules, every time I started to catch on to the way of one. One teacher, instead of encouraging me, chastised me for mispronouncing my *a*'s: "There's an *a* in that word! Grass, not grawss." She was trying to correct my English accent. No wonder I had a problem. The students weren't any better. In winter I had a fast little sled, a Flexible Flyer, and that was fun. But at one of the schools the old students threw all the sleds of the new students into the river. They were there in plain view in the water, but the teachers ignored it. Teachers just didn't seem to have much awareness of justice. Or of education. That was over fifty years ago, but I'm not sure it has changed much.

One of the schools was in New York state, with beautiful grounds. It was a boarding school. I was later to see some of the bright caring reports it sent back to my family. They were fantasy; the reality was something else. My main early entertainment was playing in the adjacent garbage dump, because the good facilities were off-bounds to us. As a first grader, I was the lowest of the low. Older students took me into a room and told me to take off my clothes. I did so, but gradually became suspicious; to be slow is not to be entirely out of it. So I dressed again and managed to break away, es-

caping to my own dorm. That night we were watching a movie, and suddenly someone was wading into me, hitting me, pummeling me, beating me up. The teachers paid no attention. I fled out of the building, into the surrounding forest, escaping the beating. I hid behind a tree, wary of pursuit. Indeed it seemed incipient, because as I watched the building, I heard frequent yelling and pounding, as of a gang about to break down the door and charge out. I was terrified. It continued for a long time, and finally I realized that they weren't actually coming out. So I sneaked around to the other side, and up the stairs, and into bed, and they never spied me. Why should they? I hadn't even been missed. Later I realized that what I had seen was the outside of the indoor basketball court; the pounding had been the ball and people hitting the wall as they played. If only I had realized that earlier, I would have been spared an evening of terror. So what of the boy who was beating on me? It took me years to put that together: I think he was the one who had been guarding the door during my "initiation"; I had pushed by him and escaped, and that made him mad. Bullies don't like to let anyone escape. So next time he saw me he waded into me. A first grader couldn't stand up to a second or third grader. I lived in fear of him, until finally other students decided that enough was enough. They brought us together and had us shake hands, declaring peace. "But what if he goes after me again?" I asked. "Then *we'll* beat *him* up," they said. That did indeed take care of it; they weren't bluffing. Justice had come, no thanks to the teachers or school administration.

Yet such things seldom happen of their own accord, and I suspect there was more to it. An older boy befriended me. His name was Craig Work, and he was the child of a black father and white mother, and his IQ had been tested at 180. I realize, in considerable retrospect, that he must have had thorough experience in the rough and tumble of life among children. I didn't know of racism then, and didn't care that his skin was brown, but surely there were others who did. He was a great friend, and once he started associating with me, things started turning better. I think he had something to do with it. His mother later reported something he had said to her: "Mom, I'm a peaceful kind of guy, and I don't like to fight. But they *make* you fight." Yes indeed. Craig helped teach me how to fight, and that in itself made a difference. I was no longer such an easy target. In fact it got so that I never lost unless my opponent was substantially larger than I. I wasn't weak, just small. So later, when others tried me out, and found me tougher than expected, they became friends instead of enemies. But at the beginning, at boarding school, I'm sure the considerable shadow of Craig protected me more than somewhat. And of course there were always boys who *were* substantially larger, so I wasn't yet out of the wilderness.

My experience with Craig was to affect my social attitude. No one ever had to tell me that racism wasn't nice; I knew it from the time I first learned of it. My best friend really *had* been black. When I see racism, I have a kind of mental picture of filth and grubs exposed under a rock. I have trouble understanding how such folk can stand their own company. I don't believe in Hell, but if by some mischance it exists, I think it must be stocked with racists.

But school was only one of the growing problems of my life. I had been toilet trained in England and Spain, but in America I started wetting the bed at night. This continued for several years. I was checked into a hospital, and that was another awful experience: periodically a group of adults would enter my room, and that was always mischief. Sometimes they wanted to poke a finger into my various orifices, including the rectum—the entire medical establishment seemed to be fascinated with that orifice, so that they even had pretty nurses take my temperature that way. Sometimes they brought deadly needles, inflicting pain on me in the manner that doctors always did to children. Once I woke to hear a cluster of nurses just outside my door, whispering avidly. "Just take it and *shove it in!*" one was saying. I was terrified; what were they going to do to me? Was it my turn to be tortured the way my sister had been in Spain? Surely it must be a knife they would use. But nobody said a word to me. I realized that they were planning to do it by surprise; without warning would come that sudden thrust, while I screamed helplessly. All in all, I was never able to truly relax, even in sleep. Since I wet my bed only when soundly asleep, I didn't do it in that hospital. In the end they reported to my parents that there was nothing organically wrong with me; no physical cause for my bed-wetting. They were

The author circa 1980

right, in their fashion, but what they didn't know could fill a volume. I learned later that it was supposed to have been a briefer visit, for observation only, but that there had been a delay in the insurance payment, so they had held me as it were at ransom for several extra days, until they got their payment. I had suffered all that extra time because of a bureaucratic snarl. So what was it with the nurses? I think now that they had merely been exchanging stories in the hall, and it was sheer coincidence that my room was the closest one, so that I could overhear. No surgery had been scheduled for me; that fear had been groundless. If only I had known!

So what was the matter with me? My bedwetting did not abate. Then I began to suffer twitches. Every few seconds I would fling my head around, or give a hard shake to both my hands. Why did I do it? It was like a cough: you can hold it back only so long before it has to come out. Naturally these actions brought further ridicule down on my head. It was evident that I was a pretty fouled-up child. Oh, I would have loved to be normal, but I wasn't. Yet that, too, was not the major thing.

It started innocently enough, while I was still in that long first grade. This was in New Hampshire, I think. We went to an amusement park that was all inside a big building, another novelty to me. All kinds of things were going on there. There was a huge hollow man-statue with an entrance at the base and exit at the top; I think there was a spiral stairway inside. People were constantly going through it. Every so often the statue would go HO HO HO and wiggle just a little, and the folk inside it would scream. I think that from inside it seemed that the whole thing was falling. My father went on it while we watched, and reported on what he experienced. At one point, beyond the statue, was a room with a table full of nice watches, and a sign saying TAKE ONE. But when he tried to, he found that it was fastened to the table, and electrified; he got a shock. One has to be wary, in a fun house. Later fun houses had jets of air that blew up girls' dresses so that their underwear showed; somehow the girls didn't find that as amusing as the boys did. Then my father took me on a ride through the horror house. This was weird and exciting. Ghostly creatures appeared and launched at the cart, scaring me. Then suddenly a stone wall appeared before us, and we were headed right for it, about to crash—and the cart dropped an inch or so to a lower track, feeling just like a crash. We swung on around the wall, safe after all, and in due course emerged from the darkness. It had been a phenomenal thrill.

But that night I had a terrible dream. It consisted of just four pictures, or brief scenes. In the first, my sister and I were walking along a city street with our mother. That was all; nothing remarkable. In the second, she stopped at a standing structure, like a telephone booth. She entered it, but then the door wouldn't open, and she was caught inside. The third picture was a forest glade, with an altar, and a woman was lying on it. I knew it was my mother. At the edge of the glade stood a man, and beside him was a lion. The fourth scene was just the man, lifting the lion up in his arms, as if hefting it for weight. That was all—but it so terrified me that I woke screaming. My mother was soon there to comfort me, but it was not possible to expunge the awfulness. I don't nor-

mally believe in dream interpretation; I think that most of it is fantasy, and that even the experts know almost nothing of the real nature of dreams. Right: I alone know their true nature, and I'll cover that in a moment. But this particular dream, simple as it seems, had formidable meaning, and is the very essence of terror. Here is the interpretation: the first picture is just the introduction, and it was taken from experience. The setting was Spain, and my sister and I did walk along the street with our mother. The second picture refers to the time she made a phone call from a booth, and the door stuck; she did get out, but for a moment I was worried. This connected to something that was preying on my mind, even then: she had said that she might have to have an operation. Little was explained to the children, leaving much to the imagination. Just as when she spoke of seeing a book that had been made into a movie, and I thought that meant that they projected the pages of the book onto the screen for everyone to read, I thought that the operation meant that they would stretch her out on a table and cut into her body with knives. It was horrible to contemplate. The memory of the phone booth was twined with the thought of that operation, as if first they had to catch her so they could do it to her. So, later, when that memory returned in the dream scene, the horror was building, for this time she was indeed caught. The third scene was crafted in part from an experience I had had when walking in the country: I had come across an animal skull. It was the vast, bleached, hollow-eyed bone of a cow, and I understood that death had come to this creature, and this was all that was left of it. That setting, between forest and field, was in my dream, and so it was a place of death. My mother was laid out there for the knife. Her absence from the fourth scene was significant: she must have been eaten by the lion, and now the man, who might have been the anonymous surgeon or perhaps was really my father, was weighing the lion to see how much it had gained. My mother was horribly dead.

So this dream was crafted from several assorted memories, assembled into a horrible whole. But why did it occur? The immediate trigger was the emotion of the horror house ride; it had shaken loose deeper fears. But those fears had been building before then, and they were related to my bed-wetting and compulsive twitches. This is the root of the larger story. For our family was coming apart. My parents were in the process of separating, though they themselves may not have realized it at that point. The marriage had not been ideal from the start; they were two intelligent, liberal, socially conscious Quakers, but their subtle differences doomed their union. As I see it, he was a creature of the country, while she was a creature of the city. He liked the self-sufficiency of the farm and forest; she preferred the civilization of the city. He could work quietly logging or gardening alone; she longed for the thickly clustered conveniences of the populated metropolis. He liked being largely free of the works of mankind; she couldn't stand a house without hot water or internal sanitary facilities. Note how the dream sequences with the woman are in the city, and with the man are in the country. Their ideal life styles were poles apart. There was of course more to it than that, but that was enough; he was headed for the farm and she for the city, and ultimately their marriage sundered, leaving them free to find their ideal habitats. There were quarrels, there were reconciliations, there were negotiations, there were compromises, but the end was inevitable. Later this divergence was to be expressed in my fiction: there was the planet Proton, with cities and pollution, and the magic land of Phaze, with forests and unicorns. Yet they were merely aspects of one realm, the city and the country merging. I liked both, and wanted the two to be joined, but they kept separating.

Meanwhile, it was hell on the children, as divorces usually are. I liken it to standing on a mountain, but then the mountain quakes and collapses, and becomes an island in a heaving sea. I was standing there, and my footing was eroding. It became an iceberg, floating in that treacherous sea, and then the ice split so that one of my feet was on each section. The sections separated, leaving me no way to escape the fate of the icy water. So while I was not physically mistreated, emotionally I was suffering. I spoke of root pruning when I lost the nanny in England; now I was pruned again, having lost the second country—Spain—and the remaining foundation of the unified family. No wonder the stress manifested in various ways, such as bed-wetting and twitching; I had no legitimate way to handle it. They say that stupid folk don't have as many emotional problems as smart folk, being too dull to realize how bad things are. The way I was reacting, I must have been far smarter than I seemed.

So how did I survive? There came a point when I realized that my problems were really not of my own making, but stemmed from the stress between my parents. I declared, in effect, emotional independence. I weaned myself away from the family, emotionally, and began building my own framework. It was a long and difficult job, like a climb from a deep and treacherous pit, but in time I got there. My parents were shocked when I stated that they were people I knew and liked, but did not love, yet it was the truth. That was the state I had needed to achieve for emotional survival. It wasn't ideal, it wasn't pretty, but it was the only way. I don't regret the decision; I regret the necessity for it. How would it have been if Joyce, my father's early love, had lived, and they had married, and I had been their child? I suspect I would have been far happier as a child—and never have become a writer. So I can't really fault the circumstances that brought me into this realm and made me what I am, however uncomfortable they may have been.

Now on this matter of dreams: I have an insatiable curiosity about the nature of the universe and mankind's place in it, and my profession of writing allows me to explore it all, seeking answers. I have fathomed a number of things to my satisfaction before they were clarified by the scientists, and this is one of them. This discussion will get somewhat intellectual, but I'll try to make it intelligible. It has been said that we waste a third of our lives in sleep. Baloney; nature doesn't work that way. It has been said that we use only ten percent of our brains. Baloney, again. While we are up and about we are constantly receiving impressions. Now consider what happens to them: are they just dumped into a virtual vat in the brain and stored for future use? It may seem that way at first blush, but a little thought shows that this is impractical. If you buy groceries for the next week's meals, do you just dump them pell-mell into the freezer? Chances are you sort them and put them carefully in a number of spots reserved for them, so that you won't find week-old milk squished under the canned beans, or fresh lettuce coated with cocoa powder. So that when you need butter in a hurry, you won't have to unload the whole freezer to find it, and then have to

At home with horses Sky Blue and Misty, circa 1980

thaw it on the stove. (That reminds me of the story my mother told of the day the refrigeration was too cold: "The ice cream's been in the oven for twenty minutes, and still isn't soft enough to cut." It also reminds me of the time I took a pat of butter and dropped it on my plate, and it clinked.) It takes time to sort things properly, but you learn to do it, because it's better than the alternative. The same is true for anything else; you separate it and sort it and store it for future convenience.

So is it any different with memories? Obviously they are well organized, because all our past experience can quickly be brought to bear on a present event. If we spy a small red roughly spherical object before us, we know almost immediately whether it's the dog's rubber ball or a giant cherry bomb, and treat it accordingly. But when did we do the massive sorting and filing of memories that allowed us to classify it so rapidly? For such work does take time. I was for some years a file clerk, and I learned that there is no paper so lost as one that has been misfiled or mislabeled. If you're using an

unfamiliar program, with a deadline for an obnoxious assignment, how do you find an article on cooking squash, if the file isn't organized? Under C for Cooking, or S for Squash, or F for Food, or U for Ugh—who wants it? In fact you have not only to file accurately, you have to cross-reference, so that under COOKING is a note saying SEE SQUASH, along with other notes saying SEE POTATOES, SEE BROCCOLI, SEE BALONEY, and so on. Also under FOOD, and under UGH. That way you can quickly find anything when you don't know how the ditsy file clerk classified it. Well, your brain has to do that job too, only it's a lot more complicated than just a list of recipes. Your entire ongoing life experience has to be sorted and classified and filed in memory for instant retrieval. It doesn't just happen; it has to be organized.

When do you do it—in your sleep? Yes, actually. Part of that ninety percent of the brain that ignorant experts think is unused is actually used for that considerable cross-referencing and filing chore. And since you are way too busy in the daytime to do it, the chore must wait for the brain's downtime: at night. Think of a computer that has some really hot features you'd like to play with, but someone else is using it now; what do you do? You schedule a session during its downtime, when no one else is using it. That's what your brain does. When you sleep, precious little is coming in from outside. So it calls up the fresh memories of the day, that have been held in temporary storage, and processes them. It takes one memory, such as that of the personable person of the opposite gender who smiled at you during lunch, and compares it rapidly to your prior lifetime's experience, in the manner of a computer checking for a word beginning with WOW. Whenever there's some sort of match, it looks farther, and when there's a significant match, it considers the matter and strengthens the neural pathways that actually make memory. But this aspect takes intelligence, because most of the day's impressions are not very important in terms of the rest of your life, and you don't want to clutter your memory with them.

For example, if that person was your sibling, you can dump that memory right there. But if there are matches to a similar smile yesterday by a person you well might want to get lost with in a stranded elevator, this bears further consideration. How would it be, if the two of you are going to the sixth floor, and the power fails, and one of you is a bit scared and the other is a bit protective, and you mesh rather nicely, and then a kiss sort of happens, and then the alarm goes off and it's morning, and all you remember is a rather pleasant dream about an elevator. And so you process everything, and the occasional images that take more serious form as you explore their bypaths are what you call dreams. It's not wasted time at all; it's vital to your well being. Your whole future may be guided in your dreams. But you can't afford to remember most of them, because they are the sorting process, and any dream you remember has to be treated as a memory and run through that classification mill itself. You would rapidly encounter the phenomenon of diminishing returns.

Now you know what dreams are for. Don't bother to tell your science teachers; they're not ready for this yet. Just be smugly satisfied in your secret understanding of what modern science does not yet know. With luck, you'll dream

about that elevator again tonight, and the alarm won't go off so soon.

And so I survived the horror of my devastating dream, though it haunted me every night for three years thereafter. When I closed my eyes I saw that corpse and knew its identity. I tried to make it go away, and in my imagination it would move off-screen, but another would appear, and another, until they were cruising by like the cars of a long train. It may sound funny, but it was killing my sanity. If I seem a bit crazy here, well, now you have half a notion how I got that way. I had an active imagination, and it didn't stop with corpses. By day I saw monsters. They followed me as I walked home from school through the forest alone, and hid behind the trees when I turned to look. They lurked under my bed, ready to grab my ankles if I was careless enough to put them in reach. They were everywhere. I had to have a night-light, for light was the only thing that kept them at bay. Today I put those monsters into my fiction, and I love them. But fantasy monsters don't chase adults, only children. So the dominant emotion of my later childhood was fear. Fear of bigger kids at school, of a monster in the forest, and fear of the corpse. Fear, really, of life. I hated being alone, but others neither understood nor cared, so I was alone a lot. That is, often physically, and almost always emotionally. Today when I get a letter from a reader who feels almost utterly alone, I understand, because I remember.

That wasn't all. One doctor had a simplistic remedy for my bed-wetting: I was to have no liquid after 4 P.M. So to my accumulated discomforts was added that of thirst. The bed-wetting continued unabated, but I longed for a drink of water. Later in life I had a kidney stone, and I wonder whether it could have started long before, during my years of dehydration.

Meanwhile, I endured, having no alternative. Each morning I would wake soaking in urine, because the rubber sheet that protected the mattress caused the brine to pool around me. I would get up—I remember dancing on the floor in winter, because it was so cold on my feet—go downstairs to the bathroom, which had no toilet but did have a basin of cold water. Once I had to break the ice on the water before I could use it to wash. I would soak the washcloth, grit my teeth, and start washing my chest. After a few strokes my body would warm the cloth, and it would be easier. I would wash my midsection, getting the urine off, then run back shivering upstairs to my room to dress. Sometimes I couldn't resist putting the wet cloth to my mouth and sucking a little of the water out, to abate my thirst, feeling guilty because I wasn't allowed anything to drink until breakfast. Ironically, I now must drink more water than I like, to keep my urine diluted so that I won't have another kidney stone. I developed a real hatred of being cold, having experienced so much of it so unpleasantly; that's one big reason I now live in Florida. Later in the day I would wash out the sheet, a tedious chore with cold water. My parents didn't call it punishment, but it was my penalty for my persistence in wetting the bed: I had to clean up my own mess. I got the message in this and other ways: I was a burden to the family.

My fondest imagination was that one day I would wake up and discover that it had all been a horrible dream, and I was really back in England with the nanny. But it never happened. I pondered my life, and concluded that if I could be given a choice to either live it over exactly as it had been, or never to exist at all, I would prefer the latter. The net balance was negative; though I had never been verbally, physically, or sexually abused, by conventional definition, my existence simply wasn't worth it. My past was unpleasant, and my prospects for the future bleak.

But it wasn't all bad. My parents did care, though they did not understand how the world seemed from my perspective. They encouraged me to paste up gold stars on a chart for every night I remained dry, motivating me to change my behavior. Unfortunately they did not address its true cause, which lay closer to their own behavior than they would have cared to admit, so such things weren't very effective. But there was one thing that did impress me. My father offered two remedies: he could arrange for a sympathetic group to pray for me, or he could take me on a trip to the city to talk with a knowledgeable woman. I never did have much faith in the supernatural, so I chose the trip. It was always a pleasure to get away from the wilderness and into civilization. I think my love of trains, especially the old steam engines, stems from that: a train was the big, powerful, fascinating machine that carried folk to interesting places. That doesn't mean that I hated the country; today I am an environmentalist,

and live on my own tree farm. But I also have central heating, TV, radio, a telephone, computer, car, and the other benefits of civilization.

I forget whether the trip was to New York or Philadelphia, but the woman was Mrs. West. She explained to me how you could not see electricity, or hear it, or smell it, but nevertheless it existed, and you knew that when you turned on a light or some appliance. Similarly, she said, you couldn't see or hear God, but he nevertheless existed. Now that's a rationale I can accept, and it may be the reason I became an agnostic rather than an atheist. I remember being told about Santa Claus: a jolly fat man who squeezed down the chimney and brought presents to all the children in the world, in a single night. I didn't buy it. Then I was told about God: a big old white man with a long white beard sitting on a cloud, looking down at mortal folk. I don't buy that either. I make my living from fantasy, but I always knew the difference between fantasy and reality. I am a realist. But I understood the difference between lack of evidence, and proof. If you're driving on a mountainous road, and you want to pass the slow car ahead, and you don't see any oncoming traffic, you don't just assume that none exists. You don't pass on a turn. You wait until you can see ahead on a straight stretch. To do otherwise is dangerous.

So while I have never seen persuasive evidence of the supernatural, and really don't believe in ghosts or flying saucers, and like the great playwright George Bernard Shaw I am wary of a man whose god is in the sky, I don't feel free to declare that there *is* no God. So I am agnostic, not presuming to define the nature of God. And if you define God as Truth, Justice, Compassion, Beauty, Honor, Decency, and the like, then I do believe. But the bigotry I have seen in so many religions prevents me from joining any of them; I don't think that any great religious leaders, including Jesus Christ, ever intended their followers to practice anything like the Inquisition or the Crusades or jihads, converting others by sword and torture. In fact I think that if Jesus returned to the world today, his tears would flow to see what has been wrought in his name. He was a man of tolerance and peace, and he welcomed even a prostitute to wash his feet. I think that he and I could have a compatible chat, and he would not object to my philosophy any more than I object to his. And I think that the bigots would crucify him again, in the name of religion. So I am agnostic, and satisfied to be so. When I grew up, I married a minister's daughter, and we don't have any quarrels about religion. My background was Quaker, hers Unitarian-Universalist, both "liberal" religions, and I like to think that when good work is quietly being done, there is apt to be either a Quaker or a U-U person involved.

So I appreciated Mrs. West's rationale, without being persuaded of the existence of God. After that she took me to a bookstore and bought me a book. No, not a religious one; it was a storybook with games. On one page a little dog had gotten its leash hopelessly tangled in the furniture: could I untangle it? That was an example of a type of fiendishly challenging puzzle I have encountered also in other settings. To solve it, you have to fashion a loop elsewhere, pass it through a couple of holes, and around the dog; then it can be freed. I, being slow on the uptake, must have struggled with it for months. So it was that wonderful book that was my prize from that trip. Perhaps it contributed to my love of books—I, who had had such trouble even learning to read. Today I earn my living by writing books, and many of them incorporate challenges and puzzles.

But the thing that impressed me most about that trip was the proof it represented that my father really did care. He had taken a lot of trouble to make that trip with me, and I enjoyed all of it. When I had children of my own, I made it a point to take them on similar trips, giving them the experience of airplane flights (today's equivalent of the train), hotels, restaurants, and far places. We also read to them, just as my father had read to my sister and me every night. I think that nightly reading, and the daytime storytelling when we worked together outside, was the most important influence on my eventual choice of career. I knew that books contained fascinating adventures, and those stories took me away from my dreary real life. Today I spend even more of my time away from real life; my very name, Piers Anthony, is a pen name relating to the things I imagine. I have entered the realm of stories, and hope never to leave it. So that trip was fundamentally reassuring in a vital way, and I think it helped lay the foundation for my emotional recovery.

And the truth is that though I would not have cared to live my early life over, today the balance has changed, and I would be satisfied to live my whole life over, rather than never to have existed. Because my physical life improved too, and though progress has never been easy, taken as a whole my life is a good one. Two major things contribute to that well-being: my wife and my career. Those who seek advice for happiness can have mine: find the right spouse and the right career. Unfortunately today's world makes the achievement of such things difficult.

It would be tedious to detail the rest of my schooling, so I'll skip it, and just say that of the ten schools I attended through college, the third best was Westtown School in Pencil Vania, were I boarded four years and graduated with an indifferent record; the second best was The School in Rose Valley, also in Pencil Vania, where I completed grades five through seven in two years, and Goddard College, in Vermont, where I got my degree in creative writing. In fact Goddard was like entering paradise. It was at the time perhaps the most liberal college in America, with fewer than seventy-five students, no tests or grades, informal clothing, and a pervasive egalitarianism. That is, there was no hierarchy of students, no initiations or discrimination, everyone was friendly and helpful, and teachers were called by their first names. That doesn't mean that everything was perfect, and I did have some severe problems there. At one point I was suspended for a week for opposing a regressive faculty policy, and as with other conflicts I have had, I think it is now generally conceded that I had the right of the case. But overall, Goddard set me on course for my future, with my practice in writing, and my wife, and I now support it generously financially, being one of its richest graduates.

Ah, yes, romance. When I was eleven I loved a girl who was twelve. I'm not one to sneer at puppy love or crushes; it was the most intense love I am aware of experiencing, and it lasted for three years despite a complete lack of encouragement on her part. She was slender, had long brown hair, wore glasses, and was a smart and nice person. She taught me to play chess, and today I still work the daily chess puzzles in the newspaper. So in certain respects she defined my interest in the opposite gender. Let's pause, here, for a statement about terms: technically, gender means the grammatical identification of certain classes of words, while sex refers to whether a person or animal is male or female. But because sex also means the activity of procreation, this gets confusing and sometimes embarrassing. There is the story of the woman who filled out a job application form, writing in the box marked SEX "Occasionally." There is the suspicion that the Equal Opportunity Amendment to the Constitution, that would have protected women from discrimination, failed to pass because some people thought it meant sex as in copulation. So I prefer to use the word gender, where there is no confusion, and to hell with the purist grammarians. I never liked the subject of grammar much anyway. At any rate, when I later encountered a smart brown-haired girl with glasses in college, I married her. Now you know why. (My wife says that's an oversimplification. I can't think why. It's been forty years and she still has glasses and brown hair, and handles the family finances and goes online with her computer, something I'm not smart enough to do.) She was a tall girl, standing 5'9" in bare feet, while I had been the shortest person, male or female, in my high school classes. But in five years, from ninth grade to the second year of college, I grew almost a foot, so I was a full inch and a half taller than she. I tease her about that: I had to do it, to be ready for her. Men judge women by their figure; women judge men by their height.

After college, life was rough. My wife and I spent most of a year trying to make a living in northern Vermont, and I had trouble getting work because I insisted that I needed fifty dollars a week to support my family, and most jobs didn't pay that much. I finally landed a dollar-an-hour, fifty-hour-week job with American News, delivering magazines and paperback books to stores. Then, at the end of the summer, the boss approached me as I was punching out my time card on Friday. "Don't come in Monday." That was it. It seemed it was a summer job, not the permanent one I had been told. No advance notice, no severance pay, just gone. After that the only job I could get was selling health insurance—and you know, it's rough if you represent the policies honestly and are in an economically depressed region. When driving, I took my eye off the road to verify the address, and at that moment hit a reverse-

Anthony in his office, 1995

banked turn and started to go out of control. I hit the brakes—and they locked, and the car sailed off a six-foot bank at forty miles an hour. I remember wondering whether I would recover consciousness after landing. It rolled over, and I found my head in the back seat. The roof had caved in six inches—which was exactly the head clearance our VW Bug had. I was lucky; I came out of it with only a bruised shoulder. That was in the stone age, before seat belts; you bet I've always used one since. My grandmother Caroline sent money to enable us to get the car repaired, and my mother sent what money she could spare to enable us to live. Meanwhile my wife was pregnant, but having trouble. I took her to the hospital, where she lost the baby. Suddenly we had no prospective child, and I was eligible for the draft. Since I wasn't making it economically anyway, I volunteered to go in immediately. At least it would guarantee a paycheck for two years.

I was lucky, again: I was in the army from 1957 to 1959, between Korea and Vietnam. My wife joined me at Ft. Sill, Oklahoma, where I was an instructor in basic math and survey. It was an artillery base, and it takes calculation to survey in the big guns, so that they can fire exactly on target. You have to know where you are, before you know where you're going.

Later they tried to make us all "volunteer" to sign up for savings bonds, at two-and-a-half percent interest, but we needed the money for groceries and rent, so I didn't sign. So they harassed my whole unit, trying to make it put pressure on me to sign, but the others supported me instead, because nobody likes getting pushed around. Remember, once I got free of childhood, I got ornery about being bullied. I even went to the battalion commander with a charge of extortion against the first sergeant. The Lt. Colonel heard me out courteously for an hour and a half, but did not feel the evidence was conclusive. So I didn't get the sergeant canned, but I made him sweat, and I suspect he got a private reprimand. It was one more notch in the minor legend I became in the army. Strangers would come up to shake my hand. But the authorities were not amused. They booted me as instructor and sent me to another unit, as well as depriving me of any promotions. It's the army way. They didn't care as much about quality instruction—I was so effective a teacher that they wouldn't give me leave time to visit home, and in the end they had to pay me extra for over a month of unused leave—as they did about 100 percent bond participation. So, taken as a whole, the army was a waste of time for me, but it did pay my way, and covered my wife's month-long hospitalization and second miscarriage, a medical expense that could have bankrupted us otherwise.

After the army, we moved to Florida. I like to say that I traveled from Vermont to Florida the hard way: via two years in the army. That's how we came in out of the cold. I worked in industry as a technical writer for three years, and later I was an English teacher in high school. But what I really wanted to do was write, and finally we took the plunge: my wife, having suffered her third miscarriage, went to work, and I stayed home and tried to be a writer. The agreement was that if I didn't make it in a year, I would give up my foolish dream and focus on earning a living in Mundania. I had a fifth cousin who did just that; after failing at writing, he became an executive at Sears Roebuck and did well. But I made it: I sold two stories, and in that year earned a total of $160 from writing. Now I'm slow, but finally it penetrated: that wasn't enough income to sustain a family. That's when I actually became a teacher. But I kept writing stories on the side,

selling one every six months or so. Finally, in 1966, I retired from teaching, which job I liked no better than the others, and returned again to writing. This time I focused on novels instead of stories, and the larger amounts of money earned from novels enabled me to make a living, barely, though my wife continued to work. So it was lean, but it was writing, and that's what I wanted.

Thereafter, with the help of modern medicine, we were finally able to have two children we could keep. I think of this blessing as being like the monkey's paw. That famous story was about an old couple who had a severed monkey's paw that would grant three wishes, but it granted each wish in such a way that the result was worse than before. So they wished for money—and got it when their son was killed and his insurance came to them. Horrified, they wished for him to return—so the corpse was roused and heading for their door as one of the walking dead, before they wished him gone again and were done with it. I would never have been able to take the risk of staying home and writing, if my wife had not been free to earn the family income instead—and she was free only because all three of our babies had died. Had we had a choice, we would never have let them go. But now I was a successful writer, and we got our two daughters too. Thus we had everything we had wanted: success in writing, and a regular family.

But I was never a regular person, as this autobio surely makes clear. My life as a writer was just as problematical as my life elsewhere. I'm a square peg, and life offers mostly round holes. I think I didn't have the most trouble of any writer in the science fiction/fantasy genre, as that dubious honor belongs to Harlan Ellison, but I think I can fairly claim second place. (Harlan himself was somewhat baffled by me, and our relations have been mixed.) A publisher cheated me, so I demanded an accurate statement of account. Instead, I got blacklisted: publishers refused to buy from me. Even a writer's organization, which supposedly existed to help writers against errant publishers, tacitly sided with the publisher, though they were in a position to know that I had the right of the case. Writing is not necessarily a nice business, and justice is not always served. I dumped the writer's organization, called Science Fiction Writers Association, and have been hostile to it ever since, for good reason. The blacklist was rough; I accumulated eight unsold novels. But one publisher didn't honor the blacklist, so I survived. Also, I got a literary agent, the same one who handled Robert Heinlein, then the genre's leading writer. That messed up the blacklisters, because they knew that if they annoyed that agent, they'd never see work by Heinlein. Then something remarkable happened: apparently the errant publisher cheated one too many writers, faced legal retribution (I hadn't had the money to make a real case), and the proprietors had to flee their own company. The new administration hired editors who were friendly to me; they checked the company books and realized what had happened, and invited me to return. I was wary, but tried it, as I really wanted to work with their editor, Lester del Rey. He was in charge of fantasy, so I wrote a fantasy book. That was *A Spell for Chameleon,* the first Xanth novel.

None of us knew it at the time, but fantasy was about to take off for the stratosphere, and the "Xanth" series rode that rocket right on up. This was, as I see it, for two main reasons: Lester del Rey was an apt editor who knew a commercial novel when he saw one; he developed Stephen Donaldson, Terry Brooks, David Eddings, and others, in addition to me, and became arguably the most successful book editor the genre has seen. The other was his wife, Judy-Lynn del Rey, who named Del Rey books. I call her a giant, and I wrote her into Xanth as the lovely but deadly Gorgon, and she even sent in puns for it, like Gorgon-zola cheese, and was duly credited in the Author's Note, like any other young fan. "I *am* a young fan!" she said. But the humor went beyond that, for physically Judy-Lynn was a dwarf, standing something like three-and-a-half feet tall. But she was smart and tough, and she could really promote her books. She was the publisher who first put *Star Wars* into print. So Lester's editing and Judy-Lynn's promotion made a publishing phenomenon like few have seen in our time, and Del Rey Books soon dominated the genre. The fifth Xanth novel, *Ogre, Ogre,* became the first fantasy original paperback (that is, one that never had a hardcover edition) to make the big national bestseller lists. My income moved from that initial $140 to more than a million dollars a year, and all our financial problems were behind us. The blacklist was gone, destroyed at its source; all the editors who had blacklisted me were out of power, and not eager to advertise what they had done. I wasn't actually responsible for getting them canned, not directly, but I believe that none of them cared to mess with me again. It's that bully syndrome; when the tables turn, the bullies flee.

With success came fan mail, and I do my best to answer it, though about one third of my working time is now taken up by it. Sometimes it seems that half my readers want to become writers themselves; unfortunately, only about one in a hundred will ever sell anything, because the competition is great. A number of the letters are serious, such as those from suicidally depressed teens. I understand depression, because despite my phenomenal commercial success (not critical success; critics claim that I don't write anything worthwhile) I remain mildly depressive. It seems that most writers and artists are depressive; I guess I'm lucky that it's not worse for me. So though I am old and most of them are young, we relate well. A number have credited me with saving their lives, just by responding and understanding. I drew on what they told me to make the character Colene in "The Mode" series: age fourteen, smart, pretty, and secretly slicing her wrists. Many have told me how well they relate to her; they wonder how I could know their inner truths so well. I don't know, really, but I listen well. I also have a novel, *Firefly,* that is apt to freak out school officials, because it deals graphically with sexual abuse, but I have had many letters from women who thank me for bringing this ugly matter out into the open. So readers should beware; not all my work is frivolous fantasy. Some of it is savage.

But no glory lasts forever. Judy-Lynn had a stroke, and died. Problems caused me to leave Del Rey Books though I really didn't want to, and in time my career crested and diminished. Publishers made promises and then reneged, to my cost. It remains a perilous business, and as in life, writing skill is not always rewarded, and justice is not necessarily served. There seems to be a small anonymous cadre of critics whose purpose in life is to spread false stories about me. I tackle these head-on when I encounter them, but it's like dealing with pickpockets: they are hard to catch in the act. It started when I was accused of being an ogre—at conventions I had never attended. It hasn't stopped. I have been called a Satanist, maybe because Satan is a character in a couple of my novels, and a possible child molester, and some even hint that I must be into bestiality because there are mythical half-human creatures in my fiction, like centaurs and mermaids. Some accuse me of unethical behavior, though they can't document it. I presume that other successful folk have similar problems; those who are not successful want to drag down those who are, and are not choosy about their methods. But the great majority of those who write to me are supportive. Still, it's more fun climbing up the mountain of Parnassus—that's what the literary establishment is called—than tumbling down it! Today other fantasy writers are surging ahead, and I wish them well, though I am sorry to be left behind. I still write funny fantasy, and I have answered an average of 150 fan letters a month for a number of years, but my real interest now is in historical fiction. I regard *Tatham Mound,* about the American Indians who encountered the Spanish explorer Hernando de Soto, as the major novel of my career, and the historical "Geodyssey" series as the major work of my career. I am now in my sixties, and know I won't live forever, so I'm doing what I always really wanted to do, and that is to explore the whole human condition, and to help others to understand it. I like to think that those young readers who like funny Xanth will in time graduate to my historical fiction, and find it as satisfying in a different way. I love writing, and when I die I expect to be halfway through a great novel.

BIBLIOGRAPHY

BOOKS OF INTEREST TO YOUNG ADULTS

Science fiction/fantasy novels:

Chthon, Ballantine, 1967.

Macroscope, Avon, 1969.

Race against Time, Hawthorne, 1973.

Rings of Ice, Avon, 1974.

Triple Détente, DAW Books, 1974.

Phthor (sequel to *Chthon*), Berkley Publishing, 1975.

(With Robert Coulson) *But What of Earth?,* Laser (Toronto), 1976, original unrevised version published as *But What of Earth? A Novel Rendered into a Bad Example,* Tor Books, 1989.

Steppe, Millington (London), 1976, Tor Books, 1985.

Hasan, Borgo Press, 1977.

(With Frances Hall) *The Pretender,* Borgo Press, 1979.

Mute, Avon, 1981.

Ghost, Tor Books, 1986.

Shade of the Tree, St. Martin's, 1986.

Balook, Underwood-Miller, 1989.

Total Recall (screenplay novelization), Morrow, 1989.

(With Robert Kornwise) *Through the Ice,* Underwood-Miller, 1990.

Firefly, Morrow, 1990.

Dead Morn, Tafford (Houston), 1990.

Mer-Cycle, Tafford, 1991, published as *Mercycle,* Ace Books, 1992.

(With Philip José Farmer) *The Caterpillar's Question,* Ace Books, 1992.

(With Mercedes Lackey) *If I Pay Thee Not in Gold,* Baen, 1993.

Killobyte, Putnam, 1993.

With Robert E. Margroff:

The Ring, Ace Books, 1968.

The E.S.P. Worm, Paperback Library, 1970.

Dragon's Gold, Tor Books, 1987.

Serpent's Silver, Tor Books, 1988.

Orc's Opal, Tor Books, 1990.

Chimaera's Copper, T. Doherty, 1990.

Across the Frames (omnibus volume; contains *Dragon's Gold, Serpent's Silver,* and *Chimaera's Copper*), Guild America Books, 1992.

Mouvar's Magic, Tor Books, 1993.

Final Magic (omnibus volume; contains *Orc's Opal* and *Mouvar's Magic*), Guild America Books, 1992.

"Battle Circle" series:

Sos the Rope, Pyramid, 1968.

Var the Stick, Faber, 1972, Bantam, 1973.

Neq the Sword, Corgi (London), 1975.

Battle Circle (omnibus volume), Avon, 1978.

"Omnivore" series:

Omnivore, Ballantine, 1968.

Orn, Avon, 1971.

Ox, Avon, 1976.

Of Man and Manta (omnibus volumes), Corgi, 1986.

"Magic of Xanth" series:

A Spell for Chameleon, Del Rey, 1977.

The Source of Magic, Del Rey, 1979.

Castle Roogna, Del Rey, 1979.

The Magic of Xanth (omnibus volume; includes *A Spell for Chameleon, The Source of Magic,* and *Castle Roogna*), Doubleday, 1981.

Centaur Aisle, Del Rey, 1981.

Ogre, Ogre, Del Rey, 1982.

Night Mare, Del Rey, 1983.

Dragon on a Pedestal, Del Rey, 1983.

Crewel Lye: A Caustic Yarn, Del Rey, 1985.

Golem in the Gears, Del Rey, 1986.

Vale of the Vole, Avon, 1987.

Heaven Cent, Avon, 1988.

(With Jody Lynn Nye) *Piers Anthony's Visual Guide to Xanth,* illustrated by Todd Cameron Hamilton and James Clouse, Avon Books, 1989.

Man from Mundania, Avon, 1989.

Isle of View, Morrow, 1990.

Question Quest, Morrow, 1991.

The Color of Her Panties, Morrow, 1992.

Demons Don't Dream, Tor Books, 1993.

Happy Thyme, Tor Books, 1994.

Geis of the Gargoyle, Tor Books, 1995.

Roc and a Hard Place, Tor Books, 1995.

"Cluster" series:

Cluster, Avon, 1977 (published in England as *Vicinity Cluster,* Panther, 1979).

Chaining the Lady, Avon, 1978.

Kirlian Quest, Avon, 1978.

Thousandstar, Avon, 1980.

Viscous Circle, Avon, 1982.

"Tarot" series:

God of Tarot, Jove, 1979.

Vision of Tarot, Berkley Publishing, 1980.

Faith of Tarot, Berkley Publishing, 1980.

Tarot (omnibus volume of three-part novel), Ace Books, 1987.

"Apprentice Adept" series:

Split Infinity, Del Rey, 1980.

Blue Adept, Del Rey, 1981.

Juxtaposition, Del Rey, 1982.

Double Exposure (omnibus volume; includes *Split Infinity, Blue Adept,* and *Juxtaposition*), Doubleday, 1982.

Out of Phaze, Ace Books, 1987.

Robot Adept, Ace Books, 1988.

Unicorn Point, Ace Books, 1989.

Phaze Doubt, Ace Books, 1990.

"Bio of a Space Tyrant" series:

Refugee, Avon, 1983.

Mercenary, Avon, 1984.

Politician, Avon, 1985.

Executive, Avon, 1985.

Statesman, Avon, 1986.

"Incarnations of Immortality" series:

On a Pale Horse, Del Rey, 1983.

Bearing an Hourglass, Del Rey, 1984.

With a Tangled Skein, Del Rey, 1985.

Wielding a Red Sword, Del Rey, 1987.

Being a Green Mother, Del Rey, 1987.

For Love of Evil, Morrow, 1988.

And Eternity, Morrow, 1990.

"The Mode" series:

Virtual Mode, Putnam, 1991.

Fractal Mode, Putnam, 1992.

Chaos Mode, Putnam, 1993.

"Geodyssey" series:

Isle of Woman, Tor Books, 1993.

Shame of Man, Tor Books, 1994.

Science fiction short stories:

Prostho Plus, Gollancz, 1971, Bantam, 1973.

Anthonology, Tor Books, 1985.

(Editor with Barry Malzberg and Martin Greenberg) *Uncollected Stars,* Avon, 1986.

Hard Sell, Tafford, 1990.

Alien Plot, T. Doherty, 1992.

(Editor with Robert Gilliam) *Tales from the Great Turtle,* Tor Books, 1994.

Martial arts novels:

"Jason Striker" series; with Roberto Fuentes:

Kiai!, Berkley Publishing, 1974.

Mistress of Death, Berkley Publishing, 1974.

The Bamboo Bloodbath, Berkley Publishing, 1975.

Ninja's Revenge, Berkley Publishing, 1975.

Amazon Slaughter, Berkley Publishing, 1976.

Other:

Bio of an Ogre: The Autobiography of Piers Anthony, Ace Books, 1988.

Pornucopia, Tafford, 1989.

Tatham Mound (historical novel), Morrow, 1991.

Letters to Jenny, edited by Alan Riggs, Tor Books, 1993.

Contributor to anthologies, including *Science against Man,* Avon, 1970; *Nova One: An Anthology of Original Science Fiction,* edited by Harry Harrison, Delacorte Press, 1970; *Again, Dangerous Visions,* edited by Harlan Ellison, Doubleday, 1972; *Generation,* edited by David Gerrold, Dell, 1972; and *The Berkley Showcase,* Berkley Publishing, 1981. Contributor, with Robert Margroff, under joint pseudonym Robert Piers, of a short story to *Adam Bedside Reader.* Also contributor of short stories to science fiction periodicals, including *Analog, Fantastic, Worlds of If, Worlds of Tomorrow, Amazing, Magazine of Fantasy and Science Fiction,* and *Pandora.*

Eth Clifford

1915-

*Eth Clifford at a surprise birthday party with her daughter Ruthanne
and husband David Rosenberg, Indianapolis, 1966*

When one sits at the typewriter (yes! I am still that far behind the times!), creating a small new world, and peopling it with a variety of characters, that world and those people are so real and alive, it comes almost as a shock when the manuscript is finished.

For some time after, I find myself still continuing to write dialogue in my mind, or visualizing new scenes, even introducing new characters. Inevitably, of course, these particular people you have lived with for so long a time, that special world you have moved about in with such familiarity, now give way to new creations.

In an author's life, there are always many endings and new beginnings.

It used to be an ardent wish of mine that I could somehow rewrite my life, change all the hurtful things that happened, the wounds and grief of growing up. I realized, of course, that you cannot change what has already happened, nor can you ever know exactly what lies ahead.

My father died when I was eight years old. I understood that I would never see him again, never hear his voice, never see him smile. Even though he was often away from home, I felt secure for he always returned. This absence was different, an absence I could not accept. He

"My older brother Maurice in England," 1942

would come back, I told myself stubbornly. He had to, because I wished it so strongly.

Sometimes, when I peered out a window, or sat outside on the steps, a figure would rush by. My heart would begin to pound. I would race after the passerby, crying, "Papa! Papa!" It never was Papa, of course. After a while, I stopped hoping and dreaming.

I think that somehow that was when I became a writer. Making up stories gave me power—power to create people and situations, power to control what they said and did. It gave me something else as well—a way to reach people and give them some moments of reading pleasure.

Reading pleasure was important to me, because I was, and still am, first and always, a reader.

My mother encouraged us to read, especially (perhaps you will find this hard to believe) at mealtime. I remember a neighbor dropping in one evening when my brothers and I (there were five of us; I was the only girl) were having our evening meal. Each of us had a book propped up in front of us. The neighbor was shocked.

"You let them read while they eat?" she exploded. "Who ever heard of such a thing?"

My mother smiled. "I enjoy the silence," she said calmly. "They're improving their minds

as well as feeding their bodies, and I don't have to settle arguments. It's the best time of the day."

The neighbor left, shaking her head. My mother knew the neighbor would never understand. You see, she was not a reader. My mother was.

We were poor when it came to material things. Food was carefully doled out, toys were unheard of, our clothes came from the thrift shops (my mother found marvelous bargains at the Salvation Army stores), but we had books!

We didn't own the books, of course. They came from the library, a remarkable institution that encouraged us to come as often as we wished, that let us take the books home. I loved the library then. I still do!

Now, knowing the books I write are in libraries, I feel that I am repaying a long overdue debt. And when I see children at tables in the library, reading or being read to by a librarian, I am delighted, for it tells me there are still many, many readers among us.

Sometimes, after I have spoken to a group of people at a seminar, people will ask me why I want to be an author. Isn't it hard work, they ask. Doesn't it take up a lot of your time? Yes. It is hard work. And yes, it does take up much of my time. But to me, doing what you love to do is a reward.

Books have helped me to escape when I have felt sad and lonely; they have made me even happier when I feel good. Books have been my teachers and my friends.

I thought people who wrote books were very special, for they made me forget myself and my problems, even if only for a little while. Authors created other worlds for me to live in for a time. They taught me so many things I knew nothing about; they showed me how people lived, what they felt, how their dreams came true, and even how their dreams fell by the wayside.

In today's world, we get all the information we can possibly want to know via television and other electronic marvels. But I still find that a book is closer, more intimate, a real friend in need. You can take a book anywhere. You don't have to depend on programs you might or might not enjoy. In the world of books, the choice is always yours.

When I was a child, I decided that if for some reason I could not become an author, I would, when an adult, be an actress, or a dancer, or a singer. I even considered the idea of becoming a criminal lawyer. I could see myself on the stage, weeping in some extraordinary dramatic moment, and having the audience sob along with me. Or perhaps the theater would be hushed and absorbed by the breathtaking beauty of my dancing. I could almost hear them shouting "Bravo! Bravo!" and throwing bouquets at the stage.

I rather favored the idea of becoming an actress. I was very good at weeping. Then someone mentioned that an actress had to be tall. Who, that person asked positively, had ever heard of a peanut acting on a stage? Who would even see you on a stage? That was a blow! I had joined the dramatic club in school when I was in fourth grade. I realized I was always part of a group, standing in front of them so I would be visible. The good acting roles always went to taller girls.

It didn't help at all that the other kids would say, "What happened? Did you shrink in the wash?" Or, "Hey, why are you standing in a hole?" Names like "Shortie" or "Peewee" or "Shrimp" or "Two-by-nothing" gave me a very poor image of myself. I got the idea that being small was a kind of deformity.

I am still small, and people still say a variety of things about my height, or lack of it. I find that I no longer mind, for I discovered some time ago that your physical appearance doesn't prevent you from writing books, if that is what you want to do, or acting, or arguing cases in front of a judge.

When I did my daydreaming, I sometimes decided it might be very pleasant to be a princess, to live in a castle in a far-off land, wear fine clothes, eat chocolate without limit (that was the nicest part of the dream), and be gracious and kind to all my subjects, no matter how tall or short they were. This last daydream I soon realized was impractical. To begin with, I would have to marry a prince, and princes were in short supply in my neighborhood.

I never, ever thought I would be a writer. Writers I regarded as a race apart. They were tall, and handsome, and male. They were brilliant, and witty, and flawless. They could speak several languages fluently, and knew everybody and his brother. They always traveled, and were so rich they hadn't the foggiest notion that everyone didn't live as well as they did.

Then I made an extraordinary discovery. All writers were not necessarily male! I found

Louisa May Alcott, and later, Edna St. Vincent Millay, Elizabeth Barrett Browning, Emily Dickinson. . . . But of course, I told myself, these women were all tall and beautiful. I was tiny, and certainly not beautiful, so I automatically disqualified myself.

What's more, I told myself, authors—male or female—lived wildly adventurous lives. They scaled mountains, explored the underworld of the seas, dived for coral in lagoons, ate exotic foods, and never got out of bed before noon!

I could not see myself moving in such exalted circles.

Then what was left for me to write about, should I decide to become a writer?

When I was a little girl, my family (my brothers and mother and I) lived in the country for about two years. Pines filled the air with a sharp, pervading scent; the woods were alive with birds; tiny creatures I could not identify scrambled from beneath dead branches; and a silent walk on a dusty road was heady adventure.

*"My next older brother Martin
at age twenty-three," 1933*

I attended a one-room schoolhouse. What I recall most vividly were the orchards—a pear orchard and an apple orchard—that enclosed the school in aromatic parentheses. Lunchtime, I sat with my back against one of the pear trees or an apple tree, opened my brown bag, ate lunch indifferently, and read.

Naturally, I understood that I could not be a writer with so simple a background, but I could be, and was, and still am, a reader. As a child, a teenager, an adult . . . always a reader.

I wrote, of course, very early on. I accepted the fact that this did not make me an author. Authors were very special people. I was very class-conscious!

But oh, the joy of being asked to write! When we were given assignments to hand in a "composition" for English class, groans filled the air. I was always surprised. Writing a composition beat arithmetic, which plagued me, or geography, which bored me. Did I really care that Wisconsin was the dairy state, and Indiana the heartland state of America? (I cared a lot about that when my husband and daughter and I moved to Indiana, to live there and love it for more than twenty years!)

Though I was born in Manhattan, I was whisked away (with my family, of course) to a small town in New Jersey. I do not remember that period. My father then got a job in Philadelphia, where I spent my early years. We moved on from there, after my father's death, to Brooklyn, New York, where we had relatives. And there, fate stepped in!

I met my husband-to-be. I was seventeen, he was nineteen. We met purely by accident.

Two friends and I, sharing an equal love for books, decided to start a poetry club. At that time, one of the Brooklyn newspapers ran a social column. People were invited to send in announcements of "get-together clubs" for people who shared the same interests. Since I lived in a small apartment with my mother and brothers, there would be neither space nor privacy for our (we hoped) new club. So after the one friend who lived in a house persuaded her parents either to sit in the kitchen or go upstairs and listen to the radio, or better still, go out to see a movie, we had "open house" for our hoped-for guests. We waited and waited. We gave each other earnest reasons why no one had come. It was a Saturday night. Most people would prefer to go see a movie. It looked like rain. Maybe we shouldn't have called it a "poetry club." Maybe the word "poetry" had scared people away. Maybe . . . maybe . . . maybe.

And then the doorbell rang!

Several people were waiting on the porch. The president of the United States would not have received a warmer welcome. In moments, the living room was crowded. Who would have believed there were so many poetry lovers in Brooklyn? Many brought their favorite poems. There were lively arguments about verse versus poetry. In fact, some of the arguments grew so loud, it seemed people were more exercised over what was and was not poetry than if they had been arguing politics!

Only one young, handsome fellow sat quietly in a corner of the room. He had black curly hair and hazel-blue eyes that he kept fixed on me. I didn't know it then, but I was staring at my future husband.

At that point in time, I didn't know that someday I would be the author of eighty-two published books. The eighty-second book is titled *Family for Sale* and is scheduled for publication in April, 1996.

We did not know that my husband would become a publisher and art director of his own company, to create and produce children's books (mostly educational, to be used widely in schools across the nation), that he would come up with ideas for dictionaries and encyclopedias that would eventually be sold to Encyclopedia Britannica and other well-known publishers.

I was delighted to be able to share in his work as both an author and editor.

It was a most exciting time in our lives.

Of course, this publishing company of ours began at first only in our minds and hearts. Though my husband had worked for a large and well-known publishing company in New York as an art director, starting from scratch with very little money was exciting but scary.

Our "company" was just the two of us. We rented two fair-sized rooms over a small barbershop. One room remained empty of furniture for quite a while. The other room we filled with secondhand items—two secondhand desks that looked as if they had been in someone's garage for years. We brought my typewriter from home, which meant I had to do all my stories and books in the office from then on. But it worked out fine, because the clickety-clack sound of the keys made it seem

*"My younger brother Edward, age twenty,
with Maurice's daughter in England,"* 1942

we were really in business. We even bought a file cabinet (secondhand, of course), which took us a long time to fill. That first year, we were hardly able to fill half the space in one drawer. But we did buy a brand-new coffee maker!

We lived a year-and-a-half on our life savings.

And then our hopes began to be realized. We actually began to earn some money.

Within three years, we had a staff of ten people—editors, authors, researchers, and illustrators. My husband originated and (with the help of the staff) developed a range of books and educational programs from the beginning of an idea to finished illustrated and designed books.

In the twenty-one years of our existence, we developed many innovative programs, some of which are still in use in some schools around the country. We would have stayed in our office, gladly have continued creating new programs, but the fates decided otherwise. President Richard Nixon cut off federal aid to the schools. Without that help, schools no longer had enough money to buy new (or old) books or series of books. As simply as that, we were out of business.

It was David, my husband, who set me on the path of becoming an author of children's books. Before that, I had begun my career in writing for adults. I started out slowly, not sure who I was writing for and what I wanted to write about. It took me a while to find the right direction. At first, I began with poetry—no, it wasn't poetry. It was verse. I got early training in verse at my various jobs—dashed off a few lines for someone in one of the offices I worked in who hadn't purchased a birthday card to enclose with a gift and in desperation asked me to come up with something—anything—as long as it rhymed!

I did; she loved it. After that my ambition was to write material for greeting cards. I honestly thought that was as far as I could expect to go as a writer. Fortunately, not a single greeting card company was the least bit interested. Suppose they had been! I might never have written anything else! The fates must have taken a hand at that point.

In 1941, two months after David and I were married, the Japanese bombed Pearl Harbor. No, they didn't do the bombing because of this act of ours. But it had an effect on our lives that went on for more than three years. David enlisted in the navy. My eldest brother joined the coast guard; my next oldest brother volunteered for service in the air force; my youngest brother went into the army. He was just eighteen at the time. Suddenly they were gone, to different parts of the world, my brothers to Europe, David to the South Pacific.

Though I didn't suspect it, that was a turning point for me, as far as my career would go.

I became a writer who came in the back door, for I was the self-appointed go-between for the family. My letters went out steadily, giving each of my brothers and husband news about one another, news from home, and stories—very brief ones—to keep them interested. They were my first fans.

After a while, David urged me to start writing short stories for magazines. I thought that was a wild idea. Who would want to buy them, I asked myself, and why? I was reluctant even to try, but David was insistent. He made me promise I would at least make the attempt. I promised,

"Eth the reader waiting for David," 1938

remembered one of the stories I had written for him, and decided to lengthen it before sending it on. I so little expected anything other than a quick rejection, I forgot about it. Two months later, the editor of the magazine sent me a check for ten dollars! Ten whole dollars for a story that had taken me no longer than a half hour to dash off. And it was to be published several months later.

I didn't want to cash that check. I wanted to have it on hand, and wave it at everyone, and shout, "Hey! Everybody. Look at me! I'm a writer." Did I save the check? Of course not. It was wartime, money was scarce, and ten dollars could buy a lot of food in those days.

I began to write short stories steadily after that, sending them off to a variety of small magazines. My stories were published. I had proof, because I was sent a copy of each magazine. I needed that physical proof, because I had a hard time convincing myself that I actually had a foot in the door of the publishing world. One magazine began to put my name on its front cover!

David urged me not to stop there but to try some of the important magazines that had a national impact. I was convinced my stories would come back so fast it would convince David he was wrong. But David had a way of being right. One magazine published four of my stories. How lucky, I wondered, could one get? I could see a future for myself in the magazine world.

And then a miracle (so I thought then and still do now) happened. I received a letter from Simon and Schuster, a large and successful publishing house. The president of S & S asked if I would make an appointment to see him. Overwhelmed, I was almost afraid to reply. I was rather shy in those days. I also knew the kind of magazines I wrote for were probably never seen at S & S. Curiosity, and my husband's urging, made me respond.

When I arrived at the offices of S & S, I was tempted to turn around and leave. What was I doing in this place? Here only real writers belonged. The president's greeting soon put me at ease, but what he had to say stunned me.

"I've read your four stories," he began, "and I thought they were marvelous. I think you should put those characters in a book, and I would like to publish that book."

I'm certain my jaw dropped down to my knees. Me? Write a book? A full-length book? Impossible.

"Why are you shaking your head?" he wanted to know.

"I can't write a book," I stammered. "Not a whole book. I only write short stories." I stopped to think. "Even if I tried, it would only be sort of a book," I explained.

"Okay," he told me. "Go home and write a sort of a book."

"You can do it," my husband said, when I was home again and full of surprise and delight and fear. He always told me that!

And I did write it. It was called *Go Fight City Hall.* Under the title was the phrase "A Sort of a Book."

Holding that book in my hand was an extraordinary experience. "I did it. I actually did it," I said.

The book went on to be a best-seller. *The Reader's Digest* purchased it and featured it as their Book of the Month.

I even wrote a sequel to it, which S & S also published.

I was overwhelmed by the response to my simple story. Servicemen as far away as

Korea sent me letters. "You must have met my Uncle Joe or Tom or Joseph," they would tell me. "You gave me a touch of home," others said.

And then, suddenly, my direction changed. My husband listened each evening as I told stories to our daughter at bedtime. She snuggled down in her pillow, thumb in mouth, ready for story time. One evening, when she was fast asleep, David told me, "You ought to write those stories down."

"Why would I do that?" I wondered. "What would I do with them then?"

"You would send them to a publisher. You enjoy telling them so much, I'm sure other kids would like to hear them."

I was pleased and touched, and also quite curious.

My first children's book was called *Red Is Never a Mouse.* It was a book about colors for young children, and it was in verse, my first love.

Eth and David Rosenberg on their wedding day, 18 October 1941, in Brooklyn, New York

The reaction to that book was incredible. The *New York Times* Children's Book Review, Special Section, and the *Saturday Review of Literature* chose *Red Is Never a Mouse* as one of the 100 best books of the year, 1961. Those reviews, and my husband, of course, convinced me I should devote all my writing time to creating books for children—of all ages.

Added to the great joy of the writing itself were the awards for which I was nominated and some of which I won. In 1971, my book *The Year of the Three-Legged Deer* was a nominee for the Newbery Award. Alas, I did not win it, but the thrill of being that close has never left me.

My book *Help! I'm a Prisoner in the Library* was published in 1979. It is still being sold! When it was published, it was nominated for a number of state awards. It was one of the 104 Detroit's Choice Books for the year, selected by the Detroit Public Library System.

My book *The Remembering Box* was selected by the American Library Association (their Children's Editors' Choice List) as one of the most outstanding books of the year, 1985. It was also chosen by the National Council for Social Studies as a notable book in social studies for the year 1985.

One of the special rewards that makes me glow with pride is the response I get from readers. Many of them write, mostly in scrawls back then and now with more sophistication, beautiful calligraphy, thanks to their school computers, to say, "You're a great writer!" "You really write good." "You must be nice. Can we be friends?"

I also receive arguments. "Why did you let Chilili die? Can you write the book over again and let her live?" one child begged. Chilili was an Indian girl in the book *The Year of the Three-Legged Deer.* Or, "You said a mouse is never red and it is so. I saw a red mouse on my front step." Or "Why is Harvey so mean to Nora?" All authors, I assume, receive mail, not necessarily favorable. Young children write from the heart, and these letters can be funny, or sad, or chiding, or—yes—even insulting. Usually they want something from you, because they often begin a letter with "You are rich and famous, so. . . ."

Rich is doubtful, and fame is fleeting, but you can't help being touched and/or amused by the honesty with which they speak to you.

"You are rich and famous," one letter from Hawaii began. Obviously the letter had been written in great haste, because spelling and the words on the ruled sheet bore no relation to each other. "So," the writer continued, "You probly know Mikel Jackson. I have to have his fone number rite away. It's not listed. Please anser rite away."

As an afterthought, the child added, "I don't read your books, but I will if you give me his nomber."

Another child wrote, "I think your books are stupid."

I could imagine the smile on her face as she penned these words; how daring she felt; how triumphant that she could put this author in her place.

The letter went on, "My best friend Peggy thinks they are stupid, too. Can you send me one of your books," she added, "and sign it. And Peggy wants one, too."

"You're not going to reply to that, I hope," David said. He was outraged.

"Of course I will respond," I told him. "She has a right to her opinion."

"She does not have the right to be insulting," he insisted.

Nonetheless, I did respond. I told her she was certainly entitled to her opinion, was free to express it, and everyone has the right to dislike a book, or a movie, or a TV program, etc. She did not have the right, however, to be rude and insulting. She could have given me the reasons why she disliked my book without resorting to name-calling.

Children also come up with some strange notions. Schools have special displays, or auctions, or book sales, or whatever, in which something from authors is displayed. One child asked me for one of my socks. I wrote an apologetic reply. "This sock was given to me by a friend to send to you. I borrowed it from her, but she says you can keep it." I thought a sock from a close friend would be almost like having the real thing.

I have been asked for recipes, for photographs of me and my family, for a neck scarf, and, of course, for free books.

Free books, I had to inform them, were not free. I had to purchase them from my publisher, buy a mailer, write a covering letter, address and stamp the package, and then drive to the post office to mail it.

I am also invited to "drop in" to their schools, especially if I just happen to be passing by. Since I live in Florida, the chances are remote that I will happen to be in the vicinity of schools in other states.

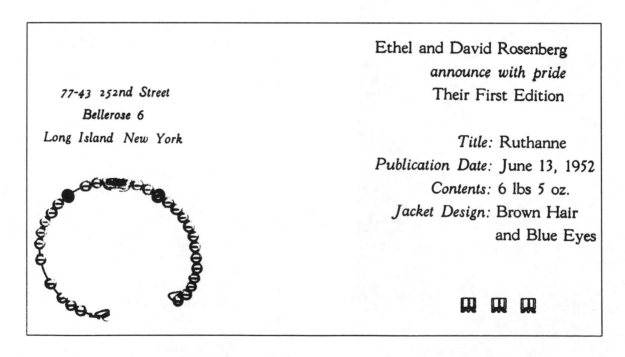

77-43 252nd Street
Bellerose 6
Long Island New York

Ethel and David Rosenberg
announce with pride
Their First Edition

Title: Ruthanne
Publication Date: June 13, 1952
Contents: 6 lbs 5 oz.
Jacket Design: Brown Hair
and Blue Eyes

Birth announcement for Ruthanne Rosenberg with her bracelet (at left)

Children who write want to be pen pals. I must then regretfully explain why this is not possible. I know the disappointment is deep, but I remind these would-be pals that I do have other obligations.

They are eager to know more about the author. Are you married? Do you have children? Do you have pets?

I answer as fully as I can. Yes, at one time we owned three dogs, not all at the same time. Tippy was a terrier. Noodles was a poodle. Bissela was a miniature poodle. All the dogs were named by our daughter. We also had three birds. Smarty was a lively green parakeet whom I taught to speak a few words. He loved to say "Smarty is a good boy." And well he might, for he was good. His cage was always open, and Smarty understood he had the run (or should I say flight) of the house. He only went back to his cage to eat and sleep.

He enjoyed playing "golf" with a small Christmas bell I bought for him. He would hit the bell with his beak clear across the room and race after it. "You can fly, dummy," I would sometimes remind him. But Smarty had his own way of doing things. He dearly loved it when we sat in the living room reading the newspaper. He would fly to us at once, perch (and sway madly to maintain his balance) on the rim of the paper, and nip it from one side, across the center, and down the other side, leaving an interesting border. Probably his motto was "All the news that's fit to nip."

In a moment of weakness, we bought a companion for him, a beautiful bright blue bird we called Beauty, because she was lovely. Beauty was aptly named for she never ever left her cage. She preferred to sit and admire herself reflected in the small mirror we had placed there.

The third parakeet was green. Because he had boundless energy (he, too, flew about freely), we named him Peppy.

When we moved from New York to Indianapolis, we decided to ship Smarty by train, for we were not going directly to our new home. When we finally picked him up at the station, poor Smarty looked as if he had been in a war. He was bedraggled and dirty; his spirits drooped; he told us reproachfully "Smarty is a good boy." When we opened his cage, he flew to my shoulder, and stayed there until we reached home.

There, in the tiny tub we filled with tepid water, Smarty took a refreshing bath, shook his

The author's beloved dog, Noodles

feathers heartily, ate till I thought he would burst, and then took a leisurely fly-around his new quarters.

We also had two other birds. The canary was a bright yellow, and a singer of songs. It was a joy to listen to him. Because of his color, our daughter promptly named him Sunshine. The other bird was half-finch and half-canary. His feathers were a rich deep red. So, naturally, our daughter dubbed him Sunset.

As time went on, and our pets grew old, we faced the sad fact that they would not be with us much longer.

Tippy had to be held on a leash, for he was the most curious creature in the world. He often tried to yank free. It was inevitable that he would make it one day. He was gone in a flash of disobedience, disregarding our calls. Though we searched for him, we never saw him again.

To console our daughter, we purchased Noodles. Her registered name, believe it or not, was Heloise. The papers that came with her stated that in black and white. We grinned at the idea of standing outside and shouting, "Here, Heloise." While David and I were trying to think of a more appropriate name, our daughter called her Noodles. She lived to a ripe old age. Then she fell ill. One night she came into our bedroom and tugged at my hand. Quietly, I slipped out of bed and followed her. She went to the living room and stood looking at me, as if to say, "Come down to my level."

I slid down to the floor. Noodles came trembling into my arms. I rocked her back and forth, as if she were an infant. After a few moments, Noodles made a small, soft sound, settled deeper into my lap, sighed once again, and was gone.

I sat on the floor, clutching her close to me, and stroked her. "It's all right," I told her. "It's all right." I let the tears run unchecked down my cheeks.

David found us there early in the morning. Gently, he lifted Noodles from my grip. "We'll take her out to the cemetery," he told me softly, as if Noodles might wake and be fearful.

When we came back, I said almost violently, "I don't want to have another pet, ever again." But we did have, of course, mostly for the sake of our daughter. Bissela (little bit) was a miniature poodle.

She brought bounce and beauty and good cheer back to us. She lived a long time. When I brought her to the vet on her last trip there, he shook his head.

"Let her go," he said. "It's time."

I left, with David, and didn't say another word until we arrived home, our suddenly very quiet home, although Bissela had been a gentle, quiet pet.

"We can go to the kennel on the weekend," he began.

I shook my head. "No," I said finally. "No more dogs."

David agreed; they left a void in our lives that was never filled again.

Then we lost our little publishing house, we felt at very loose ends. The only activity that still went on was my writing.

How strange it is to be a writer, I thought. My mind teemed with story ideas when everything was going smoothly. In difficult times, I turned to my typewriter as if to salvation. Writing was a safety valve. I could lose myself in the mythical lives of characters I created. David constantly encouraged me. I would say, suddenly, "I'm all written out."

David would repress a smile and reply heartily, "Good. That's the way to go."

"Then you agree with me?"

"You can no more stop writing than you can thinking," he said. "I know that. You know that."

"I'm all written out," I went on.

Ruthanne, age five, at Poconos Stroudsburg Wild Animal Farm, August 1957

"I know," he told me sympathetically. "You haven't had a new idea in," he studied his watch, "oh, I'd say in at least the last fifteen minutes."

I thought back to the days when I was in high school. I took a class then called Rapid Advance English, primarily because the teacher encouraged us to write, write, write! I looked forward expectantly to that class each day. I don't recall the name of my teacher, but I do remember how much she encouraged me to write. She would sometimes read what I wrote to her other classes. When I met them in the hall, her students would shout after me, "Yoo-hoo, Writer. She read us another one of your great works today."

I liked being called Writer. It sounded as if it fit me beautifully.

The following semester I had a different teacher. It was an accelerated English class, and much was expected of us. I felt I would shine here; I was eager to begin.

Unlike the previous teacher, this gray-haired, stern-eyed woman gave us no latitude in what we could write. She gave us assignments on certain subjects, ruled how short or lengthy a submission could be, and counted the words to be sure we had followed the rules she laid out.

When I handed in my first assignment in her class, she looked at my submission, looked at me and said, "Oh, yes. I've heard about you."

I was flattered. She had heard about me. The writer!

Whether she had a feud with the other teacher, or simply needed a scapegoat, I soon became the target of her whiplash tongue. Nothing I wrote pleased her. Then she began to read my essays or short, short stories aloud.

The tone of her voice as she mocked my phrases or story line or descriptions made me curl up inside. The students all threw knowing glances my way. Though, she never mentioned my name, they knew who the object of her scorn was.

I never wrote anything else in her class again. I forced myself to enter the room, take my seat, sit like a stone image, trying not to betray how deeply hurt and destroyed I felt.

She had taken from me the only precious thing I owned—my overwhelming desire to be truly a writer.

It was not until I met David that a resurgence of hope sprang up again. His encouragement, his unshakable belief in my talent, his belief that I would someday be a published author gave me back hope and ambition.

All through our life together, he has steadied me with one laughing but steady phrase. "You can do it. You can do anything."

Over the years, there are certain questions put to me that have become quite repetitive. One query, of course, which I am certain every author is asked is, "Where do you get your ideas?" Ideas abound—small news items in papers or magazines can create an idea. Listening to people talk about themselves and the things that happened to them when they were children is fertile ground. One has to learn to listen, to absorb, to abstract.

Once I saw a TV interview with a bright youngster on television. The boy, twelve years old, was a genius and presently in college. That gave me the idea for my book *I Hate Your Guts, Ben Brooster.* Suppose, I told myself, just suppose a genius comes to stay with a family whose son is bright for his age, but at age eleven is in sixth grade. And suppose this genius, Ben Brooster, is nine years old, could speak four foreign languages, and planned to be an astrophysicist.

To keep the pot boiling, suppose I threw in a mystery as well.

I couldn't wait to write that book. I always hoped afterward that readers had as much fun reading the book as I had writing it. Often children who write to me want to know if any of my books are based on personal incidents in my life. The answer is, most of the time they are just fiction. I have, however, written books that have been inspired by events in my own life. My book, *The Man Who Sang in the Dark,* is one such story.

The house I describe we actually lived in; the woman in the story was based on my mother; the boy was my youngest brother. There was a man who sang in the dark. The darkness represented the man's blindness. The girl in the story was based on me and my recollections of how I felt, way back then. Of course, since this is a book of fiction, some things were made up out of whole cloth.

The Remembering Box sprang from the stories my mother would tell me of her life in Romania before she came to America as a young bride. *The Remembering Box* was a good title, because here I was, grown up, remembering some of the things my mother had remembered!

Search for the Crescent Moon, although I created many of the characters and some of the events and, of course, all the dialogue, was based on hard facts. I wrote to two librarians in Australia, and they very kindly sent me mimeographed material which helped me get the background and the time and speech accurately.

The Killer Swan was made up. I knew of no such action as described in the book, except for the fact that I did check carefully that what I wrote about the birds was accurate. That book, to my great joy, was listed by the Library of Congress as a Children's Book of the Year, 1980.

The books I wrote for the "Arizona Highways Nature-Adventure Series" were all factual. *Ground Afire* was the story of Death Valley. *Wapiti: King of the Woodland* was about a deer. *The Wind Has Scratchy Fingers* was about erosion. *Unusual Animals of the Southwest* was exactly what the title implies.

These four books that I wrote were part of a twelve-book series. All the beautiful photographs in the books came from the *Arizona Highways Magazine* files. This series won Honorable Mention in 1964 at the Indiana Authors' Day Conference awards dinner.

Postcard of the Corner Prairie Settlement and Museum, Noblesville, Indiana. Clifford notes, "A trip to the Corner Prairie Settlement inspired my young adult book The Year of the Three-Legged Deer.*"*

One thing you learn early on in your writing career is that people are curious not only about where you get your ideas, how you plot the story line, how much money your books make (and, unfortunately, how much money did your publisher deduct from your royalties because your book didn't sell!), but feel free to ask personal questions. Some authors don't seem to mind. I do! I am a very private person. I answer each and every letter I receive, although this sometimes cuts into time I need for writing my books. I do not respond to personal questions because I think this is an intrusion. Often people have no compunction asking—how much money have you made on this book? What was your advance payment from your publisher? What percentage in royalties do you receive?

Sometimes people who want to be writers feel you should take time to read their manuscripts, give them advice, send their manuscripts to your editor and insist the editor publish them at once. Being an author does not necessarily turn you into a good editor. Often writers are unable to look at what they have written with an unprejudiced eye!

Editors do not appreciate having unsolicited manuscripts sent to them. Publishers receive more unsolicited manuscripts through the mail than they can possibly publish. A single publisher can often receive more than ten thousand such manuscripts a year.

When I worked as an editor in my husband's office, I often was submerged in unsolicited manuscripts. Sometimes a would-be author would drift into my office and demand I read his or her manuscript. The individual would sit at my desk, prepared to watch me read the manuscript, react to it at once (and favorably, of course), give that individual an advance against the royalties that would come rolling in.

I would explain it didn't work that way. Furthermore, our books were not of a general nature. Primarily, they were educational books, targeted for schools.

Working as an editor gave me an appreciation of the amount and kind of hard work that goes into preparing a manuscript for publication. On the other hand, as an author, I found that I couldn't appreciate the editor's problems compared to mine.

On the whole, I preferred to be the author, because as a writer, I had a special commitment to words. Words are the bridges in communication. Words on the page say to the reader: listen, I've been thinking and I want to share my thoughts with you. Perhaps you've had these same thoughts (and feelings) but haven't been able to express them. But when you read these words, you can say to yourself—that's it. She's got it exactly right.

When I wrote my book *The Rocking Chair Rebellion,* I was interested in depicting the relationship of a teenage girl to her parents. I took it a step further and examined her relationship to a group of people in a home for the aged. You might suspect that this is not the kind of book to which any young person would respond. And you would be wrong. For a serious subject can be treated with a light hand. Many a truth can be delivered with laughter.

What was the reaction of the critics? One reviewer commented: "This fast-moving story has humor along with one girl's understanding that the elderly are still human beings with rights and needs. The seriousness of the problem is alleviated by a crisp style, sharp characterization, and humor."

Several months after my book had been published, someone sent me a clipping. It seemed that a group of elderly people in Chicago had acted just as the elderly people in my book did. They moved out of the Home for the Aged, bought a house for which they all shared the cost, and settled down to be masters of their own fate, and in charge of their lives again. Fiction turned into fact! That was a joyous moment for me.

I was even more thrilled when I was told this book would be an "NBC After School Special." David and I viewed the film along with some friends. They had not read my book, so they had no idea what was coming. When I glanced at them from time to time, I was surprised to see how absorbed they were in the story. I was touched to see tears in their eyes as the story progressed. I, too, was moved, in a different way.

To have one's characters suddenly come physically alive, to see them move off the page and become real people, to hear the words I wrote spoken aloud, gave me an extraordinary sensation. David kept looking at me and smiling.

I was satisfied with the treatment of the film, but I couldn't help thinking a reader would gain more insight into the story by reading the book. I suppose an author is like a mother hen, very protective of one's chicks—my chicks were my words.

I have not experienced this excitement since. That was the only story of mine that was translated to film. It was a very special moment that I will never forget.

I received some fan mail, but none of it compared to the pleasure I get when children write to me, confiding in me, asking questions, complaining about a variety of problems. One child told me he hated school. Had I hated school, too? This is what I told him.

I was one of those kids, I explained, who loved going to school, because it was a place where you learned extraordinary things. One dark, rainy, dismal day, back in second grade, our teacher told us that, though we couldn't see it, the sun was still up in the sky. Imagine that! I figured when it rained, the sun just skipped off to the other side of the world, or even vanished completely. On my first plane trip, when I was grown, we left the airport on a dark, rainy, dismal day. But then we soared over the clouds, and there was the sun, just as my teacher had promised those years ago.

In third grade, I learned about the water cycle. The sun, my teacher said, sucks up water from oceans and rivers and lakes. The water rises as a fine, invisible mist. Winds blow the mist across the earth. Then some of the mist forms clouds. When the water droplets become too heavy they fall back to earth as rain or snow. The rivers and streams carry the water back to the oceans. And the cycle begins all over again.

The water we drank at the fountain, she said, was the same water that was on earth in ancient days. Why the water we were drinking could have fallen as rain on George Washington!

As I went from grade to grade, I learned and discovered more new and wondrous things. Skip school? Not I. I didn't want to miss anything. I still don't, for there are always new and wondrous things to discover.

It's raining, this dark and dismal day, as I write this. But that's okay. I know the sun is still up there, and the raindrops beating so hard against my window might have come from the Nile in ancient Egypt!

BIBLIOGRAPHY

FOR CHILDREN

Fiction, as Eth Clifford, except where noted:

The Year of the Second Christmas, illustrated by Stan Learner, Bobbs-Merrill, 1959.

Red Is Never a Mouse, illustrated by Bill Heckler, Bobbs-Merrill, 1960.

(With husband David Rosenberg, under name David Clifford) *No Pigs, No Possums, No Pandas,* Putnam, 1961.

A Bear before Breakfast, illustrated by Kelly Oechsli, Putnam, 1962.

A Bear Can't Bake a Cake for You, illustrated by Jackie Lacy, E. C. Seale (Indianapolis), 1962.

(As Ruth Bonn Penn) *Mommies Are for Loving,* illustrated by Ed Emberley, Putnam, 1962.

Pigeons Don't Growl and Bears Don't Coo, illustrated by Esther Friend, E. C. Seale, 1963.

(With husband David Rosenberg, under name David Clifford) *Your Face Is a Picture,* E. C. Seale, 1963.

(As Ruth Bonn Penn) *Simply Silly,* illustrated by Joseph Reisner, E. C. Seale, 1964.

The Witch That Wasn't, illustrated by Jean Dorion Kauper, E. C. Seale, 1964.

(With Leo C. Fay) *Curriculum Motivation Series: A Necessary Dimension in Reading* (contains *Blue Dog, and Other Stories, The Flying Squirrels, and Other Stories, The Almost Ghost, and Other Stories, The Barking Cat, Better Than Gold,* and *Three Green Men*), illustrated by Carol Burger, Lyons and Carnahan, 1965.

Why Is an Elephant Called an Elephant?, illustrated by Jackie Lacy, Bobbs-Merrill, 1966.

The King Who Was Different, illustrated by Francoise Webb, Bobbs-Merrill, 1969.

The Year of the Three-Legged Deer, illustrated by Richard Cuffari, Houghton, 1972.

Search for the Crescent Moon, illustrated by Bea Holmes, Houghton, 1973.

Burning Star, illustrated by Leo and Diane Dillon, Houghton, 1974.

The Wild One, illustrated by Arvis Stewart, Houghton, 1974.

The Curse of the Moonraker: A Tale of Survival, Houghton, 1977.

The Rocking Chair Rebellion, Houghton, 1978.

Help! I'm a Prisoner in the Library, illustrated by George Hughes, Houghton, 1979.

The Killer Swan, Houghton, 1980.

The Dastardly Murder of Dirty Pete (sequel to *Help! I'm a Prisoner in the Library*), illustrated by George Hughes, Houghton, 1981.

The Strange Reincarnations of Hendrik Verloon, Houghton, 1982.

Just Tell Me When We're Dead, illustrated by George Hughes, Houghton, 1983.

The Remembering Box, illustrated by Donna Diamond, Houghton, 1985

I Never Wanted to Be Famous, Houghton, 1986.

The Man Who Sang in the Dark, illustrated by Mary B. Owen, Houghton, 1987, published as *Leah's Song,* Scholastic, 1989.

Scared Silly, illustrated by George Hughes, Houghton, 1988.

I Hate Your Guts, Ben Brooster, Houghton, 1989.

The Summer of the Dancing Horse, Houghton, 1991.

Will Somebody Please Marry My Sister?, illustrated by Ellen Eagle, Houghton, 1992.

Never Hit a Ghost with a Baseball Bat, illustrated by George Hughes, Houghton, 1993.

Family For Sale, Houghton, 1996.

"Flatfoot Fox" series:

Flatfoot Fox and the Case of the Missing Eye, illustrated by Brian Lies, Houghton, 1990.

Flatfoot Fox and the Case of the Nosy Otter, illustrated by Brian Lies, Houghton, 1992.

Flatfoot Fox and the Case of the Missing Whoooo, illustrated by Brian Lies, Houghton, 1993.

Flatfoot Fox and the Case of the Bashful Beaver, illustrated by Brian Lies, Houghton, 1995.

"Harvey" series:

Harvey's Horrible Snake Disaster, Houghton, 1984.

Harvey's Marvelous Monkey Mystery, Houghton, 1987.

Harvey's Wacky Parrot Adventure, edited by Patricia MacDonald, Houghton, 1990.

Harvey's Mystifying Raccoon Mix-Up, Houghton, 1994.

Nonfiction:

(With Willis Peterson) *Wapiti, King of the Woodland,* Follett, 1961.

Ground Afire: The Story of Death Valley, photographs by Ansel Adams, Follett, 1962.

(Under name Ruth Bonn Penn) *Unusual Animals of the West,* photographs by Willis Peterson, Follett, 1962.

(With Raymond Carlson) *The Wind Has Scratchy Fingers,* Follett, 1962.

(With Richard E. Kirk and James N. Rogers) *Living Indiana History: Heartland of America,* illustrated by George Armstrong and David Kinney, David-Stewart, 1965.

(With Leo C. Fay) *Curriculum Enrichment Series: A New Dimension in Reading* (contains *Look at the Moon* and *Tommy Finds a Seed*), illustrated by Carol Burger, Lyons and Carnahan, 1965.

(With others) *War Paint and Wagon Wheels: Stories of Indians and Pioneers,* illustrated by David

Kinney, Bill Harris, and Polly Woodhouse, David-Stewart, 1968.

(Compiler) *The Magnificent Myths of Man,* edited by Leo C. Fay, Globe Book Company, 1972.

Show Me Missouri: A History of Missouri and the World Around It, illustrated by George Armstrong, Russell E. Hollenbeck, and Gene Jarvis, Unified College Press, 1975.

Also author of four books in the "Now You Know" series.

Editor:

The Third Star: The Story of New Jersey (fourth-grade history textbook), Third Star Publishing, 1974.

Contributor:

(Lexicographer) *Compton's Illustrated Science Dictionary,* Compton's Encyclopedia Company, 1963.

(Lexicographer) *Dictionary of Natural Science* (2 volumes), Compton's Encyclopedia Company, 1966.

(Lexicographer) *Discovering Natural Science,* Encyclopedia Britannica, 1967.

Basic Science Series, McGraw-Hill, 1968.

Reading Incentive Series, McGraw-Hill (Webster Division), 1968.

Pacesetters in Personal Reading, Lyons & Carnahan, 1969.

Health and Safety Series, Globe Book Company, 1970.

Living City Adventures, Globe Book Company, 1970.

Pathways to Health, Globe Book Company, 1970.

Pre-Primer Stories for Series 360, Ginn & Company, 1971.

Also a contributor of four books to "Reading for Concepts" series for McGraw-Hill (Webster Division), 1970, now distributed by Phoenix Learning Resource Company.

FOR ADULTS

Fiction:

Go Fight City Hall, Simon & Schuster, 1949.

Uncle Julius and the Angel with Heartburn, Simon & Schuster, 1951.

(Under name Eth Clifford Rosenberg; with Molly Picon) *So Laugh a Little,* Messner, 1962.

Nonfiction:

(With husband, David Rosenberg) *To 120 Years: A Social History of the Indianapolis Hebrew Congregation,* Indianapolis Hebrew Congregation, 1979.

Contributor:

(Louis Untermeyer and Ralph E. Shikes, editors) *Best Humor Annual, 1949–50,* Holt, 1951.

(Louis Untermeyer and Ralph E. Shikes, editors) *Best Humor Annual, 1951,* Holt, 1951.

(Nathan Ausubel, editor) *A Treasury of Jewish Humor,* Doubleday, 1951.

(Jerry D. Lewis, editor) *Tales of Our People,* Bernard Geis Associates, 1969.

The Rocking Chair Rebellion was made into an NBC-TV "After-School Special." *The Dastardly Murder of Dirty Pete* and *The Curse of the Moonraker* have been translated into French. Some of Rosenberg's manuscripts and papers have been collected by the Division of Rare Books and Special Collections of the University of Wyoming, the Bicentennial Library of California State College in California, Pennsylvania, and the Kerlan Collection at the Walter Library of the University of Minnesota.

Patricia Coombs

1926-

"Betty and Don and I, Boston, c. 1929"

Books. Books are what I remember, the stories, the pictures. It was as if I had been born in limbo, just waiting around until I could read.

My father was a civil engineer and my family had lived in many places. My sister Betty was born in Washington state, while my brother Don was born six thousand feet up in the Andes Mountains in a copper mining camp during the first World War. My father was working for Shell Oil, and the family was living in Los Angeles when I arrived in style in the Hollywood Hospital. Betty was ten years old, and Don was eight. My first birthday was in Honolulu, my second in Berkeley, my third in Bos-

ton, my fourth in Larchmont, New York, my fifth in St. Louis.

Memory begins in Larchmont. A single image. A scene like an icon, as vivid, as powerful now as it was sixty-five years ago. I am alone, on the stairs, looking over the banister. There is a corner of the living room. Sunlight is pouring in through a white framed window; it lights the slanting front of the desk, the rush-bottomed chair, and under the chair, the thick, thick wool rug with its pattern of diamonds in sky-blue and rose. I stopped in my tracks, spellbound. I had encountered something beautiful. I didn't know what it was, this feeling, but it would lead me all my life.

A second memory from that year. Winter. Snow. I'm on a sled, going faster and faster. I collide with a tree head-on. I am in a strange house with my mother. A woman pours red wine into a goblet. The red wine goes all the way to the base as it fills. It has a hollow stem! I had never seen anything so astonishing. No act of legerdemain would ever seem as magical as that goblet, it was the stuff of Dulac and Rackham.

The move to St. Louis would be our longest stay in any one place, nine years, broken only by a change of houses after five years. We were in a plush hotel while a house was located. For some reason we three siblings were alone in the hotel suite for a brief interval. My brother, bored and curious, wondered if the electric fan would slice a banana. The result was amazing! Squashed banana on the walls, the ceiling. This may have been the instant that my brother became my lifelong hero. The thrill was not shared by either parents or management, but they hadn't seen it happen.

We moved into a large, three-story house in Webster Groves. As well as the furniture from Boston, the books arrived and went into the bookcases. All the books that Betty and Don had outgrown, waiting for me to learn to read, already beguiled by the illustrations.

When I was ill with a high fever that summer, my mother read to me, and I floated with her voice in and out of stories, surrounded by images that went in and out of dreams and back again. Happily, my mother liked to read. My brother had gone through several crises in his early childhood, and mother "read him" through them as I would do years later with my own children. The voice is like the rope on a balloon, or across a chasm, keeping the child connected to the world.

The first book I remember reading on my own was *Poogie and Sibella.* Poogie was a dog, Sibella a cat. *Raggedy Ann* and *Raggedy Andy* I read so many times the books became more raggedy than the characters. Hugh Lofting's Doctor Dolittle books, my brother's favorites, were enjoyable but not as much to my taste as the Oz books. I doted on the Oz books. If a philosophy of life could be rooted in an Oz book, mine surely was. They are in a box in the attic. I like knowing they are there.

A book I have never seen again was a favorite, *At the Foot of Windy Low.* I don't even remember why it was so completely satisfy-ing, but each time I finished the story I felt happy.

The Twin books by Lucy Fitch Perkins were mine. They were illustrated with fine, ink drawings that fascinated me. In *The Irish Twins* a wicker laundry basket was drawn with such detail and panache I've never forgotten it. I would draw it, with less success, in lots of illustrations—it's in that basket that Dorrie finds the Goblin.

It was in Kipling's *Just So Stories* that a passion for language, for the merging of sound and humor and affection, was awakened. Who could not be enchanted by that "great, grey-green, greasy Limpopo river, all set about with fever trees"? The rhinoceros loosening his skin as he tries to scratch the itchy cake crumbs. There is such a tangible warmth toward his readers that it seems as great a part of Kipling's genius as his exuberant inventiveness.

One book that must have eventually succumbed to my nearsighted attentions was Grimms' *Household Tales,* illustrated by Arthur Rackham. I went from illustration to illustration, examining every detail. Their power was inexhaustible. I struggled to read the stories long before I had sufficient vocabulary, doggedly searching out meanings from the context of specific words. Entrails. Entrails of a goat. I asked my mother. She claimed not to know. And gave me that look that conveyed definite disapproval. My mother had grown up with strong Victorian influences—the outsides of goats were okay, but not the insides.

Once settled in Webster Groves, my sister went to the public high school, my brother to a private school, John Burroughs. I was enrolled in a small, local kindergarten. This was my first encounter with children my own age. At once I fell in love with a curly-haired child named Billy. What an amazing experience! Like Miranda in *The Tempest,* "O brave new world, That has such people in't!" I couldn't wait to tell my family all about my feelings, all about Billy.

Instead of sharing my happiness, they teased me and dismissed it. What I felt wasn't special, it was commonplace. Whatever else I might have learned in kindergarten, this was a lesson in Don't Tell Anybody Your Feelings. I didn't have a chance to fall out of love, because my mother was afraid of germs and took me out of kindergarten. My religious education foundered on the same reef. When my mother came to pick me up at Sunday school, she heard one of the children coughing. After that, I sat in a pew with my parents examining the dandruff on the shoulders of whatever dark suit was in front of me. All I could see of the service was the processional and then the recessional. It was an Episcopal church so I did get to stand up and sit down and kneel a lot.

Without kindergarten, I was once more at home with just my mother, the maid, and my brother's airedale. I made up an imaginary friend, a girl who lived in the brown-shingled house next door. She played dolls with me on our screened porch. I found her infinitely satisfying as a playmate. I invented all kinds of scenarios, chattering away to my invisible friend and the dolls.

The porch where I played opened into the entry hall. One afternoon as I came into the hall I found my mother in the middle of disclosing, to the amusement of some women guests, a conversation of mine she had overheard while I played. It was devastating. I have never forgotten the shock, the outrage, and pain of that betrayal and belittlement of my feelings, my privacy. It was worse than being teased about Billy. It would become the central theme underlying all the stories I have written: respect for the child as a person, honoring their feelings.

I was, in effect, silenced. I vowed never to speak about my private feelings. As Peter Høeg wrote: "No one is more covert than a child and no one has a greater need to be that way." And it may have been this bottling-up that would make writing and drawing such imperatives.

When my brother was home, the atmosphere opened up. He was full of energy, projects. I was a willing slave. I trotted all over, from the basement to get tools, up to his third-floor rooms, down to the kitchen and back again. He built a magnificent hotel for white mice in the garage. The mice ran up and down tiny stairs from floor to floor. His love of puns was my introduction to verbal wordplay. We would have punning matches. At the dinner table we would go back and forth until even my patient father groaned and made us stop.

On very rare occasions a relative would come for a visit. One such visitor was Grandma Coombs, who lived with an uncle in California. The first night she was there, I woke up in the middle of the night and went down the hall to the bathroom. I turned the light on. In front of me, on the washbowl, was a glass of water. In it, a complete set of teeth with pink gums. I had never seen anything so horrifying. I raced back to bed and dove under the covers and hid. Grandma Coombs was awake and had heard me running full tilt back into my room, and she knew what had happened. She was highly amused.

I was sent to a private, "progressive," elementary school. From the moment my mother dropped me off, I was up against odds I didn't like. The other children were being brought by uniformed chauffeurs in very large cars. This was the middle of the Great Depression. For a child, there is no wide view of the world; it is one's peers that determine our status. The sight that filled me with foreboding filled my mother with elation. Her interesting conviction was that the wealthy do not have germs. If you should come down with chicken pox and measles, at least it has arrived by limousine.

The groundwork for a future appreciation of Dante's *Inferno* was about to be laid. Almost immediately my inadequacy and ignorance would be exposed. Toward the end of the morning class, the teacher chose a child to look at the clock and tell everyone the exact time. Every day dread gripped me; passed over, I would nearly faint with relief. But the inevitable moment was coming closer, and closer, day by day. There was no escape. She was looking around. Her look landed on me: "All right, Patty, today it's *your* turn!"

I was the only kid in class, probably in the universe, WHO DIDN'T KNOW HOW TO TELL TIME.

True to my vow of silence, I said nothing to my mother about what had happened in school. The rest of the afternoon and evening, not a word, as misery heaved and boiled inside me. Suddenly, on my way upstairs to bed I started sobbing and couldn't stop. Then I told my family my terrible secret. They were amazed. They hadn't noticed what felt to me like a huge hole in my brain. My father sat down with me, took out his round gold watch from his vest pocket, and showed me how to tell time.

More trouble lay ahead. Hot lunches were served, set out on long tables, a teacher at the head. Left-handed, sitting right between other children, I drank the wrong milk. An outraged howl went through the lunch room: PATTY DRANK MY MILK! PATTY DRANK MY MILK!

The worst was yet to come. A gangly child named Janet had been sensing my vulnerability, my all-encompassing shyness. Sent to the girls' room to relieve ourselves and wash up before lunch, Janet had me targeted. She grabbed hold of the stall door and refused to let me close it. She held it open, and laughed and invited the other girls to come and look. And gradually, day by day, more of them joined in. Even those who had been my friends.

One morning I refused to go to school. The limits of my endurance, as well as that of my bladder, had been reached. This period is a sealed room to me. I've tried, but there is no window, no door. Whatever symptoms I displayed, they were taken seriously. Otherwise, my refusal would have been countered by an insistence on obedience and the endless reminder of exactly how much money that school cost.

Weeks went by. My vow of silence even more firmly entrenched by the humiliations at school, I refused to tell my mother anything. One afternoon, Miss Towns, the principal, came to the house.

"Miss Towns has come to see you. Take her out back and show her the ducks," said my mother. Miss Towns took my hand and we walked across the backyard to the duck pond. She asked me if I would tell her what had happened at school. I shook my head. She then offered several different scenarios of what *might* have happened. It made me smile. And then I told her.

Miss Towns took both my hands in hers. She had lovely eyes behind glasses that glinted in the light. You can come back, she told me. You don't have to worry. Nothing like that will happen again. *She was on my side.* For a child in extreme adversity to feel an adult is truly on their side is an unforgettable experience. And I made another lifelong vow that day. I would never, ever, be unkind to anybody.

I went back to school. Janet wasn't there. She'd been sent to the city branch of Community School. It was literally years before I realized it was because of me.

Happy discoveries as well. One of them was the existence of rows and rows and rows of *books I hadn't read!* Because of germs, my mother had kept the existence of public libraries a secret. As far as I knew, a library was a place where my sister went to study after school. Now I was in classrooms with shelves and shelves of books.

Art class was utter bliss. Paints. Brushes. Fingerpaints, as well as the usual crayons. Praised for my paintings, I was more embarrassed than pleased. It was just one more thing to set me off from others. I was absorbed in finishing a night scene, the teacher stopped, and said, in an annoyed tone, "WHY do you always make stars PURPLE? Stars aren't PURPLE!"

Not purple? At the first opportunity I stood on the front porch and looked up at the sky. The teacher was right. They were yellowy-white. I tried to see them again as purple. I couldn't. It was a very puzzling, strange experience. A version of it turned up in *Dorrie's Magic.* By misadventure Dorrie turned everything in the house blue, and the Big Witch's dinner guests sit around the table offering their opinions on the color blue.

It was an incredibly unchauvinistic school. All our sports and activities were mixed boys and girls. Soccer was an all-out, glorious melee. Having gotten my growth early, I excelled in wrestling. There was only one boy in class I couldn't beat. My classmates and I built an Aztec temple and took turns being priest and human sacrifice. We took shop and made cedar boxes for our mothers, who were also the unfortunate recipients of coffee cans tucked all around with painted wooden clothespins.

After school: books, drawing. Gradually I was able to read more and more of the Grimms' tales, figuring out meanings from contexts. Stumped, I might ask my mother about a word. There was no way of knowing ahead of time if it was a word I shouldn't ask about. A chilly silence and then she would say that she didn't know. And I knew that the word somehow teetered on the edge of respectability.

Annoyed with my reading, she would send me outside to play. Thus I learned the art of smuggling, finding out which books were smugglable, going undetected inside the top of my leggings, under waistbands. The Oz books were too big, the Bobbsey Twins just right. Between the garage and the neighboring fence there was just enough space to sit and read. The garage was a possibility but it smelled because of the mouse hotel.

We were given IQ tests. It would not have been memorable were it not for the final oral question. The examiner asked me what I would do if I came home from school and my house was on fire, and nobody was around. I explained that it was impossible. My mother always picked me up after school. He asked again, and again, he gave cues about neighbors. My exasperation was building. He asked me other questions, but kept returning to the burning house with me alone in front of it. I can't GET home unless my mother drives me, I kept saying. He gave up. If he had told me the situation was in a story, and what I thought the Bobbsey Twins would do, I could have told him. Fortunately, he decided I was too immature to skip a grade. With all the trouble I was in right where I was, a change in class would have spelled disaster. My mind was an ordinary mind magnetized by an extraordinary vocabulary.

Field trips. We were taken to hear the St. Louis Symphony play *Peter and the Wolf*. We

The author with her father and brother, Potato Lake, Wisconsin, 1932

toured factories, and in the process got a searing look at soot-blackened St. Louis in the middle of the Depression; as a scene from hell it could have had no equal.

We were taken to see the film of Admiral Byrd exploring the South Pole. I'd left my glasses at school in my desk, and couldn't tell the Admiral from a polar bear.

In third grade we began French lessons. Our French teacher was young, she was beautiful beyond belief. She had no problem in holding our attention; we were rapt. This was my introduction to the Babar stories. They were our textbook. The illustrations were unlike any I had seen before and provided a very different delight—these were comical, simple, exaggerated. Yet the simple lines conveyed a full range of feeling, the sadness of the Old Lady as she stands alone on her balcony watching Babar disappear down the boulevard in the red car she gave him, then the joy of the elephant reunion, Arthur dancing on top of the trunk and tooting the horn. These books made a lasting impression and widened my awareness of the ways pictures and text could interact. French class became another bright spot in the gloom. At home I tried to draw beautiful princesses that looked like the French teacher; the eyelashes were always so long and thick the eyes looked like hamsters.

My aptitude for art pleased my mother. I think it was always a relief when I did something other than read. For a year, every Saturday morning, I went to an art class. There was even a kiln for firing clay figures and tiles. We did batik. Remembering that is remembering the smell of dyes and melting wax, and looking with wonder as the green parrot I'd painted emerged from the background.

At school I discovered a new humiliation. We were given the task of reading about an animal, writing a short report, memorizing it, and then telling the class about it. Lion cubs. I wrote about lion cubs. No problem. I memorized it. No problem. My turn came, I stood up in front of the class, announced the title of my report—and my mind went blank. That one part of me could betray another part was a shock. This was the beginning of a lifelong aversion to public speaking.

But there was no way around doing things in front of the class, or worse, with adults in the audience. At a parents' day affair we each had to make a short speech describing one of our school projects. The terrors that gripped me beforehand were indescribable; I just knew this was going to be another lion cubs fiasco. I memorized and memorized and memorized. The night before the event, I knelt down beside my bed to say the Lord's Prayer, as we had been taught to do. I was almost at the end, when I realized I hadn't been saying the Lord's Prayer, I had just given my speech to God! It was so embarrassing. I knelt there, blushing in the dark, apologizing to Him. Would I never learn to do *anything* right?

This recalcitrant mind of mine had other tricks up its sleeve. Like most children, I had to go to bed long before I was tired enough to sleep. Lying on my back under the covers looking up at the ceiling, I imagined myself writing my name on the darkness the way I wrote it in chalk on the blackboard at school. Patty Coombs. Patty Coombs. Over and over again. Gradually something strange was happening; my name began to separate itself from me until it was no longer attached. I was just this awareness in an enormous whirling emptiness. It was so terrifying, and at the same time so exhilarating! It became the Great Secret of my childhood. It was such a powerful experience that I didn't practice it often; but always knowing it was there was like a talisman, a hidden treasure, a realm of secrets.

After that first summer in St. Louis, we went away to cooler places on vacation. To rented cottages in Wisconsin, and then Michigan. My father would come with us for a week, then go back to St. Louis, coming back again briefly and intermittently. It must have been Don who taught me how to swim, to dive. He also taught me that to qualify for his company, I could not ever cry, complain, or tattle. Since I would have walked on hot coals to be able to go with him and be part of his activities, that was no problem. I was also good for pranks of devilish devising. He once wired up a shovel to a battery to dig up night-crawlers for fishing, then had me feel the shovel to see if it was "hot." I got a shock that made my hair stand on end like Orphan Annie's. He laughed so hard I ended up laughing too.

He took me along to help spot pike in the shallow, reedy water at the edge of Portage Lake. He had made a harpoon and decided he'd spear pike and Mother would cook them. I knew she wouldn't. She wouldn't touch raw meat, ever. One of these mammoth fish would give her fits. While not successful, these pike hunts were a tremendous pleasure. Wading in the shallows has always been like wading at the edges of the unknown, mind and eyes alert to every shell and pebble, every moving shadow a guess, and the sand ribbed like the roof of our mouths.

After summers of renting, and having grown to love this area of Michigan, my parents decided to build a cottage. My father had wanted to take all of us to Europe. My mother was aghast. Europe was dirty, full of germs, she would *never* take the children there. So instead of Europe, we ended up with a large log-sided cabin. It was log because Don was a fan of L'il Abner. He made a rough wood sign, painted "Dogpatch" on it, and hung it over the gate. He had long been in revolt against the phoniness, the artificiality of upper class "society." This put him at loggerheads with my mother. His best friends were from the public high school, not his own private school.

The summers at Portage, those first few years, were idyllic for all of us. After twenty-two years of living in construction camps, then a mining camp, then a dozen rented houses, my parents actually owned their own land, their own house. My mother was happy, as happy as I had ever seen her, or would see her again.

A retired boat captain, "Swede," had pitched camp in the woods beside us. We met through the good offices of our second airedale, Smokey, who came running through the yard with a roll of toilet paper. Swede had a boat. He asked me if I would like to learn to sail. Would I!

The sailboat was freedom, a freedom I had never known before. He taught me the names for the different parts of the boat, how to fasten the lines; luffing and tacking and coming-about entered my vocabulary. There were enough sailboats on the lake to have races every weekend.

My brother had a large inboard motorboat. He liked engines and could take them apart and put them together again. He had rapidly acquired friends and we all learned to aquaplane—this was before water skis. This led to seeing how difficult they could make it. Don stood on his head on the board, on his hands. Then they found a wooden kitchen chair and rode standing on the chair. He rode with me the first few times to show me how to get the board over the edge of the wake. I rode on his shoulders, as well, and then standing on his shoulders. It felt as if I were fifty feet in the air.

Sometimes Betty joined us, but she didn't want to get more freckles so she spent most of her time until late afternoon under a sombrero. Don would take all of us in the boat for rides in the evening. Sometimes we went into Lake Michigan through the channel to have cookouts on the beach. Nothing ever tasted quite as good as those slightly scorched hot dogs with mustard and a few grains of sand.

Betty had boyfriends and girl friends her own age. Watching her get ready for a date was fascinating. It involved a steady stream of complaints about her beautiful auburn hair, her freckles, her hands, her feet, her figure. She was lovely. She was learning to cook. One night she made gingerbread and it came out black. Not from overcooking, but something funny with the ingredients. It tasted quite good. Ever after, the connection between magic and cooking stayed in my mind—they are both rich sources of the unexpected.

Betty was already attending Lindenwood College, and in the fall of 1936 Don went to Purdue. I missed them terribly, so I took up letter writing. Until then the only letters I'd written were the obligatory thank-you notes. This was different. This was like talking to him but without his interrupting me. As I wrote I made a discovery that changed my life: I could write letters that not only made me laugh, they made my brother laugh. When a ten-year-old can make an eighteen-year-old laugh, that's POWER. I was hooked for life. A life piled high with boxes of letters.

Desolate without Don, my mother decided to take me out west to see her parents, Mama and Daddy Joe, her sister Betty and my cousin Elizabeth, Uncle Bill and Aunt Jenny. Except for a brief visit by Bill and Jenny in St. Louis, we had not seen them for years. We would go first to California, to see Grandfather Coombs, who was dying. My father had never reconciled himself to this man, who had left my grandmother and six children, forcing my father, at eleven, to leave school and find work to support them. Dad's bitterness toward him was the only deep anger he ever expressed. It may have fueled his dedication to both his own family and to his career.

Falling asleep to the click-clack of the rails, the distant hoots of the locomotive as we swayed around curves, plunged into tunnels, sheets and pillow cases starched and ironed, a train ride across America was an incredible adventure for a child. The roar and racket as, with great effort, the door from one car was opened and we walked in windy gusts of soot to the next car, and standing on the observation platform at the rear of the train watching as forests and cliffs and farmlands unrolled on either side of the shining rails. And always, cinders in the eyes.

The visit to my Grandfather Coombs was eerie. All I knew about him were the stories, bitter ones, that my father told us. Here was this gaunt, waxen, almost motionless old man lying in a bed. He was the oldest person I had ever seen; he confirmed my belief that my sister and I would die young, because I had never, ever seen an old person with freckles.

In Washington state we went to my Aunt Betty's place first. My mother was more relaxed with her than with anyone else. She was warmhearted and full of laughter and fun. They liked to tell about the time they got so fed up with their brother's teasing, they tried to drown him in the horse trough—and almost succeeded. My cousin Elizabeth was there. She cut her hair like a boy, wore suits and white shirts with neckties. Their collie and I followed her around like shadows. They had apple orchards all around, and a big kitchen with a wood stove. Aunt Betty made toast on top of it that tasted marvelous. It was from the memory of that stove that I would draw the one in the Big Witch's kitchen.

Aunt Betty came with us to the coast, to Shelton. Mama and Daddy Joe had lived in the same place, the same simple farmhouse across the road from Puget Sound, all their lives. Uncle Bill and Aunt Jennie came while we were there. They worked together, taking in the catches of salmon from smaller boats, Jennie with her clicker clicking off the numbers as salmon slid into the hold. Childless, they were great with children. It wasn't hard to imagine Uncle Bill picking up a couple of chickens and chasing my mother or Aunt Betty all around the yard. I was glad he hadn't drowned in the horse trough.

The love and rapport I felt with Mama Joe never changed. Later it would be through letters that our relationship flourished. If I could write letters to the dead, I would still be writing letters to her.

"Mama Joe, Daddy Joe, Aunt Betty, in front; Mother and I in back," Puget Sound, 1936–37

On our previous visit, several years before, Daddy Joe showed me how to skip stones across the water, an accomplishment in which I took great pride. We walked across the road to Puget Sound so I could show him how well he had taught me. With prompting, he would talk about the lumbering days. He was not a talker. French Canadian, he had run away from home as a boy and ended up in Shelton as a logger. He never learned to read English—like the accounts, all the paperwork was Mama Joe's domain. He was successful. On payday, Mama Joe counted out the silver dollars each man was owed, put them in the wheelbarrow, and Daddy Joe wheeled it along the logging road into the woods. He was quite wealthy, but somebody talked him into investing in Stanley Steamer. They lost everything.

Mama Joe was born in California, her parents Irish immigrants. Her father, Billy Taylor, walked the continent three times. This fact is engraved on his tombstone. When Daddy Joe died at the age of ninety-three, their friends kept saying to her, "Well, Fanny, Joe really lived a long life, not many of us get that old." It made her mad; she snapped back, "He didn't die of OLD AGE! He was SICK!"

Many years later, Mama Joe became partially, then totally, blind. Uncle Bill and other relatives decided she just wasn't able to take care of herself any longer; over her protests, she was put in a nursing home. She made friends with a woman named Josephine. Josephine could see, so they hatched their plan, chose their moment, and escaped. They settled in at Mama Joe's place, where they both thrived. Mama Joe dictated all her letters to Josephine, so our correspondence also thrived.

After the trip west, we were involved in another move, this time simply to another suburb of St. Louis. Fair Oaks was an upscale development, stone pillars at the entrance gates, and long, curving roads perfect for bicycles. There were other children in the neighborhood to play with; this was a first. A girl named Judy lived right across the street. We liked to do exactly the same things. My imaginary playmate had materialized at last. The others, mostly boys, came over for endless, hilarious games of kick-the-can. In the fall the many persimmon trees dropped ripe, orange fruit and we had squashy, disgusting persimmon fights.

My brother was living at home again, enrolled at Washington University. Halfway through his second year at Purdue, he had suffered a ruptured appendix—no small matter in those days before antibiotics—and was in the hospital for weeks. And Betty had gotten married. I couldn't believe she'd gone. Every time I passed her bedroom, my heart seemed to drop a few inches. Her red hair and freckles would find a place in my illustrations, in *Lisa and the Grompet* and *Molly Mullett*.

Another change, as I went from elementary school to junior high, the same school from which Don had graduated. Puberty is difficult under any conditions, and having been inept at childhood, I would prove equally inept at adolescence. I developed great crushes that were distracting. I read Thorne Smith and P. G. Wodehouse and tried in vain to become sophisticated. I sat in class one day admiring Winnie. Winnie was perfectly groomed, perfectly poised. Her sleek dark hair was turned under in a pageboy. She had flawless ivory skin. Her clothes never wrinkled, lost buttons, or got spills on them. I realized I would never make it. There was only one thing left in life: I would be smart. It was a most heartfelt decision, but alas, transitory. As always though, art classes were islands of happiness in these stormy seas.

Destiny shook the dice again. Shell's St. Louis office was going to be restructured. My father was transferred to Chicago for a year, then retired. My mother's cherished dream of me as a debutante, attending a coming-out ball and marrying some wealthy young man of good family, was shattered. Since I had fallen down an entire flight of stairs in my first long dress, and was speechless at parties, that debutante dream was doomed to failure anyway.

Don had shattered Mother's dreams for him by carelessly falling in love with a girl he'd met at the lake in Michigan. They were engaged and planned to be married, over my mother's vehement and often expressed protests, as soon as he got his degree.

In Evanston, outside Chicago, my parents, the airedale, and I lived in an apartment overlooking Lake Michigan. It was nothing like the Lake Michigan I knew from summers at Portage. I was enrolled in a private girls' school, Roycemore. We wore white middy blouses, navy serge pleated skirts and either a red, yellow, or navy scarf. For gym we wore the same navy serge but styled as bloomers.

I learned to study. Homework assignments took up all the hours after school as well as after supper, and part of the weekend. All the gaps in my progressive education became apparent. Having had French since first grade, I knew French grammar. English grammar we were supposed to absorb from reading. The parts of speech were quite different. So I had extra

tutoring after school and struggled to learn how to diagram a sentence. Algebra was another Slough of Despond, but Latin, Latin was a treasure hunt. Finding the roots of English words filled me with a curious elation. I loved it. What I lacked in brilliance I made up for in enthusiasm.

It was a strange, sad year. A heavy weight seemed to push me down as if something had happened to gravity in Illinois. My father did everything he could to brighten matters. My mother refused to join us, so Dad took me to all the Northwestern football games, complete with a giant mum each time, and hot dogs. On Saturdays when there wasn't a game, he took me downtown to the Parker House for lunch. Mother did come with us to stage plays, the first professional stage productions I'd ever seen. My father spent more time with me than he had been able to spend with my brother and sister since they were small children. We had always gotten along, with ease and affection and humor; the same sense of humor that bonded my brother and me. It was a long time before I realized how difficult that year had been for him, trying to reconcile himself, after twenty-five years, to a retirement he didn't want and hadn't planned.

The year ended. The drama teacher, Miss Rice, and I were both all but in tears at parting. She had given me not just encouragement, but a sense of myself that was completely new. She showed me how you can move your emotions into a character and let them act on their own with different rules. The algebra teacher snorted and gave me a "C" I hadn't earned, remarking that I could take algebra over again for years, and still not be able to figure out the formulas.

What do people do when they retire? They go to Florida. While we were in Michigan for the summer, my father went to find a place in Florida to settle. The assumption was, of course, that they would rent a small place and see if they liked it. My mother thought that. My father wanted to surprise her, and he did. Without her knowledge, without consultation, he bought a very large White Elephant in Daytona Beach. It was a seven-bedroom mansion on the banks of the Halifax River. Previously housing a men's club, the amenities included a large rec room with piano and ping-pong table, plus five showers. Just the accommodation for a middle-aged couple, a teenager, and a dog. We even had a tiny island in the river, connected to the yard by a wooden bridge.

My mother was *furious,* and not without reason. The war in Europe brought about the devaluation of the British pound sterling, and the Shell Oil Company in the U.S. had all their employees' savings in Britain. My parents' life savings were cut in half.

I loved that house, I loved the place. I loved the river, stained purple from palmetto roots, that I could see from my bedroom window. Everything about it was generous. The wide, open hall faced oceanward on one side, and toward the river on the other. It had its own fireplace. There were screened verandahs with wicker chairs and hibiscus blooming everywhere. Ponderosa lemons, grapefruit, and oranges grew in the yard. Large blue land-crabs climbed out of holes in the ground and walked around on tiptoes. They could have come from the pages of *Alice in Wonderland.*

A sophomore, I attended my first public school, Seabreeze, which was a few blocks from the beach. It was close enough so that I could ride my bike. My classmates were very different from those I had gone to school with before. They were friendly, easygoing, welcoming southerners. Our house was a perfect party house. We jitterbugged, played ping-pong. We swam and walked the beach, drank cherry cokes at the local drugstore, went to movies, on dates.

That December Pearl Harbor changed the world. It changed this small, sleepy town almost overnight. Jeeps patrolled the beaches, looking for German submarines. A Naval Air training base was set up across the river in Daytona, and a WAC Cantonment in Daytona Beach.

My father offered his services as an engineer and was quickly taken on and later made Post Engineer at the Women's Army Corps Cantonment. His expertise in fuel transportation was put to use. Working again was a blessing for both my parents; he didn't adjust well to retirement, and she didn't adjust to having him around all day.

School went on much as before, but something in the very atmosphere had changed because of the war, a feeling we had to be happy while we could.

In 1944 I graduated from Seabreeze High School, one of a class of fifty. The boys were going into the services, most of the girls to college. My mother refused to stay in Florida. We packed up and moved back to the cottage for the summer, putting the furniture in storage and the house up for sale. And I would go to college, to DePauw University in Indiana. Why DePauw? The daughter of some friends at the lake had gone there and recommended it. I was being sent in order to meet an appropriately qualified mate, and to join a sorority in order to facilitate such a meeting.

The year at DePauw was reminiscent of my first year in elementary school. I joined a sorority. I learned to play bridge—very important in those days. The art and English classes kept me afloat.

Meanwhile, my parents decided to live in Grand Rapids, which was a reasonable drive from the cottage. My sister-in-law, Sandy, was from there but since my mother was barely on speaking terms with her or her family, it wasn't a family-oriented move. But my guardian angel, hard-worked though she was, floated me off to Michigan State.

At that time, there were fifteen hundred students and a great many cows. The student numbers would burgeon, however, as government training programs took effect, and then the GI Bill.

The art department was a fantastically lively place, thanks mainly to the presence of a young woman, Jayne Van Alstyne, who, though going blind, was filled with a passionate love for art, especially modern art. She talked about the Bauhaus, she brought us reproductions of Picasso, Miro, Mondrian, everything she could get her hands on. She opened the studio to us at all hours, day and night. She was not just inspiring to her students, she was inspiration itself. I had never encountered anybody even remotely like her—a young woman, single, independent, in love with her work. It was as if I had been wandering around with my life in my hands, wondering *where can I put this down?* Jayne showed what might be possible.

Quite casually, she asked me what I wanted to do with my art. Without thinking, I said, "Children's books." "Good!" she said. "Do one for your term project." And I did. The story was about a cat, and the illustrations were equally influenced by Babar and Picasso. Those third grade French lessons turned out to be helpful.

English classes were almost as informal as the art classes, providing me with an opportunity to write funny stuff for what turned out to be an appreciative group of students. This was important. Roycemore had disconnected me from writing, and Seabreeze had simply required book reports. This class connected me again to that awareness that began when I was ten years old and writing to my brother. It seemed as if separate pieces of myself had begun to coalesce.

It was too good to last. I fell into my own tar-pit. Michigan State had instituted what were called "Basic Courses." No matter what your major, these were required. These courses were given in large auditoriums to hundreds of students. I took them all, except one. The one with the innocent title, *Effective Speaking.* Even reading a paper in front of a small, familiar class was panic time. It was an ordeal, but it was in the range of the possible. But an auditorium? A stage with a podium? An audience of a hundred or more students? This is what nightmares are made from, this is unabashed terror.

The decision was taken out of my hands. My parents gave up on life in Grand Rapids. My mother's mental and emotional state was deteriorating, my father's distress and unhappiness increasing. They had both come from the west coast, they would go back, and maybe go down to California where I could finish college.

Seattle was the first stopover. Old friends from my parents' days in mining camps, the Posts, still lived in Seattle. A few others were around that they had known. They were persuaded to rent a house near the University of Washington, my parents' alma mater, and I could enroll there.

I was an art major with a minor in psychology up until then. The art department changed all that. After Jayne Van Alstyne I was not prepared for a bored young instructor who set us to drawing stuffed ducks in a museum case. Buffleheads, to be exact. I switched to English. My guardian angel was getting time-and-a-half.

Sitting in a class on the nineteenth-century novel, where I was rebuked for knitting (knitting was actually a wonderful aid to concentration, but never mind explaining that to the professor), the door opened. A large poet shambled in. "I'm Theodore Roethke," he said. "I teach modern poetry. If any of you are interested, come along." So I did, along with

perhaps a half dozen others. I would end up taking every course he taught.

Roethke had a genius for teaching that was as great as his genius for poetry. He could articulate all the passionate involvement with language that had held me in thrall since I first encountered words, words in all their rich magic. He would catch every nuance, every shift, the subtlest inflection and hold it up before us, turning and tuning our awareness. His memory was poetry. He tossed handfuls of lines that landed like sparks in that grubby classroom, to ignite later in our own lives and work.

Those of us who met in his classes continued the discussions in the coffee shop near campus—intense, highly charged, we talked and argued about poems, poetry, poets. Names swirled around us, Stanley Kunitz, Marianne Moore, T. S. Eliot, Louise Bogan, John Berryman, Robert Lowell, and the one who influenced my work the most, Wallace Stevens.

With sensibilities fine-tuned by Roethke, the poetry of other periods was illuminated, enhanced. The seventeenth-century metaphysical poets became an obsession—a well-worn copy of Donne has stayed within reach all these years. There was Shakespeare, and Milton. A scholar poet, Arnold Stein, taught Milton with subtlety and brilliance; he also taught us how to use our critical faculties to analyze and explicate any given text. This was as valuable as anything else I learned.

On the domestic front, further deterioration. After minor surgery my mother became addicted to pain pills, then sleeping pills. Taken off drugs, she slid into depression, and was hospitalized in a private sanitarium for shock treatments. The treatments had mixed results. The depression was broken, but she had retreated. She refused to talk to the psychiatrist, finding his questions in poor taste, so that ended whatever hope we had invested in counselling. They decided to go back to Michigan, winterize the cottage, and live there. My brother and sister and I knew this spelled disaster. Nine months of the year they would be isolated, neighborless in a summer resort.

My brother and his family lived fifteen miles away, but by then they had three little boys and Sandy had been stricken with multiple sclerosis. He was hard pressed to find time to check on our parents.

I spent the summers there, as always, but now it meant occupying my mother. We must have walked hundreds of miles along the beach, in the woods, all the while she talked, repeating the same litany of complaints that she had gathered up over the years. She wouldn't talk to my father. And when September came she always told me the same thing: "If you go back to school, you'll never see me alive again." Not exactly the usual *bon voyage*. I wrote to her faithfully, all the time I was in school, once or twice a week. Boxes of letters, eventually stored in Don's barn, burned in a fire that destroyed the barn completely.

Having transferred and changed majors, I completed my B.A. mid-year, and began the courses for an M.A. Arnold Stein was my graduate school mentor, and with his guidance I decided to do my thesis on the epic similes in *Paradise Lost*. Their imagery fascinated me, as did their function in the structure of Milton's epic.

I took on an assortment of part-time jobs. My experience as an inept waitress was so memorable it became the basis for a story twenty years later: *Mouse Café*. And I read for blind students—the state funded readers for them. This was immensely rewarding, because one of the students was majoring in anthropology and I was able to read the texts and write the papers. Courses I wasn't allowed to take because of the number of hours working, I could audit. One such course was French poetry, taught by Jackson Mathews. His brilliance, his wit, the incredible scope of his learning gave him such an air of gentle sophistication that we all felt the honor of his presence on the campus.

Stein asked if I planned to teach after getting my degrees. I said "yes." That was all I could envision, since that seemed to be the only way I could stay at the university forever, go on doing research, excavating images from texts, and writing, writing, writing. I tried not to think about my terror at being in front of people. Could I teach sitting at a desk in the middle of the room, begin a new style of lecturing? I did, however, trust the power of my love for literature to overcome the shyness, the panic.

In Michigan my mother was in and out of the state hospital in Traverse City. If she was unable to sleep, she took to wandering. A neighbor found her, in her nightgown, clutching an alarm clock, standing in her yard and wanting to know what time it was. It was acutely distressing.

Meanwhile, Roethke, who had become a good friend, had a breakdown and was hospitalized at Pinel Foundation outside the city. He sent me urgent messages that didn't make sense; a touch of paranoia seemed to be involved when he was ill and everything became very cloak-and-dagger. He had a wonderful doctor who, after a few weeks, allowed Roethke to "escape" once a week. In total darkness I would wait for him by the back fence. He would appear, scramble over, and we would go into Seattle for supper at his favorite restaurant—it had high-backed wooden booths so spies wouldn't find him. I felt as if I was involved in a surrealistic foreign film, directed by someone on a limited budget. Roethke always took *my* rolls, not his, to feed the seagulls when we took the ferry back to Pinel.

As summer approached, I determined to stay in Seattle. Students were being hired at Boeing Aircraft, and by working the swing shift, I could still get in two of the necessary courses for my doctorate. A group of us travelled on the same bus from the same corner after lunch in the same café. One student, Jim Fox, I had seen in classes and in the halls, but we hadn't actually met and talked. Now we were working in the same department at Boeing. We started meeting to have lunch together. Then we were going out and talking, talking for hours about art, painting and sculpture, poetry, writing. He was doing his thesis on Henry James, working on a novel, and longing to do sculpture. Our talk turned out to be a lifelong conversation. At seventy he began working on the sculpture he talked about when he was thirty, and I am painting.

After three weeks, we got married. The minister was in one of our poetry classes. There had also been a minister in another class who was Episcopalian, and I thought he was the one Jim meant. So it happened that we ended up with a Lutheran ceremony. Jim had a year of the GI Bill left, and he wanted to go back to New York—to Columbia University. He had had some of his army training at Fordham, and loved the city. I could take the rest of the courses I needed at NYU, finish my thesis, and return to Seattle for the oral exam.

We rented the living room of a fifth-floor walk-up apartment on East Tenth Street. A medical student rented the maid's room; an artist, with whom we are still in touch, rented one of the bedrooms. Two other young working people occupied the parlor and dining room, and we all shared the kitchen and bathroom. This odd arrangement was made possible—and deemed illegal—by the existence of Rent Control in the city. The woman who actually rented it paid the controlled rate, then sublet to us and made back quadruple her investment. To make it look legal, she would appear from time to time, always wearing a red hat, carrying a bag of ironing. She would collect our rents, then stand in the kitchen at the ironing board, ironing away, the red hat bobbing. That image has stuck with me. Not long ago she turned up in a story I was writing, turned up with a pig named Gerald.

The GI Bill paid the rent but not much else, so I quickly found a part-time job at Prentice-Hall, typing invoices. I had a night class in Anglo-Saxon at NYU. I quite liked it, but was in the minority. Some of the students were taking it for the second and third time. The room was hot, and tired students dozed off in the gentle hiss of the old steam radiators.

New York was stuffed full of energy, of excitement, and Jim and I were exhilarated by all of it. Even with no money, there were endless venues for students—poetry readings, museums, galleries. It was there that we heard Dylan Thomas read. We roamed the streets of the Village, which was still safe, day or night. A small art theatre offered coffee at intermission, making it possible for us to amble in, ticketless, and see the last half of foreign films. We were full of dreams, and cherished being part of what seemed to us the very center of the world.

Unable to withstand the boredom of typing invoices, I tracked down a part-time job in The Corner Bookshop—in the middle of the block on Fourth Avenue. I learned to package books for mailing, and, with less success, to spot book thieves. It was an interesting as well as a pleasant place to work, the clientele often quite wildly eccentric, and I would find myself involved in Alice-in-Wonderland dialogues. A bearded man wrapped in what seemed to be several overcoats, and speaking with an accent, asked if we had any books by Gore Vidal. "No," I said, "We don't carry foreign authors." He laughed uproariously. "Vidal!" he cried, "He iss az Hamerican az you or I!" The modern novel was not a course I had taken.

Unexpectedly, inconveniently, inexplicably euphoric, I was pregnant—and restless. A notice at the New School announced that Stanley Kunitz was teaching poetry. I made inquiries. By taking attendance at the door, I didn't have to pay. He was not only a great teacher, but his class was exactly what I needed at exactly the right time. I had been writing steadily, working every day, but I was tangled up in revisions of revisions of revisions. He gave me, I don't know how, a way of sensing the balance in a poem, of finding it, then letting it be. Handing me back my poems at the end of the last class, Kunitz told me it was time to start sending out my work to the various literary journals—*Poetry, Partisan Review,* the *Hudson Review.* Dumbfounded, I could barely speak to thank him.

The apartment below us caught fire one Sunday morning. As a result the law caught up with our landlady in her red hat. We were all to be evicted at once, and there was no place to go. Housing was critical. So we found a Legal Aid lawyer who persuaded the judge to let us stay until the end of the school year.

"Europe," said Jim. "We'll get degrees in library science and then find jobs in Europe." That sounded good. We found out that one of the best library schools was at the University of Minnesota.

Jim had also been working part-time in the stockroom of a publishing house, and we had managed to scrape a little money together. For seventy-five dollars we bought a '37 Ford. By removing the back seat, we had room for all our possessions: five cartons of books, several cartons of manuscripts and theses, two typewriters, a pressure cooker, a coffee pot, and a frying pan. We figured, well, if the car doesn't make it all the way to Minneapolis, we'll stop wherever it stops, work, have the baby, then move on. Our optimism was as great as our ignorance of what an infant would entail.

We found an apartment, and set up housekeeping the same way thousands of other students did during those years. Bricks and boards for instant bookcases, the Salvation Army for odds and ends of furniture. Every day I worked on the poetry, which was beginning to find acceptance in the literary journals.

Jim had found a job as a technical writer, writing instructions for heating systems at Minneapolis-Honeywell. A friend he worked with helped Jim rig up a phonograph from an old radio. We found some chamber music on sale, Bach, Mozart, Beethoven's Last Quartets; the apartment was filled with those sounds as I wrote. At six months I went to see a doctor for the first time. He was aghast at the delay. But I had felt fine, and without money it would have been impossible to go to a doctor in New York.

In late September, close to midnight, Ann arrived. Tiny, exquisite, in a city where twelve-pound babies were the norm, they popped her into an incubator. She'd kept me company for nine months. Coming home without her was devastating.

As soon as she did come home, she proceeded to teach us about colic. Never having been around infants, all I could do was keep reading Dr. Spock. I didn't even know enough to pin her diapers to her undershirt. Every time I picked her up, her diapers fell off. Friends from graduate school stopped off to visit. My closest friend, Ruth Anderson, a composer and flautist, was going to New York to live. Another friend was going to Austria on a Fulbright. Whoever was going east or west, went through Minneapolis, the train-track and airline center of the world.

Annie was healthy and good-natured enough to survive my ignorance. One morning, when she was about a year-and-a-half old, I got her dressed and put her down on the floor. Her left leg went out from under her. Again and again I tried. She couldn't stand up. I rushed to the phone and called the doctor's office. "Polio," I said, "It must be polio. She can't stand up." I lifted Ann back on the bed, and took her shoe off to massage her foot. A metal bottle cap fell out. Had Spock mentioned a stage where toddlers put things into other things? There was an audible groan in the nurse's voice when I called back to tell her.

Pregnant again, we moved to the second floor of an old-fashioned duplex, and in January, in the middle of a howling blizzard that sent every pregnant woman in Minneapolis into labor, Trish was born. It was 1955.

We had made some friends, mostly through Norman Sherman. Norman had taught at the University of Minnesota for awhile, until someone idly looking through the files discovered that Norman had actually never finished his course work and gotten an advanced degree. He brought Ralph Ross over for dinner. Ralph was chairman of the Humanities department at the university. Jim and I both became very fond of him. And Norman, Norman was always warm and wildly funny. Then Ralph brought a

"Ann, Trish, and me reading, 1962"

visiting poet with him one night. We opened the door, and in walked a hugely grinning John Berryman. He had taken over Roethke's classes at the University of Washington, and we had spent hours in his company, not just in class, but at the coffee-shop and houseboat parties.

After that, John became a regular visitor, coming to share our cheap red wine and spaghetti suppers, teasing me about Trish. "That's not a girl! Look at those ears! And where's her hair?" He was working on *Homage to Mistress Bradstreet* when he wasn't teaching classes. Witty, intense, prickly, and erudite, he was lively, welcome company.

Every day, while the children napped, I wrote and revised, and wrote and revised, searching with language, with images for something sensed, but hidden. William Phillips, the editor of *Partisan Review,* gave me encouragement and support, as he did to so many other young writers.

More and more, we missed New York. We felt as if we were about a million miles in either direction from anywhere, and the climate was atrocious. So it was we devoted Sundays to lying on the living room floor, a map of the east coast and the want-ad section of the *New York Times* in front of us. Technical writer wanted? Find the location on the map. Gradually, the search narrowed, the pencil landed on Electric Boat, in Groton, Connecticut. There was Long Island Sound, water! And New York 118 miles away, Boston even less.

A year after Trish was born, we arrived, accompanied now by our first cat, a calico named George-Alice, the first of approximately one hundred. We rented a bungalow near the lighthouse in New London; a stop-gap measure since we would have to move once the high-rent summer season began in June. We played on the beach, climbed around the rocks and watched the tides.

As spring came on, house-hunting began in earnest. There was a housing shortage, and it is even shorter for those with limited funds. We looked at collapsing farmhouses, at houses too small or yards too small or roads too dangerous. Everything we looked at was either unsuitable, or beyond our means. We came to the end of the real estate agencies. The final real estate agent from the final agency showed us a house that would have been all right, but it was only a few feet from a busy road. No place for toddlers.

Discouraged, we bade farewell and climbed back into our car. A scraggly kind of road meandered down on our right. There was a glimpse of water, a tilted sign that read Oswegatchie Road. Idly we drove down, over a tiny stone bridge, to see what was there while we pondered our destiny.

And there it was. It had been waiting for years. A forgotten, shabby house sitting above the road behind a stone wall, and across the road, a small tidal cove, part of the Niantic River, an estuary of Long Island Sound. An old boathouse/barn sagged between the weeds and the sun.

We climbed the steps to the front door. The For Sale sign in the window was so faded we could barely make out the name and number to call. We wasted no time tracking down a person named Jennie, a woman as affable as she was eccentric. Remarking that we hadn't seen her name listed in the real estate pages, she waved her hand airily, "Oh, I don't believe in *advertising!*" Fortunately for us. When it looked as if we might not be able to get enough money together for the down payment, Jennie offered to lend it to us. On April first, as we were getting a baby-sitter arranged for and preparing to sign papers at the bank in Norwich, George-Alice climbed onto the fifth shelf in the linen closet and had five kittens. It was an omen, of sorts.

Every morning, even now, I come down the stairs, open the sunporch door and look out at the cove. It is a modest cove, but it is an infinite miracle that fills me with the wonder of it—the light, the water reflecting the changing colors of the trees along the shore, the curving out to where the river widens with the sky. Every season has its own water birds, along with the ubiquitous swans and mallards. Like a gaunt monk with his head bent down in benediction, the great blue heron watches for a guileless school of minnows. A flash, and he's motionless again, nearly invisible against the grass and stones. If the cove has a guru, he is the one.

We worked long and hard to get the place in reasonable shape. We would get partway through one project, put it aside for lack of time or money, get on with something else only to have everything stopped by a plumbing crisis. I painted and sanded and patched plaster and glazed windows and wallpapered—things I had never done or even seen done became part of daily life. A small stream at the bottom of the yard, between the house and the woods, provided hours of entertainment for Ann and Trish—and the cats—as they took up frog-catching. Toads dwelt under the stone steps. Star-nosed moles dug tunnels everywhere.

In Michigan my mother had been hospitalized, and this time was declared incurable. My father, already emotionally exhausted from trying to take care of her, had a heart attack. He would soon be released and my brother and I had to figure out what the options were. Because of my sister-in-law's MS, they could not take care of him, and he was in no shape to live on his own out at the cottage. Dad wanted to come here. Betty offered him a place but I was the one who had still been at home during the nightmare times, and he felt I understood. So it was decided that Dad would come here to recuperate. Don didn't want to say anything to discourage me, so he skipped mentioning an alcohol problem.

These were quite difficult years. Two children under five, a half-dozen cats, a falling-down house, and a semi-invalid parent with a drinking problem. The first year, I took him for over two hundred office visits to a doctor who could have applied for sainthood. His patience and sympathy kept all of us going.

In spite of everything, Dad hadn't lost his sense of humor. He was on pills for his heart, pills for blood pressure, pills for sleeping. At night he was in the habit of scooping them up with one hand and washing them down with the last of a bottle of wine. This particular night, he scooped up his change instead, and swallowed a quarter, three dimes, and a nickel.

It was a balancing act. I would be up, off and on, during the night, taking care of Dad. If the sound of his falling woke me, then I'd have to wake Jim because it took both of us to get him back into bed. On bad nights, it would be three a.m. before I got to bed, only to get up with the children a few hours later. Dad slept until noon, and came downstairs to have breakfast while the children had lunch. I hung on to the writing like a lifeline. I had approximately an hour while Ann and Trish napped and my father read the paper.

He wouldn't drink again until nightfall. That was his rule. Only after dark. He was adamant about that. One day he came downstairs equally adamant that he didn't want to eat with the children at noon. He'd wait until they went upstairs to nap. My one hour disappeared.

My sister, her second husband, two daughters, and a friend came that summer. It was a big help having her here, even if we were stuffed into every nook and cranny of this not-very-large house. Halfway through their visit the well went dry and my back went out. Wrapped around and around with tape, I was told by my doctor to stay prone for a day or two.

I didn't have hysterics, but I felt like it. At some point, after one's world becomes totally disorganized and out of control, hilarity sets in, that touch of the surreal that has always had great appeal for me. This kind of situation shaped the Big Witch's soirees, the public events in Witchville, like the Library Bazaar and Tea where the Big Witch disappears. Dorrie says the last thing her mother looked at was a cup of tea. Squig remarks that in that case, she swallowed herself and they'll never find her.

One evening the phone rang, and a man introduced himself as Noel Gerson. "I have an old friend visiting. I understand he's a friend of yours." He invited us over. The friend was Ralph Ross, one of the last people in the world we would have expected to find in Waterford, Connecticut. Norman had told Ralph where we were when he discovered Ralph would be staying with Noel. Noel had bought that last house we looked at before we turned down

Oswegatchie and found ours. It was a three-minute walk.

Noel became one of our closest friends. Jim and I loved him and saw him at least once a week. He wanted to have a party every weekend to unwind from his concentrated work. He was the first freelance, self-supporting author we'd ever met. And he was a prolific writer, making up pseudonyms almost as fast as plots. A gifted raconteur, he had a bottomless fund of jokes. He regaled us with tales of agents and editors, publishers and publishing.

Slowly, with relapses in between, my father was getting better. The drinking pattern didn't change much, but he was physically stronger and more himself. He enjoyed the cats, which multiplied around us like a scene from *The Sorcerer's Apprentice*. People gave them to us. People dumped kittens in the woods next to our yard, from whence they speedily made a beeline for our back door and joined the others. One litter was born in Ann's closet, among them a tailless black and white number that she named Josephine. Josie wore doll clothes with a certain panache, liked being wheeled in the doll carriage, and she followed Ann and Trish everywhere.

By this time, 1959–1960, Ann was in school and reading. When she came home, she and Trish would set up their own school; Ann was the teacher (strict!) and Trish the pupil. They never seemed to get tired of this—it seemed to be Annie's way of adjusting to school. Sitting on Jim's lap one evening, while he looked at the newspaper, Trish began reading the captions out loud. In their pretend-school, Ann had taught her to read!

Our local library was very small, and each child could only check out three books at a time. Easy Readers don't last long. The children sat in the back of the car eating lettuce out of the grocery bags, and reading, then trading books. By the time we got home, they needed to go back to the library for more books, and I needed more lettuce.

A child in school meant, for example, chicken pox, with two weeks at home in bed. Immediately afterward, the second child came down with chicken pox and was in bed for two weeks. I needed more than three books at a time, and I knew just how important reading and being read to was for a child, how reassuring. I began a story, writing and draw-

The Big Witch poured more magic into a bottle. "Come along, Dorrie," said the Big Witch. "Now we will get Cook." And down, down, down the stairs they went and into the kitchen.

From Dorrie and the Blue Witch, *written and illustrated by Patricia Coombs*

ing pictures to go along with it. It was a never-ending story, pages and pages as colds and flu and measles came and went.

My father, on the advice of his doctor, found a nearby residential hotel, coming here most evenings for dinner and sometimes taking care of Ann and Trish while we went up the road to Noel's place. He made friends with a widow and she was a great help in keeping his drinking under control.

Norman Sherman called from Minneapolis. Lonely after a divorce, he wanted to see us. He came for Christmas and stayed years. He liked it here, rented a house and relished the New England place names: Oxoboxo was his favorite, but a close second was Chicken-Fat Swamp on Gungywamp Road. He spent a lot of time with us, but he never got used to Josie emerging from under a chair in her red satin

skirt with the polka-dotted blouse. Another new writer in Jim's office was Jim Hepburn, a scholar and playwright. His wife Margaret was a gifted painter, open to everything, meeting all challenges with warm and wry good humor. The children loved her. But she also puzzled them— she didn't know how to drive or swim. Every few weeks they would direct further queries, had she learned to drive yet? Had she learned to swim? Margaret liked to do what I liked to do. Armed with a crowbar and hammer, she helped me whack a door-size hole into the study; we discovered it was the original door to the room and all the framing was in place. She was a most loved companion, and when she and Jim moved to England they left a hole in my life that could never be spackled over.

With Dad relatively independent, and with Trish soon to start first grade, I made a decision. I would give myself a year to write a publishable children's book. If I couldn't, then I would take the necessary course work to teach high school English.

I wrote every morning, doodling, drawing characters, finding their names. Waterford had a big new library, with a well-stocked children's section. Several times a week, I sat there on the floor and read my way along the shelves, getting a feel for the vocabulary for six- to nine-year-olds. Know your market, that was Noel's valuable advice. The stories I read had boys as heroes; all the action, the adventure, was for them. The girls were the audience. Well, my feelings on that score had simmered a long, long time. Whatever I wrote, it would be for girls who did things.

Halloween came, a favorite holiday. Costumes and makeup, beads and bangles and long skirts and witchy hats. With the wind shuffling dry leaves around our feet, we made the rounds of the neighborhood. Knocking on doors, mingling with other groups, then off on our own again. To be anonymous, disguised, other than one's self, this was utter delight.

Witches! Where were the witches? In books too difficult to read. With her character based on Annie and Trish, I made up this little witch and named her Dorrie, whose black cat Gink follows her everywhere, the way Josie did. Except I drew the cat to look like our Siamese, Ding-Bat, because she looked witchy and Josie didn't really even look like a cat—she looked like an overinflated guinea pig. The Big Witch and Cook were aspects of myself. The Big Witch busy with her own concerns, distracted, never listening properly to what Dorrie tells her, and Cook, always hurrying, always too much to do, spilling and stirring.

I drew on the floor this time, spreading out the pages, testing Trish's response as I drew. I wanted a child to be able to follow the story through the pictures, even if they had only heard it read once. "What's happening here?" I'd ask. If she wasn't sure, I needed to change the drawing.

A week or so after I had finished the story and done the drawings—they were in pencil on typing paper—Jim was scheduled to interview a promising applicant for a writing job at EB. His name was Rod Ham, and he arrived from New York with a blizzard right behind him that shut down the trains. Jim brought him home.

Rod had published several well-regarded novels, so we talked writing. He was interested in my having written poetry, since his mother was a poet. I explained my current project. He read *Dorrie's Magic* sitting there in the living room. He looked up and said: "I have an agent who has just started taking on children's books. I just know she'd really like this story. Send it to her, and tell her I told you to." That night he slept in the guest room with one of the cats draped across his balding head. He didn't mind. He said it felt like a fur night-cap.

The manuscript went off to Toni Strassman in New York. Toni was not just an agent, she was a character and had strong opinions. She offered the manuscript to one publisher, and they wanted it but not my unprofessional illustrations. Well! Toni was indignant. They couldn't have it. She liked the drawings. She took it to Lothrop, Lee and Shepard. They liked the story AND the drawings and wanted it for their fall list.

Lothrop was then a division of Crown Publishers. Their offices were small, cluttered, and a casual sort of frenzy seemed to keep everything in motion. Stuart Benick, the head of production, gave me a crash course in illustration. He explained about "bleeding" and double spread and trim sizes, the kind of paper to use, the ink, the pens, and overlays. It would be alternate pages with color, and two colors that together would make a third. He told me I would need a light-table and where to buy Bourges paper for the color. That I didn't know

beans about what I was doing didn't seem to concern anybody there, not the editor, Bea Creighton, nor Stu, nor the art director, Miriam Downes.

Happily, Jim had experience doing paste-ups and type specking at work. All the stuff I needed to know, he had right at hand—crop marks, measuring copy, even vanishing points. *Paradise Lost* hadn't prepared me for this. I loved doing the illustrations. It could be fiercely frustrating, but the joy of it could not be diminished.

Dorrie's Magic was published in the fall of 1962. Miriam had used the picture of Dorrie reading the Big Witch's Book of Magic for the cover of their catalogue. A kind of unreality hovered around it all. It grew much more unreal when a copy of the *New York Times* children's book section arrived on a Saturday. There, on the front, was Dorrie reading the Big Witch's Book of Magic, with a lovely and long review. Their only complaint was a line Bea had snuck into the book after I'd checked the galleys: it was a moral, a sort of lecture from the Big Witch. It was the very patronizing, put-down sort of attitude that adults often use with children that I had detested and abhorred. I was upset. In 1977 when it was published in England, I was able to have my original text reinstated.

My gamble of a year had, against all odds, and with the help and encouragement of Jim and Noel and other friends, succeeded. I wrote another. It was inspired by a story Dad told. Having to take care of his baby brother, he'd put molasses on the baby's hands, then give him a feather to play with. I changed everybody into raccoons, borrowed a name from a local fishing dock—Waddy's—and called it *Waddy and His Brother*. It came out in 1963.

Driving into New York with the children one day, we glimpsed a lost, much run-over stuffed animal lying in the middle of a street. It was just a glimpse, yet the image was so evocative of childhood and the loss of childhood it would not go away. Months later, I woke up with an entire story in my head. It wrote itself. I didn't know stories did that. It was called *The Lost Playground*.

Bea Creighton was enthusiastic. "This is Dante's *Inferno* for children!" The hero, Mostly Frederick Sometimes Sam, acquired his name from Noel's daughter, who named one of their cats Mostly Black and White Meower. That was the best name ever. The hero's odd figure came from the first stuffed animal I ever made, when Annie was little. It was a medley of ill-fitting parts—a bit of bear, quite a bit of giraffe, rabbity legs. Published in the spring of 1963, *Playground* was well received by critics, including the *New York Times*. It was on their 100 Best Children's Books list. But, it was NOT a big success with children. The subject matter and the vocabulary were at odds. Children who could read at that level were beyond stuffed animals. This was a good lesson.

Rummaging through piles of notes and scratchings and other flotsam and jetsam, looking for inspiration, part of the original story I'd made up for Ann and Trish floated to the top. There was a figure of a blue witch. That was the image I needed. She belonged with Dorrie and Gink and the Big Witch.

I had the image, but not the story. I wrote, I wrote and revised and filled the wastebasket with words and ideas that didn't work. When it got too frustrating, I'd go around and polish all the lamps in the house. Dust. Cook something that simmers all day. Back to the typewriter. This went on for months. I couldn't get it right, and I couldn't let it go. For no reason at all, on a morning no different than the others, it fell into place. *Dorrie and the Blue Witch* was finished.

Published in 1964, that book was in print for twenty-five years. It was translated into German, and came out in paperback by Dell six years later, and was published in England by Heinemann in hardcover, later as a Puffin paperback. It was a favorite with children and the letters poured in, nearly always writing that the best part is when Dorrie "shrinked the witch."

That was my favorite, too. Behind the image of tiny, furious, threatening Blue Witch was the childhood memory of Don showing me how to trap bumblebees in hollyhock blossoms: you hold the tips of the petals tight, break the blossom from the stem, then shake. Held close to the ear, an angry bee buzzes with such ferocity there is a "frisson" of danger. As Dorrie says, "I bet she bites."

Dorrie's Play followed, coming directly from living room dramas put on by Ann and Trish. Rummaging through my sewing stuff, they'd come upon a length of sky-blue cotton. By cutting a hole in the middle that Trish's head would go through, they made her a splendid dress for her part as a princess. Until that moment, the blue cotton had been part of a quilt project.

Children wrote and asked: "Where do you get your ideas?" I couldn't tell them I didn't know. I had to consciously consider, which I had not done until they asked. Some parts I did know—like the funny things that happen around any ordinary household—but how they got mixed in with memories, my own feelings toward children and toward myself as a child, that alchemy couldn't be explained.

Dorrie and the Weather-Box was spawned by a school science experiment of Annie's that got out of hand. We *all* knew how clouds were formed by the time she was through. There was a cloud obscuring our kitchen ceiling. That was one ingredient. The other was the picnics the children would have in the car when it was rainy. We had no garage, so the car just sat out front near the road. They made cheese or bologna sandwiches, put them in their handbags (the fancier the better) and picnicked in the back seat.

Hurricane Esther brushed the Connecticut coast. Flood tides inundated the yard, backing up all along the streambed. When it subsided, there was a twelve-inch wood-turtle, stranded. Naming it Esther, the children made it a home in our only bathtub, the same claw-footed tub commemorated in my illustrations. They kept Esther supplied with a few inches of water, bits of lettuce, and ground beef; the latter does not take well to soaking. The agreement was that Esther could stay a week or so, then we'd find a good place for her back in the woods by the swamp.

An unexpected call notified us that Aunt Beenie was going to be in New York, en route to Boston, and she'd be visiting. Beenie had been at the University of Washington with my parents just prior to World War I. A single lady, she taught deaf students at a school in Seattle. She had visited us in Minneapolis where she sat on the couch of an evening and made pronouncements regarding our child-rearing practices. Ann, at two or two-and-a-half, had turned over the wastebasket in order to stand on it, get to the chair, and from thence to the desk. She did this often when we had company. It put her up high enough to watch the faces and gestures of the adults on the couch. Not yet talking, she did everything but articulate words—she mimicked the sounds, the rhythms, the inflections of speech. She copied the gestures, the pauses, the laughs.

"You are very PERMISSIVE!" was Beenie's verdict, delivered with a frown that Ann copied, along with the wave of the hand.

Beenie's impending arrival sent me into high-speed domestic turmoil—the vacuum, the dust mop, the duster, the polish. There were meals to plan, groceries to get. The children were sent to clean up their rooms and round up the cats, check the latches on the hamster cage, the gerbils' cage, the rabbit hutch. Whatever we found that didn't fit went under the beds or into the closets, unless it was breathing.

She came. Her train was late. A piece of luggage had gone astray on the flight to New York. Her stomach was upset and she did hope that dinner would not be too heavy for her. She had on a navy suit. I hadn't vacuumed the cat hairs off the furniture, just the floor. And Beenie didn't sit on the floor.

She went upstairs to wash up before supper. Two seconds later, a shriek, a scream, a yell: THERE'S A TURTLE IN THE BATHTUB! To say nothing of pale, disintegrating hamburger and a leaf of lettuce. We were so used to Esther, we'd simply forgotten her. This was not an extended visit.

That visit was immortalized in *Dorrie and the Witch Doctor.* Letters from boys were start-

ing to come as well as from girls. They really liked the Witch Doctor, with his MD license plate on his broomstick and his belief in the power of chocolate peppermints to cure most ailments.

All the illustrations, after *Dorrie and the Witch Doctor,* were done on mylar with colored pencils. It cut printing costs for the publisher, so they supplied me with the mylar. Tricky stuff. It couldn't be erased, except in non-printing areas; the least smudge, or fingerprint—or sneeze—could ruin hours of painstaking labor. Josie once walked across a completed double-spread, leaving a trail of little paw-prints.

Another book with a long, happy life was *Dorrie and the Wizard's Spell.* Published in 1968, it went out of print just last year. As some stories do, like Beenie and Aunt Agra, this came during a spell of thinking about a specific character. I'd been remembering John Berryman as I sat doodling assorted witches and wizards. And there he was, John Berryman as the Wizard Wink. It is him to the nth degree, lying on the library shelf in a turtleneck sweater with all his nervy wit and the hint of malice. Leaning on his elbow, grinning, he waits to view the disaster he planted among the ordinary items for sale at the Big Witch's table. Done not for revenge, or real meanness, but just to show off his own powers.

From Lisa and the Grompet, *written and illustrated by Patricia Coombs*

The following year was fraught with family emergencies coast to coast. There seemed to be so much on my mind, so much preoccupying my feelings that I wasn't able to do anything about writing. By now Lothrop had become a division of William Morrow, and there had been changes in editors. My new editor, Edna Barth, sent me a story by Gladys Yessayan Cretan, and asked if I would illustrate it. It was a dog story, *Lobo.* It felt as if she had thrown me a life preserver. Drawing. Drawing took me out of myself and that was exactly where I needed to be. Two years later, I illustrated the sequel, *Lobo and Brewster.*

The clouds opened, another story arrived overnight while I was looking in another direction. I made my mug of coffee, sat down at the typewriter and wrote it out in one sitting. It even came with a title in place, *Lisa and the Grompet.* It went into galleys without a word being changed from the original draft.

My friend Ruth had spent some time with us, off and on, whenever she had a break in teaching. Noticing Jim's perpetual battle against the bull-briers on our back hill, Ruth remarked that all we needed was a goat. We had laughed. And forgotten about it. Ruth hadn't. Our phone rang in July and a woman said: "This is Mrs. Smith on Braman Road. Your goat is ready." Our GOAT was ready?

We went to look. Born out of season, his mum took one look and rejected him, so he had been bottle-fed until he could drink out of a bowl. He was so small, he could balance on the palm of a hand, which also meant he could walk up an arm extended over the back of a chair, walking all over us as if we were geological outcroppings. Mrs. Smith asked five dollars for him, and explained that he was in the process of being neutered. To neuter her male goats, she fastened rubberbands round their testicles; shortly thereafter they would dry up from lack of circulation, and fall off. Yes, but where? In whose lap?

Ann named him Vincent Van Goat. All of us had a new playmate. He would chase us all over in wild games of tag. Hide-and-seek was a good goat game. Jim built him a small shed with a fence around it out back. He didn't spend a lot of time there. He had an ear-splitting wail which gave us to understand he was lonely and might perish without immediate attention. He napped on the patio chaise, ensconced among the flowered cushions. The

cats liked his company and took up positions on the chairs nearby, and when those got too crowded, on the picnic table. Annie had a friend come over to play, and as they came up the stone steps to the patio, the friend stopped in her tracks and gazed at the assortment of animals on the furniture. "I wish I lived here," she said wistfully.

Vincent was pure mischief. His capacity and talent for trouble was boundless. He loved trouble. He loved being yelled at, especially when people got irritated enough to leap around waving their arms. He responded by dancing up and down and shaking his head. He found a way out of his pen, and early in the morning, before we were up and about, he would trot down to the road and stop cars. This was news to us. A lady accosted me in the library and asked if I was the one with the goat. She explained that he stopped her every morning.

Meanwhile, I'd done the layout and sketches for *Lisa and the Grompet* and they had been checked out and sent back. It was time to begin work on the finals. Part of the story takes place in the woods. I wanted the woods to look like those around us, with masses of ferns, toadstools, wildflowers. Gathering up sketchbooks, pencils, erasers, and coffee, off I went, Vincent at my heels. I had been working on a clump of ferns, figuring out the pattern of the fronds. The goat got bored. He put his forefeet on my back and tugged at my hair with his teeth. He tugged at my shirt. He offered endless invitations to a goat chase.

I went on with my drawing. For a moment, silence, followed by a loud slurp. There went my coffee. Looking idly about, he spied a sketchbook. Nosing it, he discovered that the glue of the binding was delicious. He had already chewed up an eraser, but I didn't know that yet. At last I gave up, got a bucket and a shovel, dug up a clump of ferns and brought them inside to draw. So much for the plein-air school of painting.

The pencil and mylar turned out to be ideal for that story, and the illustrations were immensely satisfying. Popular with children, adults also liked it and it was reprinted in school readers, which was also immensely satisfying.

Letters came thick and fast. This was one of the best parts about writing stories and drawing the pictures: hearing from children. I answered, and still answer, every letter. They are stowed away in cartons, insulating the attic—I can't bear to discard them. The letters were also a surprise. As a child, I never wrote to an author. Nobody I knew ever wrote to an author. Authors were dead. One little girl had apparently run into that problem. At the bottom of her letter she wrote: "If you aren't dead will you please write back to me?"

Dorrie and the Haunted House was next. There was an abandoned house up the road from us, half hidden behind overgrown trees and bushes. Walking by after dark, the children and I had seen a pale light gliding from window to window to window, all along the second floor. Then darkness again. It was truly spooky. Our claw-footed bathtub is in this book. Dorrie and Gink hide inside it under an old rug. When the door-latch rattles, she thinks it's ghosts. "You can't come in," she says, "I'm taking a bath, and so is my cat."

After that it was months of writing and finding myself at dead ends. Something began to simmer in the typewriter cauldron. Birthday cakes had always been a source of comedy. I liked making them. They tasted very, very good. But they looked funny. A birthday story. Looking up weeds in a reference book at the library, weed names were still in my mind when I went to check out other books. Ahead of me, a woman had a copy of Rubin's diet book, *Forever Thin*. Turning it around, mixing in a weed, I had the character I needed: Thinnever Vetch. That was *Dorrie and the Birthday Eggs*.

My editor, Edna Barth, called and asked if by any chance I had a story around for their spring list. Stu Benick had told her about a story I'd submitted to Bea Creighton ten years ago, that Bea had rejected as being "ahead of its time." No one had ever *asked* for a story before! Excitedly, I dug out the manuscript of *Mouse Café* and sent it off. It was a story close to my heart, written out of my experience as a waitress. The irony of females dishing up food and serving people while they dream of romance and marriage, only to find themselves dishing up and serving people when their dream comes true. So with Lollymops and the crumb soup.

Edna called. A line had to be changed. It wasn't logical. "You can't slam a hole," said Edna. "But look at the picture," I said, "there is a round hole and the hole has a door." Our conversation went on and on, and eventually, I got to keep the line, which read: "And

with that, they picked Lollymops up and threw her out the hole and slammed it."

All was well. Until it was about to be published in Great Britain. The Windmill Press editor, David Elliot, sent me an airmail letter. And what did he say? "You can't slam a hole." I wrote back an impassioned plea on behalf of that line, and it stayed.

Vincent Van Goat was not with us long. He contracted listeriosis, and despite our vet's valiant efforts and our nursing care, he died. In his short life he greatly enhanced and livened our lives. He never ate a single brier. He ate the blooms off half my marigolds. Ill, he practically lived on bananas and homemade oatmeal cookies. Annie would sit by him as he lay on his bed of blankets in the basement, and feed him, talk to him.

Unforgettable, Vincent turned into a goblin in *Dorrie and the Goblin*. What does one know about goblins? They love trouble. They cannot be left alone, for they are untrustworthy. They cry piteously for attention. Caught eating candles like bananas and scribbling on the ceiling, they pretend remorse. It is pretense. They are just waiting for a chance to do more mischief.

The book came out in 1972. That same year, Akane Shobo published six of the Dorrie titles in Japanese. They did a lovely job of printing them, but we had no idea how accurate the translations were. It was indescribably exciting to see them in Japanese. Four of the stories had been translated and published in Germany as inexpensive paperbacks. The contract for one of them gave the title as "Dorrie and the Haunted Horse." This didn't inspire a lot of confidence in the German translation.

It was the 1970s, the world around us bubbling with changes, with astrology and ESP and past lives and mystical possibilities. We learned to meditate; we still do. In New York a friend of Ruth's read our charts. "Jupiter! Look at that!" she said. "Do you find things tend to multiply, expand?" "Like one book turning into a series?" I said. "That's it! That's Jupiter!" Now I knew who was writing the stories that formed while I slept.

I went home and wrote *Dorrie and the Fortune Teller*. Toni, my agent, served as the model for the fake Madame Zee.

This was also the time of alternative medicine, herbs, acupuncture. It was all exaggerated enough to be fun just as material. *Dorrie and the Amazing Magic Elixir* bubbled up, fed by my old fear of the dark. I had a lot of fuel in those feelings. So much so that Edna insisted on cutting the scariest part. Something of John Berryman is in that wizard, too, a wizard who wears green and white sneakers, and wants to be immortal.

Longing to work on something totally different, I spent hours in the library and at home, reading folktales, seeking a path that would take me back to childhood and Grimms. In one of Katherine Briggs' remarkable collections, I found a story that captured my imagination wholly. But, one of the main characters is a woman who drinks—a mean drunk at that. And drunks aren't allowed in children's stories. I would still like to do the story of Billy Biter. The comic dragon with his mouth filled with gingerbread is irresistible, reminding me of my sister, Betty, and the black gingerbread.

Jupiter did a spin, and I woke up with a folktale that just needed to be written down: *Molly Mullett.* My most cherished story, and dedicated to Trish.

Out of that same ambience came the doppleganger in *Dorrie and the Witch's Imp,* followed by *The Magic Pot,* a retelling of a Danish tale.

Years before, I had waked in the middle of night to find a small silvery Dream Witch perched on the footboard of our bed. I knew she had a story, but it couldn't be found. I worked and worked on it. Giving up in despair, months later I would try again. After seven years Jim and I happened to go to Stamford, Connecticut in search of something at the Acme Wrecking Company. The place must cover acres— acres of old bathtubs, urns, merry-go-round horses, a trolley-car, wrought iron staircases ascending toward an empty sky, cement cherubs hold basins where birds bathe, cement maidens pour empty pitchers into nonexistent pools. Bedsteads are *everywhere.* Brass beds, iron beds, wooden beds. Sleighs and sleds and snowshoes, chandeliers. I looked around and I said to Jim: "We found the Dreamyard. This is what the dreams and nightmares use for props and scenery." *Dorrie and the Dreamyard Monsters* had finally come together into a whole story.

Children often ask, in letters and in schools where I visit, "How long does it take to write a story?" They are usually stuck in the middle of an assignment when they ask. So I tell them about the ones that come in the night, and the ones that take months, and then I tell them about *Dorrie and the Dreamyard* that took seven years.

I had written a version of the Grimms' tale, "The Three Aunts," and sent it off. Edna sent it back. Feminists, she said, would eat that princess for breakfast. As a child those three old women, deformed by their spinning, thrilled and horrified me, thanks to Rackham's genius.

It so happened that not long before this, I had found a dead but barely damaged groundhog at the side of the Niantic River Road. Wrapping it in a towel, I brought it home to look at. Seeing an animal close up is a completely different experience than seeing it in a yard. The small, black leathery hands were like doll's hands with gloves on them.

Idly listening to the coffee perk, looking out at the woods, I suddenly knew the answer to the problem. Groundhogs. After all, a Groundhog Princess can be as politically incorrect as she wants. A Groundhog Princess would boss around a Groundhog Prince. Thus revised, *Tilabel* became a well-liked story for Groundhog Day.

From the immersion and absorption in folktales and books about ESP came *Dorrie and the Screebit Ghost.* Long-ago Field Days at the local elementary school returned in *Dorrie and the Witchville Fair,* enriched by all the visits we made to a nearby piggery. The whimsical owner had placed an abandoned school bus in the pig-yard. There are no words to describe the hilarity of seeing pigs solemnly climbing up the steps into the bus, trotting down the steps out of the bus, like grade schoolers upon whom a spell has been cast.

With Ann and Trish in college and the numbers of animals decreased, there was more space and time, time to write and to *paint.* Lyman Allyn Museum in New London was offering a course in oil painting. I had tried doing some painting on my own over the years, without notable success, though the first one, painted on Masonite, did a splendid job of covering a crack in the living room plaster, a memento of our first experience with hurricanes. The class was like a door opening into another part of my life, rooms I had known were there but had never explored. Instead of the mental images that had been the material for illustrations, I began to learn how to draw and paint what was in front of me. It was completely absorbing, seeming to consist of equal parts frustration and transcendent happiness.

The following year, another story. A little girl had written to tell me that she loved the Dorrie books, and her uncle did, too. He wanted her to ask if I'd write one called *Dorrie and the Swimming Pool.* Periodically, letters from boys would ask for stories about creatures and monstrous lizards attacking Witchville. Except for Black Pond, there wasn't any water there—so the Big Witch and Dorrie, Gink, and Cook fly off to a remote lake. *Dorrie and the Witches' Camp,* published in 1983, came from those letters.

This was followed by *The Magician and McTree,* my homage to our old cat Henry, whose bravado and misadventures had so brightened our domestic scene for eighteen years. And at last I got to draw a princess—and a King and Queen. As well as a truffle pig.

We drove west that summer to visit Jim's family in Washington state. We made that trip so often over the years that this time we took yet another route, going through Nebraska to see if his grandfather's place was still there, and an uncle or cousin in the area. It was, and they were, and the open farmlands reaching to the horizon came in such contrast to the small-scale scenery of New England I longed to fly over it, slowly, like a pterodactyl, to see where the world ended. Stopping for lunch in a small town, a hand-painted sign pointed down a narrow road and said: MUSEUM.

Museum? Indeed. A one-story clapboard building built at the side of a defunct quarry, the latter now filled with water and catfish so big a nightmare couldn't hold them. Created and owned by one family, it was as unlikely a collection of objects as the wrecking company in Stamford. There was a pair of white embroidered kidskin gloves, once belonging to Annie Oakley. In an ancient iron frying pan, the largest rattlesnake ever caught in Nebraska lay stuffed and neatly coiled. All the Nebraska license plates ever issued were represented on the walls, along with assorted farm tools. In glass cases fossil dinosaur bones retrieved from the quarry, a seventeenth-century English policeman's rattle—the forerunner of the whistle, bonnets from homesteading days and various types of guns and silverware and kitchen utensils. I thought, this could be in Witchville: the first cauldron, clothes worn by the founding witches and wizards, old books of magic. When we got back to Connecticut, I wrote *Dorrie and the Museum Case.*

The author in her studio, Waterford, Connecticut

In 1986, on an ordinary evening, Jim came home from work and asked how I would like to live in London for a few years. The Office of Naval Research had an opening for an editor. Trish had been living with us for a couple of years. After graduating with honors from San Francisco State, and working part-time at a brokerage firm, she had been stricken with systemic lupus. The prognosis had not been good, but her condition had stabilized. As long as she got a few hours of sleep in the afternoon, she could manage. It was a wonderful opportunity for all of us: Trish would have the house and the dog and cats all to herself, Jim and I would have a badly needed break from our routines.

Off we went. Noel, recovering from a heart attack and now living in Florida, sent us an urgent message regarding the need for WARM CLOTHES. He always gave us excellent advice. We packed silk undershirts and sweaters and turtlenecks. And art supplies. Lothrop had given me a story by Alice Schertle to illustrate.

London! We had visited London twice on brief vacations. Living there, actually moving into a flat in the center of the city and being part of a neighborhood, it was an unceasing marvel.

I worked on the illustrations all morning, then set off to explore, by foot, by tube, by big red bus. The National Gallery was a whole afternoon in itself, often twice a week. They had art lectures, they had films of different artists and periods in a small theatre with soft chairs—and they had a tearoom.

In the summer I flew back to Connecticut to see how Trish was and to mow the lawn and take care of the garden, see friends and jog with the dog. In the fall, I tracked down drawing classes. The Camden Arts Centre in North London offered life drawing, and portrait drawing. At last, I could begin to learn to draw legs, arms, heads, their joints and junctures. The only flaw in the courses was the tendency of the models to slump, slither, nod off, or slowly swivel into another position. Most of the models were drawn from the "squats" in the area, "punks" as they were called, and drugs made them less than ideal as subjects. To compensate, however, one learned that earrings are not necessarily confined to ears, and tattoos can be done absolutely anywhere there is flesh. Tea-breaks were enlivened by the instructor, Jack Yates, whose gifts as a raconteur reminded me of Noel. If a model didn't show up, he'd pose—with his clothes on. At sixty, I was back in school, and I loved it.

The next summer, I wrote *Dorrie and the Pin Witch.* The Pin Witch was a seamstress that made some of my dresses when I was seven or eight. The feel of her cold, white fingers against my neck as she pinned a collar, around my arms when she pinned a sleeve, her coal-black hair and unsmiling face made me dread those visits to her apartment. If I moved or turned the wrong direction, she'd hiss under her breath. This time Lothrop wanted full-color illustrations. The market had changed, they said, illustrations were "in." That part was fine. But when they said because of the cost of full-color, the book would be 32 pages instead of 48, I cut and revised, cut and revised. The manuscript would come back with more cuts. The story was becoming the summary of a story to go with the illustrations.

Back in London, I began the final pictures, and that was lovely—color. All kinds of colors. I had a basket full of design markers, and ink and colored pencils and gouache to use. No overlays. All of it directly on illustration board. And all the while, drawing classes for at least six hours a week.

London was three-and-a-half years of freedom, of such "lightness of being" it was hard to believe it was actually happening. The flat was small, and took no time to keep up. The garden behind it was about six feet square and paved. Changing the pot plants with the season was all that was required in yard work. It was adventures. It was being locked in the British Museum when an alarm went off. I had gone to see an exhibit of Henry Moore's bomb-shelter drawings. It was a smallish gallery, and about a dozen of us were locked in there. Gradually we all settled ourselves on the carpet and leaned against the wall to wait. There was one chuckle, then another as we realized that we looked exactly like the drawings on the walls.

En route to the same museum in December, I turned down Great Russell Street, and paused in disbelief. Coming along the sidewalk toward me was a remarkably fat white pony, another was coming along beside it in the gutter. As the man holding one of the ponies came closer, I asked: "Where are you taking these animals?" After all this was right near Oxford Street, jammed traffic, hordes of people. He waved his hand with pride at the ponies: "Them pulls the coach in *Cinderella.*" I watched. They turned into an alley behind a theatre.

London had worked its magic. We'd gotten to Amsterdam and driven through the lovely French countryside twice, the Loire valley, then the Dordogne. To Brussels, back to Amsterdam, to soak up the museums full of paintings, so those years were as special as years could be.

In Connecticut, salt and sun had wreaked havoc with window frames and doors, and rendered some of the shutters toothless. That was all I did for a few months, paint and scrape and sand and fill, which helped with re-entry problems—it grounded me when I seemed to exist somewhere between England and America. It took a year, actually, to land. Talk about lost luggage!

Jim retired. We began classes at the Lyme Academy of Fine Arts. At last, Jim would sculpt the forms that had followed him all these years.

And we both took anatomy, the nomenclature an incantation: femur, clavicle, patella.

Occasionally I was asked to do school programs for first or second or third graders. The program is drawing on a big pad of paper with lots of bright magic markers. I start it, and have the children, a few at a time, finish it while I begin another one. I empty a canvas bag of markers on the floor before we start, which relaxes all of us. Only once have I found a child who didn't like to draw. We must come into the world with an impulse to make pictures.

Classrooms brought back my experiences in elementary school, and I wanted to write about it, somehow. It took a long time, a lot of revising, and, like The Pin Witch, cuts and more cuts and more cuts. At last *Dorrie and the Haunted Schoolhouse* was ready to be illustrated. This was, as always, the happiest of undertakings. With all those colors I went crazy with striped socks flying through the air, the schoolhouse airborne against a blue sky, a tiny landscape down below. Six weeks went by, and just before the deadline, it was done. As UPS carried the package off to New York, I took off for the beach. All those hours, seven days a week, and I was free! I swam, I raced up and down the beach, splashing in the shallows, shouting to the seagulls. In September, the beach is empty, so one is free to celebrate with eccentric abandon. The following days were spent in the ritual cleanup that sets the stage for whatever adventure may follow. I sort through all the sketches and preliminary sketches and the tracing paper outlines, keeping only what might do to send along with a letter to a child.

The next week my editor called, asking how soon they could have the illustrations. The package should have arrived long before this. My heart slid down into my socks. All the offices in New York were searched, the mailroom turned inside out. Nothing. UPS reported that the package had been delivered with their usual efficiency, the receipt signed off. The illustrations had disappeared.

Since most of the sketches, the drawings, the tracings, were now part of Waterford's landfill, the task of redoing all that work was daunting. I had four weeks to do it. Jim and Trish pitched in with the housework, the cooking, the groceries, the laundry. As it turned out, I grew happier and happier as I redid those pages. Details could be added, scenes rearranged, a perspective changed or an expression. We drove into New York and I delivered *this* package in person. The book came out in 1992, exactly thirty years after *Dorrie's Magic*.

We turned the ground-level basement into a studio, where Jim sculpts and I paint. I keep on writing. Unpublished manuscripts spill from folders, lie in drifts around my feet. A different kind of story is there, demanding attention—not a children's story, but an everybody story about a very particular dog. We had had dogs, but this wasn't our dog. Chum belonged to a neighbor up the road. But he walked into our lives and simply refused to leave. I sent him home. I walked him home. I drove him home in the car. It is a love story. Like all love stories, it is also a mystery. And my life, my life has gone from witches to wags.

BIBLIOGRAPHY

FOR CHILDREN

Books written and illustrated:

The Lost Playground, Lothrop, 1963.

Waddy and His Brother, Lothrop, 1963.

Lisa and the Grompet, Lothrop, 1970.

Mouse Café, Lothrop, 1972.

Molly Mullett, Lothrop, 1975.

The Magic Pot, Lothrop, 1977.

Tilabel, Lothrop, 1978.

The Magician and McTree, Lothrop, 1984.

"Dorrie" series:

Dorrie's Magic, Lothrop, 1962.

Dorrie and the Blue Witch, Lothrop, 1964.

Dorrie's Play, Lothrop, 1965.

Dorrie and the Weather-Box, Lothrop, 1966.

Dorrie and the Witch Doctor, Lothrop, 1967.

Dorrie and the Wizard's Spell, Lothrop, 1968.

Dorrie and the Haunted House, Lothrop, 1970.

Dorrie and the Birthday Eggs, Lothrop, 1971.

Dorrie and the Goblin, Lothrop, 1972.

Dorrie and the Fortune Teller, Lothrop, 1973.

Dorrie and the Amazing Magic Elixir, Lothrop, 1974.

Dorrie and the Witch's Imp, Lothrop, 1975.

Dorrie and the Halloween Plot, Lothrop, 1976.

Dorrie and the Dreamyard Monsters, Lothrop, 1978.

Dorrie and the Screebit Ghost, Lothrop, 1979.

Dorrie and the Witchville Fair, Lothrop, 1980.

Dorrie and the Witches' Camp, Lothrop, 1983.

Dorrie and the Museum Case, Lothrop, 1986.

Dorrie and the Pin Witch, Lothrop, 1989.

Dorrie and the Haunted Schoolhouse, Clarion, 1992.

Books illustrated:

Shelagh Williamson, *Pepi's Bell,* Singer, 1961.

Noel B. Gerson, *P. J., My Friend,* Doubleday, 1969.

Gladys Yessayan Cretan, *Lobo,* Lothrop, 1969.

G. Y. Cretan, *Lobo and Brewster,* Lothrop, 1971.

Alice Schertle, *Bill and the Google-Eyed Goblins,* Lothrop, 1987.

Other:

Also contributor of poetry to periodicals, including *Partisan Review, Poetry,* and *Western Review.*

Penelope Farmer

1939-

I am a twin, the second born of two girls. I begin with this, because as for most twins, I suspect, my twinship was and is probably the most important fact about me. It explains a lot about what I am, what has happened to me, and what I've done with my life—including writing books. (Sometimes it explains what's in my books, even when not obviously about twins. But I'll leave such explanations to others.)

We were born in June 1939, three months before the outbreak of World War Two; my twin Judy was expected, of course. But nobody expected me. These days ultrasound machines look at babies in the womb before birth. That way two babies can be seen, if there are two, unless one is tucked right behind the other. Even then, long before the invention of ultrasound, the doctor and midwife could sometimes feel twins and sometimes hear a second heartbeat, but often they did not. In our case most definitely they did not. The first my mother knew about me was twenty-five minutes or so after my sister's birth, when at my urgent signs of wanting to follow her into the world the doctor cried, "My God, there's another one!" And out I came, leaving my mother doubly exhausted. The nurse ran quickly for brandy to revive her and came back with the only bottle she could find, in the sideboard in the dining room, more than three quarters empty. She emptied all of it into a large glass.

Because of the brandy my father, too, suffered a double shock. Not only did he have two daughters where he'd expected one, the bottle contained a rare and vintage brandy that he was saving for a special occasion. In the circumstances, I doubt if he would have objected to my mother being given such an expensive sip. But the nurse's emptying the remainder of the glassful—most of it—down the sink was another matter.

Presumably he forgave us in the end. But the way I've always felt obliged to shout about myself so loudly, I sometimes wonder if I've

Penelope Farmer, 1985

managed to forgive the world for denying my existence in the womb. I did not actually emerge from my mother shouting. I weighed only three pounds, so I was very weakly. But I made up for it later; starting, you might say, along with my sister, straight after our birth. The doctor's second reported comment on seeing how little and weak we were was "I won't see those two alive when I come back." But we weren't having any of that, nor was the maternity nurse. We'd been born at home; there was no incubator handy. So she put together a homemade one with a hot water bottle, which worked very well. The fact I'm sitting here writing this con-

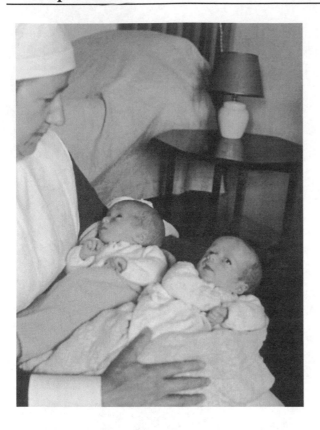

Twins with their maternity nurse, June 1939

tures or the ones in my head, my twin was always there, alongside me—in our mother's arms, in our crib, dangling from our father's hands, in our playpen, in our school uniforms—twins, a couple. And I know, though this I remember less well, for our mother always managed to make each of us feel we were special to her, that it was not looking into her eyes that told me who I was, as happens with the single born. My sister, side by side with me, told me who I was, and who I wasn't.

One of the ways we told each other who we were was by fighting, not an unusual state of affairs between twins. Jacob and Esau, for instance, started fighting in the womb. In these days of ultrasound, twins who fight each other after birth sometimes have been seen exchanging punches in the womb. If we didn't punch each other there, we certainly made up for it later. When we shared a playpen, all our toys had to be soft toys, since we used them to bash each other over the head. It's not that we didn't love each other. But love sometimes shows itself in anger and fighting. Ours certainly did.

Perhaps this is the point to say a little more about our family. Our father was a civil servant who worked in the House of Commons—the English Parliament—all his life. He had not wanted to be a civil servant; he'd wanted to be a soldier. But both his elder brothers having been killed fighting in the First World War his mother wouldn't let him join the army, and leaving university at the time of the Great Depression, he had to take any job he could get. Fortunately this one allowed very long holidays, in which he gardened and played golf and cricket, all things he enjoyed more; it meant, too, he was around us much more than most fathers, throughout our childhood.

He himself had not had a happy childhood. Not only unplanned, like me, he was barely expected—finding herself pregnant with him at the age of fifty, his mother had hidden her condition so well that the first the world knew of him was a cable reading, "Emmy has had a redheaded son." (He did not remain redheaded—though several of us have red tints in our hair.) His father was sixty years old then, his brothers in their twenties; even his sisters were thirteen and eleven years older than he was. More like a grandchild in that household, he grew up lonely, having few friends. Pictures of him

firms it. So do the burn scars still visible on my thumb and knee that I got from the hot water bottle. They are honourable battle scars, I think, in my struggle to stay alive; I've always felt proud of them.

Some people might say—my sister would have agreed with them—that after such a hazardous start, my life has been one long yell for attention. I've embarrassed myself often enough. My upbringing made much of being quiet and modest, altogether ladylike. I can still feel my shame, aged eight, confronted with one school report that claimed I was "disturbing in class." But nothing stopped me for long, to the dismay, then, of my much more retiring, more easily embarrassed sister. What else do you write for, after all, except to tell the world you're there and that what you think is to be counted? It's no profession for someone determined to hide their head; mine being hidden once was enough for me, I think.

There is this, too, about twins. Right from the start you are never alone. In all the pictures of our childhood, whether snapshot pic-

show a small boy dressed in clothes passed down from his older brothers that were by then twenty years out of date, looking understandably mournful. At the age of eight, in the way of things in England, he was sent away to school, where the headmaster beat him unmercifully. All this left him a not very talkative, if loving, man.

He and I were poles apart—growing up I quarrelled with him constantly. He didn't think girls needed a university education, and I wanted one. I had radical socialist views, and he was very conservative. When it occurred to me once that he and I never talked except to fight, I decided to ask him about his work—professors of politics came from all over the world to pick his brains, why shouldn't I? He told me he hadn't got time to talk just then; next day he brought home a book written by one of his colleagues. So that was that; he and I continued shouting at each other until I left Oxford. Though these days we get on very well, affectionately even, we still don't talk much.

My mother, too, suffered an unhappy childhood; her mother died when she was three, and she and her sister spent their early years being shunted round a series of unwilling aunts. Unlike as they otherwise were, this shared past unhappiness seemed to be what drew my parents together. I see them, still, as two orphans huddled in each other's arms, weathering the storm. They continued to adore each other until my mother died when I was twenty-three. Fond parents as they were, I sometimes think we

"The twins in their playpen in the garden of the house on the green," summer 1940

children were, for them, above all, an extension of their love and that our role was to make up by our happy childhood for the one they never had. My mother, though much less educated than my father after a disastrous school career, was much the brighter of the two, intellectually speaking, as well as more talkative. She was the storyteller in our family. The tales of her unhappy childhood—the dreadful schools she went to, the havoc she caused at them—wove themselves in and out of our much more ordered life; made the myth with which we grew up. "I was at ten schools," my mother would say; then she'd pause, draw a long breath and add, "I was expelled from nine of them." Much of this myth I put into *Charlotte Sometimes,* years later. Emily in that book was based on my mother, more or less; Clare/Charlotte on her long-suffering older sister.

My mother was altogether more unconventional than my father. Though she could put on the uniforms of her class and kind when it was necessary, left to herself she would not. She refused to join in the normal activities of middle-class women in a village like ours; she picked as her best friend one of the few disreputable women around, who, on the quiet, led her husband on more than a dance. Not that my mother would have behaved like that; all the same I've a feeling that the things this friend got up to compensated for my mother's own much more proper behaviour—even released the wild teenager still lurking within. The teenager who, according to her stories, climbed out of her Swiss boarding school at midnight and went skiing with the ski instructors, who put Epsom salts in the chamber pot of her French mamselle. Though properly behaved and dressed outside our house, at home, still, she did not mind what anybody thought of her. My university friends invited to Sunday lunch would be amazed to be greeted, not by a neatly dressed suburban matron, but, in summer at least, by a woman wearing a sunhat, an old pair of shorts, a badly dyed pink bra passing as a bikini top, and nothing much else.

There were four of us children. My elder brother, three when we were born and previously the sole, much doted-on object of my mother's attention, had his nose not merely put out of joint, but cut off, virtually, by our double arrival. I do not think he ever quite got over the shock or ever quite forgave us. Even when he was an adolescent, at school,

The twins at four (Penelope on left) with Tim, seven, 1944

we remained a disappointment to him. His more fortunate friends had sisters with fair hair, long legs, and English china doll good looks. He had short-legged, dark-haired, dangerously academic, scowling, altogether undesirable sisters, in duplicate to make things worse. Our younger, fair-haired, blue-eyed sister did him much more credit. She arrived seven years after my twin and me—there'd been a brother in between, but he'd died, aged one week. My sister would have died too had it not been for a then-new medical miracle, a process which changed her whole blood supply at birth.

Apart from her medical history and her Anglo-Saxon looks, apart from being born singly, my sister differed from my twin and me in another profound way. Born in 1947, her first six years were spent in quite a different world from the one in which we spent our first six years. Along with twinship, we grew up taking a second unusual condition for granted: war. Food rationing, air raids, a coming-and-going father, and shortages of everything seemed normal to us. And when the war ended in 1945, two years before our sister arrived, I remember feeling disappointed rather than glad. It had been fun having to get up in the middle of the night to crouch under the stairs eating biscuits and sipping hot drinks while our mother read stories to us and the German bombers roared overhead. It had been fun when we first went to school lying under a desk, most likely with someone else's feet in your mouth: this was called "air raid practice." It was fun being evacuated—that meant being sent away—from London when the bombing got bad. In our case we went to northern Lancashire with our mother, to moorland country quite different from the gentle Kent countryside we inhabited normally. We lived on a farm, moreover. Of which I remember entirely delightful things like riding home atop a load of hay or being perched precariously on tall plough horses or creeping illicitly into the big, warm farm kitchen where two-year-old Fred, the farmer's youngest child, used to be sat up on the wooden table without his knickers on, something which intrigued me hugely; we never saw our brother without his knickers on.

I also remember the bull in a field that we used to pass on walks with our mother. It always came—or always seemed to—tearing towards us, bellowing. She swore that the bull recognised her, had something against her. Who knows if it did or not. But the fact is that this bull bellowed its way into my head and stayed there, along with other Lancastrian delights. Along, most delightful of all, with the beck. "Beck" is the north country name for a stream. Quite rightly it has a different name; a stream which chatters down from the hills is a wholly different creature from the stiller brown streams of our Kentish countryside. It is busier, for one thing, and it flows over pebbles and stones and has shallow places and deep places, and stretches of pebble and stone beach. In short, unlike the average southern stream which keeps between muddy banks, it makes a perfect kindergarten for children of any age. What more can a child want than stones, sand—of a sort— and, of course, water, in this case endlessly moving water, the beauty of which may not be much noticed amid the pleasure of playing in it, but which stays in the head years later. Above all, the sound of it stays in the head. Southern streams have relatively little to say. But a northern beck is a shameless chatterbox. To this day I find wandering along the side of a stony northern beck or northern river, listening to its ever-changing conversation, one of the most soothing and comfortable—at the same time stirring—activities I know. Just as my memory of those seemingly endless summer afternoons playing in the beck, eating our tea by the beck, shifting stones, sifting sand, paddling in cold, shallow, running water is one of the best memories of childhood I have.

We only went north twice, in fact. The first time was during the blitz—when Hitler unleashed the full power of his bombers on Britain; a year old at the time I remember nothing of that. It was the second evacuation from which all the memories come. That was in 1944 after the arrival of a new range of bombs—first V-1s, flying bombs; then V-2s, rockets. These were

Penelope and Judy, two, with brother Tim, five, summer 1941

much less predictable than bombs dropped from planes. Instead of coming only at night, they came at any time of day or night. So then we went north again; it took two days on a train—we spent the intervening night in a hotel in Leeds, the first time we'd ever stayed in a hotel. The trains were steam trains, of course; the steady sound they made said, according to my mother, "To *Lanc*ashire to *Lanc*ashire to buy a pocket *hand*kercher." On such a long journey it was hard to keep us amused. My mother gave us crayons and paper to draw on; growing bored, I covered page after page with little straight dashes. "I *am* drawing. I'm drawing rain," I said indignantly when accused of wasting the precious paper.

If the war was fun for us, I doubt if it was much fun for our parents. Where we weren't frightened they must often have been. And I think my older brother learned to be frightened, too. When the war was over, my mother noticed how he would jump and turn white at any sudden noise. In some ways, of course, we were better off than many in England then. We did not live in a large city; the reason some bombs fell on us was because the planes flew over us every night on their way to London, and on the way back they jettisoned any bombs they had left over the Kent countryside. The flying bombs and rockets that hit us were not aimed at us either; they just happened to fall short. They were bad enough, but nothing like the raids suffered by people in London or Plymouth or Coventry. Nor did our father disappear into the army—the government said the work he did for them was too important. The nearest he got to soldiering was being in the Home Guard, along with other men in jobs like him or who were thought too old, too young, or too weak to go to war. Though he hated being prevented from joining up, it meant that we did not lose him during the war, like so many of our friends lost their fathers, nor was there much danger of him being killed or wounded. The only wound he suffered was when the tailgate of a Home Guard truck closed on one of his thumbs, and he arrived home next morning with it wrapped in a bloody bandage; I remember the blood.

Apart from being frightened, the hardest thing for my mother was having to keep house. Before the war, women like her had servants to cook, clean, wash, look after the children. They did not know so much as how to boil an egg. But as soon as war came, the servants were called up into the army or into munitions factories. My mother was luckier than some; she had an old nanny helping her out, a woman too old to be called up. With twins—and very weakly twins at that—my mother needed some help. But that still left her with all the work of the house, with few household gadgets to lighten the load. We had a vacuum cleaner, but that was it. There were no washing machines, no food mixers. And though many households did have gas or electric stoves, in our old house the basement kitchen was provided with an ancient iron range that had to be lit each morning and fed with coal, and that cooked very erratically. It was a beautiful house—the most historically interesting I've lived in. But it had no central heating, few carpets, the doors didn't fit, wind whistled in through and under them and up through the floorboards. The only way of keeping warm in winter was lighting big fires, but the pull of their flames made the draughts still worse. My mother had spent much of her childhood in France and Italy; she hated cold. She hated cooking, too; she didn't know how to cook, and there she was having to turn out meals for the family on this ancient, unfriendly stove, and with very lim-

At home with Penelope (on right), Judy, and Tim, 1945

ited ingredients because of food rationing, and with limited time because she often had to queue hours at the shops for everything: meat, fish, bread. The vegetable pie she produced for her first lunch took her all morning and left her in tears.

She was a perfectionist, though, my mother. What two or three servants had done well before the war, she was determined to do just as well herself. And so she did for the rest of her life, until long after the war was over. Brought up in more relaxed times, I don't feel obliged to scrub my front door step, dust the tops of cupboards, iron all the sheets, iron the dish towels even, let alone keep every piece of wooden furniture in my house gleaming with polish. But my mother, who started off, unlike me, not knowing how to do any of these things, insisted on doing all of them, or trying to at least. Hating every minute of it. Yet turning herself into an excellent cook and a good housekeeper besides. I admire her for it at the same time as I feel sad because of the many other things that she could have done, would rather have done, but never had time to.

Living next to the church meant we were right at the centre of village life. Our house, built in the seventeenth century, had originally been the old coaching inn; here all travellers came, and the weekly mail. Horses and coaches would have been driven through the big doors alongside the house, fronting the village green. Under our long back garden lay the cobblestones of the old London road. Beside and above the garden ran the churchyard. To this day, on my way to put flowers on my mother's grave, I can look down on where my sister and I played during the war; it looks much the same as it did then. Our first-floor nursery made a fine grandstand for checking on all comings and goings from the church. War or no war, people kept on being born, getting married, dying. We watched babies being carried to their christenings in long christening robes. We watched weddings—the brides in white, the grooms, mostly, in uniform. We also watched what my sister called "dead weddings"—funerals. And on weekday evenings the church bells put us to sleep—or kept us awake—during bell practice. The sound of church bells is as much part of myself as the sounds of the Lancashire beck, as much as that other sound of my early childhood, the call of the sirens which gave

The twins (Penelope on left) with their brother and father at Perrin Porth, Cornwall, on their first summer holiday, 1945

the air raid warnings. Used till quite recently in some places to muster firemen, the sirens for me evoke those early war years above all. The shudder I feel makes me wonder if I hadn't been more frightened by the air raids than I remember.

We lived next door to the butcher's assistant, Leslie—very convenient that, at a time of heavy rationing. The prime minister, Winston Churchill, lived near the village. Every so often he got our butcher to slaughter a pig from his estate. Being friends with the butcher meant getting a bit, if we were lucky, to add to our meat ration. Five doors along, even more conveniently, was the village sweet shop. Mrs. Cosgrave, the shopkeeper, wanted to be friends with the twins, just like everybody else. She used to take us for walks sometimes, and I think that often a few more sweets than the rationing allowed would come our way.

That house was a good base for any celebrations on the village green. The one I remember best came right at the end of the war, after the very last of the bombs—a V-2—fell on our village. As usual it came in daytime and with little warning. My twin and I were out playing in our sandpit when the sirens sounded; we were hurried inside and upstairs, but had hardly reached the nursery door before there was an enormous bang and the windows all fell in. No one was killed, luckily.

But a girl called Peggy—I remember because it was my mother's name, too—hurt her arm, and she carried it proudly in a sling at the party held on the village green a week or two later to celebrate our escape. The refreshments were laid out in our house; Peggy and the other invited guests crowded in for cups of tea and fishpaste sandwiches and biscuits. Best of all, Mr. Churchill came. We watched as usual from our nursery window as he stood there among the people with his right hand raised, making the victory sign. Afterwards he even drank a cup of my mother's tea.

The full VE-Day celebrations followed a month or so later, with fireworks, a torchlight procession, and a bonfire on which was burnt an effigy of Adolf Hitler. Now there were no more air raids; that was the last time we were to be fetched out of bed in the middle of the night. (Except for once or twice, much later, when my mother heard a nightingale singing in the garden and woke us up so we could hear it, too.)

We lost some sense of the village when we moved a few months after the end of the war to a much less interesting, even quite ugly, house built in the nineteen twenties. It was more convenient and warmer than the seventeenth-century house, so I can't blame my mother for wanting to move there. There were houses nearby still, but they did not stand tight-packed like those on the village green. They were surrounded by gardens an acre or more in size; the fields and scrubby woods beyond, full of bracken and brambles, made a wonderful playground for us and the children from the other houses when we grew old enough to roam by ourselves. In the beginning, of course, only six or so, we were not allowed out of our garden.

We were at school by then. The school, three miles or so away, we reached by bus, picked up after a walk of half a mile or so down a steep lane with high banks, which was dark at the best of times and almost totally so coming home on winter evenings. My parents had a car, but with petrol rationing they couldn't manage to drive it, so we went everywhere by bus or on foot, or, occasionally, by train. Even when petrol rationing eased, they still used the car very carefully. On hills, they'd turn the engine off and let the car coast, to make the petrol last as long as possible. We used to bet on how far the car would run before the ignition had to be switched on.

The author (on right) with Judy and their mother, Christmas, 1945

The school was a small one, taking only thirty or so children divided into four classes of fewer than ten. But it seemed big enough to us. We'd never been to any kind of nursery or kindergarten. Besides, it was at school we first began to learn the true weight of being twins. The headmistress got up in school assembly one morning and announced that Judy—my sister—and I had names and were to be called by them. Till then, we were both known simply as "Twin." Everyone wanted to know us, of course; we were the only twins around.

We were not identical twins. People who knew us found it easy to tell us apart. But we were more alike than many fraternal twins; our hair was more or less the same colour—mine a bit the darker—and dead straight, too. We were the same height and much the same shape, and we were always dressed exactly the same. Even if we couldn't play twin games with our friends, or with the teachers who saw us every day, we could and did confuse the teachers who only saw us once or twice a week. Miss Hoare, the gym teacher, for instance, a hearty woman always dressed in a short, brown gymslip and thick, brown stockings above white plimsolls, and Miss Edwards, the music teacher, a bony woman who wore a pinstriped suit like a man, had gingery hair, and a very disagreeable—or unhappy—expression, we confused utterly by turning up at alternate classes as each other. Also, because we were so clearly a pair, and the same size, we were in demand for school plays, as twin angels, for instance, or shepherds, or twin page boys for the three wise men. One year we were made to sing one verse of a carol all by ourselves. I don't know that we sang very well. But we did—everyone said—look sweet. (For the same reason, outside school, we were often asked to be bridesmaids.)

At the time, we took this attention entirely for granted. Unfortunately, spending your childhood as a minor local celebrity makes it hard when you get to seventeen or so and start going different ways, because then, without your twin, you're not a celebrity any more, you're just like anybody else.

Our being dressed alike was part of what intrigued people, of course. With clothes rationing, it was much easier for my mother to dress us in the same clothes. People knitted identical sweaters for us. My grandmother was in her eighties when we were born. Sitting bolt upright on a sofa like a grandmother out of a picture book, white hair piled on her head, black skirt stretching to the floor, I remember her, too, knitting us sweaters, pink-striped and in very scratchy wool which we so hated wearing that they went into the dressing-up box as soon as was decently possible. What we would have preferred to wear were the brown tunics, white blouses, brown blazers, and brown hats of our school uniform. But uniform wasn't compulsory at that school, and my mother didn't like uniforms. For us to be dressed like each other was one thing; to be dressed like everybody else was quite another. So we were sent, often, in our older brother's cast-off school uniforms instead; the brown corduroy shorts and green polo-necked sweaters were very comfortable but not elegant exactly. In this way, too, we were made to feel different from everybody else.

But even if it was school that made us more aware of our twinship, it was also the place

that began to bring out, much more clearly, the differences between us. My sister was always better at arithmetic, for instance; I once had to spend a whole week on the same sum. I, on the other hand, learned to read quite a bit before she did. I liked to write and, better still, to draw and paint, which she did not.

I remember vividly the first book I read right throughout to myself, sitting under the dining table in the house up at Farley Common. A collection of Babar the elephant stories, put together by Enid Blyton, it had an orange binding and black-and-white illustrations based on the pictures in the big Babar picture books which you couldn't get at the time because paper was too scarce. Even then, sitting under the table, I realised what being able to read meant; I sensed a whole new world lying out there, to which I had now been given the key. I started to write my own stories not so very much later. Since all my favourite books at that point seemed to be about talking animals—the Beatrix Potter books, Little Grey Rabbit, as well as Babar—not surprisingly my stories, too, were about talking animals.

We had a library in the village. Though it was only open on Saturday mornings, I spent every Saturday there I could and took out as many books as I was allowed, annoyed that I was not allowed to choose storybooks only, but had to take out some nonfiction, instructional ones as well. Even the storybooks did not look exciting; bound in green or blue or red cloth, they had no pictures to lure you inside. But within I discovered magic worlds; those of myths and fairy tales, in particular, but also of pony books and family sagas, many of them showing a prewar world quite as mythical and strange to me as the world of fairy tales. A world so miraculous you could drive in a car all the time if you had the money; in which you could buy all the sweets, all the food and clothes you wanted, and travel round France and Germany any time you wanted. Where bananas and oranges were everyday fare; where toys were abundant rather than having to be hunted out by our mother as if they were rare jewels; where you could buy, above all—for this always seemed to me the two ultimate wonders of prewar life, encapsulating its glory—Japanese shells which when put in water opened up and spilled out paper flowers, and little glass bubbles with figures inside which when shaken or turned upside down sent snowflakes whirling around the figures of the skaters or dancers, or miniature Father Christmases, whatever they contained.

When the war ended everyone had expected things to get better quickly. Rationing would end, all the things that had been available before the war would come back on the market, people would go on holiday again. Certainly we did go on holiday—the first seaside holiday of our lives—to Cornwall. I still have pictures of us sitting on the beach, hard by the tall barbed-wire barriers which had been strung around the beaches of Britain to frustrate attempts at invasion. Big gaps had been cut in them so we could go to the edge of the sea, but there had not yet been time to clear them all away. Our nanny, who always wore a hat and an apron, sat bolt upright with her legs stretched out in front of her and did not look as if she was enjoying herself much. But we clearly were very happy, our hair in bunches, our bodies clad in pink sunsuits sent by a Canadian airman our parents had befriended during the war; digging and making sand castles with buckets and spades, playing in the sea with our father, just as if, despite the barbed wire, the war had never been.

In other ways, however, things from then on didn't get better, they got worse. Two years after the end of the war came the worst winter of all, with less food and less fuel to keep us warm than ever. I do not remember much of that, however, because this was the winter I was ill.

That October my mother found a large lump in my neck and sent for our doctor at once. A morning or two later, my father turned up in our bedroom around the time we normally got up. But instead of chivvying me out of bed, he lifted me up and carried me in to see our mother, who was still in bed herself. Eight then, I was no longer used to having my father carry me about. And though getting into our parents' beds for a morning cuddle was a normal enough treat—if not on school mornings—what I did not expect was to hear my mother tell me that the lump in my neck was a form of tuberculosis and very infectious. On doctor's orders I wasn't to be allowed out of my bedroom thereafter, not even to go downstairs, let alone to go to school. Until the lump went away I had to stay in bed all the time. And I wasn't to be allowed any visitors, especially not my twin. And, as I soon learned, all

my plates and cups and forks and spoons would have to be kept separately from everyone else's, marked with little pink pieces of Band-Aid, to prevent anyone else using them by mistake.

I don't think I was upset. I was delighted that I was going to miss a test at school that day. Only eight, I did not understand what it would mean to be kept so isolated—and even when I found out I don't think I minded much. I'm a solitary creature to this day, luckily, for writers need not to mind being alone. Perhaps it was then I discovered how much I enjoyed being alone. For I liked doing all the things you can do by yourself. I liked drawing and writing stories. Still more I liked listening to the radio and more still I liked reading. On the radio there was not only "The Children's Hour," there were also all the programmes put out for schools—history and English programmes, music programmes, dance and exercise programmes—I could only wave my arms around for those, but wave them I did.

I stayed in that room and in that bed till Christmas. I read a book a day at least; my mother went crazy trying to keep me supplied. In particular I read all the Arthur Ransome books—perhaps because the children in them were so very energetic; their sailing and swimming and walking over fells much like those of north Lancashire that we'd used to know made up for all the energetic things I could not do. Reading about the Walkers—John and Susan, Titty and Roger—and the Blackett sisters Nancy and Peggy, I could imagine it was me doing those things. Or at least I could forget for a while I was not able to do them. My being naturally lazy helped: I always had preferred reading to running about.

Spending three months in bed in one room, you get to know that room very well. I still remember the tomato-soup coloured felt carpet—of which there was more to see now because my sister's bed had been taken away; there were dents in the felt where its legs had stood. I remember the little black hexagonally-shaped table by the bed, piled with my books and writing and drawing books, pencils and crayons, with glasses of lemon squash and mugs of the milk they made me drink because they thought it was particularly good for people with my condition. Unfortunately, since it was almost certainly milk that had made me ill in the first place, I had to drink it boiled—the look of the wrinkled skin on the top of boiled

"The day the plaits (braids) were cut off before the twins went to boarding school." Farmer (on right) notes that this photograph was taken in 1951 "at the house on the common."

milk sickens me to this day. I remember the rabbit picture on the wall, given to me when I was very little. Still better I remember the picture framed by the window; my only sight of the outside world. My bed had been put under the window so that I could see out. On mild days they'd open it, and my twin would come and stand on the gravel path down below and we'd shout hullo. We hadn't much to say apart from that. When you share a life and bedroom with someone, only talking when you need to, you don't think about making conversation; never having had to, we didn't know how.

Beyond my sister was the garden, rose beds in front, a few roses still lingering from summer; further down, a lumpy square of grass big enough to play tennis on; further still, an area of much rougher grass and trees, where my father kept chickens in a wire run; and beyond that the old elm tree backing the fence that divided our garden from the fields and woods. Our house stood on a hill; behind the elm tree the ground dropped away, and I could see right across the valley to the low hills on the far side. In the fields there grazed our

local farmer's herd of black-and-white Friesian cows. I could also see a strange, round, pillared building, like a little temple, called a folly. I always used to wonder at that—all by itself, with no reason for being there, or being what it was, it looked a little sorry, even a little mad. It made the familiar fields strange in a way that I now think is exactly the same as the way storytellers make things more interesting and strange. Yet somehow, at the same time, it made them seem all the more real.

Staying in bed did not cure my tubercular lump, unfortunately, and I kept on running a fever. A month or so after Christmas, I had to go into hospital to have an operation to remove it. In those days most children's hospitals refused to allow parents to visit, so my parents sent me instead to a clinic run by Irish nuns in London. The nuns—the kind that wore wide-winged headdresses—were very kind, but kindness is as much use against homesickness as a Band-Aid against a broken leg. The first night I sat in a curtained cubicle crying bitterly, feeling more desolate and abandoned than at almost any time before or since. The ward was full of old ladies; some of them groaned and sighed and were as oblivious to my distress as I was oblivious to theirs. Others whispered comfort. "There there, dear, don't cry," and so forth. But nothing could comfort me now. The only light in the ward at this time was in my cubicle. It threw my shadow against the curtains, making it look huge, making me look as strange to myself as everything else was strange.

I became more at home once the operation was over. I was moved to another, very sunny ward, also full of old ladies, to whom I showed off, sitting up in bed singing loudly, while they applauded. My mother visited every day, bringing me treats; books and fruit—a grapefruit I remember once, but grapefruit is sour; I didn't like it much. Kind as they were, the nuns weren't great ones for washing their patients; this suited me fine, but, alas, after a week or two my mother found out and complained, and from then on, every day, I was laid naked on a prickly blanket and sponged all too thoroughly from head to foot. Once, I was taken down to the men's ward to meet the only other child then in the clinic. A red-headed boy and I stared at each other with nothing much to say, until he pulled his striped pyjamas down far enough for me to see the scar of the operation he'd had to take his appendix out. Whereupon I tilted my head and showed him the neat scar on my neck, made by a surgeon who was famous for making neat scars, which was why my parents had chosen him. (He is still famous, though long dead—if you say to a surgeon now, I was operated on by Dr. — they look at you as though you are bearing on your body the surgeon's equivalent of a Picasso painting; I have been asked, very politely, if they may see what he did.)

I was in hospital three weeks or so altogether. But I wasn't allowed to go home even after that. Tubercular patients were supposed to need feeding up on rich dairy foods: cream, cheese, butter, and so on. In a country on rationing, such things weren't easily available, so in the middle of the worst winter in England for many years, I was sent to a convalescent home in the country.

I arrived in a snowstorm, in an ambulance, accompanied by my mother, who'd almost been

"A family portrait," 1952. Twins—"braids gone!"—with the author on the left, age twelve; Tim, age fifteen; sister Sally, age five, on mother's lap; father, standing behind.

prevented from getting to me by the weather. But she had to leave almost at once, and yet again I found myself alone and desolate in a strange place. It was full of children this time, all of them older than I was and most of them much iller. Many of the girls in the ward I slept in were severely disabled. The eldest, a girl of fifteen or so, lay flat on her back, paralysed for life. She, like the others, was very cheerful—amazingly cheerful—even I could see that. After lights out, the able-bodied would scurry back and forth mysteriously on the instructions of the immobile. There was much whispering, and they rarely enlightened the younger children as to what they were up to. But they made a pet of me as the baby of the ward, and I needed their kindness, because our parents were seldom allowed to visit. I hid my homesickness by being very rude and difficult, not caring that I made people dislike me. I heard the teacher who took classes in the day telling someone once I was a nasty little girl. I didn't mind. As the snow cleared and spring arrived, I lived only for my mother's visits and, still more, for the day I would be allowed to go home.

And finally, at the end of April, or thereabouts, I did go home. I hadn't seen my twin then for nearly three months. I don't know what I thought it would be like seeing her again. I'm sure I'd missed her; on the other hand, I had missed her along with everything else in my familiar life, whereas she, of course, would only have missed me. I know she missed me—but since I, as usual, was the one who'd won all the attention, I suspect her hurt was much less noticed than mine. I suspect, too, that though it never occurred to me for one minute that I would die of what I had, she mightn't have been so sure.

She arrived back from school quite a while after I got home. I was upstairs already, and there she came to find me. If she was pleased, she wasn't going to show it. I don't think I got a smile even, barely a "hallo." I remember her face as a pale glimmer in the gloom of the upstairs landing. I remember, too, the sinking feeling given me by her lack of greeting, her seeming unfriendliness. I don't suppose it took long for things to get back to normal, though. I daresay that once we had spent the first night together back in our bedroom, arguing about me wanting to sneak the light back on to read after we were supposed to bc asleep and her wanting to turn it on first thing in the morning, so waking me up—after we'd had our first fight, I suppose—things must have returned to normal.

She was so very different from me, though we were twins; it was not just her liking for going to sleep and waking up early and my being the other way about. She liked animals and natural history. I liked books and pictures. I talked first and thought afterwards, blurted everything out; she kept her own counsel at all times. I liked to eat, and she wasn't much interested in food. She liked looking after me, finding my pens and pencils, my lost hats and gloves, helping me get off to school on time. I took her help for granted and never thought of helping her. She liked going to play with friends. I liked sitting at home by myself, reading, or else going out for long solitary walks with my dog, which I was allowed to do from the age of ten or so. That was around the time our parents, who'd been intrepid travellers until the war stopped them, started heading for Europe again but now with us in tow. Which I liked but she did not.

At the time, only a few years after the war ended, package tours hadn't been invented; things weren't set up for tourists the way they are now. We drove in our own car, which quite often went wrong: the fan belt broke, or the radiator boiled toiling up steep passes in the Austrian Alps. We never knew where we were going to stay the night; sometimes there was nowhere to stay; we'd end up round nine o'clock at night staying in the private house of someone who'd taken pity on us. Once, in Switzerland, they opened up an enormous barracks of a place, used for skiers in winter, but normally closed all summer. No one, of course, spoke English, not that this mattered since my mother spoke good French and German. We ate what the locals ate. And, of course, almost invariably, we ran out of money before it was time to go home.

I loved the adventure of all this. I loved setting out in the car each morning wondering what we were going to see next. Being greedy, I loved the food, too. My only problem with that was eating too much of it and making myself ill, which I did from time to time. But my sister hated almost all of it. She got car sick, which meant she hated being in the car all day. She didn't like the uncertainties about where we were going to spend the night. She didn't like the food (except Wiener schnitzel and apple juice in Germany and Austria). She liked the seaside or sailing holidays we took in Ireland or Wales as an alternative to the European trips. But once we crossed the English Channel, all she ever wanted was to get home again.

We had a good childhood in most ways. Our family was a noisy and demanding one, crammed with family phrases, games, stories, family songs—my mother knew a vast array of songs, music hall songs, folk songs, army songs. On long car journeys we sang them full voice all the way. We lived in houses with big gardens where our father grew fruit and vegetables and kept chickens, ducks, and rabbits, which helped mitigate the trials of rationing. The gardens were perfect for playing in, hiding in. (At times, too good. Once, after a quarrel in which she nicked my finger with a pair of cutting out scissors and drew blood, my sister ran away and hid for four hours in the rhododendron bushes, where no one was able to find her.) As we grew older we were allowed to play in the fields and woods around, sometimes only coming home for meals. Our play was not always safe. We spent one holiday tobogganing down the sand slopes of a local sandpit, a pastime so dangerous it terrified our parents when they found out; one of our dogs had gone rabbiting there, dug into a hole and been suffocated.

For entertainment we had no television, but we had the radio; in particular we loved "The Children's Hour"—heard unexpectedly, the music used for some favourite serials takes me back to those stories even now. We played our family games and card games, sometimes inviting another family to play Racing Demon with us on Sunday nights. We went to the cinema occasionally, to *Pinocchio* but not *Snow White,* which my mother thought too frightening. We shamed our brother once when he'd taken us to a Lassie film on his own by wailing out loud when the dog died. We went to local amateur performances of Gilbert and Sullivan operas. At Christmas every year we were taken to the theatre in London to see *Peter Pan* or Victorian pantomimes (ordinary pantomimes my mother thought too vulgar) or a patriotic play called *Where the Rainbow Ends* in which we all had to get up and shout hurrah for St. George.

Our village held a carnival at Whitsun every year, called the Westerham Gala, with processions of floats and brass bands as well as sports and dressing-up competitions. One year my twin and I dressed up as Tweedledum and Tweedledee in the scratchy striped jumpers knitted by our grandmother, our cheeks filled with peppermints to make them look fat. (My mother had made us try dough first, but it tasted too horrible.) We won a prize for that, but had less luck in the three-legged race, where, legs tied together, running not exactly in unison, we pulled each other over and ended up fighting as usual, though more dangerously than usual, given our tied legs. Fairs came sometimes to the market field at the bottom of the village, and circuses too. But almost the best treat of all arrived every other week in the form of the local market, when farmers from the countryside around brought in flocks of sheep and herds of cattle for sale, pigs too, making a kind of mini rural zoo which, as small children, we adored.

The centre of that childhood, though, apart from my twinship, was my mother's kitchen; the Aga cooking stove made it the warmest place in the house. Pandemonium it always was. Dogs keeping warm by the stove leaped up, barking if any stranger appeared. My father banged in and out of the back door with fuel for the stove, all of us complaining at the cold air he brought in with him. My mother might be using the food mixer; the washing machine would be grinding away, a very vocal old refrigerator groaning and sighing; several of us would be talking at once; and, above all, my mother's little red radio perched on top of the fridge would be belting out music, soap operas, "Woman's Hour," whatever was on. It was good training for a writer. I had to learn to disappear inside my head, so shutting the din out. I got so good at it that to this day I am often accused of not listening, of ignoring my companions. It means I can write on trains, in cafes, anywhere—sometimes it seems the more noise there is the easier it is for me to concentrate on what I'm trying to say. I like silence. But I don't always write very well in it. Pandemonium can be better.

Going to boarding school at the age of twelve was a pivotal time for my twin and me. Even then we felt something of our idyllic childhood, our free roaming around the country,

our friends, slipping away. We walked around the common with one friend saying to ourselves, "Nothing will ever be the same again." Nor was it, quite, though there were plenty of compensations. At the new school we were once more minor celebrities. Yet again people had to be warned to call us by our proper names rather than simply "twin." But this was a bigger school. After the first term we were not even allowed to sleep in the same bedroom because our roommates were so upset by the sight of us fighting each other all over the floor. Thus, gradually, we began developing our own lives, our own friendships, apart from each other. Unfortunately, the school wasn't so big we could be put into separate classes. This was harder on my sister than me, because I was better at the subjects the school specialised in—English, history, art, languages; whereas my sister was still better at science, maths, the things taught less well at that school. She was better at music, too, and sport. She acted in school plays, which I never did. She also had more friends. But, always, I was the "clever one" and she wasn't. And she suffered from that, being clever enough in her own way—she went to university in her thirties and got a degree as good as mine. But the sense of failure she was left with from our school did her no good, nor me. It was made worse by my going to Oxford straight afterwards, while she was sent to a little local secretarial college. She should have gone to London to learn secretarial skills. But the cost of my university fees left no money for that. Added to this, I'd found a publisher for my first stories and was going to have a book published. You could hardly expect her not to be jealous, and she was.

The book came about like this. All through my childhood, on and off, I'd continued to write. I still have notebooks full of work done before we went away to school. About the age of fifteen I actually managed to finish some of the stories—fake fairy tales, you could call them. Straight after school I was sent to Munich in southern Germany to learn German, where for the first time since my hospital stay I was bereft of everything and everyone I knew. In particular I found myself bereft of my twin. To cheer myself up, to fill her place in my life, I wrote more and more stories, most of which I sent home in letters to my small sister. I'd no thoughts of them being published, still fewer thoughts of ever being a real writer

Farmer with friends in California, fall 1994

(nor did I dare imagine I was one, until I'd had several books published, many years later). Unknown to me, though, my father had my stories typed up and showed them to a publisher friend. The publisher showed them in turn to an agent—that is, a person who looks after writers and helps them sell their work to publishers. She, to my amazement, took me on and demanded I write more stories to make enough for a whole book. So at Oxford, alongside history essays, I continued to write fairy stories; the second publisher who was shown the book that resulted bought it.

I was still only nineteen, too young to sign my own contracts; my father signed them on my behalf. It meant being taken to see the publisher by my agent and sitting in the corner, looking meek, while she and the publisher discussed me over my head. It meant, once the book came out, more than two years later, being interviewed by newspapers as the latest child prodigy—all publishers at that point were looking for child writers, it seemed. I was given a double-page spread in a comic called *Girl*,

complete with pictures of me looking soulfully into the eyes of my old poodle dog. The only problem thereafter was that people expected me to go on writing, and bemused by all this attention I had no idea what to write. I tried autobiographical novels for a while, but never got further than a chapter or two. But then an American publisher saw the stories and asked if I would be interested in writing a children's novel. As it happened, I was. Taking a story which I'd put aside as seeming much too fat an idea for a short story, I wrote a first chapter, put together a synopsis for the whole book and sent it off. I don't think I expected much. But the publisher accepted what I'd written and gave me a contract, which I was still too young to sign myself, and paid me, I think, one hundred dollars. Three months after I'd finished at Oxford, I sat down to write my first children's book, *The Summer Birds,* and thus, almost by accident, became a children's writer and remained one for the twenty-odd years it took me to get around to finishing an adult book.

I haven't left much room for the years of my life since. I'm sorry about that. But as a writer, presumably, I should write about becoming a writer—and my childhood and my twinship were what turned me into a writer, after all.

For the rest, I can't quite say I've lived happily ever after. Who does that? No one in my fairy tales did either; I didn't believe in happy endings even then. I became a teacher for a while and, still more briefly, a social worker. I married a man I met at Oxford, lost my mother shortly after, had two children now well grown up, and got unmarried again fourteen years later. I moved from London, Battersea, down to London, Richmond on Thames, where I lived for eighteen years and brought up my children, and then back to London, Hammersmith, where I still live overlooking a park and next to the Underground line, meaning that these days the pandemonium I focus my thinking against, to help me write, is the sound of trains. I have remarried, acquired cats, gone travelling across the world, from North and South America to Australia to India and all ways round. Five years ago I lost my twin sister—probably the worst time of my life; the time I had to begin working out what it was to be a twin in order to learn how to live without one. But above all, I've kept on writing; sometimes successfully, sometimes not. I daresay I will be writing till the day I die. Writers don't retire, I think. This one doesn't intend retiring. She would not know how to.

© 1996 Penelope Farmer

BIBLIOGRAPHY

FOR YOUNG PEOPLE

Fiction:

The China People (short stories), illustrated by Pearl Falconer, Hutchinson, 1960.

The Summer Birds, illustrated by James J. Spanfeller, Chatto & Windus, 1962, Harcourt, 1962.

The Magic Stone, illustrated by John Kaufmann, Harcourt, 1964, Chatto & Windus, 1965.

Saturday Shillings, illustrated by Prudence Seward, Hamish Hamilton, 1965, published as *Saturday by Seven,* Penguin, 1978, Walker, 1990.

The Seagull, illustrated by Ian Ribbons, Hamish Hamilton, 1965, Harcourt, 1966.

Emma in Winter, illustrated by Laszlo Acs, Chatto & Windus, 1966, illustrated by James J. Spanfeller, Harcourt, 1966.

Charlotte Sometimes, illustrated by Chris Connor, Chatto & Windus, 1969, Harcourt, 1969.

Daedalus and Icarus (picture book), illustrated by Chris Connor, Harcourt, 1971.

The Serpent's Teeth: The Story of Cadmus (picture book), illustrated by Chris Connor, Collins, 1971, Harcourt, 1972.

Dragonfly Summer, illustrated by Tessa Jordan, Hamish Hamilton, 1971, Scholastic Book Services, 1974.

A Castle of Bone, Chatton & Windus, 1972, Atheneum, 1972.

The Story of Persephone (picture book), illustrated by Graham McCallum, Collins, 1972, Morrow, 1973.

William and Mary, Chatton & Windus, 1972, Atheneum, 1974.

Heracles (picture book), illustrated by Graham McCallum, Collins, 1975.

August the Fourth, illustrated by Jael Jordan, Heinemann, 1975, Parnassus, 1976.

Year King, Chatto & Windus, 1976, Atheneum, 1977.

The Coal Train, illustrated by William Bird, Heinemann, 1977.

The Runaway Train, illustrated by William Bird, Heinemann, 1980.

Thicker than Water, Walker, 1989.

Stone Croc, Walker, 1991.

Penelope, Bodley Head, 1993, Simon & Schuster, 1996.

Twin Troubles: Stories for Five Year Olds, Walker, 1996.

Editor:

Beginnings: Creation Myths of the World, illustrated by Antonio Frasconi, Chatto & Windus, 1977, Atheneum, 1977.

Two, or the Book of Twins and Doubles: An Autobiographical Anthology, in press.

Translator (from the Hebrew):

(With Amos Oz) *Soumchi,* illustrated by William Papas, Harper, 1980, Chatto & Windus, 1980.

FOR ADULTS

Fiction:

Standing in the Shadows, Gollancz, 1984.

Eve: Her Story, Gollancz, 1985, Mercury House (San Francisco), 1988.

Away from Home: A Novel in Ten Episodes, Gollancz, 1986.

Glasshouses, Gollancz, 1988, Trafalgar Square (North Pomfret, Vermont), 1989.

Snakes and Ladders, Little, Brown, 1993.

Back Country, in press.

Radio Plays:

Jerusalem—Finding the Thread, BBC Radio Three, 1980.

Screenplays:

The Suburb Cuckoo, 1961.

Other:

Contributor to various journals and magazines, including the *New York Times, Nova Magazine,* and *Times Literary Supplement.* Also coauthor of papers on epilepsy published in academic journals. Farmer's book *Charlotte Sometimes* was the inspiration for the song of the same name by rock group the Cure.

Dennis Hamley

1935-

Dennis Hamley with an aspiring young writer during a Lending Our Minds Out *(LOMA) course*

The first real memory I have is of a big, shiny, red figure 4 on a birthday card. I wish I could tell you how I had just lived through some of the most dangerous events of the twentieth century—the rise of Hitler, the invasions of Poland and Czechoslovakia, the Munich agreement between Britain and Germany and the fatuous cry of "Peace in our time," the start for Britain of World War Two. Well, I was around at the time all right. But I was gurgling in my pram, crawling round my playpen, learning to walk and talk, so perhaps I did not influence events as much as I would have liked.

But after seeing that shiny figure four I knew I was alive—AND THAT THERE WAS A WAR ON. I was nine before it ended. I saw

the soldiers come back from Dunkirk, listened to the German bombers on their way to London, saw the Spitfires and Hurricanes roar after them, and watched the tiny curling vapour trails in the sky. Later, I heard the U.S. Flying Fortresses and the Royal Air Force (RAF) Lancasters take off for Germany, watched the soldiers with their new tanks and guns get ready for D-Day. Oh, yes, by the time 1945 and peace came, I knew all about the war.

For nearly fifty years those memories lodged in my mind like a great exciting pageant. The war destroyed many families. Ours, thankfully, it hardly scarred. But many years were to pass before I realised how often, as people in Britain hourly expected Hitler's armies to invade us, my parents must have looked at me and wondered whether they should have brought a son into the world. Yet it all seemed so right: I knew nothing else but being in a state of war. This was how people lived: peacetime was something that, when it came, I had to get used to.

I lived my life with all these half-memories at the back of my mind. And then, with eleven books already published, I took up pen and paper to try to sort them out. The result was *The War and Freddy,* a book for which I have a great affection. From all the people in the world I could have written a book about, I found someone exactly the same age as me to the very second. "Isn't that amazing?" I often ask children when I visit schools. For just a moment they want to say, "Yes, it is. Fantastic coincidence." But then they see what I mean so they don't.

In the eight stories of that book, from war's start to end, as little Freddy becomes bigger, are the hopes, fears, misunderstandings about what was going on, not just of me but many others as well. I didn't write those stories to be about me. I asked, "What was it really like?" and knew I had to write it down before I forgot it all.

We lived in the county of Kent, "the garden of England" some say, south of London. Our home was in Edenbridge, a small town in the north of the county near Westerham where, it was reported with awe, Winston Churchill himself had a house. The road we lived in was called Westways. A few years ago when I went to see the town again after fifty years, I found Westways at once, remembered where the two railway stations were, and recognised much of the High Street. But the old tannery with its pungent smell was gone. So was the Negresco Cinema where before I was five I saw the brand new Disney cartoon *Pinocchio,* the animated *Gulliver's Travels,* and a film which really frightened me, *The Man in the Iron Mask.*

My father was a telephone engineer, an important job at home so he never had to join the army. But he went through danger all right: he looked after the telephones on an air force base, RAF Biggin Hill, which the Nazis were always bombing. On the night of the biggest raid he was badly injured and shellshocked, but won a medal for keeping the phones going in the thick of it all.

A big enough thing to happen. But it led to something even bigger for us. First of all,

he was sent away to get better. We left our little house in Edenbridge. I said goodbye to my earliest school and to my teacher, Miss Dibbs; to friends whose names I still remember—Tony Brindley, Michael Straighton, David Weaver, Shirley Christmas. I left the Westways Army that shambled up and down our road armed with toy guns and carrying Mickey Mouse gasmasks. I packed up my tin hat, my wooden rifle, my clockwork train set (a model of the Silver Link steam locomotive—how I wish I still had it: its worth now would be astronomical) and we went away on a train to what seemed the other side of the world.

I loved trains then. I have ever since. Green steam trains (of the old Southern Railway) trundled up and down the line at the back of our house and punctuated my days. But this train was different. We went to London—even then I remember an eerie, ruined place—to a vast, echoing, smoky station with a great glass roof. Here were huge trains, red, with vast clanking engines which roared, spat, and frightened me. But they were wonderful too, and one of them pulled us all the way to where there were rolling moors which edged into purple distances and brooding mountains, where fields were not hedged but had grey stone walls, where there were broad, shining, endlessly exciting lakes. There we stayed for a period which cannot have been more than a month but which hovers in my mind like half a lifetime. I have seldom been back to the Lake District—and sometimes feel I don't want to see it too much, lest it does not match that mythical time of years ago.

But we returned home. I remember our train back was stopped at Watford, just north of London. The biggest raid of the Blitz was going on over the city. So we could not finish that day's journey—and I do not remember ever going back to Edenbridge until my flying visit in 1988.

My father was transferred to another part of England. We came to a small town in Buckinghamshire: Winslow, the place I always regard as my real childhood home. Fifty miles north of London, eighty from my old home in Kent. But it seemed to me then that it might as well have been on a different planet.

It was now 1941. I remember arriving on a wheezy old bus in the rain, to a place which seemed so old, surrounded by fields which looked unkempt, wild, full of cows and sheep. People walked the streets, speaking in strange country voices which sounded weird to my ears, used only to voices from south of London.

Until we moved into the cottage the Air Ministry let to us, we lived with a family in a house with no water taps but a pump at the back shared by all the houses. I went to a school which looked rough and dangerous, full of large and raucous boys and contemptuous girls, all speaking this new and uncomfortable version of the English language. The teachers shouted a lot and, when it grew dark, big gas lamps were lowered from the ceiling and lit so they hissed like caged, watchful snakes. I was frightened and unhappy.

Things were better when we went to the little house in Sheep Street. Nearby was a big house—Winslow Hall, designed by Sir Christopher Wren, in fact—and the Air Force had taken it over. Two miles away was a bomber base, where planes took off for Germany at night and did not all return. New telephones and teleprinters were put in and my father's job was to keep them going. Soon the two

separate worlds of the Royal Air Force and the country children combined in my mind. Then I realised there was a third world: scores of children who spoke much as I did—the evacuees from London here to be safe while there was the danger of bombing.

At school, I remember, I was at first useless. I couldn't sort out the arithmetic, I made neither head nor tail of the reading. Miss Hawes, my infant teacher, was often very cross with me. I must have seemed completely thick. I do not remember when the penny dropped, when the perpetual panic about being able to do nothing merged into confidence about everything. I don't remember learning—or being taught—to read. My mother always said she knew I could read the day I picked out the headlines in the paper. I don't remember that—but the idea formed a crucial part of *The War and Freddy*.

Gradually I became more a part of the place. The Infants receded. I was in the formidable Miss Green's class—standard one and standard two in the same room. Miss Green, even with the distorting lens of childhood, remains one

Working with fellow author John Gordon (left) at another LOMO workshop

At a signing for Badger's Fate *with illustrator Meg Rutherford, "complete with badgers!"*

of the great characters of my education, with her raucous voice, weird beribboned hair, and sudden tantrums like deluges from a blue sky. What do I remember of her classes? Me-Tik the Eskimo boy. A huge, lovingly drawn map of Africa, her pride and joy, unrolled and pinned to the wall at any excuse. Singing "There's a Tree in the Meadow" and "The Tailor of Ramsey." Hearing her claim (never put to the test, at least by me) that she never needed a ruler to draw lines of absolute straightness. Another claim that she once took the salute in a big parade, standing alongside General de Gaulle, was also perhaps not to be taken as seriously as we did. Was that the sum total of my education when I was seven and eight? It seems so now.

I sometimes think I learnt far more of lasting use outside school—perhaps even including those things the school should have been giving me. For example—Christmas 1943. No money around for presents—besides, there was a war on, so there were hardly any presents. What did I want? A new model railway? Impossible. Model aeroplanes? No hope. More games? I was fed up with them. Some books? Not really. I had some.

But a book I had. I can remember now, sitting in bed at three in the morning, fishing in my pillowcase, bringing out the parcel, unwrapping it—to find a big, thick book with a strange dust jacket. Lots of little black-and-white pictures all over, with orange shading in between them. In the middle, title and author. *Swallowdale,* by Arthur Ransome. Doubtfully, I opened it. Four hundred pages of small print with not a single bit of colour except maps at the start and end. Well, there was little else of note in the pillowcase, so I started reading.

I think by evening I had nearly finished the 426 pages. I was bowled over, hypnotised, taken out of myself, living a new life in tents and on boats in the very Lake District I had been to—already, it seemed, so many years ago. Perhaps it was then that the thought first came— this book is giving me so much pleasure that when I grow up I want to give some of the same pleasure back. I don't know, but when people ask me when it was I first wanted to be a writer, that's what I tell them.

So, if that was the first book I consciously recall reading, what had gone before? There must have been a long progress leading up to it. Well, I can't remember. Until I was fourteen, I was an only child. My parents are now dead. So there's no one to tell me. I know that when I was little my parents read to me. Two things stand out. A story about two brothers called Ponder and Plod. Comic books—Mickey Mouse and Donald Duck. A series about a couple in the deep South called Eb and Flo. Only very recently did I remember that and realise the title was meant to be a joke. A poem which began and ended something like this:

> There was a little rabbit
> Who had a naughty habit
> Of eating and eating all day.
> Little bits of greenery
> He found upon the scenery.
> They went down the very same way.

Alas, the middle has gone. But I do know he was extremely ill.

> Six doctors attended
> Until he was mended,
> But then, I am sorry to say,
> That silly little rabbit
> Took up his naughty habit
> Again the very next day.

I remember stories by Enid Blyton, Rose Fyleman, and Alison Uttley, and a rather vicious version of Robin Hood that made me want to go to a fancy dress parade as the

Nottingham outlaw—to such effect that I think I won first prize. But what had as much early effect was the radio. Especially the comedians—the British ones—Tommy Handley, Arthur Askey, Richard Murdoch, and Kenneth Horne; as the war progressed and the GIs came over, there were the Americans as well—Bob Hope, Jack Benny. My earliest love in comedy were the Americans who had stayed here when the war started and did their programme *Hi Gang!*—Bebe Daniels and Ben Lyon. But most important of all was Children's Hour on the BBC, with which I grew up. Over the years great books were dramatised, such as *Moonfleet* and *The Box of Delights.* These I only read much later. Less great children's books were also broadcast and these I read at once—the Bunkle books of M. Pardoe and the Lone Piner books of Malcolm Saville. I met Malcolm Saville in 1978, just before he died. I shook hands with him—and to me it was almost like meeting God!

I suppose some might say this was a strange literary upbringing—the usual classics like Beatrix Potter and A. A. Milne's *Winnie-the-Pooh* I encountered for the first time when reading them to my own children.

Two other things important to me happened round about 1943. I started to learn (unsuccessfully, it turned out) the piano and I was made to join—unwillingly, I may say—the choir of the Parish Church. Whatever else these did, they laid the foundations of a love of music which has never left me.

Still, when I found *Swallowdale* in my Christmas pillowcase, it was 1943 and there was still a lot of war to get through. I can't claim an exciting wartime childhood. I'm glad. The war was a gigantic, exciting adventure followed in the papers and on the radio. There were soldiers and airmen all round us. And airwomen too: we always had members of the Women's Auxiliary Air Force billeted in our house. Jo, Maisie, Trudy—I remember them still. Trudy was engaged to an American GI. I recall the terrible day the news came that he had been killed on D-Day.

I remember our cat, too. Not the first cat in my life—Marco, a little tabby, was left in Edenbridge with friends. Panda, a black and white longhair of high intelligence and independent fierceness, arrived when I was six and stayed with us, larger than life, for fourteen years. I've hardly been without cats since. Emily, our Siamese, is with me now as I write.

Just once did the war impinge on us in a really big way. I said we lived near an RAF bomber base. One early morning the crew of a Vickers Wellington made a terrible error and ploughed into the roofs of a line of houses in the town. Many were killed as they slept. Among them were two boys in my class: Peter Mullis, I remember, and Victor Hobermann. The name of the second haunts me still—the irony of his parents risking everything to escape Nazi persecution, to have their son killed by the very people supposed to protect him. I never put that in a book—but years later I used the Wellington crashing into the houses as the centrepiece of a novel, *The Fourth Plane at the Flypast,* a book I've always been pleased with.

Of course, my family extended far beyond Winslow. We, after all, were mere outposts. There were two main centres. One, surrounding my mother's parents, was a village still then deep in the Surrey countryside but only three miles from where London began. Godstone, set in the North Downs, was to me a magical place of woods, sandpits, and chalk hills. Nowadays, the M25 London Orbital Motorway roars almost straight through it. But Godstone Green is still there and cricket is the big game played on it—though no longer with my Uncle Jim opening the batting. Here, Nanny and Nandad Payne lived, with an aunt, uncle, and two cousins next door but one. It was like a second home at the end of a well-remembered journey—bus from Winslow to Aylesbury, train to Baker Street, tube across London, green electric train from Charing Cross to Caterham, bus to Godstone.

Less frequently visited but more exciting because further away were Granny and Grandad Hamley, in their little wooden bungalow in the Hampshire Downs near the small town of Bishops Waltham. Here we caught a really big train out of Waterloo in London and thundered down to Winchester, where Grandad Hamley would be waiting in his prized Ford 8 and I would have a rare trip in a car. Nearby was Portsmouth, where the big ships of the Navy were, Southsea with its pier and beach (both cut off from us with barbed wire), and—brooding darkly on the horizon—the Isle of Wight, which just once or twice I attained by ancient paddle steamer.

But the war was ending. We all knew it. And, of course, we had won. I never doubted we would from the moment I had consciousness—it was a self-fulfilling prophecy. Even now I cannot quite comprehend that for much of its weary six years we were likely to lose. But by this time I knew pretty well what was going on. I had begun to understand the issues. I started to believe there was a war to be won at home as well as abroad. In 1945, after Germany had fallen but before the atomic bomb and Japan's surrender, came a wondrous thing: a general election for a new government. I believe, and nothing will ever convince me otherwise, that were it not for this first election after the war, when millions of people decided they didn't want things to be like they were before, but new and different, I would not be writing this now, would not be an author or have had a long and fulfilling career in education, would not have been to university, would not have received the priceless gift of a good education or, more importantly, the opportunity to use it properly.

I never doubted that we would have a Labour government. I can't now quite comprehend that most people thought we wouldn't. I'm quite sure that without it there would have been no free grammar school, no State Scholarship to Cambridge, nothing to give the glorious opportunities that were suddenly mine in 1945. Seeing what was built so laboriously after the war to liberate our entire British society systematically destroyed over the last fifteen years has been, quite frankly, an offence to my soul.

Anyway, the celebrations at the war's end and the first amazed holidays in faraway places like Wales had come and gone, 1946 arrived and with it a time of reckoning. In May, after a year training for it in Mr. Hall's class, I sat what we all called the Scholarship. Really, it was the eleven-plus exam and every child in the country had to submit to it. I remember that out of the thirty or so in the class, four of us passed. This was regarded as hugely good for Winslow. If you look at it the other way and say that twenty-six of us failed, you'll see why I spent a large part of my career fighting against selection at eleven or any other school age.

But I had won my passport: from September I would go every morning on the bus six miles north to the Royal Latin School, Buckingham, and the next big chapter of my life would begin.

In 1946, the Royal Latin School, Buckingham, consisted of 180 students, eighty boys and a hundred girls—numbers which mean recent statistics showing girls' intellectual superiority are no surprise to me. "What a big name for a little school" a university interviewer years later said to me. Little or not, we were proud the school was founded in 1427. In the 1960s it moved into much grander premises and continues today bigger but whether better I am not sure. I remember my first scared walk with new satchel and cap up the winding drive to the small brick buildings, past an asphalt tennis court and a long jump pit. I was a few weeks short of my eleventh birthday.

The thirty of us in Form One sat alphabetically, boys to the right of the teacher, girls to the left. I have lost touch with nearly all now—yet I could still recite the register and see them clearly before me from half a century ago.

I shall never forget our form-master either. Mr. S. G. Williams, a voluble Welshman who appeared—like many good teachers—half ogre, half licensed clown. There were so many new things to get used to. Short lessons with a new teacher each time. A piercing electric bell punctuating the day. French—and mysterious sums with letters in them instead of numbers. A mysterious and evil-smelling science laboratory. Even after a week, I felt I held arcane secrets beyond the ken of most folk. But two afternoons each week seemed purest pleasure—double games on Wednesday and woodwork on Friday. I cannot now comprehend why I looked forward to them so much. Although the head of the school then was an ex-England international rugby player, we played soccer. I loved it—ever since Uncle Jim had brought back a real leather football from his war service in India, Dad had taken me to see his (and still my) beloved Portsmouth at Fratton Park and I had started shrilly shouting from the touchline each week watching our local team, Winslow United. Later on, Dad was to take me regularly to watch games at Kenilworth Road, the ground of Luton Town, our nearest professional League club. I wanted to shine at soccer. Sad awakening. John Butler and Basil Spencer were Form One's stars in the school junior team. I was lucky to be picked for a game at all. We walked in a long crocodile to the soccer pitch a mile away: out of the corners of our eyes we watched the girls playing hockey.

On Fridays we left the school again—to the Secondary Modern School (where those who

Hamley outside Saffron Walden Youth Hostel, Essex, England, with children from a LOMO course

failed the eleven-plus in Buckingham went— our twenty-six thwarted hopefuls had stayed in Winslow). Here was the woodwork room. Once again I thought I might shine. Alas. "Tries hard but results are few" was my despairing final report before, three years later, I was mercifully allowed to give it up. How I wish, now, that I had listened more and done better. I had passed up on a true creative skill.

As for the rest, I was not aware of either enjoying or being good at it. I remember still the profound shock when the first form order was issued at the end of term and I was top. I must never have recovered from it, because I was never top again. But I was usually somewhere up there and—oddly, I know, and it was a feature of my life as a student—I enjoyed exams. Soon I discovered I could idle my time away and always come in the first three in exams: the memory formed one good reason why, in my career in education, I always supported courses which only partly depended on exams to get through. If cousework had been assessed when I was at school I would probably have

failed the lot—except that I would really have worked and learned good study habits early.

The divide in the room between the red-girdled and black-gym-slipped girls and us was rigid. That doesn't mean the two sides were not very aware of each other. There are names from that room that I well remember—Mary Bonner, Freda Colgrove, Sheila Peet. Some of us on our side—Michael Enfield and Basil Spencer (again!)—were a lot bolder than the rest of us. But, compared with today, how innocent we all were.

Well, yes, entry to the grammar school was the most far-reaching event. But certainly not the most catastrophic. Christmas was on its way. I was not aware of anything physically wrong with my mother. It was, I remember, Christmas Eve. Dad was at work. I cannot recall what I was doing when Mum appeared from the kitchen and said weakly, "Dennis, run for a neighbour, please." I did, and everything afterwards dissolves. I know I was packed off to spend Christmas with my mate from school, John Hopkins, and his family. It was one of those times, I remember, when it was best not to ask. But in retrospect, I realise everybody was trying to stop spreading a sense of crisis to me. On Christmas Day itself, in the evening, Dad appeared, haggard and unshaven. A brother for me had been born in the Radcliffe Infirmary, Oxford. He was christened Robin Richard before he died, two hours old. I cried—but I knew the tears were for Dad on his own on Christmas Day and Mum in hospital miles away. What you don't know, you never miss.

It was about now my parents stopped being the all-powerful figures of childhood and became separate human beings in their own right. My father, quick-tempered, small, stocky, bespectacled. A strong, now and again moody man, sometimes convinced the world conspired against him. This trait may have come from his Cornish father. Dad was born on an army camp in Newcastle in 1903, after his soldier father came home from the Boer War. Like me, he moved early, far away south to Hampshire. He was a boy during the First World War while his father was in France—and, unlike so many, survived. An apprentice electrician on Portsmouth Navy Dockyard, Dad found no work there after the General Strike of 1926, so he walked to London looking for work. Years later, when I read the autobiography of the poet Ted Walker and how his father had come south from Birmingham on his motorbike on the same errand, I wondered if they had passed each other on the way. At Oxted in Surrey he found the Post Office wanted telephone engineers. He queued, got the job, and was a telephone engineer for the rest of his working life.

At Oxted, he met Mum. She was a switchboard telephone operator. In those days, long before direct dialling, her voice would say "number please" when you picked up the phone. In 1927 this was a high-tech job—like computers today. They met and courted (that lovely, obsolete expression)—Dad from the piano of the Sharps and Flats, the little dance band he both played and sang for. So they said. I never heard him sing and only rarely play a 1920s tune by ear on the piano. "Those days are gone," was all I could ever get out of him.

Mum was born in Godstone in 1910. Her mother had been in domestic service. Her father was a wheelwright by trade and also managed to survive the First World War. Old photographs of my mother at her wedding and in the long skirts, demure swimming costumes, and short hair styles of the early 1930s show she was a beautiful woman. She and Dad were married in 1932 and stayed together, sometimes rumbustiously, until 1977 when Dad died.

Back, though, to their disaster of Christmas 1947. I came home: so did Mum. But for the next two years things were muted, quiet. Something had gone out of them both. As with so many events of which I was really only a spectator, there was much I had no idea about—for example, the fear and doubt which they must have gone through before the entirely successful birth of my brother Richard in 1949. Only when our own children were born did I comprehend their sheer joy.

This little tragedy had for me a small postscript. In 1971 I started my first children's novel. A third person account of that Christmas Eve kickstarted me into *Pageants of Despair*. Ironically this beginning was never published: the first chapter and a half disappeared in the editing stage. For the book, that was right. But I was sorry none the less.

Meanwhile, school continued—through the Big Freeze of 1947, when our homes, devoid then of central heating, had to keep warm throughout a coal shortage. Yet I remember a lovely time. If, as C. S. Lewis's White Witch wanted, it was always winter but never Christmas, the deep snow and impenetrable frosts would have been awful. But I had had a marvellous Christmas present: Dad had made me a sledge and for the only time I can remember winter became—in memory anyway—truly magical.

Something else good was happening as well. I had to concede I was not brilliant at football or cricket. In the school cross-country race I was so badly last they had to send a search party. But I found I could sprint. I remember winning the junior 100 yards on Sports Day against boys two years older. At last I had my longed-for sporting status. Each summer would now be lived for the great sequence: School Sports, District Sports, County Sports and—the Grail never quite achieved—representing my county in the All-England Sports. 100 yards, 220 yards, relay. By the age of fifteen I had to concede that I wasn't really that good. But if I had done what I was told when Mr. Archer the games master tried to persuade me to take up hurdling . . . in the immortal words of Marlon Brando, "I coulda been a contender." Or probably not. Who knows?

In 1949 Richard was born. I took immense pride in my new brother. I had always felt slightly unhappy at being the only one while families all round me seemed to burgeon annually. We all of us felt complete.

It is odd how this period of my life returns in snatches while early childhood and later adolescence remains clear and continuous. Until I entered the sixth form (grade twelve) my memories of school are hazy. I do not know when people started talking about my going to university. I didn't quite know what university was, except that it was large, important, and the only two I had heard of—Oxford and Cambridge—had a boat race on the Thames every year and were places for the rich and famous, so beyond my reach or understanding. Nobody in my family had ever been able to go to secondary school, let alone university. But these were the postwar years of opportunity and a new generation was being given chances unknown before. The new headmaster now took a decisive hand in my life. George Embleton was an ex-naval officer and a person of decision and ambition for his tiny school. Himself a Cambridge man, he wanted to send us there too. Overnight, it seemed, Oxford and Cambridge and every other university were possible for us all. I'd had no idea there were so many. Let's be quite clear about it—I was scared stiff of George Embleton. I wouldn't have dared fail. So my three sixth-form years started—an exclusive diet of English literature, history, and geography. Looking back, I am deeply sorry I stopped any serious study of science and angry that I dropped any more learning of languages. But the system demanded specialisation and still does and I think we are all the poorer for it.

My school life was fined down to two teachers—George Embleton himself (long hours alone with him in his study for English and history, with the smell of a paraffin heater and one-sided conversations which I gratefully soaked up and made my own) and gentle Miss Merritt, for more history and geography. Soon after I left she was killed in a car crash. I cannot begin to estimate what I owe them both.

But there were other matters as well. I played rugby for the school whether I liked it or not (I didn't). I sang in the school Gilbert and Sullivan operas. These I loved with overpowering fierceness. Ah, you should have seen my Strephon in *Iolanthe*. My lifetime operatic peak. My athletics "career" faded out—unmourned. Because, of course, a large part of my consciousness was taken up by girls.

These, remember, were the early '50s. Things were far more reserved, stuffy, inhibited, than they are now, though perhaps not quite as much as is commonly reputed. There was much admiring from afar and, all things considered, pathetically little contact. Even so, we could be deeply involved. Just before I really struck lucky I was plunged into despair by a girl whose name I cannot now remember, and I wrote a poem about it. Secretly I was rather pleased with this effusion. I wondered: Could I be a poet? I was reading enough Shakespeare, Keats, Shelley, and, best of all, gloomy John Donne to make poetry important to me. The short answer to the question, though, was "No!" Nevertheless, I remember this poem by heart and here—a definite "first edition" after over forty years—it is. (Remember, in 1952 "gay" only meant "happy".)

Love in the veil of a question,
A maggot that works in the brain
Over her so ecstatically vital,
Whom I have loved and have lost and
    her silence
Is all my requital.

Now the question is answered, the veil is
    torn
And wretchedly from her I turn
In a grey lowering sadness,
While she whom I loved and have lost
    and still love,
She is gay, and sings in her gladness.

There we are. Actually, seeing it now in front of me after all this time, I have to say—it's not bad. No matter. As 1953 approached two things happened almost simultaneously—my first real girlfriend and an overpowering wish to go to Oxford or Cambridge to read English.

The girl first. Her name was Jackie, she lived in a (to me) very posh London suburb, and was altogether (dreadful English concept) more *middle class* than me. We were introduced by a mate from the sixth form and his equally posh girlfriend. Now came a besotted year of visits to each other's homes and long cycle rides to meet at the halfway point, the town of

Amersham in Buckinghamshire. It ended in tears when I was in the Air Force, but though now far distant and as if happening to someone else, it was important in my life.

Meanwhile, university entrance loomed. Just before Christmas I went to Cambridge for three extraordinary, mind-shaking days to sit exams at a long table in the library of Jesus College, surrounded by a new breed, the people from public schools. The term "public school" in Britain signifies something completely different from its meaning in the USA. Here, public schools are in fact private, expensive, and exclusive. The nearest U.S. equivalent that I am aware of is the school in the film *Dead Poets Society* with Robin Williams. The Welsh, Scots, Lancashire, and Yorkshire voices round me from grammar schools like mine were a great comfort. Hardly was I home than I was off again, this time to Oxford for three equally dream-like days at Wadham College. At both places I lived in college, explored the cities, had trembling interviews with dons whose names I knew. Dazed, I came home to wait.

Amazing. I received by the same post offers of places at both colleges. Memory tells me I chose by tossing a coin. I'm sure I didn't really and that I knew the Cambridge English Tripos was more attractive to me than the Oxford English course. I decided on Jesus College, Cambridge—and thus made one of life's defining choices.

That summer of 1953 was a warm, blessed time, a pause between two movements. I was in at Cambridge; I'd got a State Scholarship to pay the fees and to live on; my little long-distance relationship was flourishing, it seemed. For years I had been in the school's Air Cadet Corps. Two years previously we had been to camp to learn gliding and I'd crashed a small sailplane. That was my low point in dealings with the skies—though years later I used the episode to start a novel, *Landings*. Now, though, I was at another camp at RAF St. Mawgan, on the north Cornish coast. I was given a rare, great experience. I flew with the crew on a real peacetime Coastal Command mission in one of the very last serviceable Lancasters, the classic wartime bomber of the Dambusters. There's always been a paradox here: I abominate war and regard it as obscene. Yet I love so many of the weapons which fight it, and the Lancaster was—and still is—to me a

thing of staggering beauty. What a day it was; flying over the waters of the Western Approaches, going low to investigate Russian trawlers, being allowed to take the controls (even though I was afterwards fairly sure that when that happened the plane was safely on autopilot!)—I shall never forget it. The experience really set me up for two years compulsory National Service.

Alas, the reality of actual service was far different. Thankfully there was no Vietnam, no Falklands, no Gulf. The Korean War still rumbled on but there was no chance we would have to go. Suez came and went as I left the RAF forever. I was never more than a hundred miles from home. I would have loved a time in Singapore or Hong Kong (some of us got there), but Germany or the then strife-torn Cyprus would have scared me stiff. Instead I endured a completely disorienting reception camp, the dreaded "square-bashing" at Hednesford, then a rather enjoyable trade training at Middle Wallop—I soon realised my destiny in the RAF was to spend my working hours underground as a fighter plotter. For years, when an old black-and-white Battle of Britain film came on TV and we saw WAAFs and airmen pushing little counters with sticks round big maps to show where the enemy planes were, I drove my family mad by shouting, "I used to do that, you know."

After Middle Wallop came a very strange interlude. I and a Scotsman whose name I forget, but whom we all called Buggerlugs, were posted to an obscure base in Norfolk—RAF West Raynham. This surprised everybody. We turned up on a dark, bitter January day—to find we shouldn't be there. It was a top secret place—the Central Fighter Establishment. One-off prototypes of sleek experimental planes lined the runways. Soviet spies would have given fortunes to see what we saw. We had, by a typical piece of military logic, been sent there by mistake. We never found where the two sergeants who should have arrived there ended up. Nobody knew who we were, we couldn't be sent away, we had to be hidden. Men of mystery. We were actually given an office of our own (opinion seemed to be that our new, unmarked uniforms with no badges of rank were some sort of MI5 or even CIA disguise) where we did a little work but most of the time watched what was happening round us. Buggerlugs even started giving a few orders (which were obeyed!) and we soon sent the civilian scientific adviser packing when he came off leave and claimed our office belonged to him. This is not the place for the whole book which could be written about the bizarre experience. Suffice to say we were asked where we wanted to go to get rid of us. Buggerlugs chose a base opposite his house near Edinburgh; I went to RAF Chenies not twenty miles from home.

Meanwhile, more distractions. Jackie got fed up with me. More misery. Still, Chenies—and later RAF North Weald in Essex—were great places to live a quietly subversive existence. Here I met people who would mean a lot to me in later life. Chris Wiseman, also off to Cambridge, a poet (a real one), now Professor at Calgary University. Gerry Mosbach, another bound for Cambridge, wisecracking iconoclast who couldn't give a toss about the RAF and prospered because of it. He disappeared into Ethiopia in the '60s and has only now resurfaced in Hungary. There is something inevitable in that. And others—Tony Long, Gordon Head, Jim Bishton—who kept the two years if not sane then at least relatively happy.

And then came Cambridge, longed for like some mirage on a desert horizon. The first days were in truth like a dream. Then came hard reality. It was not what I had hoped. I was cowed by the network of ex-public school people who saw the college as a right, not a wonderful gift. They were confident, clannish, exclusive. I was not of them. The RAF had taken away my study patterns: I could not settle to the work. I joined the Chapel Choir: for three years I sang beautiful church music and found good friends whom I valued—David Jago, John Smith. And there was always the consolation of the wonderful building we lived in and all the other superb places in Cambridge. Even so, come the end of the first year I went home to Winslow so disillusioned, so worried about the exams I had taken, that I seriously considered not going back.

The results came. Amazing what a difference one phone call can make. I had got a Class 2 Division 1. I could not believe it. I was definitely in the top group in the college. If I work really hard, I thought, I could get a first class degree. So I went back, enjoyed my second year much more, worked very hard—with a supervisor, David Daiches, to whom I owe a huge amount—and got another 2:1! It plainly doesn't matter what I do, I thought. I am a 2:1 sort of person. So I had a terrific time in my third year, which included realising that those awful public school people were really nothing of the sort and many became good friends—and duly got yet another 2:1.

Cambridge in the '50s was different from any university now. The colleges were all single-

The author talking to grade nine students in a secondary school

sex. Rules were strict. Over the whole university there was a ratio of ten men to one woman. A teachers' college and a large hospital only slightly redressed the balance. There had been a couple of unsatisfactory girlfriends there—the feeling was mutual—but at the start of the third year I met Anne, who was Welsh and at the teachers' college. I really felt as though my ship had come home. It was she who largely made the third year such a good one.

Yet perhaps the most important long-term event for my writing had occurred two years before. I had previously toyed with the odd unsuccessful poem and article and even had a stab at short stories, but nothing ever got so far as being published. I reviewed films now and again for *Broadsheet,* a small Cambridge magazine, but really all ideas of being a writer had been relegated to mere fancy. However, two set books for Part One of the English degree were the wonderful medieval ballad *Sir Orfeo*—fey and magical—and the Towneley play of *Noah and His Sons,* a really funny medieval drama from the Wakefield Cycle. I made translations of both and was hooked on them. Only recently has my new prose version of *Sir Orfeo* been published. But in June and July of 1957 when I was back at home I had got a temporary teaching job. This experience fixed my choice of career. One thing I wanted to do was to get the kids acting. There was not a play to be found in the place! So I turned my translation of *Noah and His Sons* into an acting version for children. I think they liked it. I certainly did. It took three years to realise this was the start of my first book.

Now, though, in 1959, I had to learn properly to be a teacher. I had got so much out of literature; I wanted above all to pass on some of the pleasure I had felt to others. I am sure that had I done another subject I would not have been a teacher. I left Cambridge and came to Bristol—lovely city in the west—with a term's teaching practice in Bath, an even lovelier city.

At Bristol, my ever-present but lately submerged wish to be a writer resurfaced. During the first term I had merely gone through the motions of lectures and essays, waiting for the weekend. Then either I would be off on the train to Birmingham where Anne was teaching, or she would be in Bristol. The relationship seemed set for life. Yet that new year it all crumbled away and even now I'm not quite

sure why. I suspect the reason was that we both knew it was a hangover from the Never-Never Land of Cambridge and could not stand the pressures of the real world. From winter to spring of 1960 the relationship struggled in fits and starts; in March it fizzled out by mutual agreement. Even so, misery struck again. Yet it was at this moment that I remembered my Noah Play. I was reading another Wakefield Play—the First Play of the Shepherds, not the more famous Second Play with Mak the Sheep-stealer. Almost to cheer myself up, I started making a modern translation from the Middle English. I hardly dared hope I was half way through my first book.

Well, Bristol passed and I took my first proper teaching job. Second English Master (how old-fashioned that sounds now) at Stockport Grammar School. This was an all-boys school—now it has long gone co-ed. Stockport is a large town so close to Manchester to the north that it is hard to find the boundary. Here in 1961 I met Agnes, a nurse from Galway in the west of Ireland, whom I married in 1965. Here I did a part-time diploma course in advanced studies in education at Manchester University. There was also acting with a company run by the redoubtable Mickey and Johnny Johnson, teachers at Stockport Grammar School and a formidable acting partnership, who did elaborate production of classic plays. I shall never forget Chekhov's *The Seagull* with them: on stage in the final act with the lights low, the wind machine howling and knowing that Nina was flitting in the dark outside the dacha, I really felt for a moment that it was actually happening. Also, there were far different plays in the tiny theatre of Manchester's Unnamed Society—culminating for me with Brecht's *Mother Courage* and the lovely singing part of the cook. In Stockport I made more mistakes as a teacher than I care to remember—but also I met many great people, including pupils with whom I have kept in touch throughout their careers, and all in all had a very good time.

Here also I started my writing career. I looked at my two medieval translations. Is there a book here? I wondered. No, not yet. I made another translation—the Wakefield Play of Cain and Abel. This did make up a book, I was sure. So I started sending it to publishers. From three it came back with regrets. The fourth?

I shall never forget picking the letter up from the mat, seeing on the envelope William

*Discussing work with students on a LOMO course;
"a bit of tension building up before all the children
read from their work at the end of the three days!"*

Heinemann Ltd. and reading the fateful words inside: "You will be pleased to know. . . ."

I was on the way. In 1963 a little book appeared—*Three Towneley Plays.* Who noticed? Very few. But for me it was the literary event of the year. Little books for schools, though, weren't real writing, were they? I now longed to be a proper dramatist, a real novelist. Ideas floated round my head, never joining up, never forming into shape. I did not know how to be what I so desired. Suffice it to say that I don't now include *Three Towneley Plays* on my list of publications. But I shall never underestimate its importance to me.

Four years passed in Stockport. It was time to leave, I thought. I looked at a few jobs—then saw the ideal. Queen Elizabeth's Grammar School in—of all places—the Yorkshire

cathedral city of WAKEFIELD! Where my plays were first performed. It has to be, I thought. So I applied, was appointed, and crossed the Pennines, the range of hills and mountains known as "the backbone of England," to this bustling city in the West Riding of Yorkshire. Here Rugby League and a dour version of cricket were the great games and I had to get used to the legendary Yorkshire bluntness.

Agnes came with me. In August 1965 we were married and set up our first house. In 1966 our first child—Peter—was born. That warm June day of waiting (nothing so far out as fathers being present at the birth in those days!) will forever stay in my mind. Here, all things to do with writing fell away again. Being married with a new baby to bring up, looking after a house, holding a job down, together took up all my attention.

Three good years passed in Wakefield. I enjoyed the city, enjoyed the school. But an intriguing job a long way off caught my eyes— training teachers and lecturing in English at a new teachers' college in Milton Keynes, the futuristic new city just about to start up in Buckinghamshire, near where I spent my childhood. Once again I applied, was offered it— and southward we moved again. For eleven years I remained there. This was an exciting time. In education generally, huge reform was taking place. Schools were being reorganised. Grammar schools were, in many areas, disappearing. Comprehensive schools catering for the whole ability range were taking their place. Education for younger children was also changing. The end of the eleven-plus meant liberating changes in the way children up to the age of ten were taught. A new type of school was emerging—the Middle School, for nine- to thirteen-year-olds, getting rid of what some saw as the awkward change of school at eleven and combining the best of primary and secondary practice. I was fascinated by it all. One thing which freeing children under ten from a big exam meant was that children's literature could at last become something which mattered in schools.

I found ample scope to reacquaint myself with this whole field of good books for children. There was a large children's literature section in the college library. I immersed myself in it, meeting again heroes of my childhood like John Masefield and Malcolm Saville, finding giants of the past new to me like George

MacDonald and Frances Hodgson Burnett. Then new writers appeared: Alan Garner, Leon Garfield, Philippa Pearce, Norton Juster, E. B. White, many others.

Suddenly, all those stray ideas of years before found homes. I knew what I wanted to write and what sort of writer I was going to be.

In 1968 our daughter Mary was born. Our family—including the little cat Pussy (unoriginally named because she had only been given to Agnes in Stockport to look after for a few days!)—was complete. Looking back, it seems fair to say that from that time the years seem to merge into one, like a long roller coaster. Professionally, with new courses—including one on children's literature which I ran for ten years—and the contact with students learning the job of teaching which I daily realised I knew less and less about, life was exciting and demanding. The Open University was being set up nearby, an institution which, through TV, radio, and printed units sent each week to students all over the country and small local tutorials, was doing what its name said it would—offering degree-level education to all. I very much wanted to be part of it.

Soon, not only was I a tutor-counsellor to Open University students in the immediate area but also taught in a scheme by which our student teachers took OU degrees full-time at the college. The old building in which the college was situated was part of Bletchley Park, where in the war all the allied decoding of enemy ciphers was carried out. Romantic in its way—but old and inconvenient and we dreamed of a wonderful new campus. In 1975 the dream came true and we moved to a superb purpose-built college in the new city. There we waited to become Milton Keynes University in our own right one day. Alas for ambition. Strange things were taking place outside. The birthrate was going down. Fewer teachers were needed and we were training too many. Colleges were being closed. "Not us, surely?" we wailed. "Not now we're in our lovely new buildings?"

That cut no ice with the government. In 1976 the announcement came. Milton Keynes College of Education, when the present cohort of students had qualified, would be no more.

At home, things were very different from this college tale of rocketing success and then abject defeat. We watched our children grow, go to school, find out for themselves what this world was like. We grieved over the death of Pussy in 1974—and then welcomed the two arrivals who took her place: Tigger, the brown Burmese genius, and Thomas, his half-Persian fall guy. And, now, finally, I started to write.

One hot July evening in 1971 I sat down with a sheaf of paper and a pen and started writing. An idea had been floating round my mind for a long time. It sprang from the Wakefield Plays and it had to be worked out. If a person from our age could have been there when the plays were first performed—could even have acted in those first performances—how would they have seemed to him or her? What would the people of the 1300s make of their visitor from the twentieth century? I saw pictures in my mind of medieval stages, heard Yorkshire voices so broad as to be beyond understanding holding forth in Middle English. I remembered C. S. Lewis's essay "On Three Ways of Writing for Children" which had made a deep impression on me (as much as his lectures at Cambridge—he had left Oxford in time for me to hear him every week). He said that one writes children's books because a children's book is the best vehicle for something one wants to say. I knew that was true here. So, that July evening, I wrote for two hours without stopping. When I had had enough I read it through. "This is not bad," I said to myself in some surprise. "I'll carry on."

So I did. A year later I had finished my first novel, *Pageants of Despair.* Getting it published proved not so long or dispiriting a process as I had feared. The British publisher Andre Deutsch accepted it in 1974 and a few months later so did the U.S. publisher S. G. Phillips. Meanwhile, on my first visit to the Deutsch offices in London I met my editor Pamela Royds, who has been my main guide in writing ever since and to whom my debt is profound.

I was very proud of *Pageants.* Looking at it now, though, I realise how bad, how amateurish, it is. By writing it I learned my trade. It was a very good idea badly carried out. By the time I wrote my second book, *Very Far from Here,* I knew how to design a plot. This book I look back on with much greater pleasure. There was a new background—1914 and the beginnings of the First World War. I was starting to realise what some of my main writing interests were going to be. I abominate war. I don't believe one single political or national end is worth a human life. But one thing war does is to simplify things: "He who is not for us is against us." Feelings run high. Fear is in the air. Emotions are laid bare. It is a wonderful background for stories.

But I still had a career to follow. The unlucky saga of Milton Keynes College was beginning to unfold as it passed its apogee. In 1974 I started doing a Ph.D. with Leicester University and in 1975 another book written with a colleague on working with fiction in schools—*Fiction in the Middle School*—was published. When *Very Far from Here* came out I was well into my third novel, *Landings*.

Here, I returned to war. Two backgrounds merge—the First World War again, but mainly 1956 and the Suez crisis. I was leaving the Air Force as that particular sorry tale unfolded. The whole country had been split down the middle as to whether we and France should go to war together against Egypt—just as we were split in 1982 over the Falklands and the USA was for years over Vietnam. In this book I returned to an earlier passage in my own life with the crashed glider, a problem for a younger brother. Meanwhile his elder brother, doing National Service in the Army, is having a much greater problem over the likelihood of having to fight in Suez. The two brothers are really aspects of myself at different ages. The boys' grandfather is—well, at any rate, here was my first use in a story of a ghost.

One important episode in the story is the brothers' grandmother's funeral. Important things for the plot happen that day. I had just written my account of it—when, after three years of ill health, Dad died. The full church at his funeral showed what an effect he had had on the town in the thirty-six years he had lived there and we remembered the British Empire Medal he was awarded in 1966 for his work over many years in his trade union. He had lived a good life and Richard and I felt proud. But halfway through the day I realised I was experiencing exactly what I had just written about. I could not do another word of *Landings* for three months.

By now, the college's closure was irrevocable. We were all scrambling for new jobs. As I finished *Landings,* I was shooting off applications all over the place and going to interviews in far-flung parts of the country. Many were the times that I came home muttering "Thank God they didn't like me." But once—

in May 1978—they did like me. In September I started what was to prove my last full-time job—County English Adviser for Hertfordshire.

Hertfordshire is a populous county—about a million people. In the south it joins London and reaches nearly to Cambridge in the north. For me, the ideal spot on this planet! The county contains the cathedral city of St. Albans and the new towns of Hemel Hempstead, Letchworth, Welwyn Garden City, and Stevenage. It is riven by railways and motorways shooting north, yet contains beautiful countryside and quiet, unspoilt villages. It seems strange to cross fields, wander through dark woods, look over green vistas, and think: We are twenty miles from the centre of London. I came to love the place.

I certainly saw a lot of it. I shared an office in County Hall in Hertford itself, where we bought a large house built in 1913 and so not quite Edwardian. Much of my working time was spent driving to schools all over the county, advising on the teaching of English and drama, inspecting the teaching and the way it was organised, running in-service courses for teachers. At the same time I advised the education officers at County Hall about policy where it applied to English and drama. I found the job satisfying and rewarding: it took up all my energies. So, between 1979 and 1984, I published nothing except some English versions of Italian texts and a little book on Shakespeare's *Julius Caesar.* I began to wonder if my writing career were not already over.

I could not see how I was going to find the long stretch of uninterrupted time needed for a novel. Then I remembered Pam Royds once suggesting I should try some short ghost stories. Tentatively, I started. First, I put into writing a story I had once made up to tell at a camp. It worked. I tried another. It worked. A disastrous experiment with short stories on a correspondence course years before had told me I couldn't write short stories. But I can, I told myself. Just to see, I took one of those old stories and reworked it. Then I wrote a little story based on a footballing ghost—a nice idea, I thought, which I vowed to return to. Full of myself now, I wrote a longer ghost story based on the long-ago Wellington crash in wartime Winslow. I sent them all off to Pam Royds, sure here was my next book.

Alas. She liked the four shorter stories— but: "I hope you don't think I'll publish that dreadful rigmarole about the acroplane?" said Pam. "But it's great," I replied, severely abashed, though deep down I knew it wasn't. "It has to be either four times shorter or four times longer," she said.

So I took it home, pondered again—and wrote five more stories of the right length. They were published in 1984 as *The Shirt off a Hanged Man's Back* and set me firmly back on track.

Why ghost stories? At first, I wrote them merely because they entertained me and I had always liked them—though I do not believe in ghosts. Writing them, though, made me realise there was more to them than I had thought. They aren't just ways of vicariously scaring people. I came to believe they have a real literary purpose—which accounts at least in part for their perpetual popularity with usually very sceptical writers. I always tell children that we are only what we are because of the past—our respective pasts define us, tell us who we are. The ghost—that earthbound spirit with knowledge from that past it must give urgently before becoming free—truly is the ultimate messenger. At least, mine are and I think the spectres in most serious ghost stories are as well. "I don't believe in ghosts," I tell children. "Except one, and he's the best ghost of the lot. The ghost of Hamlet's father in Shakespeare's play. He tells Hamlet the truth about what happened, which Hamlet needs to know. He does what every good ghost should do—brings the truth from the past so the people in the present can find out who they are."

All looked fair now. We had our lovely home. The job was going well. Peter and Mary were enjoying their schools. I was writing again. But one never knows. . . .

In 1983 I was taken suddenly, unexpectedly, shockingly ill. In August I found myself whisked off to Harefield Hospital in north London where pioneering heart operations are carried out and Professor Magdi Yacoub is king of the transplant. To the possessors of new hearts who I met there, my operation was mere plumbing; to me it was life or death. In October I emerged, shocked, frightened, weak, with a triple heart bypass.

I could not return to work for six months. Just before I was taken ill, I had been asked to write a short story on the theme of "The Outsider" for a story collection. Almost my first action as soon as I could think straight was to

want to write it. But there was only one thing I could think of, and who wanted to hear about my operation? Well, I found myself taking all my pain and terror of the previous weeks and putting them in the form of a ghost. I became a boy having an operation to replace a heart valve. So I managed to write about what had happened to me and detach it from myself, come to terms with it. Now I was even more sure that writing can be therapeutic. Finishing that story helped a lot—though not as much as the nursing given by Agnes—in getting me better. "The Bed by the Door" is an important little tale for me.

In those months I learnt a lot about myself—and a lot about writing, too. Because I also, with all these uninterrupted months, found what it was like to be a full-time writer. I took that flawed story about the air crash, decided it had to be four times longer—and at my leisure turned it into a new novel, *The Fourth Plane at the Flypast.*

At home with wife Agnes and cats: Emily and Charlotte sit with Agnes; the author holds Tigger

Now I built a proper writing regime around the work in schools. More and more I found writing and work connected. A book a year followed and work and contact with children were better because of it. In 1985, two things happened of great importance. The first was sad but not unexpected. Mum died after a long illness. We knew it was coming: in a way it was a relief. But in retrospect, now that Mum and Dad were both gone, I realised again just how much I owed them over so many years. In some ways they had been chalk and cheese together: Dad fiery, Mum gentle. But they never wavered in the support they gave me and the sacrifices they made when an extra wage coming in the house would have been very welcome. A social revolution may have set me on my life's way, but the eternal verities of love and understanding kept me there.

The second was utterly different. There was a little pot of unused money available in the Education service; I managed to grab it for my own purposes. I went to see my friend Philip Levy, who runs a conference centre in Pearse House, a lovely Victorian mansion in the nearby town of Bishop's Stortford. Together we set up the very first of the *Lending Our Minds Out* courses—residential creative writing courses for nine- to eleven-year-old children (grades six and seven) in Hertfordshire. Three days away from everyone, working with poets and novelists. We had little difficulty in finding fifty-four children to fill the first; as the courses became established annually, we were nearly knocked down in the rush for places.

These were wonderful experiences, as were the writing courses I was already running for teachers. I thought—and still think—they were important. Not everyone is going to be a professional writer. But everyone's thoughts are valid and deserve the best possible expression. To experience at close quarters the writer's disciplined creativity, to know what it is, makes better teachers. It makes better pupils as well. Tolstoy's writing processes are no different from those of a ten-year-old on a *Lending Our Minds Out* course. The differences are in degree and not kind. Writers who read are readers who write. Both activities are sharpened by experience of the writing process. This is almost completely forgotten in the utilitarian view of education which holds sway today.

In other ways, life in education was becoming less inspiring. Money was running out; everything was a fight. A view of what schools should be was coming from the government with which I—whether wrongly or not—was fundamentally out of sympathy. A big reorganisation—mainly to cut costs, partly administrative, partly ideological—was coming in Hertfordshire. I had to think hard about what I wanted to do.

The writing was burgeoning. After *Haunted United*—another footballing ghost—and *Dangleboots,* in 1987 a book came out for which I shall always have a special affection, *Hare's Choice.* Here I tried to look at the natures of animals, children—and also of stories and the whole process of making them. A big agenda for a little book! The story ended on a question mark. Repeated enquiries from children told me I should answer my own question—which led to *Badger's Fate* and *Hawk's Vision* and thus the completion of *The Hare Trilogy.* In 1994 I was told the Children's Book Council and International Reading Association had made the U.S. paperback edition a "favorite paperback of 1994," which pleased me a lot. But not as much as the correspondence I started with the students of Nancy English in Public School 29 in Brooklyn after they first read *Hare's Choice.* As a result, I dedicated *Badger's Fate* to them. In 1989 came my only picture book for young children, *Tigger and Friends,* a true story about Tigger, Thomas, and the beautiful Siamese Claudia. All those books were beautifully illustrated by Meg Rutherford.

Then came *The War and Freddy,* based on those far-off wartime days, which amazed me with its effect. Shortlisted for the Smarties Prize in 1991, bits of it read on the radio, talked about by children on television—why did such a little book make such a stir when longer, more elaborate books dropped as quietly as dead leaves? No matter. I enjoyed it all.

By 1992 I had made up my mind. I applied for early retirement as the whole education service was cut. Now I could start the latest phase of my life.

And thus it has been for three years now. Agnes and I are still in the house in Hertford. Peter and Mary are both long through university. Peter, now married, is a research chemist living and working in Leicester. Mary is an editor with a children's publisher in London (no, she doesn't publish my books!). I write full-time now and, with Phil Levy and his staff, run the *Lending Our Minds Out* courses for children in

Youth Hostels all over the country, from the Lake District to East Anglia and the South Downs. Through these courses I meet and work with not only many super kids but also other writers—novelists and poets—who are firm friends now. It is a great thing to realise one is not alone in this solitary enterprise of writing.

There are also visits to schools to be made and talks to be given to teachers and librarians. Regular contact with children is, I think—though I know some would disagree—absolutely vital to the children's writer. I would be much the poorer without it. A regular "give and take" with the teachers and librarians who decide my writing fate just as much as the publishers and the child readers is also very important. Besides, I am still an educator even if not working full-time in it any more.

But the writing comes first—or rather second, after family, now including the cats Charlotte and Emily, Persian and Siamese respectively. We sometimes travel: our one visit to the USA came in 1992—a fortnight in Philadelphia to visit Peter when he was doing a postdoctoral year at Penn State. Together, we cycle a lot—tours of East Anglia and the Cotswolds in England, down the Rhine from Cologne to Heidelberg in Germany and an epic ride through France from Cherbourg to the Dordogne to stay in a medieval tower owned by a fellow children's writer. We often go to the west of Ireland via Dublin, one of my favourite cities. This is besides holidays in settings like Barbados, another place we love.

Back at home I try to write one big young adult novel a year and a younger book each winter, plus short stories when asked—or sometimes just for fun. And lately there has been another departure. In 1992, Scholastic, home of the Point books, took over Andre Deutsch Children's Books, my long-term publisher. I was then asked if I would like to try my hand at a Point Crime, a new British list set up beside the famous Point Horror. Why not? I thought. There were a few who were surprised at my willingness. Why should they be? Here was a chance to try my hand at a classic genre, the murder mystery. From Edgar Allan Poe, Wilkie Collins, and Sir Arthur Conan Doyle, through Raymond Chandler and Agatha Christie to really fine contemporary writers both American and British, these books have entertained and teased millions. And I have been one of them. Scholastic had given me a real challenge which I enthusiastically took up. Chandler and Ruth Rendell for teenagers! Now I write a Point Crime every fall. Three are done already. And now—going right back to my writing roots—I am planning a whole mini-series of Point Crimes set in the Middle Ages.

So there we are—if still in the middle way, then certainly well towards the end of it. But there's much to do yet—books to be written not yet even dreamed of, courses to be run, children to be met. It's a good life; long may it continue.

BIBLIOGRAPHY

FOR CHILDREN

Fiction:

Pageants of Despair, Deutsch, 1974, S. G. Phillips, 1975.

Very Far from Here, Deutsch, 1976.

Landings, Deutsch, 1979.

The Shirt off a Hanged Man's Back (short stories), Deutsch, 1984.

The Fourth Plane at the Flypast, Deutsch, 1985.

Haunted United, Deutsch, 1986.

Dangleboots, illustrated by Tony Ross, Deutsch, 1987.

Hare's Choice (first novel in trilogy), illustrated by Meg Rutherford, Deutsch, 1987, Dell, 1990.

Tigger and Friends, illustrated by Meg Rutherford, Deutsch, 1989, Lothrop, 1989.

Blood Line, Deutsch, 1989.

Coded Signals, Deutsch, 1990.

The War and Freddy, illustrated by George Buchanan, Deutsch, 1991.

Badger's Fate (second novel in trilogy), illustrated by Meg Rutherford, Deutsch, 1992.

Hawk's Vision (third novel in trilogy), illustrated by Meg Rutherford, Deutsch, 1993.

Death Penalty, Scholastic, 1994.

Tales from the Underland, Longman, 1995.

The Railway Phantoms, Hippo, 1995.

Spirit of the Place, Scholastic, 1995.

Deadly Music, Scholastic, 1995.

Dead Ringer, Scholastic, 1996.

Out of the Mouths of Babes, Scholastic, in press.

Contributor of short stories to numerous books, including *The Methuen Book of Sinister Stories*, edited by Jean Russell, Methuen, 1982; *Outsiders*, edited by Bryan Newton, Collins, 1984; *An Oxford Book of Christmas Stories*, edited by Dennis Pepper, Oxford University Press, 1986; *Twisted Circuits*, edited by Mick Gowar, Century Hutchinson, 1986; *Electric Heroes*, edited by Mick Gowar, Bodley Head, 1987; *First Impressions*, edited by Jim Sweetman, 1989; *Oranges and Lemons*, Blackwell, 1989; *An Oxford Christmas Storybook*, edited by Dennis Pepper, Oxford University Press, 1990; *Mystery Tour*, edited by Mick Gowar, Bodley Head, 1991; *An Oxford Book of Scary Stories*, edited by Dennis Pepper, Oxford University Press, 1991; *It Isn't Over until the Fat Lady Sings*, edited by Mick Gowar, Bodley Head, 1992; *Animal Stories*, Simon & Schuster, 1994; *Point Horror: Thirteen Again*, Scholastic, 1995; and *The Oxford Funny Storybook*, edited by Dennis Pepper, Oxford University Press, 1996.

Other:

Three Towneley Plays (adapted into modern English), Heinemann, 1963.

Pageants of Despair (radio play based on novel of the same title), British Broadcasting Corporation (BBC) Radio, 1979.

Court Jester (radio play), BBC Radio, 1979.

(Adaptor of English text) Gian Paolo Ceserani, *The Travels of Columbus*, Kestrel, 1979.

(Adaptor of English text) Gian Paolo Ceserani, *Travels of Livingstone*, Kestrel, 1979.

(Adaptor of English text) Gian Paolo Ceserani, *The Travels of Marco Polo*, Kestrel, 1980.

(Adaptor of English text) Gian Paolo Ceserani, *The Travels of Captain Cook*, Kestrel, 1980.

Julius Caesar: Study Guide and Cassette, Argo, 1982.

Cat Watchers, illustrated by Kim Palmer, Basil Blackwell, 1988.

The Railway Passengers, illustrated by Kim Palmer, Basil Blackwell, 1988.

FOR ADULTS

Nonfiction:

(With Colin Field) *Fiction in the Middle School*, Batsford, 1975.

(With Mick Gowar) *Living Writers: Novelists*, Nelson, 1992.

(With Mick Gowar) *Living Writers: Dramatists*, Nelson, 1992.

(With Mick Gowar) *Living Writers: Poets*, Nelson, 1993.

Contributor of articles to reference books, including *Twentieth-Century Young Adult Writers* and *Twentieth-Century Children's Writers*, both St. James Press. Contributor to periodicals, including *English in Education*. Reviewer for *School Librarian* and *Times Educational Supplement*.

X. J. Kennedy

1929-

X. J. Kennedy

Childhood was punctuated with explosions. Dover, New Jersey, the small town where I was born and raised, depended on war efforts. Most people worked at Picatinny Arsenal, Lake Denmark Naval Station, where rockets were tested, and the Hercules Powder Company. Before I was born, the arsenal had blown up, and a meteor shower of fireworks had rained on the town. One day when I was in fourth grade, the powder company also decided to explode. That blast rocked the town like an earthquake and knocked the glass out of the windows of Northside School, so we kids had a sudden holiday. Another time, a man hired to dynamite the ice on a frozen pond used too powerful a charge. Again, out leaped our school windows. Besides, every Fourth of July,

you could buy your own fireworks and set them off, often at great risk to life and limb. My father liked to set match to an evil red stick called a cannon cracker and throw it into an empty five-gallon can. We'd retreat to a safe distance and the old can would shoot ten feet into the air, with a BOOM twice as loud as that of a naked firecracker.

It was a world that might seem poverty-stricken to kids of today—a world without television. Not feeling in the least deprived, we bent ears to our radios. Each afternoon I would faithfully tune in the exploits of Dick Tracy, Little Orphan Annie, Don Winslow of the navy, and Jack Armstrong the All-American Boy. Loyally, I sent in box tops for my decoder ring which, when twisted to the right numbers, displayed letters that translated a secret message heard on the air, like, "Get your minerals from Wheaties daily." Darkness would fall, bringing thrillers such as "I Love a Mystery" and, on Sundays, "The Shadow," about an invisible crime-smasher whose disembodied voice intoned, "The weed of crime bears evil fruit—crime does not pay— the Shadow knows!" And he would snigger evilly. Radio drama is immensely suggestive, like hearing a book read aloud. I'll never forget the night of October 30, 1938, when Orson Welles dramatized "The War of the Worlds," H. G. Wells's story of an invasion from Mars. Welles' make-believe newscast had immediate local interest, for it claimed that Martians had landed not far from Dover. Believing its report of tentacled monsters zapping people with death rays to be a blow-by-blow description of current events, one of our neighbors bundled his wife and children into his car and lit out like a streak for Pennsylvania.

The world of my childhood had no shopping malls. Busy Blackwell Street, with its three five-and-ten-cent stores, was the town's central artery. Supermarkets, decidedly un-super, supplied little of our food. Only a block from our house stood a wonderful one-man store. It sold purple Popsicles and small Dixie cups full of vanilla and chocolate ice cream, whose lids, when licked, revealed photos of baseball players and cowboy movie stars. You could stand before a tremendous case of penny candy that held licorice shoestrings and sugar dots on paper strips, debating how to invest your nickel, until finally the grocer, waiting with a little paper bag, would growl, "Hurry up, make up your mind."

A steady stream of people brought things to your door. Mr. Kramer, the milkman—we called him Mr. Creamer—brought Grade A in glass bottles. On a winter's day the milk would freeze and the cream rise in the bottle for two inches and push the paper cap up into the air. Then you could scoop the frozen cream into a saucer, splash it with vanilla, sprinkle sugar on it and—presto! You had homemade ice cream. Apple-cheeked Farmer Albertson delivered peaches and pears and tomatoes, old Mrs. Schwartz brought fresh eggs and chickens (at Eastertime, always some boiled purple eggs for me), gaunt Sylvester Hendershot kept us in daily bread, aspiring actor Leo Shepps brought coffee and tea and news of his latest plans to open on Broadway, and two characters we called

Popeye and Wimpy came around selling supposedly fresh fish that my mother never bought because she suspected that they'd had it in their wagon for too long.

I was born on August 21, 1929, just before the Wall Street market crashed, banks failed, and people lost their savings by the carload. By luck, my father had sold most of his stock in order to build our little house at 84 Baker Avenue, and so avoided a dire loss. Franklin D. Roosevelt gave radio talks designed to cheer people. He had been president for as far back as I could remember, and he stayed in office until I was sixteen. Secretly, my father worshipped Mr. Roosevelt, though his several Republican brothers and sisters would speak with contempt of "that man in Washington."

Not far from where we lived, a village of shacks made of tarpaper and old advertising signs sprang up beside the railroad tracks. Hungry men would come to our back door and beg a meal, and my mother would bring them out a plate of whatever we were having. People went

Father, Joseph Francis Kennedy,
in his early twenties

around selling things—cookies they had baked, things they had knitted—anything to make a little money. I felt especially sorry for a girl in my class who, along with her mother, rang our doorbell one day, peddling homemade doughnuts. She blushed when I recognized her, and shrank back and hid behind her mother. Once I noticed that my black pal Benny Pollock wore a shoe with its sole flapping loose. I asked him why, and he said, "That's just to let in the air." At a birthday party I went to, the only present the birthday boy received was the fifty-cent game I had brought. For refreshments we had a one-pint brick of ice cream with eight spoons.

Throughout the Great Depression of the 1930s, although my father's pay had been slashed to twenty-five dollars a week, we always had enough food on our table—thanks in part to my aunt Effie, who handled the money for her husband's busy garage and towing service. Every now and then she would dump out a bagful of coins on our kitchen table and say, "Here, save me counting this. Can you use it?" We always could.

I should tell you about my parents. They hadn't married until past forty years old, and I was their only child. As a young man, my father, Joseph Francis Kennedy, had worked as a freight agent for the Erie railroad, and I believe he often wished he had remained a railroad man. He would talk of distant places, seeming wistful, but the farthest from Dover he ever went in his life was on a honeymoon to Montreal. During long Sunday walks with me, he would stand beside the tracks whenever a chain of boxcars rolled by, identifying the exotic railroads they belonged to. Incidentally, he liked poetry, had memorized bales of it in school, and used to recite from John Greenleaf Whittier's "Snowbound" and other classics. He was the official poet laureate of the Kennedy family, charged with making up and reciting a poem on the occasion of any birthday, wedding, or anniversary.

My father was a gentle man who liked to make friends with all. On our walks, he would always greet strangers, declaring, "It never hurts to say hello to anybody." He didn't like to pay his bills by mail; he preferred to walk all over town and pay them in person, so that he could talk with people. Mindful of his middle name, my mother called him "Saint Francis," after that friend of wild creatures, for each morning he

Mother, Agnes Rauter, high school graduation, about 1907

would distribute bread to the backyard birds. All the while I was growing up he worked as paymaster for the Dover Boiler Works. In those precomputer days, payrolls had to be figured out by hand, and my father could add a column of numbers with a speed that used to astonish me. The Boiler Works paid its workers in cash, and when my father would carry a black bag containing several thousand dollars from the bank to the office, he had to carry a loaded revolver. "What would you do, Joe," some amused coworker asked him, "if a man jumped out at you waving a gun? Shoot it out with him?" "Well," said my armed-to-the-teeth father, "I guess I'd throw him the bag of money and run like blazes."

Although he could grow pole beans and tomatoes, I don't believe my father could hammer a nail without smashing his thumb. He never solved the mystery of driving a car, and when a neighbor once tried to teach him, he backed our old Plymouth into a peony bush and tore it up by the roots. When the driving lesson was moved to a ball field where he couldn't run into anything, he succeeded in making the Plymouth whiz around in circles. My mother remained the chauffeur in our family.

My father stood in awe of Whoever had made the world. He never discussed religion, but one time when Reuben Farr, the village atheist, was haranguing a bunch of people in the street, objecting to the existence of God, he suddenly turned to my father and challenged him, "What do you think, Joe Kennedy?" My father reflected a moment and said, "Well, I don't believe it was Thomas A. Edison who put them stars up in the sky."

Now about my mother. While my father had grown up in a large happy family, Agnes Jane Rauter had been raised in a large unhappy one. Her mother, an Irishwoman, had died in childbirth, and her father had remarried, as in those days a working man left with a flock of children quickly had to do. This stepmother, a German like himself, came with kids of her own to whom she was partial, and she treated my mother badly. As a girl my mother used to shed empathetic tears over books about a little orphan named Elsie Dinsmore, who endured awful humiliations.

Just as soon as she was old enough, my mother fled her family. She worked in Morristown Memorial Hospital and eventually won her cap as a registered nurse. Before she married my father, she had been a school nurse in Morristown for many years, and had been a private nurse for a while, once caring for the children of the French theatrical director Jacques Copeau on the estate of a millionaire patron of the arts, Otto Kahn.

Though my mother had had more schooling than my father, who was a high school dropout, she didn't rub it in. I always felt lucky to have a nurse for a mother. Some of my happiest days were spent sick in bed with mumps, measles, chicken pox, or scarlet fever. She'd bring me meals on a tray, give me a bath in bed hospital style. Once when I had an earache, she borrowed a pack of cigarettes and sat by my bedside, gasping and coughing, blowing warm smoke into my ear.

As you can gather, I was spoiled rotten. To the best of my recollection, I was generally a contented child. Baker Avenue was a long

"My grandparents Mike and Caroline Kennedy," about 1925

straight street lined with maple trees, only a two-block walk from the Rockaway River, with its popular swimming holes. It was fun to imagine that a couple of sticks were boats, then to drop them off the bridge and dash to the other side and see whose boat had emerged in the lead. One day "Snaker" Thorsell, so called because he kept pet reptiles, dredged up out of the river the little white arm of some rubber doll. He convinced me that it was a piece of a real baby and, dangling it on a stick, chased me all the way home with it. (For a poem about this nightmare, please see "The Arm," in a book called *Dark Horses*.)

Where the river ran, the Morris Canal had once carried barges laden with iron ore, drawn on ropes by mules who trudged along the shore. When my father was a boy, local smelting furnaces had been active, but the supply of iron had dwindled and now they were abandoned, leaving the towpath to pedestrians. Like some landscape on the moon, mountains of gray slag still stood, providing us kids with dangerous locales for games of cowboys and Indians. The area had been settled largely by people from Cornwall, the westernmost district of England, who, being miners, had sought the same kind of work in the New World. Mining had brought to America my grandmother's family, the Brays, and along with them came curious legends and lore. From my grandmother, I learned odd superstitions, like the custom of placing a silver coin outside your door on New Year's Eve and taking it in again in the morning—a practice supposed to bring you wealth in the new year. It was bad luck, though, if your first new year's visitor had red hair.

My Cornish grandmother was an important, much-loved person in my young life. She lived with us in her last years, surviving all but three of her ten children. She remembered having heard, as a teenager in Cornwall, her father read aloud a newspaper account of the American Civil War. From Cornwall she had brought culinary knowledge: how to make heavy cake (a kind of hard biscuit baked with butter in the middle), saffron buns, and pasties, this last an aromatic turnover holding beef, sliced potatoes, onions, and white turnip. She was a devoted reader of the King James Bible, whose stately language gave her everyday speech a certain weight and pithiness.

My aunt Effie had high ambitions for me. She would make me into a child movie star like Shirley Temple. And so I was obliged to spend hours by the piano, belting out Shirley's hit songs, "On the Good Ship Lollipop" and "Animal Crackers in My Soup." I must have been pretty terrible, for at last she gave up on me. Aunt Effie meant well. She tried to teach me to play the piano myself, but I never did care much about it. At the time, I was more keenly interested in learning to play the typewriter.

My close pal Webster Thayer Gault was destined to be a wordsmith, too: in later life, an editor for the *Hartford Courant*. He had been named for his grandfather, Judge Webster Thayer, who had passed the controversial death sentence on the accused anarchists Sacco and Vanzetti and had had his house bombed in retaliation for it. Thayer, as he was then known, and I used to act out plays on stages made from big pasteboard boxes, with movable curtains. We invented dialogue as we went along, manipulating toy animals and saying their lines for them. In this manner we would pass whole mornings. Our plays didn't impress my uncle Jim Rauter, a fisherman, hunter, and gruff outdoorsman, who stayed with us one summer. I'll never forget the day he leveled his contempt at me. While I was down on my knees, moving a china dog or cat around the makeshift stage and talking for it in a squeaky voice, Uncle Jim strolled by. He glared down scornfully and said, "What are you doing, Seppi?"— he always called me by that nickname, short for Giuseppe—"playing with dolls?"

Not permanently discouraged, Thayer and I collaborated on a real show one summer—a circus with a cast of ten. An older lad, Jack Yale, condescended to take part, and because the circus was to be held in my backyard, it was christened the Kennedy & Yale Brothers Circus. Jack and I weren't really brothers, of course, but we figured that, since the Ringling Brothers' circus had been such a hit, our show needed to have Brothers in its name too. We set about recruiting talent. Snaker Thorsell would appear in a skit about a bum slapped by a lady, and Thayer enlisted his performing dog, Blackie, who, when you placed a cookie on his nose, would at a signal catch it in his mouth. The Tallest Man in the World would stand atop three packing cases, behind a bed sheet that came down to the ground. What to do for publicity? Luckily, a crony of my father's was a job printer who, when told of our coming show, donated handsome posters proclaiming KENNEDY & YALE BROTHERS CIRCUS in large professional-looking type. We nailed them up on phone poles throughout the neighborhood, only to have them torn down by jealous enemies. But at least one survived, the one in the window of Mr. Duffy's corner store.

When the great day came, we trimmed my backyard with paper streamers and set up bleacher seats, a row of folding chairs borrowed from an undertaker. My Sears Roebuck tent was pressed into service as a dressing room. A two-man drum and bugle corps began to play, and people streamed in until the backyard swelled with an overflow crowd. The *Dover Advance* sent a photographer. The show went off without a hitch, and the patrons clapped and cheered. The only weak note was the pink lemonade. There was such a run on it that my mother had to keep diluting it until it ended up colorless. "Huh!" snorted one irate customer, "you might's well be drinking water!" We gave him his two cents back.

My mother believed that every solitary boy should have a pet, so, doing the best she could do with her pin money, she bought me a series of pathetic creatures. There was a sad-eyed puppy that lasted about a month and finally expired from constipation, despite my mother's nursing skills. I was fonder of my pet white rats and my large black-and-white rabbits, which I kept in a cage in our basement. However, their high death rate—our neighbor "Auntie" Griffin said that every time she looked out of her window she could see my mother going down to the garden with a shovel and a bag— led us to suspect that fumes from our coal furnace hadn't been good for the poor things' health. So I gave up trying to keep mammals myself and cultivated friendships with Spotty and Buttons Griffin (pets in our neighborhood always took their owners' last names), two healthy dogs who lived next door, and made do with a canary and two turtles.

Always the most thrilling moment of the year came in late summer. Our family would make a brave and strenuous journey. We would drive for a whole hundred miles to Ocean Grove, on the Jersey shore. Marco Polo could not have prepared for his expedition to China more carefully. The week before we left, my mother would deliver our aged Plymouth to my uncle Norman's garage, and my uncle himself would go over it from front bumper to rear, making us ship-

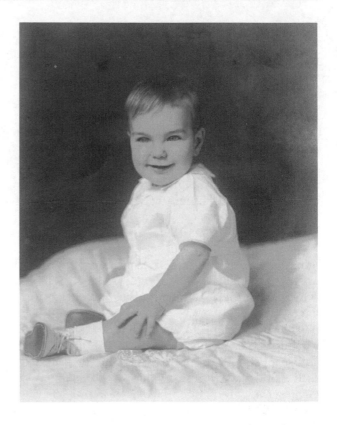

Kennedy in 1930

shape lest we break down on some distant road. My father, with an air of importance, would go to the bank and draw a hundred dollars out of his savings account to cover our week-long stay. On the fateful morning, the Plymouth tanked with gas, we would set out very early, my mother driving. She had mapped out a long and twisting route that would take us over country roads the whole way. My mother distrusted highways. I believe she had once driven through the traffic of Perth Amboy and had vowed never to do it again. Taking our farewells from all the neighbors, we would head south at thirty miles an hour—"as fast as God meant people to go," in my mother's view. After hours that seemed endless, half strangled from the dust and heat of back roads, we would reach tree-lined Princeton, where we would stop for sandwiches and sarsaparilla. At last, just before dark, we would chug into Ocean Grove, hearing the welcoming creak of seagulls and the boom of the Atlantic.

Ocean Grove must have been the lowest-priced resort on the Jersey shore, and my parents knew of rooming houses where a family could stay for a week for as little as fifteen dollars. One of these didn't have any fire escapes, but just a rope to lower yourself to the ground from the fourth floor. In my mind's eye I could picture vast flames breaking out, devouring the dry old wooden frame building in a gulp, while my father, hanging to the rope with one hand, carrying my mother and me in the other, would have to slide like Tarzan to the ground. The notion was terrifying.

"A lot of old fogies looking at you over their glasses," was how my uncle Jim described Ocean Grove. It was, and still is, a Methodist summer encampment with a large tabernacle for holding hymn services. My father and I didn't go to the services; we were Catholics. Instead, we would venture over to the sinful city of Asbury Park, to play Skee-ball and hike the boardwalk and watch prizes slip from the grasp of steel cranes in the penny arcade. One beautiful thing about Ocean Grove, besides its nearness to Asbury Park, was that on Sunday all the cars had to get out of town. You could stroll right down the middle of the street without being nudged by a bumper, unless it were that of a fire engine or the car of a doctor rushing to save a life. Ocean Grove had a strict code of morality. Card playing in public was forbidden, as was the sale of anything stronger than soda. Bare flesh was suspect. I must have been large for my age, for one day as I was playing on the beach, a policeman told my mother that I was on the wrong side of the law. "Why," she said in surprise, "this boy is only eight." "Well, he looks older," said the cop. "The law says that all men have to have their chests covered, so you'll have to put a shirt on him." Luckily, in her beach bag my mother had brought along one of my old undershirts to mend, and I was promptly rendered decent. Then my father (in trunks and a bathing shirt) and I triumphantly jumped waves.

Another high point of the summer was always a visit to my cousins Bob and Bill Rauter in Chatham, not far away. They lived on the edge of a large swampland crisscrossed by rough dirt roads. My elder cousin Bill, a teenager, loved cars, and although too young to drive on public roads, he had got hold of an abandoned early-model Ford and restored it to running condition. He and his pals would chip in fifteen cents for a gallon of kerosene, and on that low-cost fuel the old Ford would whiz over winding dirt roads at a reckless speed, for as long as the gallon lasted. One day Bill offered Bob and me a ride, so we climbed up and installed ourselves on a big squashy cushion in the rumble seat. Away shot the Ford, as if fired out of a cannon, jolting over rocks and stumps in the road. One jolt was so hard that Bob and I sailed backwards out of the car, still perched on the cushion, side by side. We hit the ground with a thump and sat there unharmed, and continued sitting there until Bill noticed we were gone and came back for us. But somehow I didn't feel like riding any more that day.

Bill Rauter was a budding capitalist. On a busy corner, he set up a stand selling homemade root beer in glass bottles, kept cold with dry ice. This excellent drink made money hand over fist, thanks in part to the patronage of passing truck drivers. Much of its success was also due to kids buying it not to drink but to hold duels with. That homemade root beer was powerful stuff. You could shake it up and squirt a jet of it for ten or twelve yards, drenching your opponent to the skin. Somehow, those stout old bottles never exploded. (I wouldn't try that kind of warfare with any soda containers made today!)

Two institutions loomed large in my life—school and church. Church was St. Mary's in nearby Wharton, where my father and I would walk for Sunday Mass. I was the child of a mixed marriage—my mother, like my paternal grandmother, was a Methodist—so that, while free to attend public school, I had to go to church and Sunday school. I didn't want to go to parochial school. The nuns in their flowing black robes filled me with dread, for they looked to me like sheeted ghosts. Besides, I had heard terrible tales of teaching nuns who would rip out their students' hair and rap rulers across their knuckles. When I had to make my First Communion and rehearse for the event under the supervision of Sister Agatha, I was scared. As that imposing nun glared down at us, we kids had to march up a side aisle of the church and take our seats, exactly as we would do when the great Sunday came. I missed a cue and started piling into my seat too soon, and Sister Agatha exploded with a torrent of abuse. I stared up into her furious face, her lips working. It was too much for a public school kid like me. I bawled. To my surprise, the good sister's rage suddenly melted. She hugged me to her white-garbed breast and decided that I had rehearsed enough for that day and should go home, and she sent another boy to see that I crossed the street safely. That nuns were human after all came as a revelation.

Sunday school wasn't so bad. It was taught by my father's cousin Marie McCarthy, and we simply had to memorize a lot of answers out of a catechism, reciting back the facts about Who made the world. One day, however, Father Mahoney, the stern-looking old priest whose sermons told how sinners would be roasted in a fiery furnace, dropped in on our class. He must have felt benevolent, for he tweaked me by the ear playfully, and said, "Now, here's a boy who would rather be watching a movie show, isn't that right?" "Yes, father," I answered, for I had been told never to argue with a priest.

School obliged me to write poetry. In third grade, Miss Smith assigned us to write a poem about Christmas or Hanukkah, and I wrote one heavily indebted to "A Visit from St. Nicholas," a similar account of a visit from Santa Claus. It began,

> The people were out in the street one night
> Waving the beautiful lantern light
> And in the window was little me
> And all around me was the Christmas tree.

There was more of it. Impressed, my teacher sent it to the local newspaper, which printed it in full. From that day on, boys in the schoolyard used to taunt me ("You must be a poet—your big feet show it!"). Smarting from the disgrace of being a published poet, I let a few years elapse before attempting another poem.

School did, however, revive my interest in the theater, which my uncle Jim had squelched for a while. With my friend Charley De Shazo, I wrote a play for Halloween called "The Treasure of Sindew Forest," whose best character was a wicked witch who kept snickering, "Yak! yak! yak!" When this melodrama was staged in the school auditorium, it was so well received that two other kids and I were assigned to write another play immediately, one for Thanksgiving. With my collaborators, I drafted a script, working all Saturday. Unfortunately, we got carried away with the giggles, and I kept throwing in jokes of dubious taste. In one scene, the Puritan maiden Priscilla Mullins was asked by Miles Standish, "How's your kidneys, kid?"

And she replied, "No soap, dope." I thought that was hilarious.

But Mrs. Booser didn't. Before our Thanksgiving play went into production, our teacher thought to show it to the principal. Mrs. Booser was horrified. Sternly, she descended on our classroom and gave the whole class a lecture on the meaning of Thanksgiving, heaping disgrace upon us three playwrights in front of everybody. "How could you write such a travesty?" she marveled. My coauthors, who hadn't contributed any of the bad jokes, were totally humiliated. Poor Blanche Detwiler was reduced to sobs, while Jimmy Gross turned red as a boiled lobster. As for me, I sat there glaring at Mrs. Booser. If she hadn't liked our old play, why hadn't she just tossed it into the wastebasket? If she had had anything to say to us, she should have said it in private. I don't know what ever happened to our script, but it was never produced. Our teacher was assigned to write a new Thanksgiving play, which she didn't get around to until it was practically Christmas.

"At age eight"

In Mrs. Booser's favor, though, it must be said that she took an interest in budding creative artists. Once when I had to write another poem for English class, she called me into her office and gave me some instruction in correcting the meter of it. I listened politely, but in truth I didn't care nearly as much about meter at that time as I did later. Northside, under her charge, was a demanding school. The most challenging subject I had was math, taught by Mrs. Tecla Wildrick. Mrs. Wildrick was a stickler for our getting fractions right. She divided the class into rows according to their current grades—an A row, a B row, and so on down to an E row, to which she consigned the disgracefully ignorant. I usually sat in her B or C row, for Mrs. Wildrick knew my father, and she treated me gently. One day I asked my father if he remembered her. "Oh, sure," he replied, "Tecla used to be sweet on your uncle Ed." Uncle Ed was a handsome man. He had married not Mrs. Wildrick but my aunt Ricky. I guessed my father must have been right, because once in a while Mrs. Wildrick would roll wistful eyes and ask me, "How is your uncle Ed?"

I must have been a naive kid. One day at recess in the school yard, it was snowing steadily. Entranced by all that feathery white stuff falling, I stood with my back against a cement wall with my mouth hanging open, letting the snowflakes settle on my tongue. The sensation was quite lovely. When some bigger boys came up to me, I shut my trap, but one of them begged, "Hey, Joe, do like you was doing before." Innocently, I opened my mouth wide again, and he popped a large gritty stone into it. I stood there spitting dirt. The whole school heard of my gullibility.

At twelve, I had to get glasses. Suddenly the world leaped into focus. Through my new spectacles, I began to look more closely at girls. I wished one of them might become my girlfriend, but none of them ever did. However, Mrs. Forsythe, a neighbor who drove a mail truck, threw a birthday party for her daughter, at which, to my great excitement, we played the kissing game of post office. In a darkened parlor I ventured to kiss a moon-faced beauty named Gloria Long. I had never kissed a girl before, so I sort of smacked and slobbered on her cheek. "That's not how you do it," she snapped, and crushed her lips to mine. For the next few days, I could hardly believe that this tremendous event had really taken place. I kept suspecting that it had all been a dream. That, however, was as far as our romance went.

At sports in school, when our class divided up into teams, I was always chosen last. I enjoyed swinging at a baseball, but scored only one run in my whole career, and that run on errors. At wrestling, though I could get into positions so odd and stubborn that I couldn't be pinned, I never could pin my opponent. Nobody ever explained what basketball was all about. I would run aimlessly around the court, trying to keep out of the way of the others, watching the clock until gym period was at an end. I never figured out the rules of football either. I was given ice skates, but had wobbly ankles and couldn't stand up in them. As a fisherman, my only catch was a sunfish two inches long. No sooner had I landed it than I slipped on the muddy bank and toppled into the fishpond. My companions circulated the report that the sunfish had dragged me in after it.

What I really liked was making comic books. I invented a phalanx of superheroes and spun out their adventures in sixty-four-page magazines that I drew in ink and colored with crayon and showed to my few friends. There was Bounco the Rubberman, whose body was shaped like a ball and who traveled along the street by bouncing on his stomach. He had a sidekick named The Candle because a candle grew from the top of his head. It had to stay lit and whenever it blew out he would fall down unconscious. Another character was Oceanman, who pelted villains with big globs of water. Like heroes in the real, printed comic books that all my spare dimes went for, my characters started beating up on Nazis around 1940, as World War II drew near.

Comic books weren't quite my only reading. Ours was not a family of book buyers—in those days, we couldn't afford such luxuries—but I early acquired a thirst for fifty-cent boys' series books: Tom Swift, the Rover Boys, the Hardy Boys, Roy Rockwood's Great Marvels series, and the good-humored books of the now almost forgotten Leo Edwards, such as *Jerry Todd and the Oak Island Treasure* and *Poppy Ott and the Stuttering Parrot.* One Christmas someone gave me Robert Louis Stevenson's *The Black Arrow* with pictures by N. C. Wyeth, and I cherished it. Once in a while I would go to Dover Pub-

Kennedy (third from left) with fellow science fiction fans George Fox (far left), Gerry de la Ree, Lloyd Alpaugh (far right) at a meeting in Westwood, New Jersey, about 1947

lic Library and bring home one of the adventures of Doctor Dolittle. At the library I came upon a book called *Albanian Fairy Stories.* Wonderfully weird, its tales made a deep dent in me.

In seventh grade, I discovered the hectograph. This marvelous instrument was a flat pan like a baking sheet, full of gelatin. You drew pictures in a special purple ink that left stains on your hands and got all over everything, then sponged water on your hectograph and pressed the original down on its surface of quivering jelly. Peeled away, the original left an impression, and you laid typewriter paper down on the jelly, rubbed the paper flat, peeled it off, and you had a copy. The more copies you made, the dimmer they became, until about the thirtieth copy became completely unreadable. Armed with this splendid tool, I began producing comic books in quantity, and tried to sell them for a nickel to my classmates. Sales were slow until the teacher, cheerful Miss Haviar, grabbed a stack of *Bounco Comics* and went up and down the aisles, hawking them for me, shouting, "Get your comics here! Comics, for the young and intelligent mind!"

Publishing always intrigued me. My earliest publication had been a woman's magazine with a circulation of one—my mother. In eighth grade my friend Meyer Okun and I put out a newspaper run off on the school duplicator. My first full-time summer job was working in the back room of our twice-a-week newspaper, the *Dover Advance,* where I swept floors, baled leftover newsprint paper, packed up used boiler plate (the little filler items that came all set in type, like "The duck-billed platypus is found only in Australia"), and once descended into the pit under the presses to retrieve scraps of metal type. From that assignment, I emerged with hair and skin gummed black with printer's ink and had to be soaked in turpentine.

I came to know and respect the printers, a salty-talking crew. They had the power to lock up tons of miscellaneous type into pages and churn out newspapers. Once, though, I saw a printer let fall a whole form—a page of type, ready for the press—and shatter it on the print shop floor. His remarks nearly chipped the paint off the ceiling. The aristocrats of the print shop were the linotypists. While others sweated, lifting the heavy forms, they would saunter in, sit down at a keyboard with masterful aplomb, and jauntily start tapping away. Down a little chute would topple sticks of warm lead with words on them. I regarded them as sorcerers.

When I reached full adolescence, my taste in trash switched over from comic books to pulp magazines, so called for their cheap pulp paper. These were thick, square-bound periodicals with garish covers showing handsome strongmen rescuing beautiful women from villains with scimitars. You could find them in any drugstore, stacked in a wire rack with their spines showing. I devoured *Doc Savage,* whose every number featured a new novel about a dashing hero, *Jungle Stories,* and *Dime Detective* (which during World War II had to raise its price to fifteen cents). Then I discovered the science fiction pulps—*Amazing Stories, Planet Stories, Thrilling Wonder Stories, Astounding Science Fiction*—and felt like some watcher of the skies when a new planet swims into his ken. Other, imaginary worlds seemed more vital, for a time, than the pedestrian world I knew.

Writing letters to the editors of these magazines, which they printed, I learned that there existed a whole underground culture of devoted science fiction fans. These youths, loners who, like me, didn't feel quite at ease with normal kids at school, published mimeographed fanzines and held conventions. Through the mails I was soon getting to know fellow SF fans all over the country and soon made friends with a contingent who lived in Brooklyn and the Bronx.

In those days New York was a decidedly tamer place, and my parents thought nothing of allowing me to take the Lackawanna railroad in to see my chums in the city. I found myself thrown into the society of teenagers whose interests were new and strange to me. Their idea of fun was to go to an art museum or a foreign movie or a remainder bookshop. They introduced me to exotic fare: pizza in Italian trattorias, cheesecake in East Side delicatessens. Hanging out with them, I was invited to a Sunday gathering at the Forest Hills apartment of the celebrated Donald A. Wollheim, editor of *The Pocket Book of Science Fiction,* in later years the publisher of DAW Books. At Wollheim's I met famous SF writers and editors: Damon Knight, Cyril Kornbluth, James Blish, and Robert "Doc" Lowndes. Two best friends of my own age were fellow New Jerseymen, and we have stayed friends to this day: Lloyd Alpaugh, poet and technical editor, and George Fox, novelist and screenwriter, whose most famous work may be the film *Earthquake.* When I was not quite fifteen, Fox and I helped an older SF fan, Sam Moskowitz, organize the First Postwar Eastern Science Fiction Convention, held in Newark, which attracted an array of famous science fiction authors and editors.

This early exposure to science fiction filled me with a fresh desire to write for print. Part of this urge was gratified by my publishing fanzines, starting at age fifteen with a hectographed gazette called *Terrifying Test-tube Tales,* which enjoyed by mail a national circulation. By and by I graduated to a Speed-o-print duplicator, which printed in black ink from stencils, like a Mimeograph, and used it to publish a more ambitious fanzine, *Vampire,* which to my glee won a poll as number one SF fanzine in the country. Of course, the poll was conducted by a friend of mine. But I kept aspiring to write stories that some magazine would pay for. The nearest I came to early success, at age fifteen, was a grim tale submitted to *Planet Stories,* which the veteran pulpwood editor Malcolm Reiss liked well enough to order me to rewrite with a happy ending. But the story had been the fruit of adolescent gloom. Somehow, the happy ending killed it. Much later, when I was twenty-one, other pulp editors bought two stories for a penny a word: Raymond A. Palmer *(Other Worlds)* and "Doc"

Kennedy as a navy journalist on liberty in Norfolk, Virginia, 1955

Lowndes *(Science Fiction Quarterly)*. To my chagrin, I never sold anything to John W. Campbell, Jr., revered editor of *Astounding,* even though my mother's cousin, Catherine Tarrant, was the magazine's assistant editor. After I finished college, my dreams of becoming a professional science fiction writer gradually evaporated, and I retired and left the field to Ray Bradbury and Isaac Asimov.

At last, bombs showered on Pearl Harbor and, as expected, World War II was declared. Some of the young men in our neighborhood went away. I was twelve at the time, too young to serve. There were ration books and little blue and red coins with which to claim a share of scarce items like meat, butter, shoes, and gasoline. There were blackouts, when we would turn off our lights and sit in the dark, waiting to be attacked by Nazi bombers. My mother brushed up on her nursing skills and joined the Civil Defense Corps. During blackouts she would venture out to find people pretending to be injured, and put bandages and splints on them. One night, a victim never did get found, and finally, after lying for hours in a ditch, he rose in disgust and went home.

If at first the war seemed distant, having little direct impact on my dreamy life, it made itself felt gradually. In the beginning I worried that the Axis powers might win, and for a while it seemed that our forces in the Pacific were no match for the Japanese. But as the war went on, America's chances brightened. I would grab the afternoon paper, the *Newark Evening News,* as soon as it hit our front porch, to follow the progress of Patton's army in Africa. When I entered high school, every boy in gym class was expected to toughen up, like a Marine. We had to scale walls, jump hurdles, do calisthenics. I didn't mind—such routines were easier than trying to understand football. Mr. Roosevelt continued to be president, looking grimmer and grayer as the war went on. At last he died, to the nation's regret, and the horrific atom bomb leveled two Japanese cities and the war was over. My uncle Ed's son, cousin Lloyd Kennedy, a few years older than me, did not return home from the air force in Germany. He had been the most promising young artist I had ever known. High school kept me busy learning French from warm, friendly Miss Mary Toye and some classic English poetry from

cool, reserved Miss Cornelia Boyd, who did us a good turn by making us memorize passages from Chaucer and Shakespeare. In retrospect I wish I had taken Latin, but my counselor advised me to take general science. All I learned from the science course was that if you pump the air out of an empty varnish can, it will collapse.

I finished high school in 1946 and, to my surprise, was expected to go on to college. I didn't know my father had that kind of money, and indeed, he didn't. Nevertheless, I made my way to Seton Hall College in South Orange, mainly because the tuition was low and I could live at home and commute on the Lackawanna railroad. With my Speed-o-print duplicator, I earned my train fare by running a copy service.

Only a handful of my college classmates were, like me, fresh out of high school. Most were ex-soldiers or sailors going to school on the GI Bill. Some of those ex-servicemen hadn't cracked a book in years and had a terrible time with their lessons, so that I had an unfair advantage. In high school, I had rarely made the honor roll—I was too busy drawing comic books—but at Seton Hall I must have looked like a serious student. I became editor of the student newspaper and wrote a column of wretched jokes for it.

In my senior year of college I took education courses and practice-taught English and history at Dover High. One lesson plan was designed to teach the causes of the First World War. I borrowed a tape recorder and told the class we'd do a radio broadcast recreating the burning of the Serbian embassy at Sarajevo, emulating a popular radio program of the time, "You Are There." All went well until, during the taping of the broadcast, I smelled real smoke. A boy in the class who talked mostly in grunts—I hadn't known what to do with him, so I made him the sound man—had tossed a match into a wastebasket full of papers. "What do you think you're doing?" I yelled. "I was trying to make it sound real," he said lamely. The wastebasket, which was made of tar or something, melted down, filling the building with thick fumes. Bells rang. The principal came running. A fire extinguisher settled the blaze, but when, a few weeks later, I applied for a job at Dover High, the superintendent didn't bother to answer my application.

Let me fast-forward. Unable to compete for a teaching job with all the returning veterans, I decided to acquire more schooling, so I enrolled in Columbia University in New York, still commuting on the Lackawanna, taking the ferry boat from Hoboken to Barclay Street and then catching the subway uptown. Nearly five hours of each school day had to be spent in travel, but I managed to cram all my classes into three days. On days off I substitute-taught at local grade schools. I loved taking over a class of third graders. They were wonderfully easy to galvanize. In June 1951 I acquired a master's degree in English and, having run out of draft deferments (this was during what was then called the Korean Emergency), enlisted in the navy for the minimum hitch, four years. *Moby Dick* must have lured me to the sea, and the memory of Ocean Grove's crashing breakers.

I ended up a navy journalist, after a course of training at Great Lakes, Illinois, located between Chicago and Milwaukee—cities I was happy to be acquainted with. I would spend weekends in Chicago, sometimes economizing by bunking for free at the Jesus Saves Mission on South State Street, on a cot beside homeless men, and at dawn listening to a sermon over coffee and doughnuts. Eventually, the navy packed me off to Newport, Rhode Island, to the staff of the Atlantic Fleet Destroyer Force aboard the USS *Yosemite,* a destroyer tender that ventured out onto the ocean only once a year. I began seeing the world, though, by making cruises on destroyers—top-heavy little ships that shuddered and rolled and pitched their way through storms. Armed with a cumbersome Speed Graphic press camera, I would photograph each crewman for his hometown newspaper. One such assignment took me on a five-month cruise aboard the destroyer *Compton.* We toured the Mediterranean from the Rock of Gibraltar to Izmir, Turkey, with more stops in Cannes, Naples, Taranto, Venice, Athens, and Oran, Algeria. If World War II had once seemed distant, its lingering effects were now clear. In port in Augusta Bay, Sicily, hungry men fought with seagulls for our ship's garbage, and in the street little begging boys would cling to the sailors' arms. One of these clingers made off with my wristwatch, but I figured he needed it more than I did. On other cruises, the navy provided my first glimpses of London and Paris, two cities in which I would later spend whole years; Scotland, Holland, and the Caribbean.

"At the time of my first adult book," 1961

Going on cruises was such a soft job that I almost felt guilty. All my picture-taking done, I would be left with nothing to do. When the ship was at sea, I published a daily news sheet, copying Associated Press news stories received on the ship's teletype, adding jokes and cartoons, and had the joy of seeing the crew eagerly jostle for copies. What writer wouldn't delight in having an audience so enthusiastic? But with spare time still, I found myself writing verse. All it took was a pencil and paper. For inspiration I reread the poems of the great Irish poet William Butler Yeats, whose work I had first encountered at Columbia.

During my last year in the navy, while shorebound at Norfolk (Virginia) Naval Air Station, I sent three poems off to a magazine I knew printed poems, the *New Yorker,* and two of them were taken. Encouraged by this success, I dreamed of one day writing enough poems to make a book. To distinguish myself from the better-known Joe Kennedys, I had stuck a fictitious X on my byline and, ever since, have been stuck with it.

The dream of having a published book didn't become real until 1961, while I was a graduate student at the University of Michigan. I began work on a Ph.D. in English there in 1956, after a post-navy year at the University of Paris. Michigan holds an annual Hopwood Contest, named for Avery Hopwood, author of popular Broadway farces like *Up in Mabel's Room,* who established cash prizes to encourage writing less profitable than his own. In the year my collection won the poetry contest, a literary agent from New York, Naomi Burton, a bright, kind, tough-minded Englishwoman, came to town scouting for talent, and she picked up my winning poetry manuscript and tried to sell it. Within a year or two Naomi moved on to the publishing house of Doubleday as a senior editor, where she brought out my poems, *Nude Descending a Staircase,* whose title poem is named for a painting by Marcel Duchamp.

X. J. Kennedy caricature by Hinton for the Los Angeles Times Book Review, *1985*

Emboldened by having a book accepted, I plucked up courage to propose marriage to Dorothy Mintzlaff, a fellow graduate student from Milwaukee whom I loved very much because she thought I was funny. We were married in January 1962, dropped out of Michigan's doctoral program together, and lived poor as church mice for the next few years. Determined to make my way as a teaching poet, I took a job at the Woman's College of the University of North Carolina. The shining star of the English department was a celebrated poet and critic also known for his children's books, Randall Jarrell. He didn't much like my poetry, but he was gracious. Almost exactly one year after we were married, our daughter Kathleen was born. We used to wheel her baby carriage down magnolia-lined Spring Garden Avenue. North Carolina has one of the world's lovelier springs.

One of the rewards of being a parent is getting to read books aloud to your kids. Over the years, I got to read a whole bunch of wonderful books that way, books I hadn't ever read before—the adventures of Babar and Madeline and Curious George, the picture books of Bill Peet, Ezra Jack Keats, Richard Scarry, and John Burningham. I was obliged to read some of those books over and over so many times that to this day I practically have them by heart.

After that year in Greensboro, I was offered a better-paying job at Tufts University, in Medford, Massachusetts, and we moved into a ground-floor flat in low-cost housing near campus. The neighborhood overflowed with small children, fostered by the faculty, so many that students soon nicknamed our block of West Somerville's Curtis Street "Rabbit Row." While we lived there, two of our four boys were born. I was assigned to teach a year-long course in modern poetry and the poetry-writing workshop. I taught at Tufts for fourteen years.

After work on textbooks became so time-consuming that I had to quit teaching, we remained in the Boston area. Still, we have had memorable departures. One year we lived on Balboa Island in Newport Beach, California, while I guest-taught at the University of California, Irvine. Another year we lived on a grant in London, in postal zone Northwest 2, and drove all over the South of England and around Ireland and vacationed in Venice. The kids had a great time riding in gondolas and feeding the pigeons in St. Mark's Square. Still another year, I was invited to teach at Leeds Univer-

*"Visiting Hastings School, where students made statuettes representing characters
from* The Owlstone Crown," *Lexington, Massachusetts, 1985*

sity, and we lived in Baildon, a village in Yorkshire on the edge of a rocky moor. That was
a stupendous year for the kids, though they
had to wear school uniforms and sometimes
lunch on pilchard, an unengaging fish. On
weekends, all seven of us would pile into our
used compact car, which wouldn't start unless
we got out and pushed it, to visit the steep
hilly village of Haworth, where the novel-writ-
ing Brontë sisters had lived, or climb around
the stones of ruined abbeys.

In the early seventies, I was feeling downcast about my poetry for big people. Rhyme
and meter, which I loved, had gone out of
style, and the loud howls of the Beat Generation now echoed through the land. Then an
amazing thing happened. I had included two
poems for children in my *Nude Descending* book.
(I must have been inspired by a number of
American poets of a generation before mine
who wrote much fine verse for kids—John Ciardi,
Theodore Roethke, William Jay Smith.) One was
called "King Tut":

King Tut
Crossed over the Nile
On stepping stones
Of crocodile.

King Tut!·
His mother said,
You'll get wet feet.
King Tut is dead

And now King Tut,
Tight as a nut,
Keeps his big fat Mummy shut.

King Tut,
Tut, tut.

This nonsensical ditty had the good fortune to appeal to the noted poet and anthologist for children Myra Cohn Livingston, who
put it into one of her compilations. She wrote
and asked me if I had any more where that
came from, so I sent her a few samples. Mrs.
Livingston showed them to her own editor-pub-

lisher, Margaret K. McElderry, who to my astonishment asked whether I had enough poems to make a whole book. Heartened, I came up with the manuscript for *One Winter Night in August,* which Margaret published in 1975, illustrated by David McPhail.

The book drew invitations to visit elementary schools, an experience that opened my eyes. Though I had been feeling downcast about the future of rhymed verse, meeting kids cheered me greatly. They and I seemed to share a fondness for the chime of a rhyme and the bounce of a regular rhythm. Those are among the most spellbinding possible elements of poetry, I believe, and although many serious poets of the day had dismissed such formal constraints as old hat, I felt renewed in my faith that they work upon a reader or a listener unconsciously. I found out another thing in reading to kids. They are disarmingly frank in their reactions. If poems bore them, they immediately act bored. On the other hand, they are quick to display their approval.

One Winter Night in August soon led to another collection, *The Phantom Ice Cream Man.*

Dorothy M. Kennedy

Mail from kids started to arrive, not all of it assigned by teachers, either. I was hooked. More books of verse for children followed, including the three-book series *Brats, Fresh Brats,* and *Drat These Brats!,* and two books of more or less realistic verse about childhood, *The Forgetful Wishing-Well* and *The Kite that Braved Old Orchard Beach.* An eleventh book of verse for kids is forthcoming: a series of limericks about a man who does everything backwards, *Uncle Switch.* Margaret McElderry has persisted in her encouragement. She is an editor of the old school. She really reads manuscripts closely, and goes over them firmly yet sympathetically. I couldn't have got far, either, without the kind and persistent efforts of my longtime literary agent, Marilyn Marlow, of Curtis Brown Ltd.

People often assume that writers can't have made up anything, and they ask whether my verse about kids and families is all based on our kids and our family. A few experiences may have suggested poems: taking car trips and staying in motels, flying a kite at Maine's Old Orchard Beach, watching melting snow flood our backyard. One poem, "A Different Door," is about our cat Smoky, who, when forced by rain to stay inside, used to prowl restlessly from front door to back door. Several experiences as a parent have set off poems, like one about a mechanically incompetent father trying to fix a kid's bike. And some derive from memories of my own childhood—such as "Art Class," in which a boy chafes when an art teacher orders him to draw a tree in a dull, mechanical way. But most things that happen in my poems never happened in life. In the nonsense poems, wherein characters jump into cement mixers and dryers and things blow up and hurl people through roofs, there is no truth to speak of. Most poems, I find, don't begin from ideas, but from a line of words that swim into my head, which I then try to rhyme. Poetry for me is a matter of fooling around with words, seeing what will happen. Often whatever happens will take me by surprise.

One book, *The Beasts of Bethlehem,* has a curious history. In 1963 when we lived in Greensboro and I was wondering how to pay the doctor for delivering Katie, the literary editor of *Glamour* magazine invited a poem for their Christmas issue. So I had an idea: there's a legend that on Christmas Eve animals can talk. All those animals said to be present at the Nativity—

"Our growing Kennedy family: (back row, from left) Matt, Dave, Kate; (front row) Dan and Josh," 1980

what would they say if they spoke? *Glamour* published the poem, and the doctor was paid for assisting at Katie's nativity. Then, many years later, my good friend Michael McCurdy, the splendid woodcut artist, who was once a student of mine at Tufts and who loves to draw animals, asked me if I had any animal poems he might illustrate. After a false try, I remembered the Christmas poem, which I had always wished had gone on longer. I went back to it and imagined some other animals who might have been spectators at Bethlehem—a camel, a bat, a mosquito, a donkey, a beetle, even a worm. Michael plunged into the task and a Christmas book resulted, exactly thirty years after the poem first appeared in brief form. Some books just don't happen overnight.

The only novel for children I've published to date wouldn't exist if it weren't for our family. One time, we were vacationing on Cape Cod, only to be cabin-bound by days of pouring rain. To pass the time, I began spinning a yarn about a strange country whose center is a giant moon-

flower. It was overrun by menacing stone owls, who rolled along like upright ballpoint pens. The main characters were a couple of twins, Timothy and Verity Tibb. Together with their friends Fardels Bear and Lew Ladybug, a tough-talking private detective no bigger than a split pea, they finally overcame the bad guys and at the end found mind-blowing happiness.

For years after that blighted vacation, our kids kept asking, "When are you going to write down the story about the moonflower?" The eventual result was *The Owlstone Crown*, which Margaret McElderry brought out in 1983. It took a long time to write and rewrite. Some scenes presented difficulty, like one told from the point of view of Verity, who is legally blind. But of all my books, it remains my favorite. At the Ethical Culture School in New York City, where the kids give a prize every year to the new book they themselves like best, it was their choice. Besides, they invited Margaret McElderry and me to come see them act out a scene from the book, in which the twins first meet the villains Raoul Owlstone and the Baroness Ratisha von Bad Radisch. Although at this writing *The Owlstone Crown* is out of print and findable only in libraries, some teachers and librarians still read it aloud, and I continue to get a trickle of letters from people who care for it.

In constructing *The Owlstone Crown,* I was a bumbling amateur. I tried to cram the story with every interesting thing I could imagine, including a giant invisible eagle and a wonderful aircraft that the kids fly around in—a little blue blimp. In its first version, the book ended up too long by about 15,000 words. Margaret plied her wise blue pencil and I chopped the manuscript down to size. The final version was a much brisker story. But I had this big chunk of wordage left over. After too long a delay—by now, some kids who first read *The Owlstone Crown* in 1982 must have kids of their own—I wove the leftover part into a new Tim and Verity adventure, *The Eagle as Wide as the World,* which Margaret plans to bring out. Luckily, my daughter Kate had spent time in the desert, watching bald eagles nest, working for the State of Arizona, and she saved me from a lot of mistakes about eagles and helped make the descriptions of them accurate. A story may be fantastic as a green-cheese moon, but to convince a reader its smallest detail has to sound true.

As a writer, I've sometimes felt like Gaul: divided into parts. Besides doing verse for adults and verse for children, and some fiction for both audiences, I have ground out enough book reviews and literary criticism to choke a horse, as well as several college textbooks. The longest-running textbook is *An Introduction to Poetry,* first published in 1966 and currently in an eighth edition, now with Dana Gioia as coauthor. Over the years, more than one and a half million students have used it. The book deals with one element of poetry at a time: elements such as rhythm, sound, formal shape, and imagery. And I wondered: Couldn't a book for children do the same?

This line of thought led to *Knock at a Star: A Child's Introduction to Poetry,* written together with wife Dorothy. It tries to offer an engaging way into poetry for kids of eight to twelve to read on their own. Dorothy and I had heard it said that when reading poems with kids you shouldn't analyze, shouldn't take things apart. To do that to a poem, went the conventional wisdom, would be like crassly tearing the wings

off some delicate butterfly. We didn't know why that should be so. In our experience, kids often like to tear things down to see what makes them work, and they like to look closely at a bird or a colored rock or a pet animal. How could it hurt to analyze poems, we figured, as long as you didn't run on boringly long, and you put the poems back together again?

Encouraged by the reception given *Knock at a Star*—the little book has remained in print since 1982—Dorothy and I went on to gather a bookful of poems simple enough to read aloud to small fry: *Talking Like the Rain.* As an anthologist, Dorothy has much better taste that I do. She has since brought out an anthology on her own.

For more than twenty-seven years, we have lived in Bedford, Massachusetts, a colonial town in between Lexington and Concord, not to be confused with New Bedford, the former whaling port, to which our mail is sometimes misdirected. Our kids are now grown. All five are terrific people, I think, though I admit I'm prejudiced, and they all have keen, offbeat senses of humor. Whenever they assemble, the laughs are plentiful. Kate has held a series of outdoor jobs, including a stint as a nature lecturer at the bottom of Grand Canyon. To go down there and visit her by muleback, I had to lose ten pounds. She is, incidentally, a capable writer and at the moment works in a bookshop in Exeter, New Hampshire. Son Dave is a married math teacher at Glenville State College in West Virginia. Son Matt is a travel consultant in Colorado Springs. Son Dan is a rock drummer, a composer, and a music teacher. At the moment the youngest, Josh, twenty-three, is working to become a cartoonist and book illustrator. He and I have just done a picture book together, *The Enchanted Roller Coaster,* which I hope will appear sooner or later.

Every once in awhile, I pass through Dover, visit my mother and father's graves, and drop in on Betty Griffin, now Mrs. Sebold, who still lives in the same house next door. Betty is like a sister to me; her brothers Neil and Bud like big brothers. Betty used to push me around in my baby carriage. It was Bud who taught me to drive a car and not dawdle when turning a corner. The New York metropolis has crept out farther into New Jersey now, practically swallowing Dover, but Baker Avenue still looks very nearly the same, and the Rockaway River still flows dependably.

Writing verse, even verse for children, brings in hardly enough money to keep a bird alive, unless the bird's name is Shel Silverstein. In recent years, Dorothy and I have earned most of our daily bread by writing textbooks. Most of our textbooks were begun under the stewardship of Charles Christensen, former English editor for Little, Brown and later publisher of Bedford Books, a genius at his trade. Writing textbooks is a task far different from writing poems and stories. It isn't what you might call creative writing, for your goal is to supply teachers not with what *you* want, but what they want. And, unlike children's books, textbooks have to be revised regularly. Lately, Dorothy and I have turned over most of the work of revising our textbooks to skilled collaborators, so that nowadays, after thirty years of steady textbook-writing, I have the freedom at last to write whatever I like.

Enough ideas are steaming on the back burner to keep me working for the rest of my days, or until the advent of senility. I'll die happy if I can churn out a few more children's books, one or two more collections of adult poems, a book or two of essays, a book of short stories, a novel, and—who knows? Some mornings when I get up and contemplate all the work still to be done, I feel as ancient as a sea turtle. Other mornings, I feel eighteen again, on the brink of a fresh career, and I run lickety-split downstairs to my study and eagerly fire up my word processor.

BIBLIOGRAPHY

FOR CHILDREN

Fiction:

The Owlstone Crown, illustrated by Michele Chessare, McElderry/Atheneum, 1983.

Poetry:

One Winter Night in August and Other Nonsense Jingles, illustrated by David McPhail, Atheneum, 1975.

The Phantom Ice Cream Man: More Nonsense Verse, illustrated by David McPhail, Atheneum, 1979.

Did Adam Name the Vinegarroon?, illustrated by Heidi Johanna Selig, Godine, 1982.

(With Dorothy M. Kennedy) *Knock at a Star: A Child's Introduction to Poetry,* illustrated by Karen Ann Weinhaus, Little, Brown, 1982.

The Forgetful Wishing-Well: Poems for Young People, illustrated by Monica Incisa, McElderry/Atheneum, 1985.

Brats, illustrated by James Watts, McElderry/Atheneum, 1986.

Ghastlies, Goops, and Pincushions: Nonsense Verse, illustrated by Ron Barrett, McElderry/Macmillan, 1989.

Fresh Brats, illustrated by James Watts, McElderry/Macmillan, 1990.

The Kite that Braved Old Orchard Beach: Year-Round Poems for Young People, illustrated by Marian Young, McElderry/Macmillan, 1991.

The Beasts of Bethlehem, illustrated by Michael McCurdy, McElderry/Macmillan, 1992.

(With Dorothy M. Kennedy) *Talking Like the Rain: A Read-to-me Book of Poems,* illustrated by Jane Dyer, Little, Brown, 1992.

Drat These Brats!, illustrated by James Watts, McElderry/Macmillan, 1993.

Uncle Switch: The Topsy-turvy Man, illustrated by John O'Brien, McElderry/Simon & Schuster, forthcoming.

FOR ADULTS

Poetry:

Nude Descending a Staircase, Doubleday, 1961.

Growing into Love, Doubleday, 1969.

Bulsh, Burning Deck (Providence, Rhode Island), 1970.

Breaking and Entering, Oxford University Press (London), 1971.

Emily Dickinson in Southern California, Godine, 1974.

Celebrations after the Death of John Brennan, Penmaen Press (Lincoln, Massachusetts), 1974.

(With James E. Camp and Keith Waldrop) *Three Tenors, One Vehicle: A Book of Songs,* Open Places (Columbia, Missouri), 1975.

French Leave: Translations, Robert L. Barth (Florence, Kentucky), 1983.

Missing Link, Scheidt Head Press, 1983.

Hangover Mass, Bits Press, 1984.

Cross Ties: Selected Poems, University of Georgia Press, 1985.

Winter Thunder, Robert L. Barth, 1990.

Dark Horses, John Hopkins University Press, 1992.

Jimmy Harlow, Salmon Run Press, 1994.

Textbooks:

(With James E. Camp) *Mark Twain's Frontier,* Holt Rinehart, 1963.

An Introduction to Poetry, Little, Brown, 1966, eighth edition with Dana Gioia, HarperCollins, 1994.

Messages: A Thematic Anthology of Poetry, Little Brown, 1973.

An Introduction to Fiction, Little, Brown, 1976, sixth edition with Dana Gioia, HarperCollins, 1995.

Literature: An Introduction to Fiction, Poetry, and Drama, Little, Brown, 1976, sixth edition with Dana Gioia, HarperCollins, 1995.

(With Dorothy M. Kennedy) *The Bedford Reader,* Bedford/St. Martin's, 1982, fifth edition with Dorothy M. Kennedy and Jane Aaron, 1994.

(With Dorothy M. Kennedy) *The Bedford Guide for College Writers,* Bedford/St. Martin's Press, 1987, fourth edition with Dorothy M. Kennedy and Sylvia A. Holladay, 1996.

Editor:

(With James E. Camp and Keith Waldrop) *Pegasus Descending: A Book of the Best Bad Verse,* Macmillan, 1971.

Tygers of Wrath: Poems of Hate, Anger, and Invective, University of Georgia Press, 1981.

Other:

X. J. Kennedy issue, *The Epigrammatist* Vol. 5, No. 2, August 1994.

Constance Levy

1931-

Constance Levy, 1991

Poets are always poking their minds into things, feeding their curiosity. Their antennae twist in all directions. Nothing is safe from their probing eyes, their sniffing noses, their alert ears. This is particularly true of poets who write for children, as I do. Like children, we delight in discovering the world, and no matter how much we grow up and grow wiser, we try to hold onto the childhood enthusiasm—playfulness and sense of wonderment—that follows along with the curiosity.

There may be some people who can keep their enthusiasm and discoveries to themselves. I knew very early in life that I was not one of them. When I had things to tell, the words refused to be contained; out they poured with barely a breath taken, and so rapidly and in such a jumble that my mother or father would say, "Slow down, we can't understand a word you're saying." When I learned to write I discovered a new way to use some of the words. I could arrange them into poems. I'm still bursting to share what's on my mind, and I still like to do it in poems.

I'm still curious, too, about all things, including people. If we were to meet, I would be as interested in knowing about you as you would be of me. (I assume you would want to know about me because you are reading this.) I, too, am curious about writers. I like to read about them and see if we share some characteristics. Reading about other poets for children, I have cried out, "So do I!" or "I feel that way, too!" or "I've said the same thing!" Even though we may have vastly different life experiences and backgrounds, some mysterious element in our chemistry seems to match. I like mysteries like that.

Now then, who am I? Researching myself for this autobiography, I'm finding out. A quick history by way of hair would go like this: I started out with light brown hair that turned dark as I grew older and has become a soft silvery shade of gray that I rather like. The light-haired person began writing poems, but it was the silvered one who got her first book published. Inside the head that has carried the hair through all its changes are memories. Some have their emotions still attached and stir my senses, flooding me with warm recollections (even tears) and letting me feel undercurrents of old fears. It was surprising to find there was so much there, eager to be revealed.

What an amazing little cabinet the brain is to contain so many old things and keep them so fresh! All you have to do is reach down deep and there they are. As I dug them out I realized that even some of the new poems have old roots, and that my memories of elementary school years have kept their color best. It may be no coincidence that this is the age group I write for most of all, and that is where I will begin.

I can still feel myself as a child walking to Lachterman's grocery and meat market at the corner, down a long street of apartments bordered with large sycamore trees (beware of birds overhead was my motto). I'm on my way to pick up our order, enjoying just looking around, carefully avoiding stepping on the sidewalk cracks ("Step on a crack and you'll break your mother's back" was a childhood chant) and maybe finding a penny, or a nickel. Once I found a dollar! A dollar, then, would buy a whole pound of corned beef (and you could watch it being sliced by the machine) or one hundred pieces of penny candy at A. P. Cohen's drugstore where, straight ahead as you entered, there stood a large glass display case containing the jewels of my childhood. Among the many selections were jawbreaker balls in rich colors that changed as you sucked the layers off, Buttermill caramels (I called them car-mels, but radio commercials pronounced it car-a-mels—the more delicious-sounding way), Tootsie Rolls, miniature soda bottles of chewable wax with juice inside (the taste didn't last, though), and Fleers Double Bubble bubble gum with a comic sheet insert. I still get carried away by the sight and taste of the memory.

Now I'm at the meat counter in the back of Lachterman's, entranced by Al the butcher's preparation of veal chops or ground beef. There is the heavy door of the cooler, the large slabs of pink-red meat (that to me were never dead cow, just meat), Al's artful and brave wielding of the saber-sharp knife, slicing perfectly through smooth meat, hacking bone with one of his mighty cleavers—whack! I follow every movement, the brushing aside of scraps, the grinding of hunks of chuck pushed into the hand grinder—ground twice, my mother always requested. It was all so practiced, so sure, even to the wrapping in oiled brown paper that completed the production.

Why do I recall that so vividly? It was, as I think about it now, a polished performance of an artist working with his hands, a sculptor of sorts in an exotic medium, and a real adventure for this attentive viewer. I'm still drawn to skilled hands: pianists, string players, carpenters, cooks, even spiders who use their feet as hands:

Technique

I watched a spider wrap her gnat
With such a flood of tidiness.
She twiddled all her nimble feet
And seemed to do a dance in place

While tying round a stream of thread
As pale and white as soft-spun milk,
So careful not to miss one step
Or spill a single
Drop
Of silk!

(in *A Tree Place
and Other Poems*)

The Cook

With a twist
of hand and wrist
in one smooth stroke

he flips
two slippery eggs
in the pan
without breaking
a yolk!

(in *When Whales Exhale
and Other Poems*)

Going to the grocery was my job every day after school, down the three flights of stairs from our apartment at the top of 5793 Westminster Place in St. Louis, just a few doors from Hamilton Elementary School in a neighborhood I loved for all of the twenty-one years I lived there. Ours, like most of those in our neighborhood, was a three-story, six-family apartment, and for reasons of economy (the depression of 1929 was not yet over when I was born) my parents, older sister, Gloria, and I shared an apartment with my maternal grandmother, Sarah Seigel, the only grandparent I ever knew, and mother's brother and sister, my much loved uncle Maury and aunt Freda. I almost knew mother's father, but he died shortly after I was born. Even though the furnace often failed us and the plumbing left much to be desired (and the roaches terrified me), it was, for me, the perfect place to grow up, with playmates in abundance, the school nearby, and within walking distance of the city's major park, Forest Park.

Constance with her older sister Gloria, about 1934

Because my grandmother lived with us, we were the extended family headquarters. Family get-togethers meant good food and piano playing by Uncle Jake (who could play anything if you hummed the tune), singing by everyone, jokes and laughter and lively conversation. Uncle Maury was quite clever with words and a good writer. He was the one who would help me with writing assignments. Aunt Freda, who was very pretty (ninety-one years old at this writing, she is still pretty), had a beautiful trained soprano voice and loved reading books. She was like another older sister to me as Maury was like an older brother. Mother and Grandma were the cooks, Grandma unquestionably the matriarch. It was she who called Mr. Frumson, the landlord, if the furnace wasn't working, and people listened to her. It was only later as I grew older that I began to know of her history, the story of a courageous woman, like many of her generation of immigrants.

If you were to ask me what I would change about myself at that time in my life I would scream out, "Practice the piano!" which I, who showed promise, did not do seriously. How I have regretted my laziness; how I wish I could play the piano now! Believe me, I have told my children and grandchildren that they should not make the same mistake.

I know now that the seeds of my love of laughter and jokes and my delight in the playfulness and pleasures of words and lively conversation were planted and nourished in those early years. I feel so fortunate to be able to enjoy such delightful times now with my own family.

Poetry, too, was introduced early. From my earliest memories my mother recited poems to me that she had learned in school. She loved the lines "Hearts, like doors, can open with ease / with very, very little keys." I knew the poems of Eugene Field, Robert Louis Stevenson, Rachel Field, Christina Rossetti, Vachel Lindsay, and others. Teachers read us poems often, and every season, every holiday, was celebrated with at least one poem. I was moved to write my own verses when I was six years old, and from first grade through elementary school I was known as the class poet. Each poem was a game, a word puzzle to solve, a rhyme to satisfy my ear. I wrote about everything I saw and thought about.

I had only a few toys and needed no more. A miniature grocery store, of three sides made of painted tin with some tiny cans and boxes of grocery items was one I vividly remembered. I had the out-of-doors and books from the library. I liked fairy tales and folktales best. I fondly remember *Peter Rabbit* by Beatrix Potter, *Little Black Sambo* by Helen Bannerman, *Millions of Cats* by Wanda Gág, and *Snipp, Snapp and Snurr and the Red Shoes* by Maj Lindman. Later, as I was growing up, I read books like the "Nancy Drew" stories. Most of these are still read and loved by children today, which shows that good literature is timeless. We had a set of *The Book of Knowledge* that had information and stories I enjoyed. I had paper, pencils, crayons, and a set of watercolor paints. My father entertained us with riddles and hand and finger games and tricks. Mother could make toys from scraps, such as a lively mouse from a handkerchief or an old sock, and I could go outside and almost always find someone to play with.

Inside, we played board games like checkers and Monopoly and many card games. Decks of playing cards were also good for building card houses, which required careful balancing and a light touch. A breath would blow them over. I remember practicing that a lot.

The seasons provided the same kind of pleasures that children still enjoy. Winters were sledding, ice-skating on the lakes in Forest Park, snowmen, snowball fights, snow forts, all leading to hot chocolate and warming our frozen feet by the hissing, clanking radiators. Heat was coal, burned in the basement furnace. I learned, even before school lessons taught me the names, that coal was either hard (anthracite) or soft (bituminous) because only the soft was good to write with. We scavengers scrambled for left-over scraps when the coal truck dumped its load. Soft burning coal was later banned as a terrible air pollutant.

Summers were the best of all. We begged ice from the milkman, who used it to keep the milk cold. If it looked dirty we'd wait un-til the dirt melted off to suck on it. When it was terribly sticky-hot we would run and play under the lawn sprinkler or beg the janitor to fill a washtub with water for us to sit in.

The Lawn Sprinkler

We dash to the sprinkler
that sputters and spouts.
We scream from the cold stings,
run and shout.
Like bees to a flower,
we spend the day
buzzing around
in the waterspray.
Then, in the sun,
we lounge about
like a family of frogs
who are all croaked out!

(in *When Whales Exhale
and Other Poems*)

We sold lemonade, as children still do. Our lemonade stands taught me many things about the selling game: fresh, homemade lemonade did not sell as well as the newer novelty, Kool Aid; you had to pick a spot where many people passed by; you should not drink too much of it yourself; sending the younger kids around to attract customers with their cuteness was good business practice. There was more, too, and we carefully employed every strategy we learned. We'd divide our profits and race to Cohen's to spend it on candy.

The summer activity program at Hamilton School provided all sorts of crafts, games, and shows to perform in. One year they had audi-tions for a new radio program sponsored by the St. Louis Board of Education. I won one of the parts. I had always wanted to be an actress, and at last I was! I was eleven or twelve, I think. The weekly program was called "The Davis Family" and was on radio station WIL.

We rehearsed in a school far from where I lived and broadcast from a real studio in a tall office building. It was exciting for me, who wanted to be a Bette Davis or a Barbara Stan-wyck. After the first summer I grew tired of it, though. The scripts were boring to me, and the long distance to go for rehearsals kept me from other activities. The second year I de-clined the honor in favor of swimming lessons at the Y.

What I really wanted as an actress (and in my pretend life) was to be elegant and charm-ing and dress for dinner, like Bette and Bar-bara, and have long cigarette holders and trays of breakfasts in bed; however, all my dramatic roles, even in high school, were as little sister types.

My happy childhood was not without its wor-ries and fears. Fears are as much a part of childhood as joys. Children have special fears, often due to only partly understanding adult kinds of things. One of my sons, for example, feared volcanoes, which is a stretch of the imagi-nation living in Missouri. I had my secret fears, too; leprosy was one (after reading about it in *Life* magazine). I ran hot water over my fin-gers daily in the tub to be sure I had feeling (a symptom if you don't) and imagined the worst. I feared the basement where our stor-age lockers were, having once seen a rat there running alongside a dark wall.

When quite young I feared the three "men": the sandman, who in story and verse made you sleepy by tossing sand in your eyes; the bogey-man, reputed to be terribly dangerous to chil-dren because he might get you, whatever that meant (I never dared ask); then there was the old clothes man, who rolled his wooden cart through the neighborhood calling, "Alt Closs, alt Closs" as he shuffled along. He looked rather ragged to me, tired more likely, but I equated him with the bogeyman and stayed close to home when I heard his call. And there was the bulldog, Dike, who lived on the first floor, and though he was always on the leash out-doors, terrified me. When he sat in the win-dow he threatened me with his eyes. I tried to avoid his comings and goings.

And there were the annoying things: sticky hands (especially from eating oranges with lots of sweet juice; I'd try to lick it off but never successfully), wet sleeves, sock heels creeping down in my shoes, balls rolling into the sewer or flying over the back fence to the large yard full of streetcar tracks where the city streetcars were kept when off duty. One of us would have to crawl through the loose board, run out on the tracks and race back before being noticed. And there were my frequent illnesses. I still recall the frustrations of missing school and play and looking out of the window at the world of the well, as a hungry waif might look into a restaurant window.

We never lacked for games to play out-doors, games of skill and games of imagination, and hide-and-seek games. My favorite hiding game was "kick the can." Someone not yet found could run in and kick the can before "it" did, and everyone already caught would be free to hide again. Poor "it"! Trees always made great hiding places.

Hide-and-Seek

It's hide and seek.
I climb a tree
and from a leafy limb
I watch my seeker seeking me
and sneak a look at him.

The trunk is strong
to lean upon.
The leaves leave room to peek.
If it had apples for me, too,
I'd stay up here a week.

(in *A Tree Place and Other Poems*)

There was baseball, flipping baseball cards, "cops and robbers," and "cowboys and Indians." Our weapons were our hands used as guns, and somehow we could usually agree on whether or not our invisible shot actually "gottcha." No one wanted to be the bad guys because the good guys always won, so we took turns. What collective imaginations we had! I was pretty good at marbles and always had a special shooter, maybe a milky or agate. I can still hear the marbles clicking in their leather bag. They were such an assortment of beautiful jewel-like colors. When I watch the clustering of huge carp in the Japanese garden described in my poem "On the Bridge at the Japanese Garden," my mind drifts back to that other image and connects the two.

On the Bridge at the Japanese Garden

Fish of every color
in a splashy flashy show
gathering to catch the bits
of fish food that we throw.

Jostling acrobatic carp
jumbled in a bunch
in and out and underneath
eager for some lunch.

Even some on tippy-tails
mouths so opened wide
we can toss the food to them
right straight down inside.

(in *A Tree Place and Other Poems*)

Jacks and jump rope were reserved for girls. Boys rarely played those games, but girls could play boys' games, as I liked to do. I had little interest in dolls, except briefly a Betsy Wetsy strictly for the novelty; you fed her a bottle and she wet. After a few days she was all but forgotten.

My bicycle, a blue, balloon-tired Schwinn with coaster brakes, took me all over the neighborhood. There were fewer cars and, therefore, safer streets. With my friends I roller-skated, biked, or walked to Forest Park, often to the art museum, set in a beautiful spot on the best hill for sledding in winter and for rolling down in summer. I loved rolling down hills, and so did my children when they were small. Sometimes when I see a particularly appealing hill I still get the urge. Here are some lines from "On Rolling Down Grassy Hills" in *When Whales Exhale and Other Poems:* "It's the 'almost like flying' / feeling; / it's the speeding without really / trying; . . ."

Most of all, I liked the mummy in the museum. It had one ragged toe, showing something black underneath. My eyes bored through that spot trying to see the real mummy, exotic, scary—a real honest-to-goodness ancient dead person. So the first time my husband Monty and I visited the British Museum in London, where do you think I began my tour?

In the evening we had a schedule: clean up before dinner and listen to the radio programs, such as "Tom Mix" (he was a cowboy), "Little Orphan Annie," and "Jack Armstrong the All-American Boy." Don't laugh, it was my favorite. He went on great adventures to exotic places like the jungles of Mindanao. I could not only see the jungles, I could feel the fronds and moist heat and the fear of dark shadows. We had no television and developed our imaginations with those radio programs, creating our own mental images from the words and sound effects. Evening programs like "Suspense" and "The Shadow" linger with fond chills in my memory. I am still a great radio fan and avid supporter of public radio.

All the kids went to the Saturday matinee at the movies. I always hoped for a scary one, the scarier the better. Even if some parts were so terrifying I had to close my eyes, I still liked them. At least one short adventure serial accompanied every movie. They would always end with the hero in a terrible predicament that he could not possibly get out of, but always did in the next week's episode. Milk Duds chocolate-covered caramels (I still called them car-mels) were my choice of movie candy.

I was very thin and was told I ate like a bird, probably a sparrow. While the chubby kids heard the taunt "Fatty, fatty, two by four / can't get through the kitchen door," we skinny kids were called what sounded like "skinny-genected gas pipe." Now I think that must have been referring to the pipe on the gas stove that connected to the wall and should actually read "skinny connected gas pipe." Then, as may be true now, I was given to excesses in enthusiasm if I liked a certain food. Once, so hungry after an afternoon of swimming, I ate ten hot dogs. They were small ones, but ten is a large number for a "skinnygenected gas pipe." I didn't even feel full. I found a fly in one of them, but I was so hungry I pulled off that part and ate the rest. I was always finding foreign objects (mainly flies) in food. For that reason I would never eat raisins in anything. Loose ones were safe, but only after careful examination.

The only vegetables I liked then were raw ones. I still like to munch on raw carrots, turnips, broccoli stalks, and others, but my favorite was, and is, raw peas, English peas right out of the pods. Poetry is a wonderful outlet for things you want to shout from the rooftops so everyone will know. The poem "Rah, Rah Peas!" is a cheer for peas. It was written to tell the world how I feel about them, and though I wrote it when my children were small, my love affair with raw peas began long before, when I was small myself.

Rah, Rah Peas!

Don't say,
"Awww, peas!"
Try some
Raw peas!

New peas!
Sweet peas!
Great fresh
Treat—peas!

Zip the pods and
Pop 'em in
You won't stop
Once you begin!

You'll scream,
"More, Please!"
Rah! Rah!
Raw peas!

(in *I'm Going to Pet a Worm Today and Other Poems*)

Speaking of hair—as we did earlier—my hair was totally, completely straight with not a curve or a bend. Mother would roll it up in rag curls using strips of old cotton sheets or underwear, whatever was available. I wanted curls! Sometimes I was so vain I'd suffer the pain and sleep with the lumps all over my head.

My favorite things to do when I was outside with nothing to do were digging holes (when I was quite young) and watching ants (when I was young and all the way to now). Here is an excerpt from one of my ant poems:

Enough Is Enough

This little brown ant
found a blue jay's feather.
He is trying to do
what he can't—he will never
carry that feather away.

His mandible clamps on the barbs
like a lion to attack,
and he digs in his toes for the pull,
but the feather fights back! . . .

(in *I'm Going to Pet a Worm Today and Other Poems*)

Except for an awful kindergarten teacher (I still remember how mean she was), school was a pleasure I looked forward to each day. Hamilton School was just two more apartments and across a small street from our house. Women teachers could not marry and remain teachers then, a silly rule if ever I heard one, so some of the young teachers would stay only a short time. Most, however, had been there for many years and were really devoted to our education and welfare. In Miss Yule's first grade I taught myself to spell the longest word I ever saw, when she wrote CHRYSANTHEMUM on the blackboard. I liked the way it looked and sounded, and I was the only one who could spell it. My secret plan was to use the rhythm of each syllable and memorize it as if it were a poem: c-h-r-y(pause) s-a-n(pause) t-h-e(pause) m-u-m. I still have a fondness for the word.

Also in the first grade came my first experience with editing. I agonized over one line of a poem. Some things don't change; I often spend hours, days, even months working over a single line. The poem was titled, I believe, "When Winter Comes." I got stuck on the last line because of the question of whether to rhyme or not to rhyme. Here it is: "When winter comes the snow will fall / on trees and hillsides near. / The birds on wing achirping will sing / a goodbye song of—cheer?" No! They wouldn't be cheery, I thought; they were leaving for a long journey. I decided to sacrifice an easy rhyme for the sake of the integrity of the poem. The word I inserted after much struggle was "parting." I learned that lesson early. I love to rhyme, but it isn't rhyme alone that makes a poem.

In Miss Smith's third grade class I wrote more poems per day than at any other time in my life because she encouraged my writing and let me write to my heart's content. She loved poetry, too. I had received a double promotion into her class and skipped the part of second grade with weights and measures. I'm still weak on how many pounds and how many ounces and that sort of thing. All through the grades we memorized poems. It was easy and fun for me, even when the poems were beyond the interests and language of our age level. I never minded. I still carry some of them in my head and find them very good company.

How could I ever forget Miss Parker, and the exciting moments in her class? She was tall, stiffly corseted, and not one to show any emotion. There were two stunning events. One

"On the running board of Father's car,"
about 1939

was the episode of her horribly bloodshot eyes, the cause of which she chose not to share with us. I could not take my eyes off them, or hear what she was saying; a teacher who suddenly acquired mysterious red eyes can really be distracting for a child. What had happened, I wondered, does she know they are bloody? It seemed to last months, but it was probably a few weeks. Even that was not the best thing about Miss Parker. It was the day she opened her black handbag during a lesson to remove a handkerchief and suddenly let it drop to the floor as she screamed and jumped back. When it landed, a large, black cockroach crawled out in a big hurry and had the good judgment to make a fast getaway. I don't remember what happened next. All I remember to this day about that whole year were the bloodshot eyes and the way Miss Parker screamed and how that scared cockroach scrambled away. I still relish that memory.

Perhaps my favorite subject in school, and one that I am most grateful for, was diagramming sentences. These were skeletal reconstructions depicting the way words work in a sentence. There was a main line with subject on one side and predicate on the other. Phrases and clauses, adjectives, adverbs, and everything else hung on below or sat above in their proper places. We could see the bones. Patterns and rules became a game, with many occasions for heated debate about usage and placement. Much to my disappointment I have yet to find a classroom that still employs that effective method. I make mental reference to it frequently to solve usage problems. I'd like to shout that from the rooftops.

Throughout my childhood things were happening in the world that I didn't quite understand. We were always reminded that there were starving children in China; that is how we were urged to clean our plates and not waste. (I always felt guilty because I rarely cleaned mine.) Our parents spared us as much bad news as they could, but no one can hide a war. Even they were not fully aware of many of the horrors of World War Two. We didn't know the real extent of the Holocaust, but suddenly we stopped hearing from relatives in Russia and never heard from them again.

Everyone did what they could for the war effort. We saved cooking fats to be used for explosives, and all of the children made tight balls of tinfoil from gum wrappers to recycle for war materials. They were beautiful silver balls, and I competed with my classmates to have the largest, smoothest, most round one. Mother made bandages for the Red Cross. Meat was rationed, so "meatballs and spaghetti" meant spaghetti with one miniature meatball on top. German immigrant children entered our classrooms, some wearing odd styles of clothing, like leather short pants. I didn't understand why and probably never asked. They were just new children to play with. I accepted things the way they came; for a child, so much happens that he or she doesn't quite understand. Uncle Maury was called for his army exam. He was anxious to go and fight Hitler, as all the men I knew were, but he was rejected because of his broken nose. He was so disappointed. My best friend's older sister grieved for her fiancé who was killed in battle. After the Japanese bombed Pearl Harbor (on December 7, 1941), I listened to the United States Congress vote to declare war on Japan. Someone voted no, and that upset me very much. Did they want us to just give up? I wondered. And I remember one day arriving at the bicycle store to have a flat tire repaired just as the radio declared that President Franklin Roosevelt had died. I was devastated by the news and raced home immediately, walking my bike flat and all. Now I can fit my childhood memories into history.

On a wall of my home are formal portraits of both my parents' families, taken when my mother and father were children. I look at their faces and try to imagine their thoughts. My maternal grandmother wears a beautiful locket, not her own, however. It was one that the photographer let subjects wear so they would look prosperous. Mother, the oldest child, also wears a borrowed locket. Aunt Freda's locket was from a Cracker Jack box. But they look fine and proud and happy. In that photograph my grandfather wears a handlebar mustache and a broad smile, and he has a twinkle in his eye. He was a jovial fellow who enjoyed life and liked to tell jokes, I was told. He reminds me of my oldest son, Bob. My father's family portrait is in a darker shade and looks more formal, though that may have been the photographer's style. But my father's face shines out; his good nature shows.

My parents emigrated to this country when they were children; my mother, Esther Seigel, from Russia when she was seven and my father, Samuel Kling, from Lithuania, both around 1900. He was fourteen when he arrived with his older sister, Eva. The rest of his family, his parents and two brothers, arrived later. He took a job in a luggage factory and eventually saved enough to open a men's clothing store in East St. Louis, Illinois, across the Mississippi River from downtown St. Louis. My maternal grandfather worked in East St. Louis shoeing horses for a time until horses gave way to automobiles, and then he opened a grocery. It was he who introduced my parents to each other.

There must have been bitter times in my father's town of Kupishek, as he never seemed eager to tell much about his life there. He was a gentle, loving father to Gloria and me, and he just seemed to understand what children liked to do. He enjoyed taking us places, perhaps as he would have liked to do as a child. Every Sunday we went somewhere spe-

"My parents, Esther and Samuel Kling, with my firstborn, Robert, about 1954"

cial. Living near the major city park was an advantage, and he loved nature, but he had a car so we could also venture off on our jaunts. Many of his customers were farmers who brought their livestock to the stockyards near his store. My sister and I, city kids that we were, had a real education visiting a farm belonging to one of these customers, Ben Worth. We picked strawberries, fought off the bees and other bugs pestering us, and were fascinated with the chubby, pink-cheeked Worth children. Their aggressive pet goats frightened us a bit. They were always in the front yard so you couldn't avoid them, and they would eat, or try to eat, just about anything you had in your hand.

Most of our trips were to places out of doors. The park was my parents' favorite, and they took Gloria and me often. The zoo was there, and we knew all the animals and interesting parts. My favorite spot was the seal pond when the keeper arrived at feeding time with a bucket of fish and tossed them one by one for the seals to catch in their mouths. Not far from the zoo, at Art Hill Lake, we fed stale bread to the catfish, and, much to my annoyance, Mom or Dad would hold the back of my shirt like a leash so I wouldn't fall in. A gen-

eration later I did the same thing to my children. The car I remember most was big, square, and black with a running board—a Chevrolet, I think. Everyone had the same car. When you parked it, there would be a long string of identical cars, and people were always getting into the wrong one. Later the square design of cars changed to rounder, and running boards disappeared; too bad, I thought.

My mother was seven years old when she arrived in St. Louis from Fostov, Russia, with her mother and two younger brothers (three more siblings were born later) to join her father. My grandfather preceded them here by more than a year, which was a common practice. Sarah and the children had to follow later on their own, leaving their faithful dog Sirka behind as he tried to follow their departing wagon. Mother told me how they had a dangerous journey from one safe house to another, hiding in hay wagons and farmhouses along the way, slipping across borders at night to avoid the Russian soldiers. My grandmother was a brave and resourceful woman, as she had to prove many times in her early life. What they left in Russia, poverty and pogroms, in which members of her family were killed, was worse

The author with her twin sons, Donald and Edward; her mother (left); and her mother-in-law, Anne Brick

than the risks and hardships of coming to America. I often wonder if I could have been as brave and resourceful. Many times I have tried to imagine myself as my grandmother or my mother, living the lives they lived. When I see immigrants to our country now, I feel somehow connected to them and understand the difficulties they face.

Poetry played an important role in my mother's life. She said memorizing poems helped her learn the new language. The rhythms and shorter lines made words and sentences easier to remember. Immigrant children received no pampering when they enrolled in school. They were put in their classrooms and had to learn to speak the language. Life was very different here, and they all had much to learn. Mother told me many stories about their neighbors, the Rooneys, an Irish family who were very kind to them and taught them American ways. She spoke so lovingly of the Rooneys that I would pretend stories of meeting them and thanking them for their kindness.

They never went hungry, mother said. My grandmother could make delicious and filling meals, like magic, from very little. One chicken would feed the family of eight for dinner on Friday with plenty of leftovers the next day. She would make her mashed potatoes mouthwatering appealing with browned onions and a little schmaltz. She and my mother were both wonderful cooks. I, however, learned how to cook only after Monty and I were married, so the poor fellow had to suffer along till I polished my skills. I recall how Mother would sit on the edge of her chair at dinner, poised to jump up and serve someone. That always annoyed me; I wanted her to sit back like everyone else. When my children told me that I was doing the same thing, I laughed. I hadn't even been aware that I was sitting that way, ready to spring and fetch, too.

Mother had a knack for making scraped knees, disappointments, and fevers seem less daunting. She introduced me to the power of positive thinking with this chant that I would say over and over when I was sick: "Every day in every way / I'm getting better and better." And her delicious, crisp, brown-around-the-edges poppy seed cookies had a taste and crunchiness that fit my mouth perfectly and always made me feel good. There must have been some secret ingredient that she put in them. Maybe it was love.

I remember as much or more of my high school years but not with the same attachment, the same sweet nostalgia, as the earlier years. There is a certain magic that fades with so many new things that come into our lives. Mrs. Bridges, my favorite English teacher, still glows in my memory, though. She, too, loved poetry and had a voice and charm when she read a poem that made everyone listen because it came from her heart; fifty years later I can still picture her lovely face and hear her rich voice reading *Rime of The Ancient Mariner.* A child on one of my school visits told me that she liked the way I "told" the poems because I made them sound so delicious. I think that was what Mrs. Bridges did.

When I turned sixteen I was eligible for my first job. My friends and I all went downtown to the big department stores to apply for jobs as salesgirls. We were known as "extras" and worked on Saturdays. The salary was small, the benefits substantial (25 percent discount on all purchases), and I was feeling quite grown up and independent. I continued working there until I graduated from college and became a teacher. All learning is not from school; I found the experience very profitable in many ways, just as I did in my lemonade-stand days.

Washington University was within walking distance from home, a long walk but a nice one. I would take in the sights as I had on my walks to the grocery when I was small, and I let my thoughts wander and develop as I do to this day when I walk. But I wasn't thinking poetry then as I often do now when I walk; in fact, though I enjoyed reading poetry, I don't remember writing poems any more until I began teaching.

Monty (his real name is Monroe) and I met at a party given by a mutual friend when I graduated from Washington University. Monty had graduated a few years earlier and had been a navy fighter pilot in World War Two, which would have impressed me, I'm sure, but I barely noticed him that evening and didn't remem-

ber him at all sometime later when he called for a date. I was reluctant to go but finally accepted; a month later we were engaged. By that time I was teaching first grade. Monty had been a physics major and was working as a solid-state physicist. I had never taken a course in physics, so I wasn't quite sure exactly what that involved. Even many years later when he started his own company I hated it when someone asked me what my husband did for a living. It was too complicated to explain, and they never really understood it anyway. "He's in optoelectronics," I would say. "He makes photo detectors and light-emitting diodes and such," and I would be greeted with blank expressions, "Oh." Our children, on the other hand, have basic, easy-to-describe occupations: dentist (Robert), civil engineer (Carol, retired to be a mom), and three physicians (Kenneth, Donald, Edward).

Our brief courtship included a rally for Adlai Stevenson, who was running for president against Dwight Eisenhower. Monty presented me with a Stevenson button, which I wore proudly. Senator Joseph McCarthy was designated our evil person of the times, ruining the lives of many innocent people in government and in the arts whom he labeled dangerous communists. How I detested that man.

The day after we decided to get married, Monty received greetings from the U.S. Navy. It was the time of the Korean War, and they were calling up former pilots from the inactive

With husband Monty in Acadia National Park, Maine, 1994

reserves. A month after we were married he had to report for active duty. I left my teaching job before the semester ended to join him in Coronado, California, which is not a bad place to go if go you must! On our return, I took another job teaching second grade and retired when Bob was born. Then came Carol, Ken, and, together, Don and Ed. It was just the family we had both wanted.

Poetry was in the air again. Now I had my own children to enjoy, to play with, to teach, and to learn from. It was such fun to watch the way they related to each other (forgetting for the moment the illnesses, sleepless nights, spilled milk, worries, fights among the siblings, competition) and to see the world fresh and new again through their eyes. Just what a poet needs!

One day Don and Ed were petting worms and let me have a turn. They were fascinated with the way a worm would shrink and curl when touched and stretch out again afterwards. From this came the first draft of the poem that would years later become the title poem of my first book, *I'm Going to Pet a Worm Today and Other Poems:*

> I'm going to pet a worm today.
> I'm going to pet a worm. Don't say,
> "Don't pet a worm"—I'm doing it soon.
> Emily's coming this afternoon! . . .

The Emily of this poem was a childhood friend of mine, and somehow she and my sons' worm-petting joined forces to form the poem. One of the many mysteries and delights of writing poems is that they take on a life of their own as you write, and they surprise you with how they turn out.

With the children had come a renewed urge to write. I won a third prize in a *Writer's Digest* poetry contest for adult poetry, but I preferred the first- and second-prize poems to my own and decided my heart was really in writing children's poetry. And there it has remained. The volume of poems I had produced grew and grew, and I entertained thoughts of a book. Bob's nursery school teacher showed me a book of little poems by Myra Cohn Livingston, her first. Maybe I can do that, I thought, though I knew nothing about how to go about it and had no one to ask. I went about reading what I could find, checking the companies that published books I liked, and in my own amateur-

ish way began the process of submitting a manuscript. I had been successful in having a few poems published in teachers' journals beginning in 1959, but all I received from book publishers was rejection.

Meanwhile I was collecting books of children's poetry and began to volunteer at our elementary school to bring poetry to the children. I had been appalled to find that my children got almost no poetry in school. It seemed the teachers didn't know much about it. I carefully chose poems I felt children would enjoy listening to and would whet their appetites for more. The effort exceeded all my expectations. After my first visit in the classroom they anxiously awaited my next visit, eager to hear their favorites again and wanting new ones. Individual preferences became apparent and often surprising, and they were memorizing their favorites on their own. I received another wonderful surprise. Children began to hand me scraps of paper with their own poems that they had written during my visits. Once, reflecting on an un-

In the garden at the Peggy Guggenheim home and museum on the Grand Canal, Venice, Italy, 1994

usually cold day in spring, a first grader wrote: "In April it is spring / but winter takes a peep." Another first grader wrote these haiku-type observations of spring: "Spring / Kids are playing games / And the green grass." There was no doubt in my mind that children and poetry belonged together. Somehow I would have to do something to bring that about.

When the children were in school, I decided to go back to school, too. I wasn't sure about a master's degree, which I eventually earned, but I knew I wanted to take literature courses, poetry classes, and workshops that I had not taken before. I was hungry to learn. When I read that the poet Howard Nemerov was coming to St. Louis to teach at Washington University, I was determined to take his poetry class and enrolled as a part-time student. I was the only older person in my class, and I knew my skills were rusty after being out of school for twenty years. And there were fear, insecurity, and my old undependable typewriter to cope with.

On the first paper I wrote in that class, Howard Nemerov attached a note informing me that it wasn't a bad paper and had some merit, but that it was a good thing I had used two paper clips to hold the paper together (meaning I hadn't clearly said what I wanted to say). The next paper returned with a note informing me that I did "some pretty things with language" but still had a "good deal of slovenly construction and careless syntax," and my sentences, he remarked, had little "bite or balance." Still, he regarded it as much better than the first. When the last paper was returned I was informed it was "full of knowledge, and far more aptly put together" than the others, and, best of all, held together quite well without the need for two paper clips. I proudly showed Monty and the children my A and felt that now I could handle taking another class. I never could summon up the courage to show Howard Nemerov my poems, but I did ask him once if he ever wrote poems for children, perhaps to amuse his two young sons. He replied, "Oh, no; it's much too difficult." It was Nemerov who first commented in class one day that jokes and poetry were related in several ways. It didn't surprise me, but I hadn't thought of it.

Donald Finkel was another poet I was privileged to learn from in writing workshops, and I credit him with helping me loosen up and

With her children—Carol, Kenneth, Donald, Robert, and Edward—at the beach at Coronado, California, 1970

be more daring in my imagery and for many other insights and practical editing tips that I refer to often. I took many literature classes, a linguistics class, even a painting class just to experience creating in another medium. Painting a picture and writing a poem do have many things in common. Eventually I had to make a decision on what I would do next.

I followed my heart back to the education department and enrolled in a master's program. The learning of reading fascinated me, but I felt something was missing in the methodology, and that the use of literature, poetry especially, was being overlooked.

Workbooks had filled in too much space in the reading program, creative writing was not utilized properly. I became an advocate of methods that incorporated literature and writing in meaningful ways.

I wrote paper after paper focusing on literature, especially poetry, and its value in the classroom, and became more convinced that I had something important to do in that regard. I spent some time visiting classrooms and reading poetry, and once again found an enthusiastic response.

With my new degree in 1974, I was certified to be a reading specialist, but I knew I

Constance and Monty at the ceremony for the Boston Globe—Horn Book *Awards at which* A
Tree Place and Other Poems *received an honor book designation, 1994*

couldn't think of a full-time job, not with five children. I stayed on for two years as a supervisor of student teachers at Washington University (you can be sure my students learned about poetry), and when someone at the university suggested the Missouri Arts Council's program called Writers in the Schools, I knew that was for me. Several of my poems had been published in teachers' magazines and journals, which made me eligible. It was part-time, and I could be home when the children arrived from school, and I could be a real Johnny Appleseed of poetry.

For seven years I taught poetry workshops in many of the local school districts, going into classrooms, teaching children and teachers. I had no book of my own at that time, but I brought books by other poets and accumulated a vast resource of the best poems available in many subjects and forms. As much as I brought to the children, they gave at least that much to me. It was wonderful to hear a teacher, surprised at what a child had written, tell me,

"I didn't know he could do that!" Teaching is always learning, and this time was a valuable enrichment period for me. I have saved volumes of the children's original poems.

I also became an adjunct instructor in children's literature at Harris-Stowe College, a city college, and managed to bring poetry into my curriculum there. The students thrived on it; it was an awakening for many of them. Several of them found a talent they never knew they possessed.

My own writing profited, my collection grew, and I found a new outlet to try. *Cricket* magazine had just begun publication, so I sent groups of poems, ten or more, and at last they chose two to publish, and then two more. I felt wonderful. The poems appeared and were reprinted in other books, and I went into the classrooms feeling more comfortable about being called a writer. That is, until a second grader asked me one day, "Where is your book?" I replied by showing a *Cricket* magazine or two, which didn't satisfy him in the least. "If you're a writer," he insisted, "why don't you have a book?" He was right; where was my book, indeed?

My book was in files, in drawers, in boxes, on my desk, and in my head. The time had come to put a manuscript together again and suffer the agony of rejection along with the daydreams of success.

I don't know how many times I sent manuscripts over the years, changing the contents, revising, waiting. I know I always had high hopes when a manuscript went out; even the lady at the post office could have noticed that. I know I watched for the mail truck, felt pain when my own handwriting appeared again on my own brown envelope which had been returned. Poetry, some of the rejection notes said, doesn't sell. Of course not, I thought, how can it sell if you don't put it in the bookstores! Sometimes a note was encouraging, mostly it was a form note. The mail truck became a symbol of my failure.

Somehow, I had not yet sent a manuscript to the much loved and respected Margaret McElderry, who had her own imprint at Mac-

millan Publishing Company, later to become, as it is now, part of Simon & Schuster. I admired her authors and her reputation, and I told myself, "She already publishes several fine poets so she probably doesn't need me." One's self-esteem wears down with repeated rejection. But I sent it and waited. After many months, I inquired and was notified by letter that my manuscript was still being considered. Well, that was encouraging, I thought. Weeks passed and no letter came in the mail, but neither did my rejected manuscript. One bright and beautiful day (I don't remember if it really was, but it seemed that way) a letter arrived from Margaret K. McElderry, Margaret K. McElderry Books. My hands shook as I tore it open, but my eyes could barely focus. Fortunately Monty was home. "I think it is good news but it's a blur. Read it to me," I pleaded. There it was; she would like to publish the manuscript that I eventually titled *I'm Going to Pet a Worm Today*. We enjoyed that moment together, both of us teary-eyed. Every book produced is a thrill for an author, but I think nothing quite com-

"With our children, children-in-law, and grandchildren," 1995

pares with the first acceptance, that affirms you as a writer and energizes you to continue to produce your best.

Our newspaper, the *St. Louis Post Dispatch,* printed an interview, and everyone congratulated me. When the euphoria subsided, the next phase entered, which was urgency to write the next book. I wanted Margaret McElderry to know she had made the right decision. I would not disappoint her or myself. Lovely reviews of the book were coming in, but I was fast at work on *A Tree Place,* and three years later in 1994 it too was published. The next was *When Whales Exhale* in 1996, and at this writing another book is in process.

Now, I write nearly every day, I edit my work heavily, and I have files full of bits and pieces and poems I couldn't quite solve. I look them over and pick out possibilities. I still write about ordinary things, and I love sharing poems and conversation with children in their schools. I love their questions and comments. Recently, in a third-grade class, I was describing the stories of how certain poems came about. I said that I keep my antennae out and notice things other people may miss. One boy was having difficulty phrasing his question and was straining to get it right. "Do you ever . . . ," he hesitated, "I mean sometimes do you not?" I understood. "You want to know if I ever give my senses a rest." That is exactly what he was concerned about. I assured him that I do relax and don't always concentrate on looking for things. I may not even be aware that I'm noticing something until it pops into my head at a later time.

Monty and I travel from time to time in the United States and abroad, he being the initiator of the trips each time. I, you see, would be content to stay at home—that is until I'm on my way, and then I'm in the mood for it! The travels give me new things to write about. Poems about my camel ride in Egypt, the whale sightings in Alaska, climbing mountains in Maine, and many others have come from those journeys. Some poems are about things like sunsets and rain and beetles and butterflies. In addition to the poems that sprouted in the days my children were young, many are memories of my childhood refreshed by moments from my children's childhood. Some come from seeing the world new again through the eyes of my grandchildren: Julie, Elana, Danny, Sara, Jonathan, Aaron, Adam, and Benjamin.

The poem "Surprises" may give you an idea about the way I see the world, with so many possibilities everywhere:

Surprises

I've learned that snakes
have cool silk skin
and earthworms shrink
when you're petting them,

That a butterfly frowns
as it dips and drinks
as if each sip
saps all its strength,

that early in a morning mist
a spider's web
is dew drop kissed,

that toads may look like
rocks with eyes,

and each new day
is a surprise . . .

(in *A Tree Place and Other Poems*)

And I have found that even a fresh radish has infinite possibilities.

BIBLIOGRAPHY

FOR CHILDREN

Poetry:

I'm Going to Pet a Worm Today and Other Poems, illustrated by Ronald Himler, Simon & Schuster/Margaret K. McElderry Books, 1991.

A Tree Place and Other Poems, illustrated by Robert Sabuda, Simon & Schuster/Margaret K. McElderry Books, 1994.

When Whales Exhale and Other Poems, illustrated by Judy LaBrasca, Simon & Schuster/Margaret K. McElderry Books, 1996.

Contributor of poetry to *Cricket* magazine and teachers' journals.

Gregory Maguire

1954-

Gregory Maguire, as an instructor of creative writing to children, 1992

One winter, when I was about twenty-two, I was vacationing with a college friend at his family home in Little Falls, New York. At 11:30 P.M. on New Year's Eve, we looked at each other and said, "We have just a half an hour left in this year—what can we do in the next half hour that we will never forget?" With his sister and another friend, we raced into the garage, hunting for some Flexible Flyer sleds. We dragged them across the street to the city park. There we spent the last thirty minutes of the old year sledding. We shrieked, we laughed, we tumbled into drifts together, we threw nets of snow over each other. We caught ourselves in memory.

It is New Year's Eve in 1995 as I write these opening paragraphs. I remember a number of other New Year's Eves. Curling up in a sleeping bag on a park bench in Geneva, Switzerland, because all the hotels were booked. Watching some Kikuyu dancers dressed only in swimsuits and fur anklets doing the hustle at the Bora Bora Club north of Mombasa, in Kenya. Playing record albums of music from the thirties and forties at my childhood home in Albany, New York. All New Year's Eves are a time of accounting of one's life: What have I done? What will I do? What need I change? What am I grateful for? It seems a good time to plunge into an autobiographical essay, to see what else the nets of memory can catch.

*

Every family has its own particular culture. Even little kids who visit the households of friends know this: Somehow the feeling in *your* house is different from the feeling in *our* house. Family culture is spun from ethnic origins, the personalities of parents, and family history. Made of good strong stuff, our family culture—such as I know it from my earliest memories in the late 1950s—was strict, respectful of books and learning, warm in some ways and less warm in others, and suffused with a sense that the world was both wonderful and dangerous.

My father, John (Jack) Maguire, had been born in Brooklyn, New York, in 1917, of Catholic stock originating in the north of Ireland. He was a gifted raconteur and had an encyclopedic memory for funny stories to deliver in his social and professional circles, but at home he maintained a grim Calvinist suspicion about enjoying life. Jack Maguire was in the army during World War II; afterward he resumed his career as a writer. He settled for a time in Albany, New York, where he met Helen Gregory, the second daughter of a Greek immigrant family.

Helen's family had had its own difficulties. Newly immigrated from northern Greece, Helen's mother had died in a hospital fire in the 1920s, leaving a husband who spoke only Greek, as well as seven children, the youngest of whom was still a baby. Helen and two of her sisters took turns staying home from school on a rotating basis, so that there would always be one sister at home to care for the little ones.

By all accounts Helen Gregory was a vivacious woman, full of fun and strong feeling. For a time she worked at her father's Greek diner, called the Famous Restaurant. When she got her pay envelope once a week, though it was the depression and times were hard, she always gave some money to the unemployed men who would come around looking for work or something to eat. And maybe they came to look at her, too: Helen was a beauty. She and my father were married in 1944, and lived in New York City, Washington, D.C., and, eventually, back in Albany. Helen bore four children. She died of complications resulting from childbirth a week after her fourth child was born. That was in 1954, and I was the baby.

For all that he made his living as a freelance writer, my father wasn't an expressive man. His sorrow and panic must have been immense, but it was tamped down by an Irish habit of stoic acceptance. In the aftermath of the disaster, Helen's sisters offered to care for the children until Jack could pull his life together again. I went to stay with my Aunt Sophia until she realized she was going to find it difficult giving me back to my father. (She told me that my father would come and mind me now and then, so she could go shopping or have some time alone; when she returned, she'd say, "But Jack, you didn't change his diapers!" "He never cried," my father answered, "he didn't fuss, how was I to know?") Though they already had two children, Aunt Sophia asked if she and her husband could adopt me. My father, hoping he might salvage something of family life for his children, didn't want to let me go. Instead, he put me in the Saint Catherine's Infant Home in Albany. The nuns and nurses there called me "Gregory the Executive" because I smiled so seldom. I didn't scowl, I wasn't bad-tempered or fussy: I simply kept my feelings to myself—had I inherited the Irish gene for stoicism? Or maybe did my silence just allow me to observe?

In time my father decided to remarry. The family lore has it that he asked Marie McAuliff of North Albany, "What would you say if I asked you to marry me?" and that she answered, "You'll have to try me and see." He asked, and she agreed. Marie had been a close childhood friend of Helen and all her siblings, and my brothers and sisters knew her already—in fact, she was my godmother, too. So the second marriage started out with some real advantages. The children of the diaspora were brought back together under one roof, and by the time I was six there were three more Maguire children, born of Jack and Marie. We rattled our family list off in nighttime prayers, at breakneck speeds, racing each other to see who could be fastest:

> God bless Daddy, God bless Mommy,
> God bless John, God bless Rachel, God
>   bless Michael, God bless Gregory,
> God bless Matthew, God bless Annie, God
>   bless Joseph.

Seven seemed a good number of kids to have in a family. We didn't feel like an especially large family—in Albany, with its substantial Irish Catholic population, there were plenty of families with eight, ten, twelve, even fourteen children. Seven seemed just about right to us.

We never forgot Helen, our first mother; even I never forgot her, though I hadn't known her. One of my earliest memories takes place at dusk on a cold winter Sunday afternoon, in our turn-of-the-century house on Lancaster Street, in the Pine Hills neighborhood of Albany. I was leaning up against the metal wall of the stove, soaking up the heat; Marie was taking something out of the oven. Had we been chatting about the arrival of a new baby in the family—Annie, perhaps? At any rate, with all the happy egoism of a four-year-old, I probably made some remark about when *I* was in Mommy's stomach. Marie replied, "You know, of course, that you were never in my stomach. You remember that I'm your second mother, and Helen was your first mother." I said, "I *know,* Mommy," in aggrieved and somewhat insulted tones. Maybe the moment is captured in my memory, however, because I had never before really stopped to think about that mysterious bit of family dogma.

Our first mother was part of our growing up. Helen's sisters were warmly welcomed in our home. Marie and Jack both told stories of Helen so that we would come to know her. In the Catholic pantheon of saints and angels we could picture so well, Helen hovered in a category all of her own—not angel, not saint, but some sort of mysterious Greek goddess of warmth, recovery, and love.

Helen watched us from heaven. Jack grumbled at us through his cigar smoke. But it was Marie who taught us to read.

*

We were not well-to-do. When we whined to find out our socioeconomic status, we received the noncommittal reply, "Comfortable. We're comfortable." And comfortable we were—more or less. Teenagers during the Great Depression, both Marie and Jack had formed lifelong habits of frugality. We children wore hand-me-downs from cousins and from each other. We drank gallons of Carnation instant milk,

Parents Helen Gregory and John Maguire on their wedding day, 1944

hoping not to get the inevitable lump of undissolved milk powder at the bottom of the pitcher. Marie bought a barber's home haircut set and gave crew cuts to all five boys as we lined up in our underwear in the basement. Five napes one after the other, five crowns, five right temples, five left temples, and drifts of brown curly hair all over the laundry floor, hiding our chilly ankles.

We didn't see these indignities as economies. We saw them as the campaign of our inventive parents to regularize and oppress us. "Our parents are so mean," we'd say to our friends. If ever some friend would make a claim for equally strict parents, we'd drag out our big guns. "Well, *our* parents won't let us ride two-wheeler bicycles until we're sixteen and we pass the New York State driver's license exam!" Which was true, and usually shut up any stunned competition.

But what we lacked in material luxury—bicycles, horseback-riding lessons, our own individual televisions or stereos, or even new clothes to show off—we made up in our reading lives. Our parents shared a love of reading and the written and spoken word, and the ceremony of a young Maguire getting his or her first library card was treated with as much solemn joy as a First Communion or a birthday.

I'm told that I was read to often as a small boy, but I don't remember it at all. I learned my letters well before kindergarten and was reading simple stories to myself and to my younger brothers and sister with panache and invention if not with accuracy. In the late 1950s, we moved to North Pearl Street in North Albany, to help care for Marie's mother, whose health was failing. In North Albany, the library was too far away for us children to walk to. So Marie went weekly, with a huge carton in which our family groceries had been delivered, and she took out forty or fifty children's books at a go. (She later learned that for years the librarians had assumed that she was the principal of a grade school.)

When I was nine, we moved back to the bigger house on Lancaster Street, and the old Pine Hills Library on Madison Avenue became the destination of most of my outings. The library was housed in a huge, bloated, late Victorian extravaganza of a private home, with a wrap-around porch, stained-glass windows, and ornate polished woodwork, balustrades, and screens. A grand staircase in the front hall twisted up and around to the children's room. There, behind the hugest desk I'd ever seen, the good women of the Albany Public Library oversaw the borrowing of thousands of books a day.

I read like a fiend. This will not surprise any reader of this essay; it would be the rare writer who *hadn't* found the love of books while he or she was a child. Once I decided to read through the entire children's collection, and brazened my way through all those thick Louisa May Alcott books on the top shelf. But I was derailed when I got to James Barrie's *Peter Pan,* for I took home all the different editions the library had. On finishing the first and turning to the second, I was disappointed to find that different covers and different artists didn't mean a different text—all four editions had the same story in it. I then decided to read just what I wanted. I loved the smell of books, the feel of their covers, even the patterns of library paste spilled on the endpapers. I loved the pictures.

My parents invented a few strategies to help us love to read. We talked about books con-

stantly, for one, and on occasion my parents would post a book chart. For limited periods of time we could write down every title we read and earn five cents for each one. But more important than this was the attitude toward the television. The TV occupied a central place in our family living room, but it was not allowed to cut into reading time. Access to the TV was limited, and access to books was not. We complained—of course we complained! Capably, volubly, constantly. But our accusation that we were being deprived went blithely ignored.

I sometimes tell this to children when I visit them in schools. (I do a lot of work as a writer-in-residence.) I point out that four of the seven Maguire siblings are professional writers, and that *reading makes the difference.* In every class there is some child with a glimmer in the eye, who nods, who knows already.

What a time to be reading, though! I was ten in 1964. My favorite book was Jane Langton's *The Diamond in the Window,* which with its blend of domestic warmth and transcendental fantasy showed me for the first time how books can expand your ideas about the world you live in. When I was done reading any Langton book, I felt I knew something crucial that I hadn't known before. Is this where a new writer really begins to hatch, at the moment of understanding the life-changing power of the written word?

I was primarily a lover of fantasy, and my favorite books in childhood are the obvious ones. The Narnia books. *A Wrinkle in Time. Peter Pan* and *The Wizard of Oz* (more because I knew the stories through the films and TV adaptations). The Edward Eager books delighted me. *Alice in Wonderland* scared me, but it captivated me too. *Charlotte's Web*—no surprise—and *Mary Poppins* and *Homer Price.* The Borrowers tales by Mary Norton, the books about Miss Bianca by Margery Sharp. A lesser known book called *Loretta Mason Potts* by Mary Ellen Chase. Eventually, books like *The Hobbit* and *The Once and Future King.* If I loved a book, I read and reread it, and eventually, with my allowance, bought the books I loved.

But next to Jane Langton's books about the Hall children in Concord, Massachusetts, the books that most caught my imagination were Lucy Boston's stories of Green Knowe. In fact, *The Children of Green Knowe* had been the first full-length chapter book I ever read. I wandered into the kitchen once again with the book in my hand. "Mommy, this is a strange book," I said.

"Is it scary?" said Marie. "You don't have to finish it if it's scary."

"I think it's a ghost story," I said, "but it's not scary. It's sort of sad. I don't know what it is. But there's something neat in it."

I remember this passage from when I was seven. The child goes to stay with a grandmother who lives in an ancient manor house in the lowlands of Cambridgeshire, England.

> The entrance hall was a strange place. As they stepped in, a similar door opened at the far end of the house and another man and boy entered there. Then Toseland saw that it was only themselves in a big mirror. The walls round him were partly rough stone and partly plaster, but hung all over with mirrors and pictures and china. There were three big old mirrors all reflecting each other so that at first Toseland was puzzled to find what was real, and which door one could go through straight, the way one wanted to, not sideways somewhere else. He almost wondered which was really himself.

What was in *The Children of Green Knowe*—though I had no words for it—was atmosphere. Literary atmosphere. *The Children of Green Knowe* taught me many things, including that the optimum growing condition for magic is the sense of mystery you develop by observing things closely.

I believed in magic. It was not hard to do, being a good Catholic boy.

*

It may seem scandalous, even heretical, to talk about magic and religion together. The type of Roman Catholicism I was raised in was rich in narrative. We read about the lives of saints, and dreamed about the chance to be put to death in some wonderfully bloody way for refusing, let's say, to spit on the Blessed Sacrament. We listened to the Gospels and to the stories of the travels and adventures of Paul. The Christmas story and the Easter tragedy and triumph gave shape and meaning to our lives— not simply theologically, but in a personal way, too. Since we carried the death of Helen in an interior pocket in our hearts, we were well inclined by personal need to accept the doctrine of everlasting life. Anyway, children don't analyze what they believe, but they do believe fervently. I believed in saints and angels. I believed in Jesus in a way that has become more metaphoric and political as I have gotten older, but no less strong. I believed in the archangel with his fiery sword at the garden of Eden, and Moses in the bulrushes, and talking animals at the manger at Bethlehem.

As an adult I find it difficult not to be a skeptic in matters of faith, at least intellectually—but I am aware that an intellectual perspective is not the only possible approach to take. Like most people, I can be impatient with hierarchy and with arcane points of dogma. But I do cherish the religious teaching I received from Catholic schools for its emphasis on moral integrity, for its strong narrative traditions, and for its giving me a language and a grammar with which to consider the crises of everyday life. When all else fails, I rely on the prayerful traditions of my parents, my grandparents, back into the dim ages further than anyone can know. The Roman Catholic tradition may be no truer than any other—but it is *my* tradition. It is a part of what I called earlier my family culture. And it is rich in mystery.

I had two best friends all throughout grade school. For different reasons I am not in touch with them now—one died of AIDS a few years ago, and the other, sadly, has been estranged from me for some years. Both of these good, dear friends helped me understand the pleasure of making things. The story of growing up to be an artist of one sort or the other always involves the meeting of soul mates, the sudden, life-enhancing realization that you are not alone.

After I had read the Narnia stories and shared them with these valuable grade-school friends, I wanted more than anything else to find a magic land of my own. Doorways to magic lands are not easy to come across in Albany, New York. I would have preferred looking in Europe, or in the Adirondack Mountains where we vacationed for a week every summer. But if faith could grow in unlikely soil, so must magic. I poked around in improbable places looking for a bit of proof. I wanted to see some tiny hint of magic, some clue—it didn't need to be much!

One winter afternoon I walked my younger sister, Annie, to her ballet lesson on Colvin

Avenue in Albany. I was with one of the friends mentioned above. We decided to explore a no man's land between the commercial strip and the Little League playing fields a half-mile beyond. Just over a pile of soil and construction debris, probably mounded there by bulldozers, we came upon a small, frozen pond. It was hidden from sight of the well-traveled street, and overgrown on three sides by stands of some sort of feathery-headed weed or marsh grass.

With something like Balboa's delight, we slid down the slope onto the ice. From the sunken level of the pond, the street and its noise disappeared; the buildings were hidden by the high grass. All that could be seen were the gray, wind-scrubbed skies, and the grass whistling around us. "It's a magic place!" I whispered. I was partly pretending, but I was also partly responding to the otherworldly atmosphere. How come this secret place suddenly revealed itself to us, who had marched up and down that sidewalk dozens of times earlier? "We were never *meant* to find this place before now," we decided. "It has called us here!"

I hope I'm not betraying the confidences of my deceased friend or of our younger sisters—his sister Sue, my sister Annie—to publish the name of our private magic land. It was Fliaan—pronounced Fly-*ann*. We made a map of Fliaan and its environs, naming sections like "The Witch's Brambles" and "The Cliffs at the Edge of the World." Our adventures there weren't much to report—we generally had running and sliding competitions across the ice, or sometimes played hide-and-seek in the overgrown reeds. When spring came and the ice melted, the place lost a good deal of its sense of mystery, but the following winter the eerie atmosphere returned, and we celebrated. We wrote a national anthem of Fliaan (mercifully, I've suppressed the memory of it). On our departure from our private paradise each week, we sang the anthem and then we said the "Our Father"—just to prove to any attendant nosy-parker saints that we weren't constructing false idols, that we knew what side our immortal souls were buttered on, so to speak.

The story of Fliaan would have no point in this autobiography except that, stirred by hope and longing, I began to write a novelistic history of Fliaan. I had written many stories before this, starting at the age of about seven. But they had been more or less realistic adventure stories, derivatives of *The Man*

from U.N.C.L.E. and Disney Sunday night movies such as *The Moonspinners.* My first invented characters had all been adults; they could drive; they were fabulously rich and adventurous; they were independent and competent and popular—all things I doubted I'd ever achieve for myself. But the characters in my stories about Fliaan were comfortably, familiarly fantastic—witches, saints, dragons, gods, dwarves, the whole gamut from fantasy's central casting. The two childhood friends mentioned above helped with the text and with illustrations. I completed four or five volumes of "The Chronicles of Fliaan." They're not very good. But they were my first attempt at fantasy. They were also my first attempt to integrate into a story some atmosphere, some mood that I had experienced firsthand.

*

It wasn't all that surprising that the Maguire kids turned to writing. John Maguire was well established as a journalist for the *Albany Times-Union;* by the mid-1960s he was writing a humorous column four times a week that was second only to "Dear Abby" in reader popularity. Through most of our childhood, he also maintained another full-time job as a speech writer for the New York State Health Commissioner. Marie was a poet whose work had been published in the *New York Herald Tribune* and reprinted in the *Congressional Record.* Even Helen had been known to scribble lines of doggerel from time to time. When we wanted to play at being our parents, we organized piles of scrap paper and stapled them together and produced newspapers, stories, plays, and cycles of poems.

With the assistance of the Gaffneys, our good friends from around the corner, we mounted theatrical productions on Sunday evenings after dinner. One extravaganza concluded with the San Francisco earthquake, which we simulated by tossing into the air every sofa cushion and pillow we could gather up. My brother Joe played a small child who was killed in the disaster. The ketchup we used for blood was effective, and the stains came out of the carpet with water and a little Tide.

When I was in fourth grade, I wrote a class play by invitation of Sister Mary Salvator. It was called "The First Thanksgiving," and it involved two Pilgrim kids, Billy and Suzy, who get lost one day late in November. A friendly

Indian named Squanto finds them and brings them home, and since all the Pilgrims are so grateful, they decide to have a big dinner to celebrate. Squanto shows them how to make creamed onions, and olives with little red pimentos stuck in them, and turkey, and crouton stuffing. "It's the first Thanksgiving!" they all decide happily. The play draws to a dramatic close when the priest arrives and the Pilgrims genuflect and cross themselves and follow him off to mass. This play was mounted in fourth grade to great critical success. No one ever told me that the Pilgrims weren't Roman Catholics; I'm not sure that Sister Mary Salvator, who hailed from County Kerry, knew much about the Pilgrims to begin with. But eight years later, when I returned to that grade school to take up my first teaching job, I found that the fourth graders were still mounting annual productions of "The First Thanksgiving," though my byline had long since disappeared from the script.

One year, because Marie was taking a course in the history of movies at the local state university, I corralled some siblings and Gaffneys to help make a Christmas present that was meant to simulate an old film. This was before the days of camcorders, nor did our family even have a Super-8 camera. So I wrote and blocked out the story ahead of time—it was called "Passion, Pride, and a Place to Pray"—and we marched on the local Woolworth's in Westgate Shopping Center. We were armed with props, costumes, and backdrops. We installed ourselves in a booth where, back in those days, you could get a strip of four photos for twenty-five cents. We thought it would make a great present, with the photos stapled down on the left of each page and a running synopsis of the action written, frame by frame, on the right.

Then we acted out the melodrama, which included a wonderful scene where the villain attempts to force the hand in marriage of a poor widow lady by threatening to foreclose her mortgage. The widow lady, played with élan by my sister Annie, shrieked her best line, "You can take my baby, but not me!" and flung her child at the villain, played with equal zest by the irrepressible John Gaffney. Luckily we used a plastic baby doll, for in Annie's zeal the infant went soaring out of the booth and over

"Young writers": (back to front) Michael, Gregory, John, and Rachel Maguire, about 1957

The author, about 1960

the heads of six Woolworth's cashiers. We were cordially invited never to come to Woolworth's again.

By the time I graduated from eighth grade, I had finished fifty or sixty stories, ranging in length from four pages to several hundred, many of them cowritten with John Gaffney. Each story was handwritten, usually in a spiral-bound notebook. I never revised my work when I was young—when I admit this to schoolchildren, teachers at the back of classrooms blanche, and frown, and purse their lips, and shake their heads. But since I was a fluent writer as a child, who at an early age had mastered the art of keeping myself interested in what I was doing, I didn't belabor finished work. In fact I scarcely looked at it again. I just went on to the next project.

I have talked earlier about the fantasies I read. In adult life I have gone on to have an appreciation for a wider range of writing. But there was another keynote event in my childhood reading, and this was the ground-breaking book of the middle sixties—for me and for many other young readers—*Harriet the Spy*.

Harriet M. Welsch maintained a spy route and wrote down what she discovered about life in her spy notebook. I had no sooner finished reading Louise Fitzhugh's masterpiece than I decided I needed to keep a spy notebook if I, like Harriet, wanted to be a writer. I still have the first dozen spy notebooks I filled up, mostly from when I was eleven and twelve. They immediately dispel any notion of my having been a child prodigy. But they also do what journals are supposed to do. They provide two pictures: a picture of the world as seen by the writer, and a self-portrait of the writer that he may not know he's constructing. I include a few sample entries, verbatim. All proper nouns refer to my brothers and sisters unless otherwise noted.

Rachel's nice. She nearly saved someone's life. Yesterday when she was in the Church she grabbed someone's sleeve out of the flames.

Joe just said I'd be a nice father to him, and he'd like it.

My mother's sipping coffee and reading the paper on the kitchen table. Rachel's eating, and Matthew's playing ball in the bathroom hall. Daddy and Joe are watching somebody make a vase on Captain Kangaroo.

Seduced—what does that mean?

Lying right here on my bed, I think I'll
    write all the sounds I hear:
The water draining out of the bathtub.
Billions of cars on Pine Avenue.
Joe saying his prayers.
My pen scratching.
Me sneezing.
Matt arguing with Joe.
My bed creaking.
A slight ringing in my ears.
A distant siren.
The side doorbell.
Rachel coming in.
Daddy talking to Rachel.
The Tijuana Brass Tijuana-ing away.
The nailbrush being plunked in the
    bathtub water.
My mother's sewing machine.
On the TV: "The day you become a
    woman, your system needs more
    iron."
Also: "Lady, take your summer kitchen on
    a date with Reynolds."

Joe's playing with a slinky which he says is his dog Money.

Matthew is in a terrible mood tonight. He said to my mother, "I pity you." I think he said that because we were in a fight. Anyway he got a great big spanking.

All alone! How wonderful it feels, stretched out on Michael's bed, with the wind rustling the leaves of the tree outside his window. I could be in a treehouse, or a balloon, or in a raft, I'm SO alone!

The tree has stopped rustling. I can see it, perfectly still. Oh blessed wind! A picture into reality. How beautiful to find your daydreams ARE reality.

[Neighborhood kids] Richie and Charlotte just walked past. Richie is turning into a pain in the neck.

We went to 5:30 mass. It was a riot. We walked in the front doors, the priest was pleading for somebody to come up and be the lector. But nobody would. (Including me.) Finally he induced this one fair, oversized youth of about twelve to read. He, the boy, had to be the worst one that the priest could possibly have chosen. He stammered, stuttered, mispronounced about every other word, and skipped lines. Whenever he stuttered or paused over a word, members of the congregation would help him out. They all must have sounded like bleating sheep. Then at another time I noticed this stout old lady occupying the pew in front of us. She wore a plaid purple dress that looked like an Indian blanket. She always was unable to find the pages from which the responses were being recited, and she kept on looking over her husband's shoulder to read from his booklet. He was more than a little annoyed at this. And then during the Kiss of Peace, about twenty seconds after the rest of the congregation had finished giving the appropriate congenial handshake, she turned and beamed at Matthew and said, "Peace be with you." After this I could see her slyly looking at her husband to see what he thought of this openness on her part. (He was indifferent.)

Tonight when we were going to swim, Annie said, "Aaahh! There's a spider in my goggles."

Joe said, "Drown it! Throw it in the lake!"

Annie said, "No, don't drown it!"

I said, "Annie, since when have you cared about the welfare of a measly spider?"

She said, "It's not that. I just don't want any drowned spiders in any lake that *I* intend to swim in."

I don't make any claims for this journal except that it was yet another way I cemented the habit of writing on a regular basis. When I was in high school, I began another journal, this time in earnest, one that has—at this writing—accompanied my whole adult life. In a few months I will buy a new spiral-bound notebook and begin volume number 48 of my adult journal—I've been keeping it since about 1970. Harriet the Spy in midcareer, just as compulsive as ever.

At the Vincentian Institute, my high school, I felt like a nerd—though we didn't use that word at the time. I wore glasses with thick black plastic frames, and began to grow my hair long. I hung around with the kids who played the guitar at daily mass in the chapel. I was a good student, but not a great one. I spent more time writing stories, painting, composing songs, or writing letters than I did studying. High school was not the disaster it can sometimes be, especially for an oddball, because the atmosphere of the times—the early-1970s—encouraged self-expression. I began to sing in a folk quintet with some good friends, and discovered that all those years of belting out the hymns at church had helped me develop a serviceable tenor. In the world beyond me—a world I was only beginning to notice—the campaign against the war in Vietnam was building, and my friends wore black armbands to draw attention to the shooting of student protesters at Kent State by National Guardsmen.

High school is a time when making friends is of paramount importance, and I was lucky to have a wide circle of interesting pals to hang around with. I'm still in touch with most of them—Annie Franze, Eileen Reedy, Mike Savage, Jayne O'Hare, MaryEllen Harmon. For a year or so in high school my habit of journal writing caught on among my friends. We all were scribbling down our thoughts and opinions and anxieties—mostly worrying about our friends, and whether or not our friendships were true and robust! Then, for a time, we started to pass our journals around for comments, and we would scrawl warm remarks in the margins of one another's notebooks, or append notes of devotion on the first blank page to follow. But too much revelation can be risky.

One afternoon I was invited to attend a music rehearsal of a rock band being organized by three guys in my circle of friends. The rehearsal was in the basement of the home of the lead guitarist. Though I preferred acoustic music to amplified, I still enjoyed hanging around with these guys. At a break, we headed upstairs to get some hot chocolate—it was the dead of winter—and we settled in the living room. The guitarist closed the sliding doors to the hall and the dining room, and said, "Greg, we have something we want to say to you."

This was not good, I could feel it. "What?"

"We've been talking about it, and we think that we guys should stop writing in journals. You, too."

"Why?" I said, but I knew what was coming.

"We think it's a pretty girlish thing to do, actually. We're not going to do it any more and we recommend that you stop, too."

I don't remember what I said. I'm not much of a fighter so I probably thanked them for the hot chocolate and got my coat and left. I do remember walking home through the snow, feeling rejected right down into the deepest private part of my self. But though I usually avoided conflict in favor of negotiation and reconciliation, I didn't for a minute stop to consider their proposal seriously. Those guys were just wrong. Writing had nothing to do with gender stereotypes. My *dad* was a writer, my *brothers* were writers. And even if those friends were right—even if I was getting a reputation for being odd—there was no way I was going to change my habits for them. Writing was too much a part of me by then.

The English novelist Jill Paton Walsh said once, "You know that you're a writer when you find it impossible *not* to write." By that definition I think I realized, that grim and lonely afternoon, that I was a writer. Perhaps I wouldn't make my living at it; there were other things I also wanted to do. But how could I *not* write?

*

I didn't have a lot of choice in what college to attend, as there was no family money to spare for dorm fees or tuition. With the help of a New York State Regents' Scholarship, I enrolled at the State University of New York (SUNY) at Albany, whose cold, unwelcoming modern campus sprawled about three miles west of our family home. I was a diligent and uninspired college student, increasingly shy in a class that numbered, I think, three thousand. I rode the commuter bus back and forth, did my work, and took no part in the social life on campus.

But my life wasn't as dismal as all *that.* To pay for textbooks and fees, I accepted a weekend job at the Church of Saint Vincent de Paul, my home parish. I was to form and direct a contemporary music group—musicians and singers. It would consist of those high-school friends still, like me, living in Albany during their college years, as well as college students living at the university and other nearby colleges. My pastor was Father Leo O'Brien, who had said the daily mass at the high school, and who had become a good friend, as had his associate, Sister Joan Byrne. My more immediate colleague in the music effort, however, was a newly ordained young priest named Father John Turner.

Almost twenty-five years later, it is hard to describe the sense of awakening that accompanied my friendship with Jack Turner. Jack was an intense man, prayerful, private, poetic. We met once a week to discuss the liturgical readings and search for appropriate music, drawing both from sacred and secular traditions. My family had taught me to respect the power of words, for which I am grateful, but Jack—more than any of my undergraduate professors—taught me to honor the power of ideas. He was only eight years older than I, but I felt like a novice sitting at the foot of an Old Testament patriarch or prophet in the making. Among many other gifts he gave me, he taught me that asking questions was more challenging than answering them. After a conversation that ranged widely over literature, art, music, theology, personal experience (mine), existential reflection (his), I would leave the parish house and walk home under the bleaching light of streetlamps. I felt more intimately connected with limitless celestial time and with the workings of my heart than all those childhood years of reading had prepared me for. I no longer hungered for a magic land.

Once I wrote a song in his honor, that said, in part,

He always got mad when I called him my
teacher.
The lessons are there in the sky, he'd say.
Don't assign me a part that I don't want
to play . . .
Oh Merlin, oh poet, oh friend of mine,
where are you now?
Oceans away, I know it . . .
Attending some marvel of God
And ascending some ladder to God
And leaving me watching you leaving me.

He laughed at it, and was embarrassed at
the starry-eyed hero worship of the song. He
asked me to sing it once more, and then he
said, "You never need to sing it to me again,
for now it exists in the world and in my memory;
you should go on and write something new."

Jack left the parish in Albany and moved
to the North Country, to a retreat center called
Barry House on Brant Lake, New York. At his
encouragement, I applied for a summer job at
an amusement park on the west shore of Lake
George, which was only fifteen or twenty miles
away. On weekends and long summer evenings
we were able to continue our friendship uninterrupted—singing, swimming, reading poetry,
wandering in to Lake George Village to poke
around the bookstore. During the day I worked
at Time Town. Occasionally, for reasons that
now escape me, I had to dress up as a rooster

Father John Turner, 1975

with a twelve-foot comb and strut about, terrifying the toddlers. However, I also ran the park's
small theater, and while I was waiting for the
films to rewind I sat on the steps of the pro-
jection booth and worked on a novel set in
the Adirondacks. I was twenty years old.

At the end of the summer Jack drove me
to the Amtrak stop at Ticonderoga—there was
so little traffic that you had to flag the train
down if you wanted it to stop—and I caught
the train to Montreal. There I took my first
overseas flight to Dublin, Ireland, to spend part
of my junior year abroad, studying for a semester and then traveling for three
months.

Incredibly naive and thunderstruck with
excitement and loneliness, I wandered from
Ireland to northern Greece. Opposite stony
corners of Europe, and the twin homes of my
bloodlines. In 1974, my brother John joined
me in Athens, and together we traveled to
Thessalonika to look for the younger sister of
my Greek grandmother—the grandmother who
had died in the hospital fire. Our communication with the Greek branch of the family had
been lost following the deaths of those in my
mother's generation who still spoke Greek. We
were the first members of the family to return
to Greece since our maternal grandparents had
left fifty-some years earlier. In a tiny house
behind a blue iron gate, we found her. My
great-aunt was a short, stout woman, who, though
not expecting us, knew at once from our familiar faces who we must be. She screamed,
"Amerikani!" and barreled into us with arms
outstretched. Tears, and hugs, and glasses of
ouzo. In my great-aunt's simple house, we found
her walls hung with black-and-white photos of
the American nephews and nieces she'd never
met, including Helen's wedding portrait from
1944.

I went back to the States to finish my degree at SUNY and to take up my music leader's
job at church again. I saw Jack Turner a few
times, but we no longer lived near each other.
I never sang his song to him again, for three
years after we met, Jack was killed in a car
accident in the Adirondacks. I went to his funeral and sat at the back, thinking, "No one
knows how important he is to me!" But the
kind of person Jack Turner was meant that
dozens, even hundreds of people in that church
were feeling the same thing. He was only twenty-
nine when he died.

The last year of my undergraduate education was spent in private grief. I was grateful for my musician friends—Roger Mock and Francisco Pabalan, particularly, and later Debbie Kirsch and Margaret O'Brien—but I felt adrift without Jack there. I felt I had lost some vital, irreplaceable key to unlocking significance in daily events. I was sad with a sadness I could hardly name, nor even much share with my family or friends.

I didn't stop writing, though. I graduated from the university and took a job as a teacher in what would now be called a middle school. I taught seventh- and eighth-grade English literature and grammar. What I lacked in teacher training I made up for in enthusiasm for the subjects and for the kids themselves. Toward the end of the academic year I organized a field trip to New York City to go to the Museum of Modern Art and to see a Broadway musical matinee. Somehow I managed to get separated from the fourteen students—during rush hour in Times Square—and I had to drive back to Albany with my pal Roger, who was serving as a chaperone. Neither of us knew where the students were or whether the sole remaining adult was even still with them. The kids all did make it home safely—thanks to Mike Savage, the responsible chaperone among us. Because I was well liked as a teacher, none of the students ever told their parents what had happened. But the mishap made me consider whether I should be teaching, especially when I realized that my year of full-time teaching was the only year I could remember being too tired to write any fiction at all.

I had decided, on my return from Europe, to look at the novel I'd written over the previous summer. It had seemed no worse than some of the children's books I still enjoyed reading, so with great labor I typed up the manuscript and began to mail it to publishers who had brought out my favorite books. I sent it to Harper, to Dutton, to Little, Brown. Each submission usually took three to four months, after which the manuscript was returned with a polite note saying that the book "doesn't suit our needs at this time." I wasn't much daunted. I told myself: It took you a whole year to write this book and type it, the least you can do is take a year to submit it. Don't be discouraged. The point is *determination.* If a publisher rejects it, just send it out to the next house on your list, whether you feel like it or not.

So I did. I sent the book to the fourth publisher, Farrar, Straus and Giroux, and when five months had elapsed, I suddenly thought: *I never made a carbon copy of the finished draft.* (It didn't even occur to me to photocopy it, as this was before the days of photocopy stores; it was also years before everyone had a personal computer.) What if the U.S. Postal Service had lost the only copy of my first real book? So I wrote to Farrar, Straus again, explaining my bad case of nerves.

They answered that they *had* read the manuscript, apologies for the delay, and they would like to talk to me about it.

A week or two later I took a day off of teaching and went to Manhattan with my friends Roger and Margy. Farrar, Straus was—and still is—a small and prestigious firm located in Union Square. I walked in to meet Sandra Jordan, the children's book editor, with my new three-piece banker's suit so crisply pressed that it could give surface cuts to anyone who brushed against it. I had a fountain pen and a hand-tooled leather notebook in which to make notes of our conversation. I was twenty-three, and still very shy. Meeting a publisher in New York seemed more terrifying to me than hiking with a backpack and sleeping roll through central Europe. Sandra Jordan wore a black hat and a cape, and she smoked thin, aromatic cigars. She was good-natured and ironic, with that brusque, New York City edge that Catholic boys from upstate find hard to read. I never knew exactly what she meant; I had perfected *sincerity* as a posture and a policy. But Sandra found a way to talk to me so I understood her. She guided me through margin notes and Post-it observations tagged onto nearly every one of the 220 pages of the manuscript. When we had finished—several hours of talking—she handed me back the pile of typescript and said, "Well, that's how *we* think it might be changed. Mull it over and if you want to revise it and submit it again, we'd be happy to look at it. Otherwise, good luck, and it was nice meeting you."

I was devastated. I was sure I had just been made a fool of. Sandra Jordan, by her own admission, was newly hired to be the head of children's books at Farrar, Straus. Probably she was just trying to fill up her workday and look busy. Why wasn't there a contract, an offer to publish? Roger and Margy and I drove back to Albany that afternoon; those good friends tried to cheer me up. However dejected I felt, though, I was determined to try, and I revised the book and sent it back to Farrar, Straus.

That same spring I had received a letter from Jane Langton, to whom I had written a fan letter, finally, and with whom a firm friendship had developed. Jane told me about a new master's degree program in children's literature that was being established at Simmons College in Boston. I left my teaching job and moved to Cambridge, Massachusetts, in the early summer of 1977, having the good fortune to find lodging with an elderly doyenne named Sarah Reginald Seabury Parker. Sarah Parker lived in Harvard Square, in a fine old federal-style home dating from the 1840s. The house was like something out of Masterpiece Theater. Standing on a table in the front hall was a coat of ceremonial brass armor from the Spanish occupation of the Philippines. A Dutch cuckoo clock dating back three centuries hung near the dining-room door. Above my bed in the back room was an original Winslow Homer watercolor. And Sarah Parker herself, frail, soft-spoken, liberal, well educated, was a wonderful new friend. The difference in our ages was only sixty-eight years or so, hardly enough to worry about. I changed light bulbs and collected the trash, and before long I also was doing modest cooking for her. Sarah paid the bills and accepted no rent from me, for, as she said, "Dear boy, if I charged you for your room then I'd have to see that everything was perfect, and if I don't charge then I don't have a care in the world, do I?"

I was happy to be studying at Simmons College. My professors there included Paul and Ethel Heins, who have both been editors of the influential *Horn Book Magazine;* Betty Levin, the novelist and sheep farmer; and Jane Langton. Barbara Harrison, the founder and first director of the Center for the Study of Children's Literature, was zealous at raising public awareness about the value of literature in the lives of children. I found new friends among the students, especially Maggie Stern (now Maggie Stern Terris) and Patricia McMahon, both of whom have gone on to their own writing careers. Even more thrilling than the chance to live in Harvard Square and study the history and criticism of children's books in Boston, however, was the news that arrived a month into my first semester as a graduate student: Sandra Jordan approved of my revisions and

Sarah Reginald Seabury Parker, Cambridge, Massachusetts, about 1977

accepted my first children's novel for publication by Farrar, Straus and Giroux.

The book was called, eventually, *The Lightning Time.* It has the excesses and enthusiasms of a first novel; it is derivative of my favorite writers, but not brilliantly so. I look back at the story of twelve-year-old Daniel Rider and his attempt to help save his grandmother's mountain home from unscrupulous developers, and I see mostly an encoding in fantasy of some of the things that Jack Turner and I talked about. Jack is a character in the story— thinly disguised as Father August Petrakis, an Anglican minister. As a character he is too wise, too lovable, too impenetrably good to get much of a handle on. I hadn't yet learned that readers best love characters who reveal their contradictions and complications, too—but then I had hardly learned to accept the complications in myself or in my own friends. I saw people as WONDERFUL or HORRIBLE, with few exceptions. In my early books I wrote them as such, too.

The publication of *The Lightning Time* in 1978 coincided with my receiving a master of arts degree in children's literature. My old friends in Albany and my new friends in Boston and Cambridge helped me celebrate my first publication. The book earned me a fellowship to the Bread Loaf Writers' Conference in Middlebury, Vermont, and that the reviews were mixed didn't bother me much. At least some wise critics saw my work as "lively" and "imaginative," and I had no place to go but up, didn't I? Still, in retrospect, I wonder what only those who published young can have the temerity to ponder: Had *The Lightning Time* and its two sequels, *The Daughter of the Moon* and *Lights on the Lake,* been turned down, perhaps I would have tried *harder* to write something more original. Perhaps I would have learned the craft of revision earlier. As it was, my earliest books were published to generally good reviews but modest sales. Alas, I had started writing fantasy at just a moment when the interest in fantasy for children, for the time being anyway, had started to wane.

For another year I lived with Sarah Parker. One evening, awaking from uneasy dreams, I had a sense of foreboding, and for the first time ever I went to check on Sarah. She was awake, but had suffered a heart attack. I called the ambulance, and while we were waiting I tried to console her. She consoled me instead. "Dearie," she said, "it has meant more to me than I can say to have you here in the house with me these two years. You mustn't get yourself stirred up for I have been very happy to know you. The gloves downstairs on the sofa belong to Mabel Colgate and should be returned to her; she left them here at tea on Saturday last."

I visited her in the hospital every day for several weeks. When she began to complain about the food I suspected she would pull through. She was well enough to spend the summer at the seashore. The last time I saw her, I took the commuter train for a day visit, bringing with me a thermos of Manhattans, because Rockport is a dry town. We sat in the gardens and looked at the sea. She died about ten days later. At her funeral, in the blistering heat of late August, the minister declared, "Mrs. Parker requested that, irrespective of the liturgical season, her service begin with the congregation singing 'Joy to the World.'" I love to sing, but it was hard to sing. Hard, and necessary.

*

In the autumn of 1979 I found myself a small apartment in Porter Square in Cambridge. My dear friend Maggie Stern had a place just up the street, and other friends lived nearby, including Mark Miller, a young research assistant at Howard Gardner's Project Zero at Harvard University. I had not attended Harvard, and for the first couple of years living near Harvard Square I hardly had the courage even to walk through Harvard Yard on my way to the Cambridge Public Library. The university seemed like a huge furnace, a dragon in bricks and slate, dangerously seething with intellectual pomp and superiority. Becoming friends with Mark helped break down that fear somewhat, for Mark was warm and open-minded, a breath of fresh air in my life, even if he had gone to Harvard.

I was increasingly devoted to my friends, but the lives we played at, rich and strange and at times daring, in the exploratory spirit of the times and of youth, weren't anything like the lives of adults in children's books. They were even less like the lives of neighbors in my solid, respectable Irish Catholic neighborhood back home. Growing up in part is realizing that you can invent for yourself the kind of adult you want to be.

One thing I knew is that I loved to travel, so whenever I had the chance I accepted any invitation to visit anyone—anywhere. In 1981 I flew off to the Philippines for a month with my college chum Francisco Pabalan, who was just graduating from medical school. In 1983 I went to Kenya with Rafique Keshavjee, a Harvard graduate student I'd met several years earlier at the card catalog in Widener Library. My writing began to show signs of greater experimentation, maybe as a result of traveling. *The Dream Stealer,* published by Harper and Row in 1983, was a fantasy like my earlier books, but it was set in a mythical Russia at the turn of the century. It featured as a central character the famous witch from the folktales named Baba Yaga. Depending on the fairy tale she appears in, Baba Yaga can be either fairy godmother or treacherous villainess. In trying to accommodate both sides of her reputation, I learned the pleasure of writing a fully rounded character. Perhaps I also was remembering the fun of the fantastic writing I had tried to do about our own childhood mythical country of Fliaan.

In the mid-1980s I continued to live in Cambridge, sharing a luxurious prewar flat with my friend Rafique. I worked full time at Simmons College as an assistant professor and associate director of the Center for the Study of Children's Literature. My former professors became my colleagues and, even more precious to me, my friends. Furthermore, due to the rigors of college teaching, I was mastering some of my shyness and trying to develop some confidence in my own thoughts. However, Rafique—who had graduated with a doctorate in anthropology and Middle Eastern studies from Harvard—took exception to my self-deprecating remarks about how weak my sense of logic was, how pedestrian my opinions. "I couldn't even get accepted into a doctoral program," I once declared, which provided Rafique with the opening he took. He said, "I don't believe you. I dare you to apply somewhere. Furthermore, I'll pay the application fee, I'm that convinced you'd be an ideal candidate."

Once dared, I had to commit: I applied to the doctoral program in English at Tufts University. I was accepted in 1986. I had thought the dare was done, and Rafique had proved his point. But the letter from Tufts announced their willingness to waive my tuition fees entirely, and a conversation with the head of the English department revealed that Tufts would also overlook the normal requirement of graduate students to teach there. I felt I had no real reason *not* to enroll. By this time I had been teaching at Simmons College for long enough that coming up for tenure was likely within a couple of years, and I wanted to give myself at least a fighting chance at that exercise.

In the middle of my doctoral studies, problems began to emerge at the Simmons College Center for the Study of Children's Literature. The master-of-arts-degree program, founded in 1977 by Barbara Harrison, had rooted itself securely and had weaned itself off the so-called "soft money" that the National Endowment of the Humanities had provided initially. But following a 1984 federal report decrying the state of teacher education in the United States, the Simmons College education department, like education departments all over the country, suffered a drop in enrollments. The president and dean of graduate studies decided to move the Center for the Study of Children's Literature into the education department to bolster enrollments. To a person, the faculty of the Center protested. We felt that the Simmons College management was betraying the original intention of the program—to be a humanities discipline—by taking away its autonomy and placing it under the aegis of education, a service discipline.

We negotiated for more than a year, to no avail. Thus, with early announcement so that our currently enrolled students might finish their degrees with the existing faculty while there was time, in 1986 the faculty of the Center resigned in protest at the administration's decision. There was some hoopla over this, both in Boston and nationally.

Soon thereafter, I helped cofound—with Barbara Harrison, Ethel and Paul Heins, Betty Levin, Jill Paton Walsh, and John Rowe Townsend—a small educational charity called Children's Literature New England (CLNE). As I write this, CLNE prepares to celebrate its tenth anniversary as an independent organization dedicated to the same ideals that the Center at Simmons College was set up to foster. I don't know for how long CLNE will continue; every organization, like every relationship, has a natural life span. For ten years, however, CLNE has gathered to its annual summer conferences a stellar company of writers and illustrators for children. Many of them have become friends as well as colleagues: Ashley Bryan, Eleanor Cameron, Susan Cooper, Virginia Hamilton, John Langstaff, Ursula K. Le Guin, Madeleine L'Engle, Katherine Paterson, Maurice Sendak—more, really, than I can name here. I've made good friends from all over the United States, as well as abroad—Japan, Ireland, England, Australia, New Zealand, South Africa. Among them, Martha Walke is one of the most treasured to me.

Every summer we meet in the new community of friends and colleagues, holding in common a belief that early exposure to literature is essential to the survival of a humane and literate society. Doesn't that last line sound like a grant proposal? But everything in my childhood prepared me to feel a missionary zeal about children and their reading. Though I was sorry to resign from Simmons after eight years of teaching fine students there, CLNE satisfied my compulsion to continue advocacy work. This time, free of the authoritarian dictates of jittery-stomached college overseers.

*

"The founding board members of Children's Literature New England": (from left) John Rowe Townsend, Jill Paton Walsh, Gregory Maguire, Barbara Harrison, Ethel Heins, Betty Levin, and Paul Heins, Oxford, England, 1992

My love affair with the Adirondacks had begun in childhood. Ever since the late 1950s, our parents had bundled us seven children into one car and driven to a camp on the east side of Lake George—what was then the undeveloped side—for a week of hiking, swimming, and living in the shadows of the mountains in summer. As an adult I have been to Nicaragua, Egypt, Kenya, Turkey, Romania, the Philippines, and all over western and Mediterranean Europe. I learned the pleasure of travel by going away to the mountains when young. But thanks to the invitation of another good friend and fellow intrepid traveler, Maureen Vecchione, I went to stay in the Adirondacks for the first time in ten years—I hadn't been there since the death of Jack Turner. We rented an A-frame chalet outside of Indian Lake, New York. A day's excursion in a hired speedboat took Maureen and me from Blue Mountain Lake into Eagle Lake. The taciturn local guide pointed to a rustic mansion on a secluded stretch of

lakefront property and grumbled, "Oh, that's where all the pinko feminists and faggots and artsy types go to write and paint."

I was just about to start my doctoral work, but I was curious. When I got back to Cambridge, I sent a postcard addressed to the postmistress at Blue Mountain Lake. If there was an arts colony nearby, would she forward this request for information to them? She did, and they replied, and so I came to know about Blue Mountain Center, New York.

Set up by Adam Hochschild, who is well known as a writer and as a cofounder of *Mother Jones* magazine, Blue Mountain Center was intended to provide a nurturing atmosphere for creative work for artists, especially those who work for social change. I hardly thought of myself as being an agitator for social change; indeed, I hardly knew whether to call myself liberal or conservative. But in my application packet I included an editorial I had written that had been printed in the *Christian Science*

Monitor—an essay on the 1982 march in New York City to protest the proliferation of nuclear weapons. And I've always had a sympathy for those who fight hard battles. Hadn't I just fought the one at Simmons College myself, and in resigning hadn't I given up my chance for a tenured position? Though my children's fantasies were not what I would consider provocative, at least on a sociological level, I was accepted for a late summer residency in 1986.

Due to a car problem, I arrived at the session late, when new residents had already had a week to begin to form a community. I let myself in the kitchen door, stumbling in the dark, not really sure I had the nerve or the right to be there. But I was willing to put up with anything to spend a month by an Adirondack lake. No doubt a children's book writer was considered only marginally an artist, so I would just keep my mouth shut, and drink in the aromatic smell of pines.

The sixteen or so residents that summer worked in areas of poverty and urban renewal, of nuclear disarmament, of AIDS activism, of ecology, of civil liberties. I hardly thought my single editorial in the *Monitor* made me an expert on anything, so I kept my mouth shut. I nearly scuttled my chances at making any friends.

But one noontime I volunteered to take the rowboat across the lake to accompany the swimmers, a precaution against disaster because of cramp or speedboats. Though I had been shy about arguing political points, I didn't mind opening my mouth and singing to entertain my fellow residents. Hymns, folk songs, Broadway show tunes, anything. As we neared the shore on our return trip, I glanced over my shoulder to navigate. The spirited and indefatigable director, Harriet Barlow, stood on the end of the dock with a look of contentment. She loved the sound of singing over water. Politics is important, but so is singing. I had arrived.

That summer session came at a perfect time in my private life. Earlier that year, my father had died of a brain tumor; also, a devastating schism had developed with one of my oldest, dearest friends. I needed a place to recuperate, and Blue Mountain Center was it—not a holiday, but a haven; not just a haven, but a home.

In the ten years since, I have been back at Blue Mountain a number of times. For a while the Center had winter sessions. Once I resigned from Simmons, my schedule was my own; I could afford to take four to six weeks off every winter in order to write. The friends I have made there—John Copoulos, Jill Medvedow, L-R Berger, Cassandra Medley, Dorothy Semenow, Christopher Sindt, Jessica Dunne, to name only a few—connect me to fields of the arts I would otherwise have no access to. More to the point, though, Blue Mountain reminded me for the first time in years that I *could* continue to gather new friends in. I had begun to behave—without realizing it—as if, blessed with good friends as I was, my dance card was filled.

As a resident last summer, I was walking back through the woods beyond Utowana Lake, and I came across an animal lumbering up the trail toward me. I thought at first it was a dog, and I called out, "Hello!" in a bright, I'm-okay-you're-okay voice. Then I saw that it was a black bear on all fours. It sniffed the air—good thing I wasn't carrying any food, Harriet said later—and it waited. I looked off to the lake, to be submissive, and again said, "Hello," in the same voice, thinking that the bear might identify this as my friendly, untroubled chirp. I looked for trees to climb—or should I rush into the lake? I, the lousy swimmer? The bear didn't move forward or backward—not until I said "Hello" again, same tone of voice. Then it backed up a few feet. Every time I said "Hello," it backed away some more, until finally it lumbered off the path and up the slope. When it was out of sight, I heard it crashing in the woods for eight or ten seconds. The noise would stop—I'd say in a carrying voice, "Hello!"—and the bear would start moving off again.

There have been times, out walking past the deer in the overgrown fairway behind the firs, that I have felt a shiver of connection with the whole world—its natural and its metaphoric aspects—such as I have not much felt since Jack Turner died. I am less and less inclined to put such notions into words, not even in my journal. It is enough that, now and then, one feels at home in one's place on the planet. Hello, indeed.

In 1987 Lothrop issued a book published for teachers and librarians called *Innocence and Experience: Essays and Conversations on Children's Literature.* I coedited it with my then-Simmons and now-CLNE colleague, Barbara Harrison; it is a massive compendium of talks on children's books and related subjects, given while Barbara was director and I was associate or acting director of the Center at Simmons College. I have done some teaching at Lesley College and Emmanuel College, and worked with teacher training through the Foundation for Children's Books, which I helped found—but my energies are always at their strongest when I get back to writing.

As a novelist I was feeling bolder, and experimented more. Partly as a result of my growing interest in nuclear disarmament, I tried my hand at a science-fiction novel for teenagers called *I Feel Like the Morning Star.* This was published by Harper in 1989. *I Feel Like the Morning Star* concerns a colony of post-nuclear-holocaust survivors trapped in their underground city. During my initial residency at Blue Mountain Center, I set for myself the task of writing a sequel, which I wanted to call *The Guy at the Top of the World.* It represented my first return to the Adirondacks as a locale since 1981's *Lights on the Lake,* and I had high hopes for it.

Alas, it never came to find its way into print; several New York editors found it too bleak a story, too dark a moral. I consoled myself by deducing that the Reagan tag phrase "It's morning in America" had made books about political corruption and moral ambiguity unpopular. In the Reagan years, whatever else you might think about them, Right was Right and Wrong was Somebody Else, not Us.

However, while working on *The Guy at the Top of the World,* I found myself one evening unable to sleep. After tossing and turning, I got up and scribbled down at one sitting the text for a picture book called *Lucas Fishbone* (Harper). I had never written a picture book before, and to date have only managed one other (*The Peace-and-Quiet Diner,* Parents Magazine Press), but *Lucas Fishbone* was a gift outright. I had jotted down the odd name in my journal several years earlier, but hadn't been able to make anything of it until this insomniacal midnight. By asking myself the question at the top of the page: "Who is Lucas Fishbone?"—I finally prompted the internal muse to answer. I'm not all that happy with the production of *Lucas Fishbone* as a book (nor were the critics, by and large). Though I admire the artwork of Frank Gargiulo, in the end I'm not sure it's right for the story. The text was poetic and open; the pictures ought to have been

concrete and specific. As it is, there's not enough to hang onto.

The book is a meditation on time and change, following the relationship of a grandchild and a grandmother through the last year of the grandmother's life. Children ask me, sometimes with glee and sometimes with irritation: "But who *is* Lucas Fishbone?" I don't want to say outright, for, outright, I don't know. Lucas Fishbone appears to be a lion, though, who derives partly from an image of Walt Whitman with his wonderful shaggy beard and glowing, loving eyes, and partly—perhaps—from the warmer of the images of Aslan in the Narnia books.

But Lucas Fishbone is also our guardian angel, our dead parent, our long-lost lover, our estranged best friend: come back, reunited at last.

*

Once in 1988—we still lived in Cambridge—Rafique showed up at Logan Airport at 11:30 P.M., to pick me up from a ten-day speaking trip in L.A. I was instantly suspicious; we had a habit of making our own ways home, on the T or in a taxi. Door-to-door delivery service, given Boston's lousy traffic, was beyond any call of duty. "What's up?" I said. I knew I was getting this first-class escort service for something.

It seemed we had some household guests. They were immigrants from Iran, and because Rafique had known their parents when he did his doctoral research in the late 1970s in a mountain village, the little family of three had shown up on our doorstep one spring evening. "For how long?" I said.

"They're very good people," he answered. "You'll like them."

I met them the next morning when I bustled into the kitchen to make my coffee. Abbas and Parvin Mirshahi were the young parents, dark-haired, solemn, brewing tea. The little one, Razi, was six: a small perky bundle with permanently arching eyebrows and a worried look. "We made you tea," he said. His English was better than his parents'.

"I like coffee," I said.

"I like our home," he answered. "I like you. Do you want to see where we sleep? I can say our phone number: 864-6094. Let's watch TV."

"We have a rule in this house, Razi," I shot out, the stillborn parent in me emerging instinctively. "No TV during mealtimes."

He caught himself in midlunge and twirled—yes, like a dervish, arms outstretched—and said, "Okay, Uncle Gregory."

My jaw dropped, and I was hooked. In one moment, Razi installed himself as a new nephew, joining the ranks that also include Stephen, Peter, and Anne-Marie MacDonell, and numerous Maguire nephews and nieces named Daniel, Justin, Matthew, Rob, Patrick, and Elizabeth. I *love* all my nephews and nieces. I didn't feel the need for an honorary nephew. But Razi didn't know that. As the son of immigrant parents, he had spent most of his young life on the go, moving from Iran to Germany to Texas to Boston. He was gifted at making instant family of the closest friendly adult. He did not stint with his affection, and suddenly there was room for Razi and his parents in my life—and I couldn't believe that I had managed *without* knowing them for so long.

Now Razi has a younger sister, a feisty, adorable little thing named Matin. Readers of my novel called *Oasis* (Clarion) will see a portrait of the young Razi in the figure of Vuffy Ziba.

With Razi Mirshahi, Cambridge, Massachusetts, 1989

*

Another New Year's memory occurs to me as I think of Razi and Matin—but it's a memory of New Year's Day, not New Year's Eve.

Rafique and I were flying to Florida to visit his niece. The plane had several stops to make, and in Philadelphia we picked up a grumpy-looking family who plopped themselves into seats across the aisle and a few rows ahead of us. Maybe the parents were suffering from too much New Year's Eve celebrating, or maybe they were sick—or maybe they just weren't good parents. The mother kept her head turned to the window and held an infant loosely, almost dismissively. The father carried on his lap a whining, restless daughter of about two, who squirmed and complained and wouldn't settle down. I watched for a while. The father set the girl down between his knees, where she wailed; then he picked her up and stood her on his lap, where she wailed. He went through this again and again, and the girl only fussed louder. "He's not paying attention to what she needs," I muttered to Rafique, who couldn't see as well as I, and anyway was deep in his book. The girl's head twisted around several times. She was panicking for something that she wasn't getting. Her eye caught mine, and though by now she was screaming, and annoying all the passengers, I smiled at her and waved. She kept flinging herself about, tantrum-struck, but when her head swiveled and she happened to look my way again, again I smiled and waved, as if I found her entrancing despite her noisy behavior.

She immediately raised her hands up over her head, the universal signal of toddlers that they want to be picked up. Before I could stop myself, I was out of my seat and saying to the father, "Shall I take her for a little walk? Give you a rest?" and reaching down to get her. The father was shocked at my boldness, and so was I, but in midair I obviously wasn't about to kidnap his child, and he was too bleary with annoyance to resist. The little girl clasped onto my sweater like a barnacle and sobbed. I began to stroll up and down the aisle, rubbing her back and singing to her, and her screams stopped within ninety seconds. In another couple of minutes she was asleep, but she was a fretful child. She kept waking up with a start and an urge to wail, and only settled down again when I rubbed her back and sang.

What is this story for? When we landed in Gainesville and I handed the girl back to her parents, the other passengers on the flight thanked me. Someone joked that they should pass the hat for me. The girl began to scream again in the arms of her father, who was probably not such a bad guy—just inattentive, maybe exhausted, maybe unsympathetic to babies. I tried to keep out of her sight, but at the luggage carousel the girl saw me again, and reached out for me, this time wailing for me to come get her. I said to Rafique as we left the airport, "If that father had said, 'Look, here, take this girl, we don't want her,' I would have happily bundled her under my arm and given her a home."

The folksinger named Bob Franke has a song that talks about "the hole in the middle of the prettiest life." My life is pretty good, but sometimes there is a hole in it about the size of a child. That hole gets filled by a bunch of wonderful kids, the children of many of the friends I've mentioned here—my own nephews and nieces, Razi and Matin, the Pabalan kids, the Mock kids, the Miller-Downey kids, the Terris kids, Conor Clarke McCarthy. I'm surrounded by a tribe of great masterpieces of childhood in their prime. But when my toothsome young friends are absent, the hole is there. I notice it at some times more than others. I think that's one of the reasons I spend so many weeks every year traveling around to classrooms as a visiting author or as a teacher of creative writing. Kids are a natural resource; I need them as I need light and air and laughter.

*

For a brief time Rafique and I lived in Jamaica Plain in Boston, where we had bought a turn-of-the-century house with skylights, exposed brick, and a bad problem of dog smell from the neighbor's yard next door. But in 1990 Rafique was offered a good job in London, and with the blessings of my colleagues at CLNE, I decided to spend the larger part

of every year in London too. We rented out the Jamaica Plain house, grateful that our dear friend Betty Levin invited me to stay at her farm whenever I needed to return to Boston for speaking, teaching, or CLNE work. With the disappointing response to *Lucas Fishbone,* my career felt stalled; I wrote several novels in a row that I couldn't interest any of my regular editors in. Having just graduated with my doctorate—and having no inclination at the time to go back to college teaching—I put my library in storage and took a deep breath, and left the United States.

Renting—and then purchasing—a flat in central London was an education in fiscal management, and I found myself learning to live without a car, without constant phone conversation with old friends and family. I missed the geography of New York and New England; I missed the informal, unplanned exchanges with friends and family. I missed the chance to help Razi become a better reader. On the other hand, I felt as if I did need a shake-up in my life. By the time I moved to London, I had

Rafique Keshavjee, London, 1992

been writing children's books for twelve years. The critical response had been warm, except for *Lucas Fishbone,* but I had the sense of treading water. Living abroad, it seemed, might teach me more about what it meant to be an American, or maybe about being an adult.

Though I have always loved to travel, living abroad could have been a dismal undertaking. Rafique was busy at his job, and as a freelance writer I had no professional circle to speak of. However, my time was made richer by the warmth and friendship of the English novelists John Rowe Townsend and Jill Paton Walsh. I had known John and Jill through Simmons and we all served together on the Board of Directors of CLNE. Up until the time I moved to England, however, I had only considered John and Jill as colleagues and august eminences in the field. John's groundbreaking work *Written for Children,* a history of children's literature, was my constant companion through all my graduate work, while Jill's brilliant novels, like *Unleaving* and *A Chance Child,* had joined that small group of titles that, in an alternative universe, I would most like to be able to claim as having written myself.

From the start John and Jill welcomed us into their social circle in Cambridge and in London. They served up a real American Thanksgiving, with turkey and homemade pumpkin pie and all the trimmings. With Rafique joining us when he could, John and Jill and I made several motoring trips across England. (I confess to the affectation of calling them motoring trips instead of car journeys, but with erudite and irrepressible polymaths like John Rowe Townsend and Jill Paton Walsh, the term car journey just doesn't carry enough literary *oomph.*) We spent weekends in Devon with Tony and Barbara Watkins; we traipsed around the Lake District in weather both foul and fair. John and Jill set for me a new standard of hospitality.

Rafique and I lived on the edge of Hampstead, which for its tree-lined streets and brick homes—and for the famous Heath—attracted other expat Americans. Though we had English friends as well, we were delighted when a social group began to coalesce in our neighborhood. With Ann and Sid Seamans, Bob Piller and Beatrice von Mach, and Susan Mashkes, we came to feel we had rooted ourselves pretty successfully. We all laughed at *Absolutely Fabulous* long before it made it to the Comedy

Channel in America. We wrangled over the relative merits of the *Independent* and the *Times,* of BBC One and Channel Four. We argued incessantly about the royal family. We found transplanted elements of American culture appealing, too, things we wouldn't have spent the time on if we'd been back in Boston—like *Twin Peaks;* and the presidential debates featuring Bush, Clinton, and Perot; and the Olympic figure-skating soap opera starring Tonya Harding and Nancy Kerrigan. We craved Reese's peanut-butter cups and American cheeseburgers, and pigged out instead on fish and chips and full-cream teas.

And then, as Rafique had predicted, many of our friends and family visited us, too. Debbie Kirsch and I zipped around Wales, playing Merlin and Guinevere in a rented Austin mini. With Mark Miller, in whose warm family circle I am so pleased to be welcomed, I trudged in the great stone circle at Avebury, lugging the great stone weight of baby Maeve or toddler Kate. I got to the Continent, too. Maureen Vecchione and I zipped over to spend a Thanksgiving in Paris, sipping pumpkin soup at Charles De Gaulle International Airport. Margy O'Brien and I met for lunch in the shadow of Notre Dame, and then strolled up and down the Champs-Élysées, singing snatches of the Joni Mitchell song about just such a carefree afternoon.

Living in England, there were inevitable reminders of my childhood reading, since England has produced so many of the great fantasists. When Roger Mock visited, we had lunch at the Eagle and Child pub in Oxford, the place where C. S. Lewis and J. R. R. Tolkien and the other Inklings had met and shared their fantastic writing. Even more thrilling, in one of my inaugural trips, John Townsend and Jill Paton Walsh brought me to visit their good friend, the elderly novelist Lucy Boston, who had written *The Children of Green Knowe* that I quoted from earlier. I had spent so many days in childhood looking for magic places, and here I was entering the building in England that the author had used as the inspiration for Green Knowe—the Manor House at Hemingford Grey, Cambridgeshire. I walked into that very hall, wondering which was myself—the young man visiting a venerable writer whose work he had loved—or the seven-year-old novice reader walking through the text into the hallway described in the book—or maybe I was Tolly, the child protagonist, all over again? The three mirrors hung

The Maguire family: Gregory in front, with (from left) John, Matthew, Rachel Maguire MacDonell, Anne, Marie McAuliff Maguire, Michael, and Joseph, Albany, New York, 1995

in the hall just as in the description I'd read as a child, twenty-five years earlier.

*

During the Gulf War crisis, Rafique and I were in Kenya visiting his parents. To show how my journal writing has changed from when I was twelve years old, here's an entry from February 1991. It refers to an overnight train journey from Mombasa to Nairobi.

> Perhaps 2:30 . . . I hear the sounds in my sleep of people running and screaming, thudding and banging along the corridor— it is a narrow gauge railway—but I don't wake up until I hear from Cabin E next door the unmistakable calm, insistent tones of a mother waking her children from their sleep because something is terribly wrong. And so I wake up, fully, and say, "Rafique, Rafique, get up, something's wrong." There is more shouting and running outside. I

think first of sabotage: a bomb, explosives, a terrorist attack—but on a train. There are British soldiers on the train too, coming back from exercises on the coast—we saw all those laughing young men leaning out the windows when we came down the platform to find our reserved compartment. But Kenya is just as much Muslim as it is Christian. A Gulf War incident? I am scrambling into my shorts. I think: fire—the car is on fire. Rafique says, "Don't open the door—" Is the corridor filled with smoke and flames? We are still rollicking along the rails. Rafique says, "Quick, climb up on the top bunk, quick." I don't yet think to feel the metal door to see if it's hot. From the top bunk I can push the screen down—can we jump safely from the top half of a broad sashed window? Can we roll away from the train? Are we passing through game park, will we be safe? The children in the next compartment are chattering excitedly, and the mother is still being calm and steely; it is all in German or Dutch but there is no mistaking the presence of danger. It is dawning on me that the sound of men's voices are raised in anger, not fear. I remember the scene from the end of *The Jewel in the Crown*, where a train is ambushed and the male passengers executed. Rafique [who was raised in Kenya] later tells me he is envisioning a band of brigands systematically breaking into each compartment; he has thought to drag the ladder onto the top bunk with us, so we could fight if we had to from there. But the noise lulls suddenly, and I think it will be easier to jump from the doorway at the end of the car than the window; you can spring with your legs away more easily. By now we have grabbed shirts as well, and sandals. Rafique unbolts the door and slides it open, looks out, right, left, moves out. I grab our satchels with money, documents, and my journal and writing, and follow him. There is a crowd of men at the end of the car, including several stocky Germans in jockey shorts. Are they jumping? Footsteps pound behind us; two uniformed attendants running. To allow them passage we step into the open doorway of another compartment. A woman in her 30's is there, in underpants and a T-shirt, weeping. Rafique pushes ahead again and rounds the corner toward the door at the end of the car, looks out and down, then pushes back. "Go back," he says, "go back," and I don't see. But once in the compartment, our door closed and bolted again, he says, "It was a thief. They were beating him."

My journal entry continues in another direction, but I recall that once Rafique had informed me of the circumstances, we agreed he should return to the end of the car and try to convince the irate travelers—some of whom were drunk—to leave law enforcement to the railway officials. Rafique can speak English, Swahili, and a smattering of German, and he is a man of moral conviction, possessed of a persuasive voice. I lay in my bunk, reviewing the drama. I sang to myself to still the pounding of my chest: "Be brave, my heart; my heart, be bold."

It wasn't the first time I have sung to summon courage, and it won't be the last. A few years earlier I had gone to Nicaragua with my friend Maureen Casey, as a member of a Witness for Peace delegation. Our itinerary took us into the mountain village of Quilalí, in a zone that Sandinistas and contras were both working to control. We were told that the road might be mined; indeed, the day we arrived

from Miami, for the first time in the civil war, a peace delegate from another country had been shot. Seeing signs of hardship and terrorism all around, we sang—"Hello, Dolly!" and "Dona Nobis Pacem" were our favorite numbers.

One night, when the power was cut, we were warned to expect an attack by the contras. There was no protection, no way out. The children of my host came under my arms like chicks, and I sang "Old MacDonald" to them, translating into Spanish as best I could. Not knowing what was coming, and only "Old MacDonald" to hold us steady in the dark. In a way, I was more terrified than ever before in my life, yet since I did not approve of the Reagan administration's policies in Central America, I was glad to be there. Singing is important—but so is politics.

In the years in which we lived in London, the economy was suffering the severe depression of the early nineties. My British agent, Gina Pollinger, worked hard on my behalf, but I seemed incapable of landing a contract with a British publisher for my children's books. I had turned my hand to realistic fiction for children and young adults—emboldened, perhaps, by the success of *I Feel Like the Morning Star*—and after several years of slogging I placed a children's novel with an American publisher. *Missing Sisters* (Margaret K. McElderry) is about a pair of twins who, though separated at birth, find each other halfway through the novel and struggle to resolve the dilemma that one is adopted and the other is still in an orphanage.

Missing Sisters is, in many ways, my favorite of my children's novels. For the first time I was eschewing any fantasy overtone and relying on my memories of growing up Irish Catholic in the Albany area in the 1960s. Alice Colossus, the main character, is well meaning, a bit dense, intends to be as holy as she can, but at the same time yearns to make connections with people in her world: her beloved friend, Sister Vincent de Paul, her newly found twin, Miami Shaw, and a pair of prospective parents who just might adopt her. In a sense, I managed to capture one of the great mysteries of life—to me—in two sentences toward the end of the book. Alice is getting ready to leave the orphanage, and in response to what she thinks is a platitudinous remark by the Mother Superior—that the sisters love her and always will—Alice comments, "'How can you love all of us? There's so many.' 'It's a miracle,' said Sister John Bosco. 'The heart has infinite room inside it.'"

That's as good a summary as any of what my childhood experiences and these twenty years of adult life have taught me so far. You think you have gone as far as you can go; sometimes you feel exhausted at the work of living, perceiving, connecting, being responsible, being reliable, being resilient. But there is always room for another person, especially one who needs you. It is one of the central miracles. I keep learning it again and again.

*

When I finished *The Guy at the Top of the World*—that book I couldn't sell—I dedicated it to Rafique with this quote freely paraphrased from the Persian poet Hafiz: "My head has no protection than your portal, my body no rest but at your threshold." The story of Alice Co-

lossus looking for a home—a portal, a threshold, a context—has echoes of my looking for a family from the Saint Catherine Infant Home. One definition of home is the place you can be most yourself, and so for some years my home has been with Rafique.

Late in 1994 we returned to Massachusetts. We bought a house in Concord, from which I write this memoir. We live only a mile or two from 40 Walden Street, memorialized in Jane Langton's books and known among aficionados as the Diamond in the Window house—as inspiring a literary site to me as Louisa May Alcott's Orchard House or the Old Manse of Hawthorne. Private lives can still be festooned with loops of significance—hinges of fate, as Winston Churchill called them. I didn't imagine as a child that I'd live in Concord one day. I have come to trust in the circularity of experience, the building up of references, echoes, reverberations of the past in the present. Of the future, who can say: the pathways ahead from now are no clearer than they've ever been. But we get more used to that as we get older.

The author with Rafique and Marie, New York, 1995

My narrative has almost reached the present day. Not all significant events can be narrated as stories—but here are a few notable moments of the past year or two.

In 1994 I was an artist-in-residence at the Isabella Stewart Gardner Museum in Boston, a mock-Venetian palazzo built in the Boston fens and stuffed to the ceiling with early Italian paintings, plants, music, statuary, and artifacts—a frothy overload of high culture all crammed into one setting, part surrealist dream, part art warehouse. Talk about magic places! For a month I slept in a flat over the greenhouses and had dreams art-directed by the Renaissance.

Recently I have also embarked on a series of comic novels for children—broad farces, you might call them. *Seven Spiders Spinning* (Clarion) is the inaugural volume. In a small town called Hamlet, Vermont, seven Siberian snow spiders defrost out of a glacier and imprint themselves most amorously on seven schoolgirls in an after-school club. The girls don't know they are being stalked by the lovesick arachnids until a spider manages to take a big luscious bite out of the neck of their teacher—and then pandemonium breaks loose. The book is to be followed by a ghost story tentatively named *Six Haunted Hairdos.* There are others in the series—I call them the Hamlet Chronicles—waiting to be written.

Though to date it has found no American publisher, a book set in France during World War II, *The Good Liar,* was published in Ireland by O'Brien Press. I like to think that my dad would have been pleased about my having an Irish publisher. I was tickled that both German and French prospective publishers found the novel realistic enough to ask probing questions about where I was during the war, was I from a German or French family, how did I know what I knew? *Careful research* was the only answer I could give, since the war in Europe ended ten years before I was born.

On another front, and following a stint doing volunteer work at an AIDS ward, I was asked to contribute a story to the groundbreaking anthology called *Am I Blue? Coming Out from the Silence*—original fiction about children growing up gay and lesbian. The critical success of the book showed that there is a gap that needs to be filled, more work that needs to be done. All children need a climate of tolerance and security in order to thrive. I credit a good deal of my adult happiness to growing up in such a climate—a climate largely created by my parents, but maintained by my loving brothers and sisters, too.

In the year before Rafique and I returned from London, I threw myself into a new endeavor. After eight months of feverish composition, I finished a draft of my first novel for adults, called *Wicked: The Life and Times of the Wicked Witch of the West.* Once the book was signed up with a new HarperCollins imprint—Reganbooks, directed by Judith Regan—I set about revising *Wicked,* relying on the careful reading and good advice of friends like Betty Levin and Rafique. *Wicked* can sound like a campy send-up of the lovable MGM film—and it is partly meant to be just that—but *Wicked* is also a serious fantasy in the tradition, I hope, of T. H. White and J. R. R. Tolkien. Living in England gave me a new distance from my American youth, and a different culture with which to understand and assess my own culture—and Oz's. My characterization of Elphaba as the Wicked Witch of the West owes a little bit to my earlier depiction of Baba Yaga, but this time the heroine is writ large, and human. She is morally ambiguous, she is brave and foolish, she is crippled, and yet she defies being labeled as merely "the green anomaly" or even "the wicked witch." Coming back to the United States with *Wicked* sold, and a national promotional tour to embark on, I found myself coming full circle once again. Throughout the United States, friends from folk music days at Saint Vincent's, from Simmons days, or from CLNE, or from Blue Mountain sessions all showed up at the readings—as did my loyal and warmhearted family. It was a chance for me to have a national reunion with most of the beloved people in my life.

There are many inside jokes that readers of *Wicked* will enjoy; I'll divulge only one here. If you look at the map printed on the end papers, you'll see an arrow pointing off the top left margin of the page, indicating that travelers heading in that direction would eventually reach Fliaan—the magic country my friends and sister Annie discovered and invented in Westland Hills, Albany, New York.

*

I have been asked to write this autobiographical essay when I am forty-one, which I

Gregory Maguire, Dublin, 1995

hope is too early for a definitive picture of my personal history and accomplishments. It is a couple of days after the New Year as I come to the end of this writing exercise, and though I'm not superstitious, I don't want to draw any conclusions about my life. I made my New Year's resolutions; that seems enough thinking about the future for one week.

The snow comes down tonight, fifteen inches they say. Rafique is working on an animation project at the computer in his study. I'm going to put on my big boots and go out in the dark, and shovel the walk, and knock some icicles from the eaves. I'll think about what I've put in here, and how I've said it, and what I've left out, and why. Maybe I'll get another chance, another time, to augment what I've said, or to update the installment. Let's just call this a chapter break, not FINIS. It is, after all, the start of a new year.

BIBLIOGRAPHY

FOR YOUNG PEOPLE

Fiction:

The Lightning Time, Farrar, Straus, 1978, Chatto & Windus, 1979.

The Daughter of the Moon, Farrar, Straus, 1980.

Lights on the Lake, Farrar, Straus, 1981.

The Dream Stealer, Harper, 1983, Green Bay Publications (Cambridge, England), 1993.

The Peace-and-Quiet Diner (picture book), illustrated by David Perry, Parents' Magazine Press (New York), 1988.

I Feel Like the Morning Star, Harper, 1989.

Lucas Fishbone (picture book), illustrated by Frank Gargiulo, HarperCollins, 1990.

Missing Sisters, Macmillan/Margaret K. McElderry, 1994, O'Brien Press (Dublin), 1994.

Seven Spiders Spinning, illustrated by Dirk Zimmer, Clarion, 1994, Harper Trophy, 1995, O'Brien Press, 1996.

The Good Liar, O'Brien Press, 1995.

Oasis, Clarion, 1996.

Six Haunted Hairdos, Clarion, in press.

FOR ADULTS

Fiction:

Wicked: The Life and Times of the Wicked Witch of the West, illustrated by Douglas Smith, HarperCollins/ReganBooks, 1995.

Nonfiction:

(Coeditor, with Barbara Harrison) *Innocence and Experience: Essays and Conversations on Children's Literature,* Lothrop, 1987.

Contributor:

Travelers in Time: Past, Present, and to Come (proceedings of the 1989 summer institute of Children's Literature New England), Green Bay Press (Cambridge, England), 1990.

Am I Blue? Coming Out from the Silence, edited by Marion Dane Bauer, HarperCollins, 1994.

Contributor of articles to *Horn Book Magazine* and essays and reviews for *Christian Science Monitor, Kirkus Reviews, Boston Review, Five Owls,* and *School Library Journal.* Also author of educational software material for McGraw-Hill Book Company and contributor of original stories and retellings to the Fisher-Price "Little People Big Book" series put out by Time-Life for Children.

John Marsden

1950-

John Marsden at Timbertop

Growing up in Australia wasn't a matter of kangaroos, surfboards, and the wild outback. Not for me, anyway. My childhood was spent in quiet country towns in the green southern states of Victoria and Tasmania. It was peaceful, secure, and often very boring.

My parents, Eustace Cullen Hudson Marsden and Jeanne Lawler Marsden (née Ray), were conservative, middle-class Australians of British origin. They were typical of their time. They'd met and married in wartime, and my father then returned to the battlefields. He was shot in the thigh but survived and returned home, where he and my mother had four children.

My father became a bank manager, my mother stayed home and raised the children. Again, it was a typical arrangement for the times.

When my father retired he was the bank's longest-serving employee in Australia—forty-eight years with the one employer. Perhaps one of the things I've done in my adult life is to react against that kind of commitment. At the latest count I've had thirty-two different jobs.

My first dim memories, however, are of the small Victorian country town of Kyneton, to which we moved when I was two. In those days the iceman still delivered to families without refrigerators, cooking was done on a fuel stove, and no one had television. I began school there

169

and perhaps there too acquired my liking for country living, a liking which has never left me.

In 1956 my family moved again, to Devonport, on the north coast of Tasmania. For four years I attended Devonport Primary School, where my interest in reading and writing really developed.

I first saw television when I was ten years old. In our small Tasmanian town an electrical shop brought in a TV and put it in their window, for the wedding of Princess Margaret. On the great day the whole town gathered in front of the shop and the set was switched on. All we saw was "snow"—grey and white static, with a few figures vaguely visible through the murk.

It didn't worry me a lot. By then I was completely in love with books. When the TV failed and Princess Margaret got married without me, I went back to reading and hardly took my nose out of books for the next ten years.

I read and read and read. Almost always fiction. Maybe the most powerful early novels for me were *Robinson Crusoe, The Children of Cherry Tree Farm, Little Men,* and the Australian books *Billabong* and *Tiger in the Bush.* When I ran out of books for boys I read the girls' books, like *Pollyanna* and *Daddy Long Legs.* I read some adult books too, including the ones I found hidden in the back of the bookcase, but I didn't really understand them. Some days I'd borrow three titles (the maximum allowed) from the town library, read them, and get them back to the library by five o'clock, in time to exchange them for three more before the library shut. I'd become a speed reader without really trying!

Of course, I did other stuff too. My favourite game was to draw a town layout on the driveway with chalk and use little model cars to bring the town to life. Perhaps that's how I first became used to creating and living in imaginary worlds. I envied a kid I knew who had a proper model train layout, powered by electricity. I decided that when I grew up I'd buy a huge railway set, the biggest in the world. I couldn't understand why adults, with all the money they seemed to have, wouldn't want to spend it on great toys like that. Somehow though, as I got older, I lost interest in those kinds of models. I still haven't bought that train layout.

Another favourite game was to whiz around the garden at high speed on the back of a tricycle. And when I was big enough I spent a lot of time riding my brother's bike anywhere and everywhere: all over town, and into the country. When my brother demanded the bike for his own use I would borrow my sister's, but it was a matter of great shame to be seen riding a girl's bike.

Nowadays it's becoming unusual for kids even to walk to school on their own, but in those days we did pretty much what we liked. After school, or at weekends, all we had to do was tell our mothers where we were going. If we then went in the opposite direction, no one seemed to notice or mind much.

School was something we had to go to. I never thought about whether I enjoyed it or not; I just went, every day. I can't remember much before grade three, except that by grade two I knew Enid Blyton's *The Children of Cherry Tree Farm* off by heart. I knew it so well that when the teacher wanted a break she'd have me stand up in front of the class and recite the next chapter to the other kids . . . from memory. She'd go off to the staff room and leave me there. I loved it! Maybe that's where I got my first taste of the power of storytelling. I was always something of an entertainer in school, the class comedian.

Grade three was pretty horrendous, with a teacher who screamed at us all year long. She threw great tantrums. One day she was screaming at us so fiercely that her false teeth flew out of her mouth. Not a kid moved. We were too scared of her to laugh.

We were caned for anything. Every Friday we had a test, and if we got less than seven out of ten we were caned. Recently I met up with a girl who'd been in that class with me. As she talked about those Friday tests she started to tremble with the memories. At the age of forty-four she was still haunted by her grade three days.

My brother was caned on the back of his legs so hard that blood ran down them. His sin was talking to his friend in the back row of the school choir. Choir was a lunchtime activity that kids volunteered for, but even that didn't save him.

When people talk about the good old days I think they're being a bit simplistic. Like everything, there was good and bad in those times.

In grade four things changed again. We got a kind and inspiring teacher called Mrs. Scott, who organised us into producing a class

In the uniform of The King's School, age twelve

newspaper. This was my first taste of publication. It was a heady experience. Seeing my name in print, having people—even adults—reacting to and commenting on what I'd written was powerful stuff.

I don't remember many of the actual lessons, but I remember the schoolyard games. Marbles were very popular, as were yo-yos. Backyard cricket was an Australian institution, commemorated by a recent popular song called "I Made a Hundred in the Backyard at Mum's." Forming clubs and gangs took up a lot of energy. We had a secret society that met in a disused laundry. To join we had to cut ourselves and use the blood to swear an oath of loyalty. I was in a shoplifting gang for a while, but that ended in disaster when we were caught by my father. Another activity that got us into trouble was yelling insults at the Catholic kids in the school next door.

In 1960, when I was ten, we moved again, this time to Sydney. In those days a car with Tasmanian number plates was so rare on the mainland that small crowds gathered around

us when we stopped anywhere. I thought Sydney was huge and exotic, and wildly exciting. I spent my first week collecting bus tickets, to the amusement of the staff in the hotel where we stayed. Riding on the escalators was as good as Disneyland. It was my first experience of city life, and we must have seemed very naive to the people we met.

I was enrolled at a private Anglican school called The King's School, Parramatta, for the remainder of my primary (elementary) schooling and for all my secondary years.

The strictest—and oldest—school in Australia, King's was run on military lines: conservative values were rigidly enforced in an all-boys boarding atmosphere. The uniform looked like it came out of a fancy dress shop. It actually came from the nineteenth century and hadn't been changed since. It attracted a lot of attention whenever we went out in public, and some of the attention was pretty ugly. Local kids made regular attempts to beat us up—I can't say I blame them. We did look outlandish. The rest of the Western world was embarking on a decade of drugs, free love, and the Beatles, but at King's boys continued to salute their teachers, drill with rifles for hours every week, and stand to attention when speaking to prefects.

In grade six I started writing what I called books. They were twenty or thirty pages long, with illustrations. They were rip-offs of Biggles and Agatha Christie, and they weren't very good! But I had fun doing them, and I was proud of them. In grade seven I spent hours editing and distributing class newspapers, underground productions that were quite popular with other students and had a good circulation. Some were to do with what was happening in the school, others were about the "new" music—groups like the Beatles and the Rolling Stones.

When adolescence hit I was caught by surprise. The world started sorting itself into new patterns, but I wasn't sure what the patterns were. I wasn't even sure that there were patterns. I lost a lot of confidence and started getting in trouble at school. The teachers' comments on my reports reflected that: "More careful work needed," "He must decide to concentrate on the work in hand and do it thoroughly," "Very disappointing—very little effort evident," "During most of the term a frivolous attitude was maintained."

A lot of the classwork was boring. When I wasn't producing illegal newspapers, I spent much of my time reading under the desk, a habit I had engaged in since grade four. I just couldn't bear to stop reading a book that had really grabbed my interest. One week I read twenty-three full-length novels.

There was no such genre as teenage fiction then. I read Ian Fleming (James Bond), Hammond Innes, John Buchan, Alastair Maclean, Nevil Shute, who all wrote terrific adventure stories. I've always been a sucker for a good storyteller. Other favourites included P. G. Wodehouse and Agatha Christie. It was a very British reading list, but some of them, especially Wodehouse, used language beautifully.

A few more "literary" books made a huge impression on me though. They included Huxley's *Brave New World,* Hemingway's *Old Man and the Sea,* Eliot's *Cocktail Party,* Orwell's *1984,* and above all, Salinger's *Catcher in the Rye. Catcher in the Rye* had me gasping for breath. I'd never dreamt you were allowed to write like that.

A typical school report, age thirteen

Holden Caulfield sounded like me! He thought the way I thought and spoke the way I would have spoken if I'd been allowed—and the way I secretly spoke inside myself. For the first time I was reading a genuine contemporary teenage voice. If I've had any success at capturing teenage voices on paper, it's because of what I learnt at the age of fifteen from J. D. Salinger.

The music of Bob Dylan was another big influence. A boy at school lent me a record called "Mr. Tambourine Man," and I took it home and played it. From the first few bars I was hooked. That strange, haunting, beautiful-ugly voice, singing such poetic and insidious images, made me restless and excited. I'm still a big Dylan fan, as are so many people of my generation.

I began to question everything: religion, education, law, parenting. All the institutions and customs that I'd been taught to accept unquestioningly. I'm still questioning them today, and hope I'm still doing so as I take my final breath.

My last two years of secondary schooling were a little more settled, but nevertheless I was one of a very small group of boys to graduate from King's without a single military award or promotion. I'm quite proud of that now, though at the time my parents were rather mortified. Still, by then I guess they were getting used to feeling mortified.

I did win a number of academic prizes, however, including one for a forty-thousand-word essay written for a competition in year eleven. It was on the topic of the poetry of World War I, another area of literature that I'd become passionate about. Poets like Wilfred Owen and Siegfried Sassoon moved me greatly. I spent an entire school vacation writing the essay and won the prize easily. I doubt if the judges bothered to read all forty thousand words.

In general, though, I'd have to say that when I finished school I didn't have much understanding of life. I thought I did, of course—everyone thinks they have a good understanding of life—but King's was too sheltered. The school was too competitive: every day was a battle for survival, and there was no sympathy for anyone who couldn't cope. I'd hardly talked to a girl for seven years, and the macho male environment left little room for students to develop an emotional life—something I later learned was crucial to a person's development.

When I left school it was to begin an arts/law degree at the University of Sydney, but I soon abandoned that for a series of exotic jobs, which included collecting blood, looking after a mortuary at nights, working in a sideshow, being a night clerk in the casualty department of Sydney Hospital, and guarding Australia's oldest house from vandals. I didn't plan any of this; it just happened. It sounds like the perfect background for a writer, but that's not necessarily so. Some of the greatest writers the world has seen didn't travel more than a few hundred miles from their homes in the whole of their lives—Jane Austen, Emily Dickinson, and the Brontë sisters, for example. I doubt if Shakespeare got around much. It's the internal journeys that are important, not the external ones.

Still, I did travel, moving from job to job as I got bored with each one. Once I mastered a job I got bored with it and started restlessly looking for the next challenge. Maybe that was a reaction to the boredom of my early life and the tedium of most of my years in schools. Maybe, as I said before, it was a reaction to my father's lifestyle. Working in hospitals was probably the most challenging job, because of the endless variety. One never knew what the next minute would bring: a burns case, a drunk with abrasions, a suicide, a hypochondriac with a headache. I saw suffering and death in the hospitals, but I also saw a lot of humour, a lot of friendship, a lot of people showing strength and endurance.

During these years I continued to read extensively and to experiment with writing. When I was about twenty-one I wrote a long book, one hundred thousand words, and sent it to a publisher. They sent it back all too quickly. It wasn't a very good novel, but it had some of the elements that my later books also explored. It was the story of two boys sent to boarding school. While they were there they discovered that they were actually half brothers. I think it was called "The Heart of Things," and it was influenced by Evelyn Waugh, with whose work I was quite fascinated.

Years later, without looking at my book again, I used the manuscript to start a fire one cold winter's night. It burnt pretty well.

I won't pretend that these were happy years in my life. From time to time I made attempts to restart tertiary education, but none of them worked. I didn't enjoy the courses, I wasn't

In the uniform of The King's School, age seventeen

motivated, I couldn't settle to study. I passed first-year law but dropped out of law school halfway through the second year after seeing a tidal wave of final-year students entering the building for their evening classes. The sight of so many grey pinstripe suits made me nauseous. I knew that I could never dress like that, could never live like that. I got up and left the building and didn't go back. I was engaged to a nurse for a short time but broke it off when she wanted me to go deeply into debt just to buy her an engagement ring. It made me realise that our values were seriously different.

I ended up as a patient in a psychiatric hospital for several months. I'd become depressed and felt that life was going nowhere. Like most depressed people, I couldn't imagine that things would ever get better. If I've learned one thing in life, it's that all moods, all emotional states, do change eventually. Sometimes you just have to sit it out and wait for the change to come. The trouble was, I didn't know that back then. It was a time of great despair.

One of the patients in the hospital was a fourteen-year-old girl who didn't speak. She hadn't spoken for eight months. I didn't get to know her very well—she made it impossible for anyone to get to know her—but I felt great sympathy for her. I don't know why she had become silent, though the rumour around the hospital was that it was a reaction to her father's remarriage.

One day another patient and I were getting our breakfasts on trays at the servery (dining hall). We were talking about the girl who didn't speak, and he remarked that she was being discharged from the hospital that very day.

"So is she talking now?" I asked.

"Yes, she's been talking for a few weeks."

We decided to have breakfast at her table. We sat with her and we talked. It was a moving experience. She seemed so much happier. Although she was still shy, she was certainly excited about going home. Perhaps because of my own enjoyment of language, the pleasure it's always given me, I was fascinated by this girl, and twenty years later she was to be one of the inspirations for my first published novel.

I eventually left the hospital myself and resumed my unsettled life. I worked for a charity for a while, then got a job driving trucks. I delivered frozen chickens all over Sydney, but with mixed success. Accidentally locking myself into the back of the truck while delivering chickens to a Red Rooster restaurant didn't help my career. Nor did backing into a car in a car park, or knocking down an overhead arch whilst driving into a reception centre.

A series of other jobs followed, until I joined General Express, a rapidly growing collection of transport companies in Sydney. I was appointed to Operations, where I got to allocate jobs to the trucks each day and direct them as they plied the highways and byways of the city. Again, I wasn't always successful. When one driver rang up to say that he didn't know if his truck would fit under a rail bridge on a major highway, I told him that the job was urgent and to go for it. The next phone call was from the police, informing us that our truck was stuck under a bridge and had caused a four-mile traffic jam.

By the age of twenty-seven, however, I had worked my way up to the position of administration manager to a group of the companies. This promotion had one serious disadvantage—it took me away from the adrenalin-pumping operations desk and put me in a quiet carpeted office in the company headquarters. Within weeks I was bored again. I wanted something more intellectually stimulating and spiritually satisfying. One day I was reading the newspaper in my office—having finished all my day's work by ten o'clock—when I saw an ad for teaching courses, in a country town named Bathurst.

I'd long been interested in teaching, so I decided to apply. I'd always had a vague idea that I might enjoy it, but then I'd had the same vague ideas about other jobs and they hadn't worked out. But I applied for a primary teaching course and was accepted, after persuading them that I was now serious about tertiary studies.

One reason I chose the course was that I thought it would be the easiest one available. I had so little confidence left that I didn't want to risk failing again.

From the first day, however, I knew I'd found my vocation. I loved the life and energy of the course and the sense that we were doing something exciting and important. I loved the fact that we were encouraged to use our imaginations. I was lucky that it was a progressive and enlightened course, taught by dedicated tutors. After the time spent in places like law school and trucking companies, the contrast was strong. Now I was dealing with people, not with millions of printed words about cases decided in 1763 or boxes of frozen chickens or tonnes of steel girders to be moved from Ultimo to Woolloomooloo.

My first lecturer in English was a man named Nigel Krauth, who was later to become one of Australia's most exciting and admired novelists. I didn't know then that he was a writer, but I knew he was an exceptional teacher. Early in the course a student asked him if he ever gave full marks for English essays. "Yes," he replied, "if I think it's written better than I could have written it myself." For my first assignment he gave me 30-30. It was one of the most wonderful fillips my confidence has ever received. I guess it doesn't matter how old you are; praise and success are always powerful.

I soon realised that teaching, working in casualty at a big city hospital, and being operations manager for a transport company were similar in many ways. Every day was different. You could never get smug, never think you'd finally conquered the job. There was a tremendous energy in the hospital and the Operations Room, as there is in most schools. You never knew what to expect from one day to the next. Although all three jobs could be frustrating, I rarely got bored in them—and that was very important to me.

In Casualty too, of course, you tend to see people as they really are—the masks drop away. That happens in schools a lot. If there's one thing that fascinates writers, it's the differences between masks and reality.

Six months into my teaching studies I moved into All Saints' College, an Anglican coeducational day and boarding school, as a resident tutor. This meant that I supervised boarding students in the evenings and did various other jobs in the school. I got free board in exchange, which enabled me to continue with my studies. By the end of my course two years later, I was editing the school magazine, teaching remedial reading, coaching football and cricket, and producing the school play. But maybe the most significant thing that happened there was that I met an English teacher named John Mazur.

John was a Canadian who had been working in Australia for many years. He taught in a way that I had never seen before. He inspired, cajoled, bullied, stimulated. His lessons were brilliant, masterpieces of creativity. He was dedicated to his job: he worked so hard that he made me feel lazy, and I think I'm a workaholic!

John was especially good with students who were unhappy, unmotivated, negative. As our friendship developed I must at some stage have been daydreaming about the mute girl in the psych hospital because I remember wondering what might have happened if she had come into contact with John. Would she have ended up in a psych hospital if she'd had an adult like him in her life? I didn't think so.

I was still eleven or twelve years away from writing *So Much to Tell You*, but I guess that was another stage in the genesis of the book.

When I finished my teaching course, the boarding school offered me the position of sportsmaster and special education teacher—the only vacancy they had. I took on these two functions but as well taught English and Divinity, ran the activities programme, curated the cricket wickets, coached four different sporting teams, coached the debating squad, continued to edit the school magazine, and began an arts

degree by correspondence. I feel exhausted now just thinking about it all, but that's what I did. I guess that's another reason I like teaching—it gives me an outlet for my energy.

English teaching was my favourite activity at All Saints', and I gradually concentrated on that more and more. You can be so creative in an English class! Everything is grist to your mill.

I stayed at All Saints' four more years, during which I completed my arts degree, majoring in English and German literature.

From there I went to a position in Australia's most famous school, Geelong Grammar School. I sent in a highly unconventional application. When they asked for three references I sent thirty, all written by students in my classes. I felt that the only people qualified to speak with authority on a teacher's competence were the students. My application was full of jokes, which make me cringe when I think about them now but which apparently appealed to the school principal because I got the job.

Geelong is a very expensive private school that attracts students from all over the world. I liked its cosmopolitan flavour and the interesting young people I met there. I became head of English at one of its four campuses and after two years moved to its Timbertop campus, again as head of English.

Timbertop is one of the world's more unusual schools. Prince Charles is its most famous ex-student, but it's a place that's had a profound effect on a lot of people. In the remote Australian bush two hundred fourteen-year-olds live in wooden cabins for a year, having only minimal contact with their families. The boys and girls spend the year doing schoolwork, but as well they hike, ski, canoe, climb, and run up and down mountains. The longest run is seventeen miles, the longest hike six days, during which the students are on their own, covering vast distances with their packs on their backs.

The staff do all these activities too. It's gruelling stuff, but it gets you fit. And it's a very real challenge, not an artificial one.

I stayed at Timbertop four years. Although there were times when I hated it, overall I thought it was a wonderful place, a life-changing experience. I've always felt at home in the bush. Many people are scared of it, and I've had times of fear, when I've been lost, for example, or when I'm being confronted by a

At Geelong Grammar School

snake. Fear is a survival device in the bush. It helps you stay alive. But I love the smell of the bush. And I love the gum trees, the subtle colours, the restless wildness, the incessant life and movement. When I'm away from the bush too long I start getting sick. My health, my life, depend on my having plenty of contact with this profoundly beautiful, profoundly Australian place.

Being in a boarding school in the bush, so far from the civilised world, is a strange experience. It's like living on a teenage island for long periods of time. You get to know the students really well. At Timbertop, without realising it, I started to absorb all kinds of information about their lives. The way they talked to each other, the way they interacted, the values and opinions they held. I admired their energy, their optimism, their idealism. I thought the girls in particular were very supportive of each other.

I began to question a lot of the myths about young people that are so commonly accepted.

Girls gossip more than boys? No. Girls are "bitchier" than boys? No. Girls are neater and tidier? No again. Boys settle their differences with a good clean fight and then it's all over? No way. Boys are braver than girls? No. There are lots of variations among human beings, of course, but they haven't got much to do with gender.

A number of factors combined at about this time to reawaken my determination to write. One was the simple problem of being unable to find good books for my students. The variety of texts available was pretty depressing. I thought that one solution might be to write one myself. I was also having another midlife crisis, of the type that I'd been having since I was fourteen. I felt that my life was going nowhere, that the dreams I'd had since childhood were no closer to being realised, that life was slipping past too quickly.

One day a magazine journalist and photographer arrived to do a story about the school. I didn't meet them, but one of my students told me the next day about a conversation she'd had with the photographer. She showed him an article I'd written for the previous year's school magazine. He read it and remarked, "This guy's in the wrong job. He should be writing."

This simple comment came at the right time. I thought, "Being a magazine photographer, he must have read a few stories in his time. Surely if he thinks I can write. . . ."

I resolved that when the next school holidays rolled around I would write a book. Because I was sick of starting projects (especially books) and not finishing them, I decided that this time I would write a complete book. I didn't care how long or short it was, as long as it was finished. My girlfriend had gone to London on a whim, to see *Cats,* and I was to look after her house, in a coastal town in Victoria. So I knew there wouldn't be too many external interruptions.

The holidays arrived, and I sat down and started to write. I made two decisions that turned out to be critical. One was to use the diary format, the other was to aim it at teenage readers. These two decisions seemed to free me to write more fluently than before. I worked in an intensity of emotion, a state that I often seem to slip into when writing.

The book that resulted, and which was finished on the last day of the three-week holiday, was the story of a mute girl who is sent to boarding school after other attempts to rehabilitate her had failed. Marina is an amalgam of two people, the silent girl of fourteen whom I had met in Sydney in 1970 and a Victorian woman named Kay Nesbitt, whose face had been badly damaged by a shotgun blast. Lindell was based on John Mazur, the inspiring Canadian teacher of English at All Saints' Bathurst.

I got the book typed, gave it the imaginative title of "Diary," and sent it to six different publishers, all of whom rejected it. At this stage no one had read it but the typist and the six publishers, but a chance conversation with a friend, Melbourne bookseller Albert Ullin, changed the book's fate. Albert offered to read it, did so, and gave it to a new Sydney publisher, Walter McVitty Books, who eventually made an offer for it.

I suppose every published writer remembers that moment when the letter making an offer to publish at last arrives. I certainly remember it vividly. The only catch was that the editor wanted the book to be longer and to have a different ending. After the usual sulking that

every writer will recognize, I sat down when the next school holidays arrived and did as he asked. I have to admit that the changes did make for a better book.

After some more minor editorial work on the manuscript, it was published in 1987 with the new title *So Much to Tell You.* To hold that book in my hands, as I did one night outside a freight yard where I had just collected the first copies, may not have been the greatest moment in my life, but it is hard to think of a greater. I kept running my hands over it, touching it, opening and closing it, almost in disbelief.

A good proportion of the first print run was bought by my students, who were smart enough to know how to improve their grades in English. Those who bought them reluctantly can at least have the consolation of knowing that their copies, being first editions, are now worth about five times what they paid for them!

The book quickly attracted favourable attention, but no one could have predicted the

The author with a colleague from Timbertop

At Timbertop

success in store for it, least of all the publisher who rejected it on the grounds that it "would have no interest for high school students." In Australia *So Much to Tell You* won the 1988 Children's Book of the Year Award, the Allan Marshall Award, and the KOALA Award, and in America, the Christopher Award. It was also named as a "notable book" by the American Library Association. It is one of Australia's biggest selling novels—ever—and has now been published in fourteen different countries in nine languages.

My everyday life didn't change much; being in such an isolated part of the world meant that I was insulated from the success of the book. But when I moved back to Geelong in 1988, I began to realise that it would be quite a battle to juggle writing and teaching. The mailbag began to get heavier, and there were invitations to give talks and workshops all over the place. These were aspects of writing that I hadn't previously considered.

But my previous lack of confidence about writing was cured, I hope forever. Before *So Much to Tell You,* I had been unable to finish the books that I started, but that now ceased to be a problem. When staying with some friends on a sheep property in New South Wales—a family with five daughters—I started a new book, a comedy in the Australian larrikin tradition, but again written for contemporary teenagers.

My only reason for writing it was to amuse the five girls, to make them laugh. Titled *The Great Gatenby,* this book was rejected by two publishers—one with the prophetic words, "Adults will hate it, kids will love it"—but was accepted by Pan Macmillan. It was not long before teenagers began to respond to it, writing comments like, "I felt as if I was a part of Erle's life," "I loved your book . . . my only complaint is that people gave me weird looks when I laughed on the bus," and "My mum had to bring my lunch and tea to my room because I refused to come out till I'd finished your book."

Many teenagers admitted that it was the first book they had read. Nothing in my writing career gives me more satisfaction than the fact that reluctant readers seem to find some of my books accessible and even enjoyable.

My third book was partly inspired by the Timbertop experience. It was very different again from either *So Much to Tell You* or *The Great Gatenby.* It had its origins in many sources, apart from Timbertop: a belief that Western society had lost its way, for instance. A concern that a lack of ritual and ceremony had impoverished many lives. A respect for Australian Aboriginal and North American Indian cultures. A fear that young people were not being allowed to grow up, were being kept as children for too long. A belief in the importance of storytelling: its mythic power and its ability to work on a number of levels simultaneously.

My strongly held feeling that many teachers and writers were underestimating young people, were unaware of their urgent desire for intellectual and spiritual nourishment, led me to write a book which challenges and makes demands upon its readers. Their powerful response to *The Journey*—it is in its fifth printing—has confirmed the ability of young people to grapple with the most complex issues.

After *The Journey* came another change of pace, with my first book for primary school readers. *Staying Alive in Year 5* is as subversive as *The Great Gatenby* and *The Journey* but quite different in content. It began in the shower: while soaping up one morning at the start of a new school year I started planning my opening remarks to the students. "You must get here on time. You must have the right books. You must do your homework. No calling out without putting your hand up." Reflecting on this, I realised how tedious this routine must be to the students, as well as to the teachers. I began to wonder what would happen if a teacher opened the year's work with a bizarre and unexpected set of rules. Still dripping, I ran from the shower and jotted down the first few pages of *Staying Alive,* a book that has been one of my most successful. It is now in its sixth printing.

By 1990 I was finding it increasingly difficult to juggle my teaching and writing careers, and it became obvious that one would have to give way. I took leave from teaching for a term and wrote my fifth book, *Out of Time,* which was published the same year. It is a book that uses discontinuous narrative to give a sense of lost and alienated people moving through a timeless landscape. Fragments and unfinished stories reflect real life more accurately than does traditional fiction and seemed particularly appropriate for the dislocated lives of the characters in *Out of Time.* In a long and thoughtful discussion of the book in the magazine *Literature Base,* the reviewer concluded, "Spending some time thinking about a well-written book

Marsden with some of his readers

like *Out of Time* can extend our experience as humans."

I guess this is one of the reasons I write, and one of the reasons I value other people's books.

I returned to teaching at Geelong for the remainder of the year but then resigned to take up the offer of a residency at the Keesing Studio in Paris. This is an apartment that a generous benefactor of Australian literature endowed some years ago for Australian writers. It was my first experience of living overseas—living, compared to just passing through a place. I wandered the streets of Paris in a daze of perpetual wonder. There were few museums, galleries, or churches that I didn't visit. Perhaps the best thing of all though was the French-language lessons that I went to every day for several months. Learning the beautiful French language was fun, but better still was the class itself, an extraordinary mix of students from all over the world—Canada, Sri Lanka, Portugal, Japan, Iran, Britain, Norway, the United States, Finland, Germany. It was an Internet forum face to face, but better than any computer!

It also amused me to see how quickly, as a student again, I slipped back into adolescent behaviours. Talking to other students when the teacher turned her back to write on the board, lying about doing my homework, writing letters when I was meant to be doing class exercises . . . the experience gave me fresh sympathy for the students in my own classes back in Australia.

After an exhilarating and inspiring six months in Paris, I came home for the launch of my new book, *Letters from the Inside.* A harrowing but, I hope, realistic novel, *Letters* is based on a number of true stories: a newspaper account of a girl who found out when she was sixteen that her father had murdered her mother, a television interview with a girlfriend of a murderer, a conversation with a girl who had a violent brother, and my own experiences in a Tasmanian prison when arrested during a conservation demonstration. The book was too strong for some: one Sydney reviewer called it "the most pernicious book I have ever read" and commented that it made "*American Psycho* look like a spotless lamb." Others differed: noted American author Robert Cormier wrote that it was "unforgettable . . . absolutely shattering," and added that "John Marsden . . . is a major

Marsden's house and garden

writer who deserves world-wide acclaim." Many adults were unnerved by the book, but young people loved it; one was moved to say that "John Marsden is the Poet Laureate of Australian teenagers."

Letters from the Inside ran through ten print runs in its first four years in Australia. It was followed by *Take My Word for It,* a "coquel," if there is such a word, to *So Much to Tell You.* By taking another character from that book, Lisa, and telling her story, I was able to explore further the lives and worlds of all the girls in *So Much to Tell You.* I enjoyed returning to the dormitories of Warrington School, but more than that, I enjoyed getting to know Lisa better. I guess all writers like strong characters, and Lisa, cold and proud and deeply unhappy, is very strong indeed.

I had decided, whilst in Paris, that I'd try my luck as a full-time writer when I got back to Australia. By then I'd been teaching for thirteen years, and I'd noticed in the last couple that I was finding it harder to summon the imagination and energy which teaching needs. In the event, however, I simply swapped full-time teaching for "itinerant" teaching. I began a series of tours, lectures, and workshops, speaking to an estimated thirty-five thousand people in the first twelve months alone. I continued to do this for three and a half years. During that time I spoke in jails, libraries, and hospitals, in remote outback communities and huge inner-city multicultural high schools, in Jewish, Catholic, Protestant, and alternative schools, in isolated Tasmanian communities and to audiences of twelve hundred in city halls. I took workshops over the radio, to children on the school-of-the-air network, but also spoke to Rotary clubs, businesspeople, retirees, teachers, and parents. I went to New Zealand, Britain, and the United States and gave talks at the International School of Paris, exclusive private schools in Baltimore, a peaceful rural school in Ohio, a heavily guarded urban school in Dayton, and two of Britain's most distinguished and ancient schools for the wealthy and aristocratic. It was a gruelling and exhilarating time.

Somehow though there was always time to write. For the younger readers who had enjoyed *Staying Alive in Year 5,* I wrote *Looking for Trouble,* a book I was especially happy with. Although this is a light and cheerful book, it also asks young people to engage with some serious issues, in particular the effect on families of greedy and dishonest adults. The humour in the book certainly worked: to this day I have never had a reader comment on its poignancy, yet it's the only one of my own books that can still bring tears to my eyes!

Shortly after that I wrote *Everything I Know about Writing,* a very important book for me. I tried to put down on paper all the things I'd slowly worked out over many years—everything I know about writing. I'd never thought much about writing when I started, but over the years I'd been asked so many questions that I gradually began to figure out just how I go about it, the things that work and the things that don't. I know I can't turn someone into a Shakespeare—I can't even turn myself into a Shakespeare—but I do believe there are specific skills that can be taught, and that will improve anybody's writing.

Well, everybody except Alan Garner, Katherine Paterson, Margaret Mahy, Robert Cormier, Gillian Rubinstein, and a few others maybe.

Within eighteen months the book had been reprinted twice.

The other book I wrote during this period was a play. A Melbourne school commissioned me to write and direct a one-act play, so I did so, choosing to base it on *So Much to Tell You.* I enjoyed the project so much that I went on and turned it into a full-length piece, which was published in 1993.

In 1992, however, I began a book that was to engage me totally for the next two years. One of my childhood fantasies had been of a world without adults, a world in which the adults had magically disappeared and the kids were left to run the place. I wasn't surprised when I recently heard the fabulous New Zealand writer Margaret Mahy comment that the first thing to do when writing for young people is to get rid of the parents. In *Tomorrow, When the War Began,* I brought to life that childhood dream and got rid of the parents on a dramatic scale. The immediate inspiration for the book, however, was the depressing news footage on TV of wars in places like Sarajevo, Rwanda, and East Timor. While the West procrastinated,

immoral aggressors like Indonesia, Russia, and Iraq continued to steal territory and destroy their fellow humans. In some parts of the world, thanks largely to geographical accidents, people live in relative safety. Australia is one of those places. We know of only two attacks on Australia—one in the eighteenth century, when the British invasion resulted in an overwhelming victory against the Aboriginal people, and one in 1942, when Japan launched brief attacks on two Australian cities.

So Australians take their security for granted. I don't think anyone seriously contemplates that this country will be invaded again. It's a writer's job to shock readers out of their comfortably held assumptions, to force them to look at issues they may prefer not to look at—hence, *Tomorrow, When the War Began.*

Like a number of other books I've written, *Tomorrow, When the War Began* soon became an obsession. I realised when I was halfway through it that one book would not be enough to tell the story. The scenario was just too big for one volume. I decided I would need, eventually, to write a sequel. And in fact, when I finished the first book I couldn't stop. To my surprise—and horror—I started the second one the next day. "Horror" because writing a book does so much damage to one's ordinary life! Everything goes on hold. The dishes pile up in the sink, the mail goes unanswered, the invitations to dinner get forgotten. Writing is a very disruptive activity!

Things got worse however. As I wrote the second book, *The Dead of the Night,* I began to realise that two wouldn't be enough either. With some reluctance I came to the conclusion that there would have to be a third one. I finished *The Dead of the Night,* and thought, "Well, eventually I'll get around to writing the third, but I'll give myself a year or two away from it first. There's a lot of other projects I'd like to have a go at in the meantime."

Over the next few weeks I started half a dozen other books. None of them seemed to work. I was restless and edgy, difficult to live with. Finally, sulkily, I admitted to myself that there was only one thing I wanted to do, and that was to return to the world of Ellie and her friends. I began the third book, *The Third Day, the Frost.* Again I wrote compulsively, passionately. When I'd written the last page something quite strange happened. I closed it feeling that at last this story was finished. There was nothing more to say. The story was out of my system.

I've had this feeling before in writing, but never has it taken me three books to achieve it. It's a bittersweet experience, the relief of knowing that something is finished, coupled with the disappointment of having to say good-bye to people I've been intimately acquainted with for so long.

The effect that these books have had and are continuing to have is hard to gauge. The passionate responses by teenagers to them has exceeded anything in my experience. They don't just read them, they live them. I think the power of the books may have something to do with the bad press that teenagers get in modern Western society. In the *Tomorrow, When the War Began* trilogy, teenagers act with courage, initiative, maturity, a sense of responsibility. These are, of course, qualities that teenagers have demonstrated many many times in many many places. The fact that we have created a society where young people are no longer given the opportunity to take on responsible roles is something which should cause embarrassment to all of us. The infantilisation of teenagers is a destructive, cruel, and dangerous process; we have reaped some of the consequences already, and we will reap many more of them yet.

Two other books complete my output to this date. One is *Cool School,* a comedy which uses the "Choose Your Own Adventure" model. Again, I was particularly conscious of reluctant readers whilst writing this. The other is *Checkers,* a novel which perhaps breaks some more new ground. It is, in some ways, a political novel, and that alone makes it a rare beast among books for young people. It uses a first-person narrative to explore a story of political corruption and the effect on the narrator, a teenage girl. *Checkers* will be published in 1996.

Obviously writing has become a big part of my life since the appearance of *So Much to Tell You* in 1987. Yet this writing life has had a number of surprises. I suppose I had a romantic view of how it would be to write full-time. I thought I would live in my little country cottage, ivy climbing the walls and roses blooming around the house, and I would think beautiful thoughts and write beautiful things.

Well, sometimes it seems like the only thing climbing the walls is me. There is ivy, but it drives me crazy. It grows so fast I have to cut it back hard every few weeks. And cutting back ivy is not easy! It's tough stuff. But it's a good metaphor. The writing life has a lot to do with ivy. There's so much to do that if you don't keep cutting and working and keeping things under control, you'd soon be smothered. In some ways writing is like many other jobs: a mixture of good and bad, of boring and exhilarating, but always requiring a lot of self-discipline and hard work.

There's so much mail, to begin with. And almost every letter is urgent. "If you could send it back later in the week . . . I would be ever so grateful," reads one that's on my desk at the moment. "Sorry but this assignment's due April 23rd, so I'd need the stuff by next week." That's from a student. "Would it be possible for an early assessment, as I would like the hardback to be printed nice and early," writes a publisher. "John I hate to rush you but the galleys have to be at the printer by the 18th, which means I'll need them by the 12th at the absolute latest," says the fax from the editor.

Anonymous strangers make outrageous demands on the phone: "I hear you're a bit of a writer," begins one man. "My daughter's written a novel, and I thought you might like to have a look at it and tell her whether it's any good or not." It turns out that his daughter is twenty-one, and I wonder why she can't make her own phone calls. At least she mightn't be as rude as her father.

There's a tremendous amount of what I think doctors call "scut work," boring necessary stuff that consumes a lot of time. Editing manuscripts especially. Checking and approving covers, press releases, blurbs, biographies, ads. Arranging schedules with publicists. Doing interviews with people who haven't read the books ("Can you just give me an idea of what the book's about, before we start?"). Replying to requests for information and invitations to workshops and conferences. Checking through contracts. Hassling publishers about delays or distribution problems or stock shortages ("My mother was in the East Cheltenham News Agency last month, and she said they only had two copies of my books").

Among the issues I have to take up with my publishers next week are a spelling error that a reader has pointed out in one of my books, a small discrepancy in a royalty statement (twenty dollars, to be exact), an expression of interest from a West Australian film company about film rights, a disagreement about sales to a book club, the need to rewrite an old contract, and the advisability of entering one of the books for a children's literature peace award. And that's a fairly typical week. I don't have an agent, so maybe I make things harder for myself by doing it on my own, but I prefer it that way.

I'm not complaining; I know there are a lot worse jobs around. And there are many consolations. The major one is the mail. Some of the letters I get are wonderful, wonderful. I read and reread them and treasure them forever. They come from all over the world, from people of all ages and both genders, and they sometimes have me blinking very hard. Opening the mail each day is a major source of excitement. I consider myself very lucky to get such letters, most of which are from strangers and all of which, incidentally, I answer by hand.

For all that, I made the decision recently to return to full-time teaching. My friends think I'm mad, but I don't. The long break from the classroom has renewed my enthusiasm for it, but to make matters more interesting I've taken on primary teaching—a new experience for me. I have a class of grade six girls, and we do a lot of maths and science and social studies and stuff like that—yes, and some language and reading and writing too! They're not very interested in books, which doesn't worry me a lot—you don't have to read to have an interesting and enjoyable life. Books are still my number-one hobby, but that doesn't mean other people have to feel the same way.

I imagine I'll always be writing, all my life, because there is something within me that needs to tell stories. I don't know that it gives me pleasure exactly; it's just something I need to do. It's been my great good fortune that other people have been prepared to take the time to read my stories. But there are things that writing has not done for me. I don't think it's made me any happier, for instance. I don't think it's given me any more confidence, though I may be wrong about that. A teenager who has read some of my books and who has been in touch with me quite often about problems in her life said to me the other day: "It's like a big chore, life, that you've gotta do. I just want to hurry up and die. I just want to fast-forward life and get to the end." I've felt like that too.

Yet at other times it can be such fun, such a warm, glowing adventure. I don't necessarily regret the depressions that have so often flooded through me—I think they give insight, helping me to understand a different dimension of life. I feel sorry for people who've never been depressed, because I think they must lack that understanding. I certainly don't feel comfortable with people who've never known depression. But the darkness and despair of depression is an awful sensation. The less often I have to feel it, the better!

Among the things that give me pleasure these days are books and teaching, obviously, but also gardening, snow skiing, driving, and television. I like to have my brain stretched, but I also like many of the elements that comprise the popular culture, like *The Simpsons,* pop music, light fiction.

Language is one of my passions in life: I love words the way some people like music. I collect words wherever I go, and rejoice in their beauty or despair over their poverty. I love words like *slurp, hiccup, oxymoron, supercalifragilistic-expealidocious* because of the way they sound. I love other words because of what they stand for—the word *chocolate*'s pretty appealing, for example! I hate words like *scenic, attractive, interesting,* because they're lazy words; *dandruff* and *tinea,* because they're ugly; *sodium triphosphate* because it's boring. One of the pleasures of gardening is being able to delight in the names of the flowers: honeysuckle, snow-in-summer, comfrey, columbines.

The language of young people is a source of constant fascination too. "I D'd in science," I heard a teenager say the other day, as she described her bad grades to a friend. "What's up her nose?" a year ten student complained to her friend about a girl who was annoying them. "Your books are so hot a heater couldn't hold them. In other words, they are cool!" a reader wrote to me. I still don't know what she meant, but it sounded complimentary. "What'd you lag on me for?" a boy muttered to another boy who'd just got him in trouble with a teacher.

All these expressions are rich and colourful and lively. It gives me great pleasure to witness language being used so poetically and imaginatively.

The other passion of my life is the preservation of life. The older I get, the more disturbed I get by the wanton destruction of other creatures by humans. I am proud to say that I have never used an insecticide or herbicide in my large, rambling garden. I keep the grass long so that insects have lots of places to hide. I don't try to stop the birds and possums from helping themselves to the fruit on my trees, even though there's never much left for me. The house is full of spiders and other insects, but it doesn't bother me: if the spiders get too menacing I capture them and release them in the garden. I do kill mosquitos and flies if they get in the house, but lately I'm getting more and more reluctant to do even that.

The result is a garden that is full of life. It's not just the birds that give me pleasure. It's the insects, who are present in enormous numbers and infinite variety. It's the frogs, the bees, the water rats, the lizards and snakes, the gliders and mice and feathertails.

Each living creature is a unique and complex organism. If I tried for a thousand years, I could not make even one of them. Yet we kill them without a moment's thought or a moment's regret. We have no right. We have no right.

This is a passage from *Checkers*:

> We started talking in the bathroom. When I went to wash my hands, standing next to her, I realised she was trying to slip a piece of paper under a silverfish that was scurrying around in the handbasin.
>
> "What are you doing?" I asked. It was the first time I've spoken directly to her. I don't talk to anyone here much, except Oliver.
>
> "Saving its life," she said. And laughed.
>
> "Saving its life? Why bother?"
>
> "Why would I want it to die?"
>
> I just looked at her and she laughed again. Laughter's not a sound we hear a lot in this place, and Esther's laugh is quite nice. She kept going with what she was saying.
>
> "It's such a complex little creature. So delicate. Imagine how long it'd take to make one, if you were a human insect-maker. You could spend your whole life working on it and still not get even one finished. And we kill them so casually. A quick squish of the finger and a moment later we've forgotten that we even did it."
>
> I started to feel guilty. "Is that why you're so fussy about what you eat?"
>
> "Mmm."
>
> We started talking about everything then. . . .

Albie, the author's beloved dog

The death of my dog, Albie, at the age of six, from kidney cancer, caused me the most terrible grief that I think I have ever experienced. Albie's death taught me yet again how precious each animal is, how dear, and gave me fresh appreciation for the creatures with whom we are fortunate to share this planet. I despise zoos, because I think they symbolize the refusal of humans to allow any life form other than themselves to have the space to which they're entitled. I hope I continue to improve in my treatment of my fellow creatures, be they animal or vegetable.

BIBLIOGRAPHY

FOR YOUNG ADULTS

Fiction:

So Much to Tell You . . ., Walter McVitty (Australia), 1987; Little, Brown (Boston), 1989.

The Journey, Pan Australia, 1988.

The Great Gatenby, Pan Australia, 1989.

Staying Alive in Year 5, Pan Australia, 1989.

Out of Time, Pan Australia, 1990.

Letters from the Inside, Pan Australia, 1991, Houghton Mifflin, 1994.

Take My Word for It, Pan Australia, 1992.

Looking for Trouble, Pan Australia, 1993.

Cool School, Pan Australia, 1995.

Checkers, forthcoming.

"Tomorrow, When the War Began" trilogy:

Tomorrow, When the War Began, Pan Australia, 1993, Houghton Mifflin (USA), 1995.

The Dead of Night, Pan Australia, 1994, Houghton Mifflin, forthcoming.

The Third Day, the Frost, Pan Australia, 1995.

Nonfiction:

Everything I Know About Writing, Heinemann Australia, 1993.

Plays:

So Much to Tell You: the Play, Walter McVitty, 1994.

Ken Mochizuki

1954-

Ken Mochizuki in Seattle, 1994

During the early '70s, there was a popular television series called "Room 222." With a multiracial cast, the show tried to be early '70s hip and cool, solving some type of problem in the school every week.

In one episode, two students take over the school's radio station to broadcast their views on an issue they feel strongly about. One of those protesting students begins to contemplate the trouble they will get into if they follow through with what they had planned. His accomplice replies, "You have to pay the price for what you think is right."

My father, watching this particular program with me, said, "You hear that, Ken?"

That was over twenty years ago when I was in high school. Now, most of my friends my age arc fathers or mothers living in nice houses and driving nice cars, but I continue to pay the price for what I think is right. As of this writing, I am the author of two children's picture books, *Baseball Saved Us* and *Heroes*. Both these books say what I have always wanted to say. I may never get rich from being a children's picture book writer, but I am doing what I want to do—and what I think is right.

I was born in and spent most of my life in Seattle, Washington. My lessons in justice, prejudice, and doing what is right go back as far as I can remember, even back to the first grade. The teacher, a devoutly religious woman, led her class in morning prayer at the same time we recited the Pledge of Allegiance. We also prayed before having our midday snack of milk and graham crackers.

I remember one day, my first-grade teacher told us about all the food and beverages we should not partake in. One of the forbidden beverages was tea. My grandparents, immigrants from Japan who had lived in America for over fifty years by that time, always drank tea. When I told my teacher they drank tea, she replied, "That's because they're not Christian."

They were. I grew up in a Methodist church in Seattle, and my grandparents attended the same church. But my teacher assumed that, since they were of Japanese ancestry, they couldn't be Christian. During that same school year, the class wrote letters to relatives, inviting them to come to the 1962 Seattle World's Fair. I tried to tell my teacher that the name of my uncle living in Chicago was "Ayao," a Japanese first name. She kept repeating, "Who?" and finally told me to call him "Uncle Al."

Being six years old, I didn't realize my first-grade teacher was trying to stamp my Japanese heritage out of me. My real, legal first name is "Ken," but other teachers later on insisted that it must be "Kenneth." Incidents such as those shaped the rest of my life: I would often have to struggle against others who thought I was somehow "different" or not American like them, just because of my last name or because of the way I look.

Luckily for me, however, I grew up in the very multicultural area of Seattle called Beacon Hill. And I attended a local church with a mostly Japanese American congregation. Whereas being proud of my heritage might have been discouraged at school, it was encouraged at church by just being around others who were the same as me. There was Sunday school, church youth groups, and a Cub and Boy Scout program that filled most of my time away from school.

Today, when I speak at schools and try to convince students that one gets more out of reading than watching TV, I tell them how I was exposed to reading while very young. At home, there were always plenty of newspapers, magazines, and a set of encyclopedias. I am often asked what was the most influential book I read while growing up. My answer is that set of encyclopedias. I ask students who have encyclopedias if—while they are looking up a particular subject—they get sidetracked by running across a lot of interesting subjects along the way.

I did. And I'm glad I did, for I learned a lot more than I ever would have by just being in school. I especially liked the plastic over-

lays, such as one of the human body where the reader could strip away the different layers of the body, or the ones of the Ice Age showing how far the ice advanced and withdrew over time, or the ones showing which countries claimed what land throughout different periods in world history.

Americans often recount where they were and what they were doing when President John F. Kennedy was assassinated in November 1963. I can remember because learning about the president's assassination was associated with books and reading.

Our fourth-grade teacher had just finished reading *Charlotte's Web* and we were all saddened when Charlotte the spider died. We walked out of our grade-school classroom for lunch, noticing the school's American flag at half-mast. I and everyone else soon learned that President Kennedy had been shot and killed.

Of course, the assassination was all we could talk about when we returned to class. Speculation and rumor flew about wildly to explain the assassination. We grew up during the height of the Cold War, when the basements of buildings were designated as bomb shelters in case the Russians attacked. Air raid sirens sounded off as they were tested once a week. National leaders encouraged us to be better students, because, if we didn't, the Russian kids would be smarter than us. Or if we didn't do our physical exercises, the Russian kids would get stronger than us. Was the assassination the start of an invasion by Russia? Was the Communist revolution beginning in America?

Then we talked about our emotional reactions to the sudden death of our American hero. What a bizarre and tragic coincidence it was to find out Charlotte had died, and then to learn soon after that our president had died, we told our teacher. I'll never forget her reply: "That's the value of fiction—it can prepare you for what happens in life."

TV shows during the early '60s also instilled in me a lifelong interest in history and current events. Re-creating different wars in U.S. history was popular then, especially World War II. The most memorable of these was "Combat," a long-running TV series which followed a squad of World War II U.S. infantrymen as they fought their way through France.

Unlike many TV shows and movies today, "Combat" emphasized the importance of teamwork, relying on each other, and the humanity

Mochizuki at seven with his favorite Civil War toys, Christmas, 1961

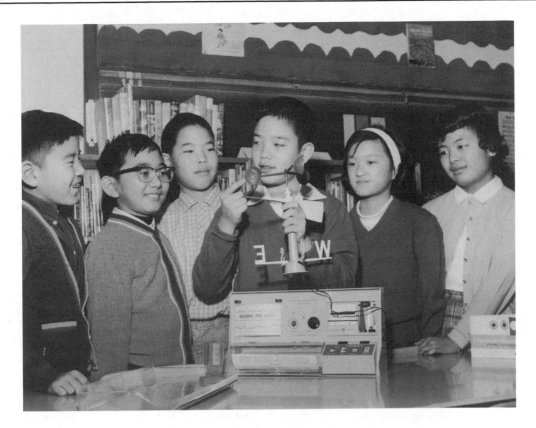

*Ken (center) in a publicity photo for the Seattle TV school competition show
"Quizdown," describing why he wanted to be a meteorologist, 1965*

that can still exist even in the most inhumane of situations. This TV show was also very story- and character-driven, and didn't rely on non-stop action and special effects. Many of its hour-long stories I still remember, and in retrospect I can say that an enthusiasm for telling stories was definitely encouraged by watching this television program.

The "GI Joe" doll made its first appearance during this time, as did a multitude of toy guns, helmets, and every other kind of military paraphernalia. I put those toys to good use in a half-acre of woods behind my family's house, as playing war with the neighborhood kids became a common after-school activity. Sometimes I wanted to play like we were in wars from different historical periods. I demanded that a machine gun couldn't be used while playing the Revolutionary War or the Civil War—only flintlock muskets, pistols, and swords.

I usually ended up having to play that kind of war by myself. My parents lectured me to get more involved with group activities, such as playing sports with the other kids. I preferred to spend a lot of time in the woods, alone with my imagination.

Then a fifth-grade teacher further instilled in me an interest in history, science, and seeking information in general, although I and the rest of the class this teacher taught were too terrorized to realize it then. As one of the rare male grade-school teachers during this time, this teacher could strike fear into any student, including the worst students in the entire school. After a school year with this teacher, those bad kids finished as good students.

With fiery eyes and quoting passages from the Bible, he didn't have to come anywhere near his students to discipline them. With one look and reminding a student that sloth was one of the Seven Deadly Sins, no one in that class dared budge an inch without permission. He addressed all of us by our last names, preceded by a "Mister" or "Miss."

Maybe it was even the third day of the school year when he made the entire class stay after school. A student could only leave when he or she came up with the right answer to a lesson. Absolutely terrified and in tears, one by one we meekly raised our hands to indicate we had the right answer.

"You sure you have the right answer, boy?" he bellowed from his desk. "Because I'm not going to walk over there and wear out the heels on my shoes if you have the wrong answer." When I produced the right answer and turned my paper in, he smiled, patted me on the head and said, "Come to class prepared next time." I always did.

This teacher was a stern taskmaster, but he was also a highly effective teacher. I still remember a lot of what he taught back them. My class couldn't go to recess or couldn't go home until we recited back to him facts such as the names of capitals or rivers in America, dates of important historical events, or could name each one of the thirty-two teeth in an adult mouth. Now when I think about him, this teacher sealed my interest in history and geography for life, and I can still name all of the teeth!

During that same school year, an event occurred that served as a forecast of what lay ahead in my life. In the Seattle area, schools went head-to-head in a popular academic TV game show called "Quizdown." Six students were selected from each school to square off on a Friday night. The show was filmed and then broadcast every Saturday morning.

By sheer coincidence, the team from my school became an all-Japanese American team and I was selected team captain. When introducing my school on the show, "Be sure to mention that our school is all portables," the principal from my school and the host of the show told me. "It would be good for passing our bond issue." This event gave me my first major experience in public speaking—with the entire city watching, and the pressure on to represent my school well!

Through a tense half hour, we scored points for our school with a correct answer. My question was: "What's the difference between a common noun and proper noun?" My answer: "A proper noun is a word for a particular person, place, or thing, and a common noun is for an 'unparticular' person, place, or thing." The host and the audience laughed at "unparticular," but I chalked up points for a correct answer.

My team felt there was a lot at stake in winning this contest, because, if we did, we would win a much-needed set of new encyclopedias for our school. At our school, the library was one portable. Each class spent their entire day in one portable, and the auditorium/lunchroom consisted of a double portable. We considered ourselves the underdogs against a more affluent school. We won easily by a score of 590 to 375.

The following school year marked the first time I departed from being a model student and into a rebellious one—my first taste of activism and fighting for what I thought was right. Our female sixth-grade teacher favored the girls. At age eleven back then, boys still considered girls the adversary.

I led the boys in a revolt, first in secret on the playground, listening to their complaints as to why a double standard existed, such as the boys being required to walk on only one side of the stairs, when the girls got to walk on whatever side they pleased. After I convinced my fellow male classmates that we were being treated unfairly, we rebelled against our teacher with harmless antics, such as smarting off or challenging her seemingly one-sided rules by just asking "Why?"

The principal heard what I was up to and, standing before her in her office, I also got my first taste of having to plead my case, of having to argue for what I believed in. The only repercussion that resulted was that the school no longer saw me as quite the model student anymore.

The end of sixth grade and elementary school marked the end of the first chapter in my life. Then came fall of 1966 and the start of junior high school, when I would be among the youngest students in school again—in awe and sometimes in fear of the older students who were physically bigger, more mature, and streetwise.

I soon knew how isolated and naive I had been; if I or any of my friends in elementary school had uttered a four-letter swear word, we thought lightning would immediately strike us. But, in my new junior high, classmates who came from other elementary schools used cuss words with shocking regularity.

Also, in elementary school, we stayed in one room all day long. But in this junior high, there were six different classes or "periods" during a school day. For physical education, students were graded by a strict point system, which meant that the faster one could do anything, the more points one scored.

We sprinted to the gym, sometimes all the way from the opposite end of the campus, swiftly changed, and hit the gym floor according to "squads." At the command of the gym teacher, squads would race from one end of the gym to the other and receive points for being the first squad back. We were so well trained that, with one bark of the gym teachers, they could make us do anything for the sake of more points. Then we had to immediately change, shower, and run off to our next class, all in about fifteen minutes.

The late 1960s and early 1970s proved to be the most pivotal and critical in my life, when my philosophies and general outlook on life were formed.

The first major change came at home. Ever since I could remember, my family always searched for a new home, to move out of our cramped, little two-bedroom house. My family and I constantly visited many potential new homes, which began for me another lifelong interest in home architecture and interior design—of how to divide and use space in the most interesting and practical ways. We kept searching until all the family members were satisfied with an empty lot to build a home on.

What a fascinating process it was for me to see a home rise out of an empty lot of blackberry bushes, and for me to see it happen in steps just like I had learned in grade school: first the planning and details finalized by a contractor, then the bulldozer came to clear the land, followed by the carpenters who built the wood skeleton of the house. Then came the plumbers, electricians, and the painters.

My younger brother, Alan, was only four at that time. My parents used my older brother, Jim, and me for a lot of the labor, not only as a cost-cutting move, but also, I think, for their sons to feel like they had a stake in the house. That philosophy, whether my parents really intended it that way or not, resulted in another guidepost in my life—essentially a varia-

With younger brother, Alan, standing in their unfinished new house, 1967

tion of "no pain, no gain." If one puts in the hard work to build something of one's own, then one will have more pride in the result.

Activities spawned within the Methodist church continued to dominate my life outside of school, especially its Boy Scout program. Many churches and schools sponsored Boy Scouts, a popular and powerful youth program in the '60s. Each Scouting organization, or "troop," had national guidelines to follow, such as the wearing of its uniform, but it was up to each troop as to what kind of activities it would pursue.

While some troops just played basketball during their troop meetings on Friday nights, the troop sponsored by our church followed true Scouting to the letter, as practically a paramilitary unit. We lined up at attention and learned how to march: "right face," "left face," "about-face." As in the military, a Scout had to advance through a series of ranks, with an Eagle Scout being the highest and rarely attained.

Troop meetings were devoted to honing some Scouting skill, such as camping techniques, first aid, survival skills; or participating in some community project such as helping out the church. Then we went off on one overnight weekend camping trip per month—in any kind of weather. There were longer trips during the summer: a week-long summer camp during which one worked on "merit badges" to advance in rank; and the eight-day, and somewhat infamous, "fifty-mile hike" through one of the rugged Washington state mountains.

We would hike about ten miles a day— mountain miles which are a lot longer than city miles. We climbed to elevations where there were no longer trees, but only vegetation no higher than our knees. All our food for that week we carried in our backpacks, which meant a lot of dehydrated and powdered food.

Sometimes conditions were miserable. Under a hastily built plastic tarp tent, while the mountain rain pounded down, we played miniature chess by flashlight. As adolescent boys, conversation eventually got down to girls that we "liked." We took turns admitting our favorites, if only by initials, starting at "Number Three"

Ken (at right) after a week of Boy Scout "boot camp" training, 1968

and eventually down to "Number One." Since we were stuck together for eight days under stressful conditions, cliques formed and became antagonists, like in *Lord of the Flies*—if only for the duration of the hike.

Mostly through Boy Scouts did I learn another of life's lessons: what one *has* to do often overrules what one *wants* to do.

As an all-Japanese American troop, we heard the occasional unsettling remarks or stares during camping trips, such as the locals joking about how they were being "invaded," or a youngster waving to us and exclaiming, "Hi, Chinese!" At our age, most of those comments went over our heads. But our adult leaders countered by instilling pride in ourselves. Our Scoutmasters and adult leaders always practiced one overriding principle: action always speaks louder than words.

Every year, there was the "Camporee," a weekend competition between all the local Boy Scout troops. Every troop and "patrol" within the troop were constantly observed and graded, beginning from when they walked onto the campsite: how our uniforms looked, how clean and organized our campsite was, how sanitary our cooking and food storage and preparation were.

Competition consisted of running through obstacle courses, or how fast we could start a fire and bring a pot of water to boil, or being able to transmit Morse Code signals, or testing our knowledge and use of rope lashings by building a log bridge over a stream. The Camporee ended with an awards ceremony on a large field, and our troop usually walked away with the bulk of the First Place awards.

Our Scoutmaster would become an important adult in my life, not just because of what he taught me personally, but because of what he taught the entire troop. He worked as a hotel custodian, but devoted all the other time in his life to Scouting and did so for years. He enforced strict discipline and wouldn't hesitate to chew us out, but also effusively heaped praise when we came through, especially if we had done well at one of those Camporees.

I remember one Camporee when we didn't win very many awards but our Scoutmaster had us march out of the campsite in a perfect single-file line, with us in full uniform and our packs strapped to our backs, heads held high. We heard comments from onlookers like, "That's a sharp-looking troop!"

High school senior class yearbook photo, 1972

Our adult leaders knew that our troop would be remembered wherever we went, in large part because we stood out by being all-Japanese American. Almost all of our adult leaders had been in the internment camps for Japanese Americans during World War II just because their parents came from Japan. Appearance was very important to us. Some of the other troops wore only part of their uniforms, such as with jeans and tennis shoes. Our policy was that we either wore our full uniforms correctly, or none of it at all.

At the conclusion of a camping trip, our leaders had us line up at one end of the campsite, and each one of us would walk in a straight line to the other end, searching for and picking up any litter in our path. Another policy of ours was not only to leave a place like we found it, but to leave a place better than we found it. If we camped on private property and the owner needed any work done, like clearing out brush, we immediately tended to that.

However, being a Scout also meant I couldn't always stay isolated within my own troop. One summer, my troop sent me to what was called Junior Leader Training—I remember it more as Boy Scout boot camp. Scouts from all over the state were formed into patrols; complete strangers had to camp out and function together for a week.

We attended classes, were graded on notebooks, and kept under constant pressure by the camp's staff. They kept reminding us how we could easily fail the course and have to go back to our troops as disgraces. During morning roll call, we stood at attention, held out our hands to have our fingernails inspected, and could not flinch as mosquitoes bit us. We had to deal with the personalities of strangers we were grouped with, and our patrol had one Scout who always tried to avoid doing work and pulling his own load. Other Scouts in my troop who had been through this training, including my older brother, warned me that this course would be psychologically tough, and by midweek I would be "climbing the walls." I was.

Patrols selected their own names, usually after some animal mascot, and made their own flags. If a patrol was negligent and allowed their flag to be captured, then the victorious patrol could dictate the terms for the negligent patrol to get their flag back.

During an evening assembly on the parade grounds, one losing patrol, named the "Nullified Nips," had to crawl on the ground chanting, "We are dumb nips." One of those was a Japanese American from my troop, and as I watched him forced to grovel and repeat a derogatory name about himself as everyone else laughed, I blurted out—actually off-handedly and unintentionally—"Hey, the war is over!" The adult leader of the camp heard me, and the next day, that patrol was ordered to change its name.

And all through my Scouting career, I loved to tell the scary stories around the nighttime campfire, or act out the characters in skits.

We could not help but be influenced by world events during the late '60s. After being away from the world during a week-long camping trip in the wilderness, we would find out that some extraordinary event happened, such as astronauts landing on the moon or the Soviet Union invading Czechoslovakia. The civil rights era had just begun and African Americans rioted in American cities.

During camping trips, we overheard our adult leaders talking in hushed tones around dying campfires at night, as we lay snuggled up and warm in our sleeping bags. We heard the concern in their voices about the assassinations of national leaders like Martin Luther King, Jr., and Robert Kennedy, about the riots and how they assured themselves that "it could never happen here."

My father and mother always discussed world events. My father, Eugene, started out as a welfare worker, then became a probation officer for the city's juvenile court and an administrator at a boys' reform school. He ended up being a professor of social work at the University of Washington and other local colleges.

My mother, Miyeko, did clerical work most of her life, mostly at the U.S. Department of Energy and the U.S. Department of Labor. Both are retired now.

The evening after Dr. King was assassinated in April 1968, I was about to go to sleep in my room when I heard my father murmur to my mother, "He preached nonviolence. Now, there's going to be violence."

And what affected everyone in America was the daily news about the war in Vietnam. We saw the grisly film footage every night on TV and the photographs every week in *Life* magazine. At the end of every week on the news, flags of the U.S., South Vietnam, and North Vietnam came up on the TV screen, and the number of soldiers killed from each country showed underneath the flags. To me at that time, the events in Vietnam seemed more like a war movie, with me cheering on the American good guys. That would change, however, when I came of age to actually be sent to Vietnam.

As the events of a turbulent time swirled around us, I stayed isolated in my own, early-teenage world of mostly school and Boy Scouts. Within the Scouts, I joined a program called the God and Country Award. In this program, a Scout worked closely with the minister of his church for about a year, serving the church, and learning about his religion in-depth.

Our church's minister also proved to be one of my most significant adult mentors. A soft-spoken man but with unwavering convictions, he firmly believed that the Christian church was an instrument for social change and activism for the good of all people. He encouraged the church's youth to express themselves, sometimes allowing us to run the Sunday service in which we played '60s rock music.

As a minister who literally practiced what he preached, he participated in demonstrations against community clubs with whites-only membership policies. He suffered ostracism from members of the church and community as a result.

In the church office, three other Scouts and I, working on this award, helped assemble the church newsletter. This became our opportunity to casually converse with our minister as he worked with us. We often talked about world events as a popular rock radio station played in the background. He was the rare adult during the time of the "generation gap" who could talk about what we were interested in. He, too, followed some of the "hip" TV shows of that era, such as "The Smothers Brothers Comedy Hour" or "Rowan and Martin's Laugh-In." Those shows, full of controversial views expressed through comedy, often became the subject of our discussions.

If anything defined the popular culture of that time, it was the music. The Latin-influenced instrumental group Herb Alpert and his Tijuana Brass were my first musical idols, probably because I played trombone. But I could insulate myself from the '60s for only so long before it caught up with me. These were the days when most radio stations were AM, and owning an AM/FM radio was a luxury. Teenagers listened to or carried their AM radios everywhere and couldn't help but be saturated by Top 40 songs.

Unlike the explicit lyrics in a lot of today's music, much of the '60s lyrics were abstract, literary, and full of imagery, with the listener left to interpret the lyrics in his or her own way. And the electric guitar dominated pop music, leaving a trombone player to fantasize about being a rock star.

My favorites—and I still listen to them today—became Jimi Hendrix because of his innovative and "psychedelic" guitar work combined with primal, catchy rhythms (and because he was from Seattle, too); the British trio Cream,

The author sporting early '70s look with family, Christmas, 1973

with Eric Clapton, and their sublime instrumental virtuosity; and the Doors, with their singer and lyricist Jim Morrison—a modern day and musical Edgar Allan Poe.

I sat in front of the stereo for hours, mesmerized by the mystical poetry and often spooky symbolism of Morrison's words. And because I didn't understand most of what he was saying, that made his words even more attractive. No doubt that the stereo would also influence me to become a writer later.

My first serious stab at creative writing came in the ninth grade. My teacher, younger and hipper than most of the other teachers and with the long sideburns of the time, played records in class by the Beatles, Simon and Garfunkel, the Moody Blues, and other popular artists. He had us keep a journal to turn in and be graded every week.

To receive an "A" grade for the journal, a student would have to write a minimum of fifteen pages. However, different types of writing were worth more per page. One could write fifteen pages of anything, even gibberish, and receive the "A." Or one could write a report, a capsule summary of anything the student experienced, like a movie or television program. One page of this type of writing equaled two pages, so composing seven-and-a-half pages received an "A."

However, a page of creative or fiction writing equaled three ordinary pages, so one would have to write at least five pages to get the "A." My thinking was, "Only five pages of making stuff up to get an 'A'? Are you kidding me? Piece of cake!" My favorite genres for story ideas were horror (influenced by the Doors, my campfire tales, and popular TV shows like "The Twilight Zone" and "Night Gallery"); spy thrillers (James Bond movies, "The Man from U.N.C.L.E." TV series); and science fiction (the original "Star Trek" series and movies like *2001: A Space Odyssey*).

Science fiction really captured my imagination, and I became a big fan of authors like Ray Bradbury and Arthur C. Clarke. And my imagination, as that of the entire world back then, was stirred by the U.S. space program. I often tell students today that, unfortunately, manned space flight now consists of only the Space Shuttle orbiting the earth. I tell them what a thrill it was to follow man's mission to the moon.

I watched on TV as the astronauts first went up in the Mercury space capsule and came

Show business resume photo, 1977

straight back down. Then they orbited the earth, at first only three times, then many times. Then came the Gemini capsules with two astronauts, then the Apollo with three. Before going to the moon, satellites did early exploration. The Ranger satellite flew right at the moon, taking pictures before it crash-landed on the moon like it was supposed to.

I remember my family huddled around the black-and-white TV set, enthralled by live pictures the satellite sent back of craters on the moon close up. Then, as the satellite sped closer, we saw craters within craters, then more craters within craters. Then the screen went black, and the famous TV news anchor Walter Cronkite would come on and summarize what had happened. Then there were the Mariner satellites which made "soft landings" on the moon and returned photographs to earth. Then came the Apollo missions to the moon, with the whole world watching as an astronaut stepped on the moon's surface and changed world history.

Students have asked me what I wanted to "be" when I was their age. I wanted to be a meteorologist, and I also considered being an astronomer because of the space program.

I tell students: imagine what it must be like to have been one of those astronauts who walked on the moon—that there are only a handful of people on this planet who can gaze up at the full moon at night, point to it, and be able to say, "I was there."

I think that's what our country, even the world, needs again—to be able to wonder and be united by a common imagination, to be assured that there is more in the universe than one's own little world.

Today, I am amazed that schools have to teach "multicultural education." When I walked into my junior high school, multicultural education began by just being there. I found high school to be the same way, continuing on with the same set of friends. Certainly, distinctions between different races existed, but more often than not, fellow students were known more for their deeds than for their races.

We knew another student as a great athlete first—the fact that he was African American was an afterthought. We associated another student to his hot car rather than his race. The guys may have considered a female student to be unapproachable for a date, not because of her race, but because her social skills were light years ahead.

Though we coexisted in relative harmony, there was no denying what was going on at other schools and in the world. African Americans set Black Pride in motion in the late '60s and self-pride became an infectious force during the early '70s. At other schools, the Black Panthers marched in to make demands and were driven out with tear gas. Some race riots broke out, but usually the struggle was between youthful change versus traditional adult authority, us against the "establishment" or "The Man."

At our school, however, the changes were mostly cultural ones. The length of one's hair immediately categorized a person: hip or "square," a part of "the struggle" or not. Lines were drawn between who had long hair and who didn't; long hair united youth across racial boundaries. Most of the young quarreled constantly with their parents over having long hair, as I did.

Since we Asian students had very few national role models and no identity of our own, we followed the lead of the African Americans, who considered themselves at the time as "Blacks" and not "Negroes." The students of Japanese, Chinese, and Filipino descent no longer considered themselves "Orientals" but "Asian Americans."

In addition to hair and clothes, music continued to be a big part of our lives. Before the '70s, pop music was either white rock or black rhythm & blues, or "soul" music—the two never mixed. In 1969 a band called Sly and the Family Stone hit the radio as an integrated group combining rock and soul. Sly and the Family Stone, a musical group I consider vastly underrated as to the influence they had on American society, also produced songs with positive, optimistic, and self-affirming lyrics like "Everyday People," "Everybody Is a Star," "You Can Make It If You Try," and "Stand." Nowadays, I ask myself and others, "What happened to songs like that?"

Even though some groups had integrated members and sounds, they were still classified as "white music" or "black music." And the type of music people listened to determined if they could become part of a group of friends or not. I delved deeply into the soul music camp, and with the appearance of big-band soul and pop groups like Chicago I could now become a part of the "scene" playing trombone.

Other than my great passion for music, I figured I would be "out of it" if I didn't participate in some kind of sport. I became a distance runner in cross-country and track. I wasn't that good in either, but that could have been in part because I convinced myself I wasn't. One incident I experienced would later lead to an important theme I would express in books for young people.

At track practice, my coach asked me what events I wanted to run in the meet the next day. I answered: "It doesn't matter—I'm just going to lose, anyway."

The coach replied, "Then you might as well kill yourself in the first event." He pointed to his head and said, "For you, it's all up here."

High school is also when I discovered the surprising inequalities existing between schools. I went on one student exchange to a high school located in a Seattle suburb. That school's lunchroom was as big as a whole floor of our school! This school had an Olympic-size swimming pool, a closed circuit TV system, and even a student senate meeting room, where delegates voted by pushing buttons by their seats. The votes were automatically tallied at the podium!

Our school was one of the neglected "South End" schools, the multicultural schools with the outdated facilities, textbooks, and often teachers. Senior year meant just marking time till graduation, with two "study" periods in a five-period day.

During the last few months of my senior year, I found myself again speaking up for people I thought had been wronged. The school's vice principal suspended an acquaintance of mine from school for violating rules he drew up *after* my friend was suspended. I became part of a small group of students who took on the school's administration. Our complaints against the vice principal and his arbitrary rules evolved into a larger struggle to establish the new Asian American identity at our school—to get more books about people of color into our library, and to establish an Asian American Student Union.

Adult community activists joined our struggle and it even received nationwide publicity. In the end, the vice principal became a principal at another school, the books we wanted were brought into the library, and an Asian American Student Union was formed.

That experience taught me a hands-on lesson in activism: I would have to pay the price for what I thought was right. So many people started coming at me at once: many of my friends criticized me for what I was doing, many remained apathetic, others said I was being used by adults to further their own ends. The isolation I felt became hard to take when seventeen years old, especially at the end of my senior year which was supposed to be the happiest of my life.

However, when my cause gained momentum and appeared close to bringing a school administrator down, my "friends" praised me and wanted to join me. This was a tough way to learn that "everybody loves a winner." And I'll never know what my activism cost me in terms of my future, when I began hearing that I probably lost scholarships to colleges for being the "radical."

During that struggle, my parents might have disagreed with what I was doing, but they never told me not to do it. I think they preferred that I follow my own beliefs, rather than stay quiet and go along with something I couldn't live with.

Turning eighteen also meant registering for the military draft. Back then, we all had to think globally about that never-ending war in Vietnam. My friends and I grew seriously concerned and contemplated what we would do if drafted to Vietnam. Could we convince Army authorities we were mentally unstable? Anybody attending college was protected by the "student deferment" and exempt from the draft. We had plenty of friends with older brothers there in combat, and a rumor circulated that the government would end the student deferment.

We received our draft cards; the draft ended that year, but the war still went on.

I received a shocking jolt of reality when I entered the University of Washington in 1972. There, students from the South End high schools realized how much they were never taught. Many of us couldn't write or speak in complete sentences. My first paper for an English class came back smothered with corrections in red ink—he wrote more on the paper than I did! Outside of the classrooms, there were almost daily protests against the war.

The guys grew their hair even longer and the Asian American students copied African American culture even more. We dressed like they did, tried to speak like they did, copied their handshake and mannerisms, liked the same music. We were into the same movies featuring African American stories and stars with titles like *Shaft* and *Superfly*. We thought those movies were "cool" back then. In retrospect, those films told us that the only future people of color could look forward to were careers as gangsters, pimps and drug dealers.

To be a glorified criminal was really just a fantasy. Those regarded as the "coolest" back then were the community activist leaders or the members of a band. These were the days of live bands with horn sections, when only a good live band would do at dances. These were the days when one really had to know how to play an instrument or sing, rather than "rap" or program a computer. I carried over my ambition from high school, to practice and practice and be good enough to get in a band. I finally did.

By my junior year in college, a new passion overtook me. I had always been a big fan of movies, and my window into that world had always been through John Hartl, the movie critic for the *Seattle Times*. Since I was an early teenager, I religiously read his columns. (He still writes for the *Times*.) I became a Communica-

Mochizuki (left) and illustrator Dom Lee meet for the first time at Purdue University in Lafayette, Indiana, 1994

tions major at school because I thought it might teach me something about making movies (it hardly did).

Then my turning point came in the mid-'70s as I saw a succession of movies with actors that got me excited: Robert De Niro in *The Godfather Part II,* Al Pacino in *Dog Day Afternoon,* and an early film by the now famous film director Martin Scorsese, *Mean Streets.*

That is when I decided to become an actor and got into every play I could in community and college theaters. Much to the disapproval of my parents, my grades at school slid and I did just enough to graduate. If I wanted to seriously pursue acting, I would have to move to either New York or Los Angeles. Figuring Los Angeles was warmer, and because I had an actor friend from Seattle already working in Los Angeles, I made the first major move of my life.

As I sat on that plane with a one-way ticket to Los Angeles, I contemplated on what I had just done and was about to do, knowing that

another chapter in my life had ended and another just started. Landing at the airport, I now saw palm trees and smelled the city's ever-present smog instead of the evergreen trees and clean air I was used to. I was baffled that people drank bottled water, when in Seattle good water came unlimited out of the tap.

Then I learned about life the hard way.

The geographical size of Los Angeles is mind-boggling, a city so spread out. Owning a car is mandatory there, and I bought one of the first used cars I saw. It proved to be a "lemon," and auto insurance in Los Angeles is astronomical. Now I had to do everything myself—buy my own food, cook, do laundry, pay bills, fix my car. Before I made my living by just being an actor, I worked a succession of bizarre jobs, the first being a bellman at a bankrupt hotel.

This hotel used to be where movie stars stayed. Now, the owner's kids skateboarded in a waterless swimming pool. The dining room chefs didn't have the food to make most of the meals on the menu. My official duty was to help carry the guests' luggage to and from their rooms, but I was pressed into service as the all-purpose hotel employee.

I was a waiter sometimes, and I remember a table full of lawyers running up an over-thirty-dollar tab (big spending in those days) and leaving me a seventy-five-cent tip. The chefs had me go to the local grocery store when they ran out of food. Guests wanted me to drive them to the airport in my own car—I eventually got smart and charged them for it, rather than just accepting the two dollars the hotel gave me for gas.

I delivered the *Los Angeles Times,* loading up my small Toyota with 400-500 papers in the middle of the night and delivering them to apartments around Sunset Boulevard. I took the elevators to the top and ran down each floor, throwing papers to the right doors. Sometimes the only way into an apartment complex was to climb over the fence. I delivered at an eerie section of the city at night. Once I passed a stained glass window of an apartment and could make out candles burning within. Then I heard chanting in Latin, like some ritual going on. I never knew I could run so fast.

Another job meant delivering meat to swanky Beverly Hills restaurants through kitchen back doors, where the kitchen help, usually Hispanic or Asian, helped me unload. Or I delivered to the homes of rich movie producers in Bel Air. Unlike the glitz and glamour I expected, I saw the real Los Angeles and the real Hollywood.

These were just ways to support myself while I pursued what I went down there for. I spent most of my time at East/West Players, an Asian American theater company led by veteran actors. The world of acting is often a dark, bleak, and subterranean world onto itself. Acting classes often involved learning to tap into your own emotions to be able to play another character's emotions. Acting exercises sometimes meant lying on the stage floor while the teacher talked us into a relaxed state. Then he led us through an imaginary scenario where we encountered some painful moment in our lives. I remember some students being so affected, they bawled and banged their heads on the wood floor.

At the site of the Minidoka Relocation Center, where the author's parents and grandparents were interned during World War II, 1994

I paid my dues performing every kind of duty in the theater, from being the janitor to setting out the props, to running the lights and sound for the shows.

As a prop person, I sat in the theater's dressing room and waited till the show was over to clean up and store the props away. Up there, I read what was to become the most inspirational book in my life—the novel *No-No Boy* by John Okada. Set during the end of World War II, a Japanese American returns home to Seattle after serving time in prison for being a "No-No Boy," one of those who refused to serve in the U.S. armed forces because the government forced his family and all Japanese Americans into internment camps during the war.

Ostracized by his fellow Japanese Americans—especially by those who served in the military—and by America at large, the bitter, cynical No-No Boy slowly learns that there are people in the world who do not condemn him for taking a political stand.

This 1957 novel dared to portray Japanese Americans in a realistic and often unflattering way. That's what spoke to me the most—the power of this writer's no-holds-barred truth. It is also one of the most romantic novels ever. However, when this novel first came out, even Japanese Americans refused to read it. John Okada passed away in obscurity, never knowing that a new generation of Japanese and Asian Americans consider his one and only novel a classic. I would later discover that John Okada's grave is practically adjacent to that of my grandparents.

I spent my first two years as a professional actor performing on the stage, the most memorable show being a touring production where the cast and equipment traveled in two rickety vans all over California. We performed in state prisons, even the one Charles Manson is at. The actresses were whistled at and verbally harassed while on stage at the men's prison, then the actors received the same treatment at the women's prison later that day.

At Fresno State University, we performed in a hallway at their student union building. When we arrived to set up, a student slept on the front row of folding metal chairs. As our show was on, Iranian students wearing masks and hoods burned the Shah of Iran in effigy outside. As we packed up to leave, that same student still slept in the front row.

Such was the life of the stage actor. I got my first taste of screen acting when a call went out for actors to play a Japanese country-and-western band in the movie *The Bad News Bears Go to Japan.* To play the band's singer, the candidates narrowed down to me and another *sansei* (third generation Japanese American like myself) actor. That was when I first experienced the competitive and back-stabbing viciousness of Hollywood.

My competitor tried everything to get the role. Because he belonged to the actor's union, the Screen Actors Guild (SAG), he went around telling anyone in authority on the movie set: "I have a SAG card," and then pointing at me, "and he doesn't!" Finally, the movie's director saw both of us from a distance, and since this other actor had longer hair, he got the part. I ended up being in the band, faking steel-pedal guitar.

There were countless interviews and auditions, as every aspiring actor and actress must go through. Some were just plain humiliating in the way they treated those of Asian descent. As many waited in a small room to be auditioned for a commercial, the casting people would pass by and comment, "Didn't we see these people already? They all look alike." The Hollywood industry calls these auditions "cattle calls," and that's exactly how an actor or actress is often treated. While I was playing a bit part as a Japanese soldier in the movie *MacArthur,* an assistant director yelled out, "We need more Jap soldiers over here!"

However, there were the exhilarating moments also. My first screen job with a sizable role arrived in 1978. I was to play a downed Japanese pilot on the TV World War II submarine comedy "Operation Petticoat." The pilot is rescued and taken aboard the submarine, where he stays unconscious (therefore, I never said a word) throughout the entire episode. I woke up early to drive to Universal Studios where they filmed the series, then put my costume on and went through make-up, only to lie down on a hospital gurney and act like I'm unconscious—and receive mouth-to-mouth resuscitation from the beautiful nurses!

I never experienced anything like it—wardrobe people, make-up people, prop people, and assistant directors catering to your every need, as usually is the case on any film or TV set. After five days on the set, I declared to myself: "Hey, I want to do this!"

Then not too long after, I played a key character in an episode of the long-running TV series "M*A*S*H." I had the role of a South Korean teenager who is dodging the South Korean draft and hides in the M*A*S*H camp. That role proved a lot more demanding than "Operation Petticoat" as there is nothing easy about screen acting—most of it is repeating dialogue or some type of action over and over, sometimes the same thing over thirty times. I could easily see why that series lasted as long as it did. The regular actors cared deeply about the show's stories and sometimes argued heatedly about the script.

I surely felt like I was on a roll when I became a series regular on a PBS series filmed in Boston, "The New Voice." During 1979–80, I spent a total of thirteen weeks in Boston, acting in this educational series which centered on a group of high school students who create and run a school newspaper. It was the rare time I was allowed input into my character, and I challenged why he had to follow the stereotype of Asian Americans—as a "nerd" or bookworm. My advice was heeded. However, the show aired and quickly disappeared.

I have not found a comparable experience to being on a film or TV set, when the cast, crew, producers, and directors who shape the show are totally committed to doing their best work possible. When one feels the team effort, it is electric!

That is, when an actor got to work on screen. For most actors who are not "stars," that is a rare opportunity. An unemployed actor has a lot of free time. Some of the Asian American actors read any popular novel with an Asian character in the story. If that novel was ever made into a movie, then those who read the book already had some idea of the character they might be called upon to audition for. I began reading a lot of books on any subject, more than I ever had before, and caught up on some of the classic novels I had never read in high school or college.

Then my writing career began. In 1981, I learned that a friend in Seattle had been shot and killed for his views as a community activist and leader. I had to walk around the block when I heard the news. I reflected on the early '70s and how that time forever affected me. How, when I first arrived in Los Angeles, people considered my dressing and speaking like African Americans to be strange.

At that same time, a playwright who had his works produced at the East/West Players theater company held workshops on writing. In his workshops, one could write anything. Did I really think I could write a novel? With morning sunlight slashing into my little apartment, while drinking instant coffee from a cheap yellow plastic cup, I began a story on an ancient Remington typewriter. I began "Beacon Hill Boys," which would follow four Japanese American guys from the last days of high school through the events of a year and a half after. I met with the playwright, my instructor, once a week, and he critiqued what I had written so far.

I became so focused on writing, creating characters and situations out of thin air, that in the summer of 1981 I decided to become a writer. As a writer, I could live anywhere, and I knew I would never consider Southern California home since I preferred the mountains, lakes, and lifestyle of the Pacific Northwest. So, that fall, I packed what I could fit into my Toyota Corona and drove—north on Interstate 5.

"Did I make a mistake coming back?" I often asked myself back in Seattle. Jobs were scarce, especially for a former actor. I took anything: digging crawl spaces beneath houses, waxing church floors, trying and failing at phone sales, being a photographer's assistant for a local TV station, and microfilming mountains of documents for the National Archives and Records Administration.

I hit a new low in my life doing that digging job. A rerun of my "M*A*S*H" episode had just aired, and the owner of the house I worked on commented to my boss: "Isn't that guy digging in our backyard the same guy we saw on TV?"

I tell our young people: "If you want to be a writer, you have to write." That's what I came back to Seattle for, and for the next fourteen years I wrote for newspapers, magazines, newsletters, brochures, educational videos—if it used words, I did it. My experience in journalism helped immensely while doing any kind of writing. As a journalist, I learned to use the least amount of words to say the most—a skill critically important to write picture books. I also learned how to edit my own work and, most importantly, to discipline myself to meet deadlines.

"Beacon Hill Boys" has not yet grown into a published book. However, it has served as the fertile soil from which other ideas grew.

In 1983, I learned nothing is impossible if the desire is there. Two Evergreen State College students approached me about turning "Beacon Hill Boys" into a movie. "Are you crazy?" I replied. They persisted and I wrote a script, converting a year and a half in the book to two nights and one day. I ended up playing the lead character and also served as the film's co-director. We raised money through grants, donations, and by selling T-shirts. With just enough money to develop the film, we used local actors and non-actors, and the crew consisted of college students and anybody who wanted to help.

The day of reckoning came for the 43-minute version of "Beacon Hill Boys." In January 1985, I sat in a small screening room with the film's other creators, viewing our finished work. Sitting a few seats away from me was the most powerful film critic in Seattle, the god of movies, John Hartl!

I nervously speculated as to what he jotted down in his notebook in that dark room. As the final film credits rolled, I sat in awe of what a dream combined with ambition could accomplish. Mr. Hartl praised our efforts in the newspaper and the film was shown at film festivals throughout the country and in Europe.

Writing still was my first love, and my future was determined by learning about my past. For as long as I could remember, getting my parents' generation to talk about "Camp" was like pulling teeth. In 1942, my father, mother, and their families were forced off the West Coast of the United States and sent to live in prison camps surrounded by barbed wire. My father and mother, who were both born and lived in Seattle—and didn't know each other at that time—lived in a camp in southern Idaho called Minidoka.

As history now shows, these Japanese Americans were never charged with any crime, except that they were the same race as the World War II enemy; the government thought they could be some kind of threat (none was ever proven).

By the mid-1980s, more information began to slowly surface about "Camp." A national movement grew to get the U.S. government to admit that the forced internment of many American citizens was a violation of the U.S. Constitution. Most of this information was acquired through the former camp inmates who just talked about what they remembered. As a journalist, I researched and wrote on this issue constantly, reading almost everything on this subject. I eventually realized why those who lived through "Camp" were reluctant to talk about that experience—it was just too painful to relive.

The U.S. Congress and the president passed a bill in 1988, officially recognizing the wrong committed on people like my parents and grandparents.

Little did I know then that all I learned about the internment camps would pay off. During the summer of 1991, I received a phone call from Philip Lee. He said he had started a new children's book company, Lee & Low Books, and would I be interested in writing a book about playing baseball in the internment camps?

He sent me a magazine article, the true story of an *issei* man (an immigrant from Japan—my grandparents' generation) who played semi-professional baseball before World War II. Within the article was a photograph of this man posing with Lou Gehrig and Babe Ruth.

After being sent to an internment camp in Arizona, this *issei* man saw how bleak life was in the middle of a desert. Families were falling apart. In a real *Field of Dreams* story, this man led other camp members in building a baseball field on the desert sand.

Mr. Lee initially proposed that I do a non-fiction story based on that magazine article. I combined the two main subjects of this story—baseball and the World War II internment camps—into a fictional story. I wanted somehow to include the lesson from my high school track coach, along with every young baseball player's dream of hitting the game-winning home run. The result—my first published book, *Baseball Saved Us*. Since I already knew all about the internment camps, this story came easily to me.

Baseball Saved Us slowly changed my life as the book became more and more popular. This was a classic case of serendipity—I had never planned on writing a children's picture book. Since its publication in 1993, schools, education organizations, and librarian's conferences have brought me to many parts of the country.

Illustrations are half of a children's picture book, and I'm often asked if I worked with my illustrator on *Baseball Saved Us*. I first met

Signing stacks of books, Los Angeles, California, 1995

and talked to Dom Lee a year after *Baseball Saved Us* came out. The publisher selected him to do my book since he had done sports illustrations before. We first met in the aisles of Chicago's O'Hare airport while traveling to an educators' conference at Lafayette, Indiana.

Dom, an immigrant from Seoul, Korea, and I immediately bonded as artists when he told me quirky stories about himself. Once, he had to prove to his children that America is a big country. So, he took his family on a vacation, driving from New Jersey to Yellowstone National Park and back.

What a luxury it was for Dom and me to talk face-to-face about our second book, *Heroes,* during our time together in Indiana. Our publisher suggested a story on the 442nd Regimental Combat Team, an all-Japanese American U.S. Army unit in World War II. Its members volunteered to join the U.S. Army while in the internment camps to prove they were as American as anybody else. That's why they ended up in the camps, they figured, because they were not seen as Americans. The 442nd fought the Germans in Italy and France, becoming one of the most decorated units in U.S. Army history. My uncle served with that unit.

In my first draft, I wrote a flashback sequence with 442nd soldiers sloshing around in the mud, snow, and freezing temperatures of France, fighting the enemy and being shot at. I wanted to show war as it really was, with friends bleeding, wounded, and dying. No way could I show any of that in a children's picture book, the publisher responded.

Then I thought about playing war when I was a lot younger, and how I was never forced to be the Japanese soldier "bad guy" because I and my *sansei* friends could prove that our fathers and uncles were heroes in the U.S. Army. Using the magic formula for creative writing, "What if?", I wrote a story around a young *sansei* boy who didn't know about his father's and uncle's military exploits, and how he was forced to be the "bad guy." How does he find out?

Heroes was published in 1995, and I always find it interesting as to what readers read into my stories. They cite themes I never realized were there. Is the book against violence, even pretend violence among young people? But at the same time, is it patriotic? Is it about the definition of a hero? Is it about the necessity of role models?

As the writer, my objective is to just get the protagonist from point "A" to point "B," which would be the story's end with the conflict resolved. These themes must have been floating around in my subconscious mind as I wrote the story, because they are certainly there.

Another theme is the necessity for generations to pass down their history and stories, their legacy, to younger generations. I and many *sansei* comment on how our parents' generation is just now telling us stories about their past or about our immigrant grandparents. They have told us about their internment camp experiences only in recent years. Why did they wait until they were over seventy years old, we wonder. Just like the young boy in *Heroes*, maybe if a young person knows of his or her family legacy sooner, they will also be prouder of themselves a lot sooner.

One of the themes I purposely inserted into *Heroes* was a criticism of the media—for its usually unflattering portrayal of people from Asia, and its lack of portrayal of Americans of Asian and Pacific Islander descent. When reviewing my adult life thus far, I realize that getting the media to portray us as Americans in America has been a major reason for everything I did—as an actor, journalist, community activist, and now children's book writer.

I'm sure that as I spend more years on the path of being a writer for young people, I will find out that it has been blazed by a pioneer before me, the longtime and late children's writer Yoshiko Uchida, who had her first children's picture book published in 1949.

In her essay in a previous *Something about the Author Autobiography Series* edition, Uchida recalled how, as a child in 1931, she was told by a white woman, "My, you speak English so beautifully." She also remembered when a stranger shouted to her, "Go back where you came from!" Many of her books recount her own experience in the World War II internment camps.

Sadly, the perception of many in America of its fellow Americans of Japanese descent has not changed much. During my visits to schools around the country, I tell students that I was born and live in Seattle, Washington; that, as of this writing, I have never been to Japan and do not speak any Japanese; that my only connection to Japan is my last name and the fact that my grandparents emigrated from Japan about ninety years ago. And, no, I do not know any martial arts!

Still, even today I can be told what Ms. Uchida was told over sixty years ago. I know it will be my life's work to try and change people who draw conclusions about others—based only on what they look like or the sound of their name. I will especially try to do that for all our young people.

I am often asked by young readers, "How many books do you plan to write?" My answer: "As many as I can as long as there are still stories to tell."

And for our young readers, I hope that they, too, are constantly surrounded by a lot of words on the printed page (and encyclopedias!), especially at home. I hope that they, too, might have their creativity awakened by words in a song, or the woods behind their house, or from writing in a journal, or by wondering what's out there on another planet or past the stars.

And I hope that ahead of them lies some interesting times, like I have been fortunate enough to experience.

BIBLIOGRAPHY

FOR CHILDREN

Fiction:

Baseball Saved Us, illustrated by Dom Lee, Lee & Low, 1993.

Heroes, illustrated by Dom Lee, Lee & Low, 1995.

Other:

On the Wings of Peace (anthology), Clarion, 1995.

Also author of the screenplay for the short film *Beacon Hill Boys,* Kingstreet Media, 1985.

Leslie Morrill

1934-

Setting the Stage

Well, here I am again, thinking about the past. Trying to piece together, for you the reader, a picture of myself that would be both comprehensive and correct. Believe me, this is not the easiest of tasks for someone who has spent his life producing images in a different and sometimes less common or certain language.

To re-create an image that could be called typical, I refer you to the familiar cartoon character that is seen from the rear view, hunched over a workspace covered with books, pads, and papers. That is the typical attitude of most working illustrators. That is the way I look and the way . . . I see.

As you read this page, I am sitting in the south corner of a room, on the second floor of a house in Maryland, just outside of Washington, D.C. I am hunched (as previously noted) above a 42" by 32" drawing board. Beside and slightly below the board stands a small mobile chest of drawers called a taboret. In it is storage space for drawing and painting supplies. Gazing beyond me and my leather swivel chair you will see a particular item of note: a tall and narrow oak filing cabinet replete with the accumulated miscellany of more than a quarter of a century of illustration-related material. In it you will find everything from past tax forms to scissored reference materials, such as pictures of children's clothes and those of professionals (Zookeepers to Astronauts), scenery, cultural research, cannibals, and assorted animals. *Lots and lots of animals.*

A light-box sits on top of a two-tiered flat file. The files are to hold sample work for my portfolio. You might call it "Bait for future projects." The large drawers also hold illustrations in progress, loose paper, and pads that will some day aid in transferring my restless thoughts into arresting (or is it arrested) images. Upon my walls are works by fellow artists. There is a computer graphics poster for a

Leslie Morrill in his studio, 1984

biennial by Lew Fifield and two paintings by perhaps the best artist I have ever known, Bela Birkas. I have above my workspace pictures of the two most influential and significant people in my life, my wife Judith and daughter Melissa. Reference books, an Indonesian rod puppet, and an ancient banner advertising "Benson's Wild Animal Farm" round out the corners of my (now) familiar and comfortable studio.

At the present time, other than this autobiographical sketch, three assignments gleefully taunt me. There are sketches for a story in *Ladybug,* a puzzle design that must soon travel to Germany, and sketches I want to begin for two books my wife is working on. (Did I say three assignments?) Oh yes, I must complete the preparations for teaching the spring semester Children's Book Illustration class at the Maryland Institute College of Art.

". . . And NOW for something completely different."

At Home

As I remember the years between preschool and today one early memory stands out. It's the memory of tables. There were kitchen tables, end tables, sewing tables, dining-room tables, card tables, tea tables, and any other table that was to be found in a 1930s and '40s working-class home. What did all these tables have in common, you ask? A place to put food? No. It was a place to put paper and pencils. In those days, eating used to come in a very distant second to most activities, but especially to any art activity. You now can see that my artistic conversion started very early in life. It shaped itself long before I had the need to find the words to describe it. (Hmm, could that be an insight into my difficulty with writing such a profile as this?)

Every member of my family except my father was interested in the arts. Everyone but Dad danced, painted, frequented libraries, museums, recitals, concerts, lectures, and plays. However, when any of his children were on stage, he was the most proud, appreciative, and tearful member of the audience. Urged on by our parents, we three boys—Grover, Loren, and Leslie—danced together and apart, acted, and attended various classes and schools for dance, drama and art. Such experiences can be defining moments in our lives and so it was with the Morrill Boys. I cannot imagine a life where the arts do not play a central role. For me dance and illustration have been the means through which I express that role.

I grew up in the small New Hampshire town of Hudson, on one side bordered by the Merrimac River and in other directions by forest, small and large family properties, orchards, dairy, poultry, and extensive truck farms. In this environment, such activities of three brothers as tap, ballet, and acting did not go unnoticed. Public attention usually leads to opportunities as well as the occasional confrontation. Teenage boys do not always appreciate the limelight being monopolized by dancers and would-be actors. To my delight I found out that unlike their male peers, teenage girls seldom share an aversion to any form of shared popularity. Between baseball, basketball, Scouting, 4-H, and

the arts, life was full and pleasant in Hudson as it was in most towns all over America.

But the far-flung shadows cast by the War Years brought to even such remote places as Hudson the uncomfortable nudging of some larger realities. Gold stars began to replace the Christmas candles in some of the windows. These were mute messages of a son-husband-brother lost forever to the family. Rumors of dark forces close to our shores and childish burnings of the Axis leaders in effigy peaked my imagination during the last years of the Second World War. Although it usually seemed disconnected from my self-absorbed daily conditions, the currents of those phantom foreign actions did intervene and sometimes disturb me. I never really understood that children my own age could really be dying, and that some were meeting their ends at the hands of boys the age of my oldest brother. I thought that war was the total province of adult male soldiers, exclusively. I assumed that the children would be protected by their parents as mine were protecting me and that young women joined the service to entertain their husbands and boyfriends. That was my view as an eight-year-old boy. Later the aftermath of the death marches and the carnage of the extermination camps, in pictures and reality, limped back even into our cozy little town. Some of the prisoners had survived.

Tripping the Dark Fantastic

I wonder if the open interest and ease with which the German prisoners were accepted as workers in the local icehouse would have been less benign if more people had been informed about the darker side of still another nation's view of Manifest Destiny. Young men, sons of German parents, volunteered to serve as American soldiers. They didn't want their patriotism questioned or their parents to be suspects. My father had to answer an inquiry about the loyalty of his own teenage son.

Yet, small towns are usually generous places, especially in times of crisis. Small armies of children armed with pillow sacks can be marshaled to gather milkweed pods (to aid in the war effort?). Children and adults gathered rags, newspapers, tin cans, and scrap metal. Children learned to knead the orange additive into the sucking mass of that new product oleomargarine. Potatoes could be purchased by the pound, dry weight, instead of the peck. In every newly devised product they forgot to include two elements: character and taste. Conservation and self-reliance became more than buzzwords.

On several occasions our town played host to still-segregated units of black soldiers on their way to war. Since we lived close to the junior high school gym where the festivities were to be held, and since my mother was one of the volunteer hostesses, I had a front-row seat. Homemade cooking, pies, and ice cream were served and then the tables were removed by the menfolk. To the records of the Dorsey Brothers, Glenn Miller, Chick Webb, Ray Noble, Cab Calloway, Ted Lewis, and Sammy Kaye, middle-aged and young women, single and married women, danced in the warmth of a summer's evening. Many of the soldiers were from the Deep South and in their experiences I suspect that black and white relationships had rarely been this open or naturally intimate. As for the women, many had never seen a Negro man before, much less conceived of the possibility of flying across a polished dance floor in the arms of some dismayed soldier. Guarded curiosity turned to good fun as the local ladies gained new stories to relate during the long hours of canning classes in the basement of that same school. Jim Crow, where were you on that warm moonlit night?

The United States Government also made its way into our measured lives in other helpful ways. Since the government was subsidizing so many domestic research programs, its efforts would eventually effect the home front in many a novel manner. We had to drink Ovaltine or pasteurized milk instead of raw milk. Condensed, evaporated, dried, and frozen foods of every description were tried upon the troops and the civilians alike. Some were positive additions to our diets and many only induced yearnings for more and better sources of native crops. So, along with the other experimentation, there came that new national pastime and passion . . . THE VICTORY GARDEN!

Suburban Farming (A Patriotic Mission) Poultry (A Small Town Enterprise)

The Government Extension Services, to aid in our newly developing farm enterprises,

From Morrill's sketchbook

would furnish reference booklets on raising anything that moved on two or four feet or anything that could be planted indoors or out. I received seeds and chickens free from the National Association of 4-H Clubs. By keeping appropriate and accurate records of my husbandry, the State rewarded my efforts with twenty-five bright-eyed chicks, free of charge. How very weary my mother became of seeing me returning yet again from the post office with a cardboard crate of peeping White Leghorns or New Hampshire Reds. We lived in the middle of town but we were soon surrounded with chickens, ducks, rabbits, fruit trees, berries, and, of course, our very own Victory Garden.

Government attempted to offer Americans the belief that by producing food in their own family plots and therefore making us less dependent on commercial sources needed for the more direct support of the U.S. troops, we were, with our home-grown markets, aiding the nation's war effort.

I believe the government had cannily tapped into the core of its citizens' patriotic psyches. This fed into our sense of social and civic responsibility as well as our desire to be self-reliant. It was an era of making commitments, only in those instances you were prepared to honor those commitments with your personal reputation. Success, we thought, would result from a unified effort, our strong sense of justice, and the inevitable triumph of what we knew to be a noble cause, and utilize what we believed to be our most potent secret weapon: what we called in New England, Yankee Ingenuity. These beliefs were not always called characteristics, but were locally referred to as Traits. It appears that they could be mobilized in many creative ways when viewed by the participants as practical and therefore positive. Victory Gardens in New England also seemed to bring out a sense of competition, idiosyncracies (style), pride, and on occasion even our perverse sense of humor. These early experiences with my attempts at egg production and the consequential egg route sales, coupled with entering standard-sized and Banties (small-sized) chickens in state poultry competitions, account for part of my initial interest in the animal world, an interest that has continued up to the present day. Until recently, I had for the most part not consciously sought out the company of pets. The one pet my family had was a purebred English setter and his name was Peter. As a child I had expected a personal loyalty that Peter was unwilling to limit to my exclusive needs. Peter was too magnanimous with his affection to devote himself to one self-centered and unreliable child. He relied instead upon all humans, adults and kids alike, to enter into his play-filled life with as much unreserved passion and good humor as he so eagerly contributed. Yet to me, his affection seemed too impersonal. During my preteen years my working experiences with animals added to my knowledge of them. But it in turn also increased my ambivalence toward them.

In these more recent years my attitude has been changing. I am still intrigued and drawn to examples of selfless, idealized, or universal love. It is one of my goals to understand and appreciate such things with the open and guileless generosity that Peter offered in his life.

Reflections on Poverty Pond

There is a time in most children's lives when their newly forming relationship with the larger Universe begins to weigh quite heavily on those slowly spreading shoulders. Perhaps for most of us its entry is always premature. In my case I know that this was especially true. I also believe that since I had so much *unstructured* time on my hands, I was even more prone to frequent wandering into such unchartered mind fields. I look back and, although I suspect that my thoughts were no more or less profound than those of most other ten-year-olds, I do think it would have been beneficial to have been able to share the immediacy of those thoughts with a peer, or a more seasoned and demanding guide than myself. This I suspect may also be the eternal lament of many young dreamers. It's a time when the scale of our physical state is dwarfed by the immense possibilities of a newly perceived reality.

The artist at age fourteen

Between Hill and Danbury, New Hampshire, is Ragged Mountain. Nestled nearby on the top of one of the adjacent hills are a series of watery depressions. One marsh-choked waterway has what always seemed to me a very ominous name. It was and I presume still is called "The Bog." That is, unless it has become a part of the surrounding forest, as may well have always been its fate. At the opposite end of the watercourse, stretched atop a dark and bottomless deep depression, lies Poverty Pond. This was the property of my paternal grandparents. As a child, my father told me, "You could not walk it in a day." I always took him at his word and never tried. My grandparents had retired or changed professions for the third time. A saw mill was being constructed, from which the lumber for our new house would later be milled (cut). Here at the "Camp," as all such unfinished interior homes were called in New England, I spent the better part of four summers. At the time my father's parents must have been in their late sixties. They lived on the edge of Poverty Pond, eight miles from the nearest main road by car in the summer and by snowshoes in the winter. Their home included barns and outbuildings, an outhouse (or if you prefer, "privy"), a well, a wood stove and kerosene lamps and lanterns, gardens, a yoke for carrying two pails of water, a draught horse (for snaking logs), a Holstein cow and calf, cant hooks, chickens, fishing poles, a rifle, a revolver, a Winchester .30-30, a canoe, a rowboat, traps, hay and bush scythes, and every other tool and antique gadget imaginable.

You might be wondering right about now why anyone, let alone two aging retirees, would live in such a primitive state. When you realize that they owned four residential buildings (two two-family homes and two single-family houses) back in Hudson, your question may be growing to really absurd proportions. But to fully appreciate the earth around you, you must have made a physical and emotional investment in that earth. The longer and closer that association the greater your commitment will be to it. My grandparents not only needed to own land, they needed to be near the land because that was their one comprehended constant in a too rapidly changing world. I think my grandparents were attempting to return to a life for which they did not need a current and calculated rationale. To my knowledge neither grandparent attended church.

Impressions

I realize that what I am writing here is speculation. I think that my grandparents' reasons for living within such a basic rhythm of survival could have been interpreted as a repudiation of their earlier urban years. But I think for some of any generation, the very repetition of their days, months, and years, governed less by transient social forces and more by the familiar and with proper preparation and predictable seasons, has its own internal logic and a reassuring rational determination. I never asked them what their real reasons for being there were, because they would have considered the question impertinent. They would say that they were there because that is where they wanted to be. Two years after the lumber had been transported to Hudson, they sold the property on Ragged Mountain and moved to Bradenton, Florida. There they grew a garden and planted fruit trees. They both lived on to the age of ninety-six.

My memories of my own relationship with those bittersweet summers are complex and still unclear. The irony of my limited social intercourse, in comparison to the unrestricted freedom and the desire to share my deepest reasoning, produced little but a warm, dull resentment of my isolation. I feel that the dynamic was so great, and thus it was my responsibility to have made of it something more than a dimmed imperfect recollection. Still, there is much to be said as an artist for: Salamanders (orange-red beneath the moist leaves) . . . Water lilies (trailing plaited from a green canoe) . . . Black mud (warmly pressed about your toes) . . . Mahogany-colored fur (a beaver carried upon your back, its head touching your heels) . . . The phantom presence (of bears, moose, wild cats, mammoths, trolls, and dragons) . . . A rabbit covered with ticks (a merciful death) . . . Discovering a field mouse nest (and joyfully reciting Robert Burns) . . . Using eight shots to kill a trapped baby woodchuck (I couldn't see through the tears) . . . The fisher (rare wraith of an animal—a streak crossing behind me) . . . Sweet Timothy (hay-aroma of the summer) . . . Sugaring Off (making maple sugar) . . . Cribbage (unsolicited lessons in math) . . . Country auctions (where colonial estates and history could be purchased without a haggle; the strange air of bargaining about still warm objects and atticed antique memo-

Brothers Grover and Loren, "on our land on Pelham Road, sometime in the 1950s"

ries) . . . Blueberries (under the power lines) . . . Swimming in brown water (high above the storied and unfathomed graves of oxen teams) . . . Haying scenes (like Winslow Homer) . . . New Found Lake (the Icehouse) . . . The flooding of Hill (the Franklin Dam) . . . Sick to my stomach (Copenhagen Snuff) . . . Cupped Cannibals (Pitcher plants) . . . Dappled water on dimpled skin and so much more.

Grandparents

On to the other side of the family. My mother's mother Clara was a woman who loved animals. Domestic animals. To be more precise, she loved one species of animal. Grammie loved goats. Toggenburg goats. None of us had any doubt that the goats responded with personal affection for her. To visit my grandmother in those early years seems in my memory to alternate between a scene of protracted hours,

of three disinterested boys quietly sitting while the adults did what adults do best—talk—and those marvelous moments feeding, touching, and otherwise watching the young Toggenburgs doing what all kids do best—play.

Odd people come and go through the skewed memories of childhood and here among them emerges the image of the man who faithfully tended my grandmother's herd. His name was Louis Poppel. A simple man who cared well for his charges but little for his own wits. Louis amused himself by butting heads with the goats. It seems that he even challenged the odorous "Billy," an event (it was said) that did little to enhance his reputation or his mind.

My grandmother and grandfather had been divorced since my mother was a child. Both of them were "musically inclined" (That would make an amusing picture). My grandfather, who by some quirk of fate was also named Leslie, played the clarinet. His wife Clara (formerly Miles and now Stone) played the banjo and loved to dance. My mother said that they performed well enough to be paid for their entertainment. I must take her word, because I was never asked to attend. That "Grammie" (The other was "Grammie" Morrill) was a practical nurse (Did people knowingly hire impractical nurses?) and again from what I was told she was a force to contend with. I was around to witness some of her less public performances. She was an inspired and sarcastic mimic. I have never seen eyes that struck with such electric energy as her black eyes. Both she and her sister Cora showed the quarter-Indian blood they inherited from their father. Cora was even more convincing. All in all, our Grammie was a high-spirited and fiercely independent woman who cultivated her friends and buried her enemies with equal ardor. In many respects she was a liberated woman and proud of it.

Two nurturing streams of influence came from my grandparents. That is to say, the parents of both my mother and father. My father's father, among other interests, had once planted and maintained one of the larger apple orchards in our town. It was both a working farm and a summer vacation venue for "City Folk" from Boston. My grandfather tended the fruit trees and entertained the paying guests, while my grandmother, who had arrived in this country from Sweden at the age of nineteen, and my father did everything else. After the sale of Sky Farm, my grandfather surrounded himself with a less domestic array of animals. He bought a wolf and trained it to accompany him around town. He purchased a pelican named Rudy that assumed the role of resident watchdog. Rudy, true to the code of his canine counterparts, hated postmen and he contested their daily intrusions upon his territory.

Show Business

In time Grampie and his brother George had acquired enough of a menagerie of live and stuffed animals plus tents, cages, rides, and "games of chance" to travel around New England with their little carnival. In the later years I remember witnessing the remnants of the show when it performed behind my grand-uncle's pavilion at Morrill's Grove on Silver Lake. Of all the animals that remained after the hurricane hit the carnival in New Haven, Connecticut, one in particular stands apart from all the others, a monkey named Tommy. I can still recall his bushy-eyed and reddened face cautiously, furtively poised at an angle that would allow him to mark your every movement without engaging in any direct eye contact. He was a large rhesus monkey, fully adult and in command of everything that was close enough to intimidate. When Tommy jerked down into a bobbing crouch and raised his brows to show the lighter skin of his upper eyelids, all in attendance (animal and human) were well advised to take seriously the intended threat. Before my grandfather finally gave him to Uncle George, Grampie had to knock him senseless with a hammer to escape from his last and most relentless attack. Of the people that came into contact with Tommy, my grandmother Hulda seemed to provide him with the most devilish outlets for his inventiveness. Among his exploits of thievery, hat stealing, and work disruption, he seemed to most enjoy waiting for the wet clean laundry to be aligned, dangling from the clothes line, followed by Grammie's departure. Eventually, from his hiding place he would stealthily climb up and across the lines, methodically removing each wooden clothespin as he maneuvered through his perverse "wire-walking" act.

In later years we three boys inherited the remains of the stuffed animals, fish, reptiles, and bird displays. We put the heavy and durable wood and wire pens and cages to new uses with our own menagerie of domestic and wild animals. It was too early for us to sample show business. We were, however, beginning to parade around the edges. Some of the stuffed animals found themselves resurrected as science projects. One eight-foot alligator (stuffed with sawdust) made its way through the streets to the Webster School and back, on the sweating shoulders of five sixth-grade students. We must have presented a unique tableau for those who stopped to watch us. Imagine all those legs, beneath an imperious grinning, stiffened reptile, toiling unsteadily toward relief at the distant elementary school. Behind us lay a long thin trail of sawdust.

We raised and released a red-tailed hawk and kept a skunk until we could remove the broken bottle that collared its inquisitive head. My father, who was as fearless as my brother Loren, lifted the skunk by the tail as the glass was carefully removed from the animal's neck. We watched as it ambled away, anxious to regain its tarnished dignity.

In those days we hunted with .22s for rats at the town dump. And it raised no eyebrows to see a boy on his way to the woods carefully carrying a .410 or .12-gauge shotgun. We seemed to live in a state of easy grace with most of the natural world that surrounded us. There was also a good deal more of it around to be intimate with.

Light and Vision

We returned to Silver Lake one golden summer day, some time after the closing of the carnival. I can still recall the joy of roaming around the farm that Uncle George and Aunt Suzy kept across the road from Morrill's Grove. There was a millrace (a stone-walled passage that forced the water to rush over the water wheel, activating the gears within the mill) and the pond where a flock of mallards, Pekings, Muscovies, and wood ducks dabbled and swam. How dashing and beautiful the males were as they shone brilliant in the sunlight. How demure and delicate were the lovely female wood ducks. It was from that flock that my first Muscovy ducklings came. Around the penned yards lay the large farm equipment. Plows, harrows, cultivators, stone boats, and all manner of machinery were around the congested barn yard. Through these I picked my meandering way and headed up the ramp that led to the high doors of the main barn. I was barely able to slip into the space between the great gates that separated the brilliance of the summer day from the captive light that heightened the barn's inner mystery. As wide as the surrounding fields and lake were, nothing could rival the depth and scope of what now confronted my imagination.

In the magical rays that descended from some celestial source I saw a complete but carefully dismantled carousel. The great room was held like a dream dance, silent, commanding, still animated by the carved splendor of horses, sleighs, boards, lights, and staging. Time can be such a meaningless limiting dimension. Captured there in that dusty cavern I had found a trove as great as Ali Baba's. Every steed that day had an opportunity to bear my weight to some imagined destination. No Near Eastern magician had ever ridden more freely above Sinbad's Araby than I did that summer day. It was one of those days that has never ended. I can return to that timeless place whenever I wish to conjure it up. Soon after, one caparisoned horse arrived to adorn our own hallway for many more journeys and years. Oh, that I had thought to save it for my own grandchild in more than just memory.

I understand and cherish the need to communicate our individual and collective histories. When we share a personal insight or a unique experience, we can give beauty and breadth of knowledge to seemingly unrelated events and people. It helps to define and personalize those we will never meet and joins us all with a shared humanity.

Past Mother, Passed Brother

My mother had been raised by her grandmother and grand-uncle, Clara Miles and Grover Scollay. "Gram," as she was called, had raised my Aunt Cora and my grandmother Clara before she assumed the responsibility for my mother Leona. The women and Uncle Grover were totally devoted to each other and the remembrances of those years are filled with happiness and caring. Gram had married a successful businessman and livery stable owner. He was the son of an American Indian woman and a white father. His mother spoke a language other than English. She had been "Brought East,"

as they said, and adopted by a Massachusetts family and educated in an Eastern school. Her husband's family, the Mileses, had among their number Colonel Nelson Miles, who participated in one of the most sorrowful moments in American frontier history: the sad surrender of the Nez Perce Indians under their great chief Joseph.

If traces of blood from a Plains Indian still are to be found in my family, it must be within my oldest brother. It is Grover who has always been called to the solitude of wilderness forests and especially to the mountains. It seems to me that they are both places of sanctuary and renewal for him. I believe, and he would state it better, such places are resources to experience through reflection those things unfulfilled or missing from his otherwise urban life. Thus he, as everyone in our hometown, received a nickname. He was aptly called "Hermit." He still sleeps upon the floor, with open windows and no heat in the middle of winter. The depth of his mind borders on brilliance. You would want him at your side in battle, both for the strategy and the engagement.

Between Grover and me there exists a sometimes sparkling void that was once filled by my brother Lonnie. To have lived thirty years within the same family and to admit that I never knew my middle brother seems at times unnatural, puzzling, and for long a disturbing reality. If anyone possessed the outward manifestations of a creative, steel-nerved and calculated theatrically, it was Loren Edwin Morrill— LEM as he sometimes referred to himself. he left high school to go to New York to study ballet and was back in a week. He joined the Navy in 1950 and returned to Hudson with a sneer, a more pronounced swagger, and a pierced ear complete with gold earring or gold stud, depending on the occasion. He often wore a Chesterfield coat and a Homburg (hat). Once while dining out with Grover, he calmly finished his meal, donned his grey chamois gloves, and went outside to confront a group of teens who had followed them to the restaurant and stood outside waiting to resume their taunts. Walking up to the group's leader, he announced that he was ready to settle the dispute. There was no answer. So he spat in his face, waited, then turned with his brother and strode away. No, he did not always escape unchallenged from all fights. Both of my brothers seemed energized by walking the thinnest and quite dangerous of lines between physical injury and calculated risk.

Benson's

Being the youngest of three boys, a position I would gladly have relinquished to either of my brothers, it fell to my lot to always be arriving later than most to the party. Although I struggled to keep up, someone seemed to have gotten there first. Even at this advanced age of sixty-one, I still feel that I am playing "catch-up." At times my brothers seemed more object lessons not to be followed or obstacles to be overcome. Still they certainly broke ground, opened possibilities, and presented some unique and exotic features to my widening vision.

Grover suggested that there was a system of essential laws that governed movement, and that the knowledge and practice of those laws would eventually bring about a spiritual and physical union with the truth of the underlying principle(s). I believe he thought that this convergence could be applied to every other related action, ending with such refinement of practice as to attain in every instance a higher state of consciousness. It was Loren who introduced me to the natural world of wings, hooves, and claws. I was twelve and apart from school and my ventures with small town adolescent capitalism, it was time to seek a "real job." After I presented the thought to the family, it was agreed that Loren would recommend to his boss that he hire his younger brother Leslie for summer employment. When Fred Pitkin first set eyes upon me I could guess at his thoughts. He was thinking, I don't know. . . . He certainly is small for this kind of work. Well, we will soon be needing more kids on the pony rides. "I'll let your brother know if I can use you," he said. Within one long week my brother announced, "Fred said to come in on Saturday. You've got to get a social security number, sign some withholding tax, labor, and liability forms." I was perplexed. I didn't know what he was talking about. I had never signed a contract or engaged in state-sponsored commitments more complicated than acknowledging the receipt for cartons of twenty-five fuzzy chicks, reciting the Pledge of Allegiance, or making promises to honor and obey the 4-H

Daughter Melissa with Duchess, 1977

or Boy Scout laws. (Little did I know that I would be signing contracts for the rest of my life.) What if I didn't succeed? I went to bed that Friday night, knowing that if I couldn't live up to whatever the high standards of a "Pony Boy" were that my brother Loren would have "*ridden me down* for the rest of my life."

Benson's Wild Animal Farm had been one of the apple orchards that perched on the higher elevations of the hills surrounding the old part of town called Hudson Centre. By some coincidence, the farm's former owner, an enterprising Yankee, had leased some space on his property for a quarantine station. At the time all imported exotic birds, reptiles, and animals had to undergo a period of confinement before they were accepted and certified as being fit for shipment to zoos, carnivals, circuses, pet stores, or laboratories in the United States. All such animals arriving through the Port of Boston had to be confined close to that port of entry. Hudson, New Hampshire was thirty-eight miles away.

The artist's wife, Judith

The Wild Animal Farm

As more animals arrived, more space was needed and was provided. As more and more animals occupied a larger part of the available space it began to attract the attention of the curious locals. Soon people from all over the New England states were paying to view the odd inhabitants that were housed and on display. So Benson, noting the diminished returns from apple production and the increasing revenue from paid admissions, did the logical thing. John Benson changed professions and went from apple farmer to impresario. He opened his new enterprise as Benson's Wild Animal Farm—The Strangest Farm on Earth.

By the time I began my six-year affiliation with The Farm, or Benson's as it was called by the townsfolk, the menagerie, personnel, permanent and seasonal residents, displays, housing, pastures, slaughterhouse, barns, show rings, concessions, and the trained cats, elephants, horses, mules, ponies, and chimpanzees, and all the supporting structures were intact. It was more than a zoo; it was a permanent and stationary circus.

So I entered the bizarre, brash, and wonderful world of international oddities, human and other. Had I realized the true odds of any twelve-year-old finding himself in such an extraordinary place, I would have cherished those years even more than I did. As it was, I loved being a part of that time and place, as did most everyone who worked there. If you were to ask us to recall the names of our equine charges, I would bet that most of my contemporaries could identify ninety percent of the forty-odd animals on the two floors of the horse and pony barn. When I think of those years, they come tumbling past me, pulling me over the familiar land like the rank six lead lines of ponies that made us fly as they raced toward the pastures of early April.

Fred Pitkin's responsibilities included all activities related to the horses, ponies, donkeys, and attendants. He demanded attention to rituals and routines but otherwise ruled benignly over the lives of every entity that worked under or about him. To my knowledge he had trained all the Palomino and White Liberty Horse Acts, the pony and mule acts, and Tootsie the Educated Pony. *"She can count up to 100. Subtract, add, and divide sums. And understand and answer simple questions."* So went the introduction to Tootsie's wonderful performance (summer or winter). In time we too learned how Fred had taught her to do her popular act. It was done through minor changes in where he stood in relation to what letter or number he wanted her to select from the rack before her. He positioned himself to her left and slightly behind her. This made it appear that he was outside of her field of vision. With a pony or horse this was taking full advantage of their peripheral vision, which magnifies objects and movements greatly. By minor movements with one hand, a slight shift to the side, forward, or back, Fred had near perfect control, despite the fact that he was sometimes six feet away from Tootsie. In her he not only had a calm and willing pupil, but Tootsie was in her own right reasoned and consistent. When out of the show ring, she always acted in a responsible manner independent of any human or other animal present.

Both Sides of the Barriers

Between the horse and pony acts came "Betsy the Elephant." After performing in the ring Betsy donned a howdah or riding platform and gave rides to customers. Carl Neuffer, who was her handler, had come to this country from the famous Hagenbeck Tiergarten in Germany. Carl and Betsy had literally, with the aid of a large metal scoop, removed the earth to create Benson's large willow lined pond—truly the earliest of "Bull-Dozers." (All elephants in circus language are called "bulls," although by far the captive females outnumber the males.) The greatest number of animal-related deaths have been caused by elephants. I can attest to their unpredictability, for I had the surprising experience of having been struck in the chest by a six-year-old named Ned, who hurled me back against an iron rail some eight feet away. His trunk was swinging loosely between his front legs one minute and the next it struck forward like a snake. Needless to say, I never stood directly in front of Ned again, even if I was his senior by eight years. There are times when "might does make right."

Before I began my work at The Farm two famous women had been employed as trainers there. They were May Kovar and Mabel Stark. It was said that Mabel had died from contracting tuberculosis from her "chimps," although it may have been more common for captive animals to develop diseases from human beings (respiratory ailments in particular). Autopsies were often conducted on our charges and some results were viewed with skepticism. One such case was a wart hog that had died of ulcers. I remember wondering, what could have so worried a wart hog? Did animals have more complex lives than I knew about?

As for chimpanzees, the unruly star of the Monkey House was an aggressive male named Junior. He had been hand-raised but, as is often the case with adult primates, he proved to be unmanageable. If the drunk who had enraged Junior and then attempted to climb over the barrier to his cage had not been subdued by the Chief of Police and several others I suspect we would have had a tragedy on our hands.

In all the years of my employment at Benson's there was never a fatal accident with a guest or employee. There were however, numerous attempts to sue the owners by opportunistic litigious customers. There always seems to exist a small percentage of the public who attempt to swindle with intimidation and feigned injury. With all the minor injuries sustained by employees I do not remember a lawsuit being brought by one of them. It was understood by most workers that beyond the truly unforeseen accident it was an individual's responsibility to be prepared for the unpredictable. We learned quickly that personal well-being could be preserved best by constant vigilance.

The Wild West That Went South

All of us had our share of near misses and minor scrapes and The Farm itself had a mishap. My brother bore on his leg the scar from at least one unhappy bobcat he had unsuccessfully tried to train. As you might have guessed, we were always trying to train something. Among the perplexed victims were a coatimundi, a baby elephant, baby chimps and bears, goats, chickens, a zebra, cockatiels, cockatoos, macaws, and pigeons. Everyone at some time seemed possessed with the vision of introducing the next star attraction. Many acts dissolved in the dusty rings of reality. Most attempts were victims of impatience, impossible expectations, lack of cooperation from the trainees, and general ineptitude on the part of the would-be trainers. As teenagers we were not allowed to work with the larger animal acts. These acts included the lion act of Joe Arcaris; the thirteen-mixed-cat act of Joe Walsh (lions, tigers, and leopards) that was leased each winter season to the Shriner's Circus; and the elephant act of Miss Zequilan. We kids did work with the baby chimps and the bird act in addition to the ponies and horses.

The most expensive and ironical miscalculation of a new attraction involved the re-creation of a "Real Rodeo" on the leveled plains of that former New Hampshire apple orchard. The construction of corrals, chutes, holding pens, and ring were started. These were followed by longhorn cattle, bucking horses, a cutting horse, and Brahma bulls. If these were objects of interest and speculation, you can imagine the talk sparked by the arrival of our first cowboy, Curly Roberts, his assisting cowgirl Judy, and "our very own real Indian," Chief Young Thundercloud. They and some others started by perfecting their forthcoming rodeo spectacular

Sketches by Leslie Morrill created for Something about the Author Autobiography
Series, *Volume 22, and featuring characters from Charles Dickens's* Oliver Twist

with small feats of roping (unsuspecting attendants), bullwhip mischief (I still have one
bullwhip), and by firing rounds of live ammunition at gun-shy flies. Later they graduated
from boredom to liquored *lickings* (another
antique term) in the bars of Nashua. In time

they limped away to more active and hospi-
table places, where the locals knew how to have
a good time. Their departure left a hole in
the hopes for the future of western-style ranch
life in the East. It also proved to leave behind
a cumbersome debt to the consortium that owned

the Wild Animal Farm. Only the Indian, his family, and the longhorns remained to attest to the passing of the failed frontier. The grasses and weeds eventually would grow to cover the remnants of the wooden posts and rails.

Two years after Judy (the resident cowgirl) received a lash across her brave and attractive face, I too met with the chance unwelcome encounter that always lies waiting for the unthinking or the lax attendant.

Lifted Faces

It was a sunny Saturday in my birth-month, February. I cannot remember if we had played an away game of basketball or if I had stayed out late with my girlfriend Claire on the preceding night. Whatever the cause, I had opened an opportunity to disaster that one of the horses, Jigger of Gold, was quick to exploit. One of my duties with the six-horse Palomino Liberty Act was to use a lunge whip to drive the horses from the rear. My job was to force them forward at the trainer, who backed up to the ring curb as he raised his whips. These movements caused the forward-milling horses to rear in unison at the finale of the act. As I ran pass the horses, flicking the whip at their bunched and uneven croups, I saw an unshod hoof, backed by 1,000 pounds of horse, making its way toward my face. As I turned my face and started to slide backwards, the world exploded in starry brilliance. I came to as I stumbled out of the ring into a small horrified audience with another assistant who was asking, "Are you all right?" What a question! I was now wearing the blood that so recently had been circulating in the vicinity of my nose. To me, all of the preceding had happened in slow motion. Although for several weeks I presented both faces of Jekyll and Hyde simultaneously, everything healed without a scar or permanent damage. I learned that fatigue is inimical to vigilance; loved ones can and do look at a disfigured face and not turn away; that the tested reflexes will usually react in a predictable and self-protective manner. I had not failed my rites of passage, as my brother before me had not.

It is interesting to note that in all those years, I never tried to draw or paint the life around me. It seems ironic that now I find my most successful artistic efforts are those that involve animals. I have found that I do have an affinity for representing animals. Perhaps it was their constant exposure to public curiosity and ignorant scrutiny or something as yet unresolved that made me unwilling or disinterested in describing my increased knowledge of them. I still remember and try to depict the easy grace and weary endurance as they traced the repetitions of their unnaturally limited worlds. And often in my illustrations their facial expressions still reflect near-human characteristics.

It's disconcerting to have had the last living spider monkey of a family run to embrace you for solace. Wasn't I, in a sense, really its captor? Yet it came to me for physical comfort and reassurance. I knew then from experience that without support it could not survive. It could never go home. All of these thoughts were disarming and alarming. To have an adult cougar hurl itself against the nearest cage wall at your every approach and then to drop onto its back, purring and rolling before you in some seeming act of submission or seduction, is food for thought. Or was it only thinking of me as food? I have always suspected that, as with human behavior, there is no one unambiguous thread that clearly or simply connects me to that monkey or cougar. I have often watched the mirrored faces attempting to bridge the distance from viewer to viewed, trying to apprehend the enigma of a shared existence. Perhaps it's best not to characterize the differences or similarities in any way but just to carefully appreciate them at a greater distance. Some things we humans find hard to do.

To the Illustrator in All of Us

I have presented to you an imperfect and incomplete image of myself and that is how it will remain. Because, you see, I intend for this to be less of an exercise in self-disclosure than it is an opportunity to appreciate the vivid colors of that common journey that we all have taken. The passage that leaves those lingering images of our own childhood. Perhaps you will see or sense the familiar in some of these personal experiences and thus be able to re-create and with time gainfully shape your own biography.

I will interject here a short synopsis of the kind you will find in most resumes. I have taught classes from preschool through high school, college and art schools. I have worked in and for commercial art studios. I have been a consultant to a corporation and a designer/ owner of a company. I have designed and illustrated for porcelain, greeting cards, and a puzzle manufacturer. I have worked for British and German companies and most of the major U.S. book publishing houses. I have worked for small presses and university publications as well as newspapers. Two video projects for television in New York and Boston have been commissioned and completed. Two works on paper drawings have been purchased for museum collections. I have two degrees in art and have received four awards of excellence for science books, library awards, and two American Institute of Graphic Arts awards. I have had my work published in several languages.

May your story possess a defining beauty at least the equal of my own. May those people whom you recognize as significant be as intelligent, colorful, varied and helpful as those whom I will now list: my mother, father, brothers Grover and Loren, and all who went before. My extraordinary wife Judith and daughter Melissa, son Mark and wife Margot and their daughter Thea, Judith's family Justin, Stella, Jud, Leslie Anne, and Joy, John Baker, Richard Bartlett, John Ball, Suzanne Beck, Bela and Chela Birkas, the Boates family, the John Briggs family, Hal and Jean Cowles, Margery Cuyler, Louis Desmaires, the Djordjevic family, Dilys Evans, Lew Fifield and family, Dick Grady, James Howe, Don and Doreen Hudson, Trina Hyman, John Keller, Barry and Sarah Landau, Len Leone, Beverly Leung, Olga Litowinsky, Bob Lowe, Sue Lu, Frank and Ann Lucas, Malcolm Mansfield, Ron McCutchan, Emily McLeod, Claire Morin, Bill Morrison, Jane and Bill Pope, Gary Senick, Paul Stonehart, Lovell Thompson, Marcy and Wally Tripp, John Tarzian, Bob and Tom Toscano, Marty Redman, Carol White, and all the others in and out of the art and publishing worlds.

ILLUSTRATOR

FOR YOUNG PEOPLE

Fiction:

Anne Eliot Crompton, *The Sorcerer*, Little, Brown, 1971.

Walter D. Edmonds, *Beaver Valley*, Little, Brown, 1971.

Mary Wesley, *Speaking Terms*, Gambit, 1971.

Pearl S. Buck, *Mrs. Starling's Problem*, John Day, 1973.

Matt Christopher, *Desperate Search*, Little, Brown, 1973.

Eve Bunting, *Box, Fox, Ox, and the Peacock*, Ginn, 1974.

David McCord, *Away and Ago: Rhymes of the Never Was and Always Is*, Little, Brown, 1974.

Margery Sharp, *Bernard the Brave: A Miss Bianca Story*, Little, Brown, 1977.

Miska Miles, *Mouse Six and the Happy Birthday*, Dutton, 1978.

Miska Miles, *Noisy Gander*, Dutton, 1978.

Eugene Pool, *The Captain of Battery Park*, Addison-Wesley, 1978.

Margery Sharp, *Bernard into Battle: A Miss Bianca Story*, Little, Brown, 1978.

Sheila Dolan, *The Wishing Bottle*, Houghton, 1979.

Beth Hilgartner, *Great Gorilla Grins: An Abundance of Animal Alliterations*, Little, Brown, 1979.

Miska Miles, *The Little Pig*, Dutton, 1980.

Larry Callen, *Dashiel and the Night*, Dutton, 1981.

Elizabeth Parsons, *The Upside-Down Cat*, Atheneum, 1981.

Margaret Laurence, *Jason's Quest*, Seal Books, 1981.

Mary Caldwell, *Morning Rabbit Morning*, Harper, 1981.

Phyllis Reynolds Naylor, *All Because I'm Older*, Atheneum, 1981.

Mary Calhoun, *The Night the Monster Came*, Morrow, 1982.

Ted Clymer and Miska Miles, *Horse and the Bad Morning*, Dutton, 1982.

Kenneth Grahame, *The Wind in the Willows*, Bantam, 1982.

Kathryn Jackson and Byron Jackson, *Katie the Kitten*, Golden Press, 1982.

George Selden, *Irma and Jerry*, Avon, 1982.

Judy Delton, *Back Yard Angel*, Houghton, 1983.

Sharon Sigmond Shebar and Judith Schoder, *The Bell Witch*, Messner, 1983.

Margarete Sigl Corbo and Diane Marie Barras, *Arnie the Darling Starling*, Houghton, 1983.

Clifton Fadiman, compiler and author of commentary, *The World Treasury of Children's Literature*, Little, Brown, Volumes 1–2, 1984, Volume 3, 1985.

(With Ted Enik) Lois McCoy and Floyd McCoy, *The Byte Brothers GOTO a Getaway: A Solve-It-Yourself Computer Mystery*, Bantam, 1984.

Lois McCoy and Floyd McCoy, *The Byte Brothers Input an Investigation: A Solve-It-Yourself Computer Mystery*, Bantam, 1984.

Lois McCoy and Floyd McCoy, *The Byte Brothers Program a Problem: A Solve-It-Yourself Computer Mystery*, Bantam, 1984.

Walter Dean Myers, *Mr. Monkey and the Gotcha Bird: An Original Tale*, Delacorte, 1984.

Willo Davis Roberts, *Eddie and the Fairy Godpuppy*, Atheneum, 1984.

Marileta Robinson, *The Big Bicycle Race*, Parker Brothers, 1984.

Judy Delton, *Angel in Charge*, Houghton, 1985.

Gary Gygax and Flint Dille, *Sagard the Barbarian: The Ice Dragon*, Archway, 1985.

Barbara Shook Hazen, *Fang*, Atheneum, 1987.

Stephen Mooser, *The Secret Gold Mine*, Troll, 1987.

Stephen Mooser, *Secret in the Old Mansion*, Troll, 1987.

Sharon S. O'Toole, *Noodles: Sheep Security Guard*, Scholastic, 1988.

Betty Bates, *Tough Beans*, Holiday House, 1988.

Zilpha Keatley Snyder, *Squeak Saves the Day and Other Tooley Tales*, Delacorte, 1988.

Kathy Pelta, *The Blue Empress*, Holt, 1988.

Stephen Mooser, *The Case of the Slippery Sharks*, Troll, 1988.

Stephen Mooser, *The Mummy's Secret*, Troll, 1988.

Margery Cuyler, *Freckles and Jane*, Holt, 1989.

Laurence Pringle, *Jesse Builds a Road*, Macmillan, 1989.

Crescent Dragonwagon, *I Hate My Sister Maggie*, Macmillan, 1989.

Myra Cohn Livingston, editor, *Dog Poems*, Holiday House, 1990.

Teri Martini, *The Secret Is Out: True Spy Stories*, Little, Brown, 1990.

Barbara Shook Hazen, *Stay, Fang*, Atheneum, 1990.

Bill Wallace, *Totally Disgusting!*, Holiday House, 1991.

Betty Bates, *Hey There, Owlface*, Holiday House, 1991.

Betsy Duffey, *A Boy in the Doghouse*, Simon & Schuster, 1991.

Susanne S. Whayne, *Watch the House*, Simon & Schuster, 1992.

Betsy Duffey, *Lucky on the Loose*, Simon & Schuster, 1993.

Betsy Duffey, *Lucky in Love*, Simon & Schuster, 1993.

Betsy Duffey, *Lucky Christmas*, Simon & Schuster, 1994.

Written by Walter R. Brooks:

Freddy the Politician, Knopf, 1986.

(With Kurt Wiese) *Freddy and the Perilous Adventure*, Knopf, 1986.

(With Kurt Wiese) *Freddy Goes Camping*, Knopf, 1986.

(With Kurt Wiese) *Freddy the Pilot*, Knopf, 1986.

Freddy and the Men from Mars, Knopf, 1987.

Freddy Goes to Florida, Knopf, 1987.

Freddy the Cowboy, Knopf, 1987.

Freddy the Detective, Knopf, 1987.

Written by Patricia Reilly Giff:

Fourth-Grade Celebrity, Delacorte, 1979.

The Girl Who Knew It All, Delacorte, 1979.

Left-Handed Shortstop, Delacorte, 1980.

The Winter Worm Business, Delacorte, 1981.

Rat Teeth, Delacorte, 1984.

Love, from the Fifth-Grade Celebrity, Delacorte, 1986.

Poopsie Pomerantz, Pick up Your Feet, Delacorte, 1989.

Written by James Howe:

The Celery Stalks at Midnight, Atheneum, 1983.

Morgan's Zoo, Atheneum, 1984.

Nighty-Nightmare, Macmillan, 1987.

The Fright Before Christmas, Morrow, 1988.

Scared Silly: A Halloween Treat, Morrow, 1989.

Hot Fudge, Morrow, 1990.

Creepy-Crawly Birthday, Morrow, 1991.

Written by Judith Whitelock McInerney:

Judge Benjamin: Superdog, Holiday House, 1982.

Judge Benjamin: The Superdog Secret, Holiday House, 1983.

Judge Benjamin: The Superdog Rescue, Holiday House, 1984.

Judge Benjamin: The Superdog Surprise, Holiday House, 1985.

Judge Benjamin: The Superdog Gift, Holiday House, 1986.

"Hardy Boys Mystery Stories" series; written by Franklin W. Dixon:

Mystery of the Samurai Sword, Wanderer Books, 1979.

Night of the Werewolf, Wanderer Books, 1979.

The Apeman's Secret, Wanderer Books, 1980.

The Mummy Case, Wanderer Books, 1980.

Mystery of Smuggler's Cove, Wanderer Books, 1980.

The Pentagon Spy, Wanderer Books, 1980.

The Hardy Boys Handbook: Seven Stories of Survival, Wanderer Books, 1980.

The Four-Headed Dragon, Wanderer Books, 1981.

The Infinity Clue, Wanderer Books, 1981.

The Outlaw's Silver, Wanderer Books, 1981.

The Stone Idol, Wanderer Books, 1981.

The Submarine Caper, Wanderer Books, 1981.

The Vanishing Thieves, Wanderer Books, 1981.

The Billion Dollar Ransom, Wanderer Books, 1982.

Tic-Tac-Terror, Wanderer Books, 1982.

Track of the Zombie, Wanderer Books, 1982.

The Voodoo Plot, Wanderer Books, 1982.

"Choose Your Own Adventure" series:

R. A. Montgomery, *Indian Trail,* Bantam, 1983.

R. A. Montgomery, *Lost on the Amazon,* Bantam, 1984.

Edward Packard, *Mountain Survival,* Bantam, 1984.

Fred Graver, *Journey to Stonehenge,* Bantam, 1984.

Shannon Gilligan, *Mona Is Missing,* Bantam, 1985.

Louise M. Foley, *Danger at Anchor Mine,* Bantam, 1985.

Susan Saunders, *Attack of the Monster Plants,* Bantam, 1986.

R. A. Montgomery, *The Owl Tree,* Bantam, 1986.

R. A. Montgomery, *The Race Horse Mystery,* Bantam, 1992.

R. A. Montgomery, *Behind the Wheel,* Bantam, 1995.

Nonfiction:

Mildred Teal and John Teal, *Pigeons and People,* Little, Brown, 1972.

Harold Coy, *Man Comes to America,* Little, Brown, 1973.

Lucy Kavaler, *Life Battles Cold,* John Day, 1973.

Russell Freedman, *Growing Up Wild: How Young Animals Survive,* Holiday House, 1975.

Mildred Teal and John Teal, *The Sargasso Sea,* Little, Brown, 1975.

Barbara Rinkoff, *Guess What Rocks Do,* Lothrop, 1975.

Delia Goetz, *Valleys,* Morrow, 1976.

Laurence Pringle, *Animals and Their Niches: How Species Share Resources,* Morrow, 1977.

Gladys Conklin, *Black Widow Spider—Danger!,* Holiday House, 1979.

Vicki Cobb, *How to Really Fool Yourself: Illusions for All Your Senses,* Lippincott, 1981.

Sarah R. Riedman, *Biological Clocks,* Crowell, 1982.

Russell Freedman, *Dinosaurs and Their Young,* Holiday House, 1983.

Pat Ruane and Jane Hyman, *LOGO Activities for the Computer: A Beginner's Guide,* Wanderer Books, 1984.

Lillian Stokes and Donald Stokes, *Mammals of North America,* Little, Brown, 1985.

Sue Alexander, *America's Own Holidays,* F. Watts, 1988.

The Plymouth Thanksgiving (textbook), Open Court, 1992.

Rico (textbook), Quarazan Books, 1994.

Jessie (textbook), Quarazan Books, 1994.

Deborah Abbott and Henry Kisor, *One TV Blasting and a Pig Outdoors: A Concept Book,* Whitman, 1994.

Other:

Sharks (puzzle), International Playthings, 1992.

Pony Racing (puzzle), International Playthings, 1992.

My Aquarium (puzzle), International Playthings, 1993.

Forest Families (puzzle), International Playthings, 1993.

Dinosaurs (puzzle), International Playthings, 1993.

Rain Forest (puzzle), International Playthings, 1994.

Turtles (puzzle), International Playthings, 1995.

Also illustrator of *Ostrich* by Ruskin Bond, 1992. Illustrator of films and filmstrips, including *Animals, Animals: Song of the Turtle,* ABC-TV, 1980. Contributor of illustrations and covers to magazines, including *Cricket, Ladybug,* and *Babybug.* Illustrator of greeting cards for Recycled Papers.

FOR ADULTS

Nonfiction:

Loren Eiseley, *The Lost Notebooks of Loren Eiseley,* Little, Brown, 1987.

Stan Steiner, *The Waning of the West,* St. Martin's, 1989.

Colby Rodowsky

1932-

Several years ago my editor at Farrar, Straus & Giroux suggested that I write a book not only *about* an only child but to be *called* "Only Child." In it, he said, he'd like me to consider especially those aspects of being an only child that distinguish it from being a big sister, say, or a little sister, or even the runt of the litter. "I want you to do it," he went on, "because you can write about—or, rather, from—the point of view of an only child better than anyone I know."

"Well, I should think so," I harrumphed, putting the letter aside and promptly forgetting about it. "I've had enough experience." As indeed I had. As indeed I have.

Besides, I've done that, I thought to myself. And a recent tally of the books I've written shows that nine have been about only children and only seven about children with brothers or sisters or both.

That said, I was born on 26 February 1932, the *only child* of Mary and Frank Fossett. And, almost from my first conscious moment, I wanted to be a member of a LARGE EXTENDED FAMILY. I dreamed of families, pretended that I was a part of one, was convinced that all my dolls and stuffed animals were brothers and sisters to each other, and sought out books such as *Little Women, The Swiss Family Robinson, The Bobbsey Twins,* and even *Eight Cousins* (after all, cousins were better than nothing, I figured). And—declared straight away that when I grew up I was going to have *six children.*

Maybe my obsession with families came about because of my parents' marriage, which was rocky at best and sometimes downright horrific. As a backdrop to my childhood I remember fights and silences and recriminations. Night after night I would curl up under the covers with my Raggedy Ann doll, talking over the events of the day and, as a kind of distraction, telling her stories, finding answers to the age-old questions "What if . . . ?" and "How about . . . ?" and "What happened next . . . ?"

Colby Rodowsky, 1989

My parents separated when I was halfway through first grade, and my mother and I went to stay with *her* parents in Cape Charles, Virginia. I don't know how long we were there, but it was long enough for me to be enrolled in school, to go off to the same classroom where my mother had gone as a child, to have Miss Scott, the same teacher my mother had had. Cape Charles, both then and in the many summers I spent there later on, was the safe haven in my life, a small town on the Eastern Shore of Virginia where my grandparents "Nana" and "Popoo" Coulbourn (hence my name, which is actually Mary Coulbourn) lived in a large rambling white house with a wraparound front porch.

Looking back in grudging honesty, I guess I would have to admit that Cape Charles was an unexceptional, almost boring town where there was nothing to do. But for me it was a wonderful, almost magical place. I remember long summer days and trips to the beach, the flat lukewarm water of the Chesapeake Bay. I remember the twelve o'clock whistle and the wail of a train at night, the cry of the fishman as he trudged with his wooden cart up and down the streets. I remember going "downtown" with my grandmother and the giant, lazy fans that hung from the ceiling of the dry goods store and stopping at the drugstore for Cokes that were served in paper cups with pointed bottoms in cold metal holders.

Most of all I remember the book-musty smell of the library, an old church with the stained glass windows slightly tilted, the floors a varnished yellow, and the fiction two steps up where the altar used to be. On the off-days, when the library wasn't open, my grandmother's attic was there for exploration. The wooden stairs were steep, angling sharply near the top, and I would inch my way up, pulling back against the swoop of an occasional bird trapped inside. The floor was spotted with pigeon droppings and the heat was stifling, but there were books my mother and grandmother had read, and scrapbooks and trunks; there were hunting boots and crocks, and funny, splotchy mirrors leaning against the studding.

Even now, I have on my desk, next to the duck-shaped pencil holder and the heap of to-be-dealt-with papers, a shell that I picked up on the beach at Cape Charles when we detoured through the town a few years ago on our way home from a trip to the south. It is neither a beautiful nor an exotic shell but it is, for me, a talisman of sorts; I have only to run my fingers along its flat, somewhat pearly surface to summon up those long-ago summers.

The importance in my life of that small Eastern Shore town can be seen by the number of times I have used it in what I have written, starting with my first book *What about Me?* In that book, when Dorrie's parents decide to leave New York City in search of a smaller, more comfortable place in which to raise their retarded son Fredlet, they head for "Tunbridge," Maryland, which was, in reality, Cape Charles, Virginia. Once there, Dorrie encountered many of the names that had peopled my childhood—the Waddells, the Wilkins, and even Aunt Sudie. Her grandmother's house was *my* grandmother's house, even down to the Tiffany lamp over the dining room table and the stuffed squirrel and pheasant on top of the china closet. In fact, her grandmother was my grandmother, "little and birdlike and she always wore high heels."

In *Evy-Ivy-Over* I set the whole book in Cape Charles, though I never specifically identified it as such. This book tells the story of Slug October and her grandmother Gussie, the town eccentric. For me at least, she evokes the memory of an old woman, also named Gussie, who was certifiably crazy and wandered the streets of town, rummaging through trash and storing her finds away in her hodgepodge of a house until she was hauled off to the state asylum in Williamsburg. The "book Gussie" was not the "real Gussie" at all and was, in many ways, much like both of my grandmothers. In fact, the way Slug felt about Gussie and Gussie felt

Colby with her father, 1932

At age four in Ocean City, Maryland

about Slug was the way my grandmothers and I felt about each other. I've often thought, though, that it would be hard indeed for those two very proper women to see themselves in a character who delights in finding an empty Milk of Magnesia bottle or who knows how yellow feels all the way through.

The town of Cape Charles turns up again in *H, My Name Is Henley* when Henley and her feckless mother Patti, after a headlong trek from place to place, head for the Eastern Shore in search of the shelter I always found there. In this book Henley finds herself immediately at home in Aunt Mercy's house which is again, of course, my grandmother's house. She wanders from the parlor, with its upright piano, its spinning wheel, and marble-top table, into the library, the dining room, and on to the office, stopping to study the picture of a lion in a heavy brown frame with silver painted bars on the outside of the glass before heading into the kitchen. She explores the back stairs, the second floor bedrooms, and, of course, the attic.

The attic (or garret as my grandmother used to call it) is the subject of a book of its own. In *Jenny and the Old Great-Aunts* five-year-old Jenny is sent to spend the afternoon with her great-aunts while her mother and father go off to the dentist and the office and to visit a friend in the hospital. After Aunt Clare falls asleep, Jenny and Aunt Abby venture upstairs to investigate the attic, which was "hot and dry and

smelled like the insides of pockets." Once there they explore the nooks and crannies and cubbyholes, discovering old boots, books, baskets, and canes as well as a piano stool that gets higher and higher the more you spin around. Their greatest find, however, is something called a Victrola that, when it had been cranked and the needle set down just so, plays a funny, thin kind of music.

Sometime after the finish of first grade my parents decided on a reconciliation and my mother and I went back to Baltimore. From second grade on I attended Notre Dame, a private school for girls where my father's mother and sisters had gone and, for the brief time that they took boys, where my father had gone as well. Despite the fact that my parents' truce was a shaky one I remember this time in my life as almost ideal. I had a dog (Taffy), a bike that I pretended was a horse, and a whole string of fairy-tale Christmases.

I also had a best friend named Patty who, I was sure, was far luckier than I because she had three older sisters and a twin brother to boot. Patty and I were inseparable, running back and forth over the two blocks between our houses many times on any given day. The only trouble with this arrangement was that her father, an alcoholic, was occasionally given to holding forth in the living room, pontificating on almost any subject, even reciting poetry, lurching from place to place, at times falling. And I was afraid of him. One time when I was spending the night at her house her parents came home late from a party and her father came into our room, stumbling and staggering around, knocking things off shelves and tables while Patty and I lay deathly still and pretended to be asleep.

Years later, when I wrote the book *Hannah in Between* about twelve-year-old Hannah and her alcoholic mother, I remembered that night; remembered my near terror and what had to be Patty's embarrassment; remembered how, though we usually told each other *everything,* we never mentioned her father's drinking. I wrote the scene into the book, trying to capture Patty's feelings in Hannah, my own in her best friend Samantha.

Shortly after the start of World War II, my father enlisted in the Army Air Corps and went off to Officers Training School in Florida and then to Texas where he was eventually stationed. My mother took me and moved to New York,

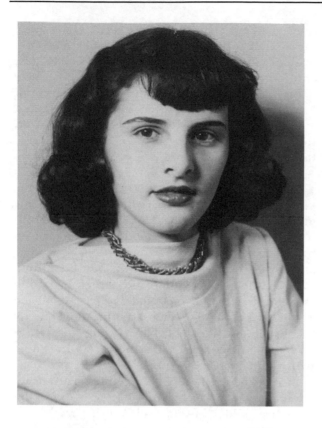

The author in high school, 1948

once a classmate took us to a Saturday afternoon performance of the Metropolitan Opera to sit in a box! We saw the circus at Madison Square Garden and the Christmas and Easter shows at Radio City Musical Hall, wondering briefly if we had what it took to be Rockettes.

It's not surprising, then, that I used New York as the setting for two of my books. When I wrote about Dorrie's apartment in *What about Me?* it was *my* apartment on Madison and 90th Street that I saw in my mind's eye. And when Dorrie went to school she was, in fact, going to the Convent of the Sacred Heart on the corner of Fifth Avenue and Ninety-first Street, though in the book I called it Miss Benson's School. Dorrie's favorite place, the Guggenheim Museum, wasn't even in existence when I lived in New York, but the way she feels about the city is the way I felt about it and her dismay at the thought of having to move away was mine.

In *H, My Name Is Henley,* when Henley and her mother go off to New York to stay with friends, Patti promises Henley one perfect day. It will probably come as no surprise that on that perfect day mother and daughter visit the zoo and the carousel in Central Park, the Metropolitan Museum, St. Patrick's Cathedral, and of course F.A.O. Schwarz—some of my favorite places in the city.

Even as a very young child I had been writing stories, trying my hand at realism and make-believe, but it was while we were in New York that I began writing "seriously," pounding away on my mother's typewriter, dipping more often than not into an impassioned purple prose. When I was about twelve I wrote my first "book" called *The Strangons* and I cringe to remember (and to tell) how my mother bundled it off (complete with my miserable typing and periodic spaces where the illustrations were to go) to a friend of hers who worked for, I think, Simon and Schuster. The friend wrote back a perfectly serious and straight-faced rejection letter saying that the paper shortage due to the war was the reason they couldn't publish my book. I knew better, but I truly think that my mother believed that a lack of paper was all that stood between me and fame and fortune at the age of twelve. The "book" was insignificant and best forgotten; my mother's faith in me was definitely significant and continues to be important to me to this day.

and it wasn't until we'd been there for a while that I found out that my parents had actually entered into a legal separation. Despite my sadness over this, and despite the fact that I missed my father and my friends in Baltimore, I fell suddenly and head over heels in love with New York.

The city during the 1940s was a friendlier and safer place than it is now, and I remember that, except for Central Park, which even then was off-limits without an adult, my new friends Libby, Judy, Ada and I seemed to have a free rein. We roller-skated through the neighborhood and took the Madison Avenue bus (for a nickel) downtown—or maybe the Fifth Avenue bus if we were feeling flush and had a dime. We went to the Metropolitan Museum especially to see the Colonial furniture as well as to the Planetarium. In winter we went sledding on the hills behind the Met and ice skating at Rockefeller Center (I wasn't very good and my ankles wobbled, but I loved *being* there). We wrote for free tickets to the Perry Como radio show and to the Prudential Family Hour;

It is understandable that several of my young heroines are would-be writers. Hannah, in *Hannah in Between,* says, "I pretend a lot. And make up stuff. But that's okay because if I do decide to become a writer when I grow up, which I'm seriously thinking of doing, then none of it will've been wasted but will be just so much grist for the mill. That's what Granddad says: all of life is grist for the writer's mill. And he ought to know because he's a writer, and kind of a famous one."

But it is Sydney (*Sydney, Herself* and *Sydney, Invincible*) who, as I was, is the quintessential aspiring writer. And just as I did at her age, Sydney thinks all writers should be misty and tragic-looking; she yearns to express "her innermost feelings" and explore "the fathoms of her mind." When I was eleven I once woke my mother in the middle of the night saying, "Who shall I dedicate my first book to?" "Why don't you write it first?" she answered before going back to sleep. Sydney, on the other hand, doesn't have any trouble with dedications. Toward the end of *Sydney, Herself* she imagines walking down Fifth Avenue in New York past a bookstore window filled with copies of her latest novel. One of the books is standing open to the dedication page and she whispers the words to herself: "*To Sam, who was there when it all began; to my mother, who believed in me; and, of course, to Wally, sans qui . . .*" Adding parenthetically, "(Which is French and means, roughly, without whom it couldn't've been done.)"

When the war was over and my father had been discharged from the Air Corps, he came to New York and my parents were once again reconciled. It was what I had dreamed of and prayed about and wished on wishbones for—and surely *this* time it was going to work. I was fifteen by then and busy with school, my friends, my writing, and trying not to hear the fights, the silences, and the recriminations that were once again going on at home. And somehow, despite all the signs and the undercurrents, I was still surprised when my mother took me out to dinner one spring night and told me that she and my father were getting a divorce. We were at the Westbury Hotel in a dining room on the second floor and we were sitting by the window. I remember looking out across Madison Avenue watching a woman and a dog and feeling that my world was falling apart while a waiter served ice cream in frosted bowls. I wanted to scream and knew that I couldn't.

Years later, when I was writing *Sydney, Invincible* and Wally's parents were getting a divorce, I used that scene and found that writing about it eased the pain even after all that time. Here it is, as Sydney tells it:

"Well," said Mrs. Martin when the waiter had brought ice cream in frosted bowls and a plate of macaroons. "There's something, some thing . . . some news. . . ."

She turned to me, speaking for a minute as if we were the only two at the table. "I've always said that Wally was mature. That he was scarcely a child at all. Even when he was small, always so funny and grown-up. And now there's something I want to tell him."

I knew I shouldn't be there, didn't want to be there, but just as I was starting to get up, Wally touched my foot with his under the table and his mother said, "No, no, Sydney, stay where you are. It's probably good for Wally that you're here." And I

College graduation picture, 1953

felt trapped, like a fly caught in a spider's web.

"I'm sure you've noticed that your father and I have been having trouble," said Mrs. Martin, turning back to Wally. "That things haven't been exactly—that we've— And we've decided to get a divorce. But don't tell Porter—not yet anyway. And your father'll stay on at the house till the end of the school year. It's just that we'll have separate rooms, go our separate ways."

All around us, people kept right on eating omelets and creamed chicken and fruit compote that tasted like McDonald's.

" . . . knew you'd understand." I heard Mrs. Martin's voice as if from far away. "That you'd be grown-up about this. That you'd see it's for the best."

I knotted my fingers in my lap and hurt for Wally, for Porter. The waiter came over and asked if there was something wrong with the ice cream, if, perhaps, we wanted a smidgen of hot fudge. We shook our heads at him and for the first time I dared to look at Wally. His face could've been made of stone, and I wished there was some magic button I could push that would let him rage, would let him hurl the ice cream and run at the potted plants and use all the words that had to be pent up inside of him, bursting to be let out. The kind of words that Sam said would take the starch right out of your vocabulary if you used them often enough.

After my parents' divorce my mother's life became more frantic and less dependable. She had recently moved to Washington, D.C., and I was supposed to live with her there, attending Georgetown Visitation Preparatory School as what was then called a "day hop." The weekend before school was to start she decided to move to New York and I suddenly found myself a boarder. Life at Georgetown Visitation was regimented and very strict—I seem to remember rule upon rule heaped upon regulation—but it was fun and, as in every place I've been in my life, it was the friends I made there that made it important.

Though my mother came back to Washington I remained a boarder, visiting her some weekends and on others going over to Baltimore, where my father had gone back to live. Gradually, almost without realizing it, I found that I was spending more and more time in Baltimore and that I had come to think of it as home. My mother eventually moved to New

York again where she remarried and stayed for awhile before going on to live in Florida.

There was a restlessness in my mother that sometimes, even when I was a child, made me want to catch her and hold her still, to tell her to stop chasing after rainbows. It is this quality that I tried to capture in the character of Patti, the mother in the book *H, My Name Is Henley.* In Patti I used the *idea* of my mother, not the person herself. Patti was younger and more Bohemian, far less reliable, but she had that same exasperating impetuosity, that same sense of fun—in an uncertain sort of way. And with Patti, as with my mother, there was always that feeling that this time things might really *be* wonderful. This is the way Henley expresses it in *H, My Name Is Henley:*

> "Are we *really* going to New York?" I suddenly felt that it might all vanish: the train, the fields streaking by outside, and the woman across the aisle with her canvas tote. I put a cheese curl on my tongue and let the yellow cheese flavor fill my mouth, then crunched it before it had a chance to soggy up. "Really?"
>
> "Really truly," said Patti.
>
> "And is it . . ."
>
> "It is."
>
> "Is what?" I asked.
>
> "Is wonderful," said Patti, holding her plastic glass up in a toast. "It's going to be wonderful for us. Finally wonderful. And I'll get this terrific job, at NBC or CBS, or maybe one of the big magazines. *McCall's* or *Redbook.* We'll get an apartment and ride in a buggy around Central Park and go to plays," she said, putting her head back and closing her eyes.
>
> All the way to New York I thought maybe this time Patti was right: this time it *was* going to be wonderful. All the way past Philadelphia and Trenton and Newark and down through a tunnel and into New York City, it was as though I had lifted up my feet and was skimming after Patti.

Life in Baltimore was becoming more and more important to me. My father and I had always been close and he was living with his mother and stepfather, my grandparents Ga and Bill. They not only made me feel welcome and literally *at home* but offered a kind of stability that I positively reveled in. After I graduated from high school I decided to live at home and go to the College of Notre Dame of Maryland, on the same campus where I had spent my first five years of elementary school. It was probably one of the best decisions I ever made.

Plain and simple: I loved college. I dove right in, taking part in all kinds of extracurricular activities even down to being the sports editor of the school paper when I knew absolutely *nothing* about sports. I was an English major, signed up for every creative writing class I could find, and wrote lots of not-so-good poetry and knew, in my heart of hearts, that I wasn't a poet. During my junior year I edited the college literary magazine and in my senior year I worked on the yearbook. And kept writing verses.

It was at Notre Dame that I met Sister Maura Eichner and had her as a teacher. Sister Maura, a fine poet in her own right, was without question the best teacher I ever encountered and had more to do with my becoming a writer than anyone else. In fact, my first book *What about Me?* was dedicated to her and, as each subsequent book comes out, I take the first copy, "hot off the press" as it were, over for her approval.

Thumbing through my books, I see that teachers play an important role, starting with

The author's maternal grandmother and mother with her children about 1963: (from left) Laurie, Alice, Sarah, and Emily.

Guntzie in *What about Me?* Guntzie, a composite of all the good teachers I ever had, is not only Dorrie's art teacher but her friend as well, encouraging her in her work and understanding what is going on in her life, empathizing with her ambivalent feelings about her brother Fredlet who has Down's syndrome.

Mary Sue Albright in *Evy-Ivy-Over* is another *good* teacher, stepping into Slug October's life when it seemed to have dipped to its lowest point, taking the place of the dreaded Mrs. Prather. For if Guntzie and Miss Albright were composites of all the *good* teachers I, or my children, ever had, Mrs. Prather spoke for all the not-so-good ones. I still remember the time in first grade when a music teacher—whose name I have fortunately forgotten—told me not to sing with the rest of the group but merely to move my lips instead. I still carry the sting of that admonition with me (I surely couldn't have sounded *that* much like a frog) and to this day am loathe to sing out in church, even on my favorite Christmas carols.

Mrs. Prather was drab and dismal and totally lacking in imagination.

> Slug didn't think Mrs. Prather looked so much mean as pulled down. It started with the top of her head, with the faded gray hair that wisped out of the bun in back straggling downward, pulling with it the drooping eyes and mouth. Then went on past the sagging bosoms, the uneven hem of her drab green dress to the black walking shoes planted firmly on the floor.
>
> But when she spoke, everything seemed to come together, as if someone had pulled invisible puppet strings. Her lips were sucked in, leaving only a thin, angry line across her face. Her voice jarred like broken glass against the murmur of the children coming in.
>
> "Fill in those seats in order. In order I say. No crowding to the back of the room. No dawdling now. The bell will ring in one minute and thirty-seven seconds and we will be ready."

But when Mrs. Prather left suddenly because of illness, Slug saw the sadness of someone who had failed to make a difference.

> Slug didn't miss Mrs. Prather, but she missed missing her. Ought to be an empty space where someone's been, just so you'll know she's been there, she thought. A dent,

sort of, to mark a coming in or going out. It was like Gussie pushing her fingers into a beer can, a funny, crunkled space that said, "I was here." Slug thought about the restless, wander-around feeling she had every time after Brian left. She thought about the space in Gussie's life left by the grandfather who was killed by the lightning bolt; and the great yawning, gaping hole that Julie made when she hopped the Trailways bus.

But Mrs. Prather was gone, and the edges she had left by going quickly ran together like raindrops on a windowpane forming a thin, unbroken stream.

But it is Sam Klemkoski in *Sydney, Herself* who best embodies all that I think a teacher should be. Sam, a wood sculptor by vocation and a teacher almost by default, was neither young nor handsome; he had a face that looked like it should have had a beard but didn't, with tufts of hair growing out of his ears that looked like Brillo pads when the sun hit them just right, a big nose, and a bald spot on the back of his head. A good teacher in spite of himself, he believed in the dictionary, good strong action words, and informed his class, at the first lapse into purple prose, that he taught writing, not Melodrama 101—and that if they want to have the vapors they should go to the infirmary. And, like all good teachers, he pushed and prodded, nurtured and cared—and got the best possible work out of his students.

During my junior year in college I went to a square dance one Saturday night and met a young man from neighboring Loyola College named Lawrence Rodowsky. Larry was a senior, a history major, and an aspiring lawyer, so that many of our dates over the next several years were spent with him at one end of my grandmother's dining room table studying and me at the other end reading or, after I graduated, working on third-grade lesson plans. We did manage to find time for parties, movies, and an occasional football game, though my year as sports editor hadn't helped much and I remained (and remain) hopelessly nonathletic. We were married at Corpus Christi Church in Baltimore on 7 August 1954.

After teaching third grade for two years in the Baltimore City Public Schools, I switched to the St. Francis School for Special Education. I loved my new job, the challenge of it, and especially the children, in particular the

Colby and Larry Rodowsky with Sister Maura Eichner

ones with Down's syndrome. I was put in charge of a small group of twelve- to fourteen-year-olds, none of whom could read or write. They were friendly and lovable, sometimes stubborn, and frequently had keen senses of humor. At St. Francis we didn't measure progress in great bounding leaps but rather in baby steps. But they were *important* steps and always a cause for excitement.

Many years later, when I wrote *What about Me?*, I called on much that I had learned from my time with the children at St. Francis. The book tells the story of fifteen-year-old Dorrie and her younger brother Fredlet, who has Down's syndrome. Dorrie's feelings about Fredlet are mixed at best: at times she thinks she hates him, his slowness, his almost constant drooling, and the way he drags an old Sears catalogue around with him. At times she wants to go to him, to hug him tightly.

During her year in tenth grade Dorrie, as part of her work-study program, signs up to go to Bellringers (Fredlet's school) to help out for a week. Here is how Dorrie describes a part of one of her days, a scene that came right out of my time at St. Francis.

I guess the things people never forget are either a lot of good or a lot of bad. And I know I'll never forget my week at Bellringers. That's what it was a lot of— good and bad.

Take the bathroom for instance. Sometimes I felt as if I spent the whole day in that bathroom on the second floor with all the pipes wrapped in plaster, and the little round sinks with rubber stoppers, and the blackish green linoleum that humped up in places. And the smell—urine and Lysol together forever in my mind and nose.

There was a sameness about the days too. Me saying the same things, like "Flush the toilet, Billy. I'm waiting to hear it." "John-Paul, you go right back in there and pull your pants up." "Sandy, what are you doing? Oh, no, not a whole roll of toilet paper."

"That's right, Billy. Put the stopper in the sink and run the water. Stop. Oh, Billy, look at the floor." And Billy looked and grinned, and he swished his hands back and forth in the brimful sink while I made a grab for the paper towels and put them all over the puddle. And with one hand I tried to get Billy's hands. But it was too late. I saw the water darkening the blue sleeves of his shirt.

"Uh-uh-uh," said Billy, holding up his dripping arms. "Uh-uh-uh." "Oh, Billy," I said. "Look at your nice shirt. Let's see if I can roll the sleeves back for you." Billy's hands and wrists were already red and chapped. As soon as I knelt down in front of him, he threw his sopping arms around my neck and we both went over backwards.

I worked at St. Francis until just before our first child, Laurie (Mary Lawrence), was born on 16 June 1956. With her arrival, Larry and I both had an overwhelming feeling that this was what we had been waiting for, not just for nine months but maybe all of our lives. Because I was an only child and had never had any experience baby-sitting, I spent a lot of time during those first few months checking the baby books and calling my friends and my mother-in-law for advice. A wise and forgiving child, Laurie took it all in stride and probably figured I would learn with practice.

Remembering my declaration that I would have six children when I grew up, and still wanting to be a part of a LARGE EXTENDED FAMILY, it's not surprising that Alice came along sixteen months later, in 1957. She was followed by Emily (1959), Sarah (1961), and Gregory (1963). By this time Larry had finished law school, passed the bar, and was in private practice. I was dealing with runny noses, bedtime stories, mountains of laundry, and the sandbox set and, except when the children had the chicken pox or the stomach virus all at the same time, I loved doing it. Much to my chagrin, however, I never turned into Marmee from *Little Women.*

Through all those hectic early years I still managed to find time to read (very late at night) and to exist on little sleep, though it's not surprising that the only writing I did was grocery lists and letters to my grandmother in Virginia.

When Gregory was almost a year old we moved from our small and suddenly *very crowded* row house to a large three-story house across the street from where I'd lived as a child. I still remember our first night in the house, sitting in the sunporch and looking out across the expanse of living room, hall, and dining room and thinking that we were the possessors of endless space. It wasn't long before we all spread out and, along with assorted bikes and trikes, roller skates, doll buggies, building blocks, a log cabin and a swing set, comfortably filled the house and yard. And when, on Christmas Day of 1965, Kate was born the family and house seemed to be complete.

Except the pets who, somehow, just seemed to keep arriving, following one or the other of us home, singling out our house and settling in for the long haul, or being picked up on a street corner because "that puppy looked cold and you just knew that woman was going to leave him there if we didn't take him." At one point, in addition to the six children, we had three dogs and two cats. And suddenly there I was—in the midst of that LARGE EXTENDED FAMILY.

Three weeks after Kate was born, my father died. Though he had been in poor health for years, it was still a shock and I don't think I'll ever forget what it was like to stand outside his hospital room while an emergency team worked on him inside, feeling a tremendous sense of loss and watching a man and a woman standing in the doorway of a room across the hall watching me watch for him. I remember wanting to rage at them, to tell them to go back inside, to leave me alone. Many years later when Fredlet dies in *What about Me?* I found myself writing that scene and experiencing the healing that writing so often gives to me.

This is how Dorrie describes what happened:

> I dropped the dime and had to crawl under the seat among cigarette butts to find

it. I had to think hard to remember Guntzie's number.

Closed in the phone booth away from sound, I could tell something had happened. It was all in pantomime. People running into Fredlet's room. Dr. Weinberg coming around the corner. I dropped the phone and opened the door.

"Dr. Blue—Dr. Blue—come to emergency."

"Dr. Blue."

A nurse with a machine of some kind disappeared into Fredlet's room. I tried to follow her. The room seemed crowded with some kind of ritual dance. I couldn't see my brother.

Another nurse blocked the door, pushing me back. "Not right now. He's having a little trouble breathing and we're trying to help him. There isn't room now. Please wait outside."

I leaned against the wall opposite Fredlet's room. I leaned on that wall as if my very life depended on it. Someone offered me a chair, someone else suggested the waiting room, a glass of water. I wouldn't move.

A man with a bloody foot stood at the door of the next cubicle; stood with his wife and watched me watch Fredlet's door. I wanted to bloody his other foot and scream, "Get back inside and leave me alone. Let me watch for Fredlet alone, you nosy old fool."

The door opened and the nurse with the machine came out and headed down the hall. Other nurses and doctors came out and melted away. No one looked at me except Mr. and Mrs. Bloody Foot.

Dr. Weinberg came out and closed the door. He looked across the hall and shook his head and put out his hands to me. "We did our best, Dorrie, the whole team. We couldn't save him. He isn't scared anymore."

Dr. Weinberg put his arm around my shoulder and we turned and walked down the hall. I saw my mother and father running toward us.

To say that the years spent raising the children were busy ones is a masterpiece of understatement. Larry, involved with his law practice, helped as much as he could, but when I look back on that time what I seem to remember are hours, days, weeks spent in the car. There were trips to the library, the dry cleaners, the pediatrician, and the veterinarian. And there were the endless carpools: to schools, to Brownies, to Girl Scouts; to swimming lessons and basketball games and lacrosse prac-

tice. Sometimes, at the end of a day, I would tally up the miles I'd driven and think that with the hours I'd spent in the car that day that I could actually have *gone* some place. And back again.

But if the carpools are remembered with dismay the rest of it is remembered as great fun. These were the years of birthday parties and Halloween costumes, of making Christmas cookies, doll clothes, snow forts, and sand castles. Of trips to the zoo and Mt. Vernon, to Williamsburg and the shore. The years of my striving mightily to be fair—and never succeeding. Of refereeing, or not refereeing (work it out yourselves) the children's fights and squabbles. And telling myself they'd all be glad, some day, that they had so many siblings. Surely they would.

And I still only wrote grocery lists and letters to my grandmother in Virginia and thought that "real" writing was probably something I wasn't going to get to.

One day, during the summer of 1972, I stopped over at Notre Dame College to visit my former teacher Sister Maura and we were talking about books, as we usually did. All of a sudden she paused, looked at me, and said: "Just think, you have all your writing still ahead of you."

I didn't say anything at the time: what was there *to* say? But I took that idea home and nurtured it and held it close. And eventually I cranked up my courage and asked Sister if I could take a writing tutorial. She said "Yes," and when I set off that first day, new notebook and pen in hand, I was as excited as any first grader ever was. Now I have to make it clear that I didn't know what a writing tutorial *actually was*. I knew it would be one-on-one, but beyond that my thoughts were vague. I envisioned some writing exercises, perhaps an informal essay, a bit of a character sketch, maybe the beginning of a short story. Imagine my shock when, at the end of the first session, Sister told me to come in the following week with an outline for a book.

An outline for a book. I wanted to scream, to say I couldn't do that, that it was asking too much. I wanted, briefly, to be a tutorial dropout. I wanted to cry. Instead, during the next week I struggled and jiggled and pieced together—and came up with—an outline for a children's book, because it didn't take me long to figure out that when you're the only stu-

*The author holding her first grandchild, Andrew, in 1987 with daughters Alice
(behind Colby), Emily, and Laurie; son-in-law Jimmy is standing*

dent in the class that old line "The dog ate my homework" just wouldn't cut it.

But the outline was only the beginning, I was soon to learn. Now I was expected to go on, to actually write the book. And so I did, working late into the night, banging my words out on my old college typewriter (until my husband gave me an electric typewriter for my birthday), too afraid to tell anyone except Larry what I was doing. Somehow the pages piled up—not easily, mind you, and not quickly— and I took a chapter a week in to Sister Maura, sitting in a state of near paralysis while she read what I had written. At the end of every session I took her comments, her admonishments, her praise home with me and—started in on another chapter. At the end of the semester I had the manuscript for a book. An unsalable manuscript, it soon became apparent, but a manuscript nonetheless.

I dug my heels in and wrote another book. Again unsalable. And now it was the rejection slips that were piling up. At this point I signed

up for a second tutorial and at the end of *that* semester had a book about a teenaged girl and her Down's syndrome brother, a book that was published several years later as *What about Me?*

One thing that made me very sad was that my mother, who, when I was little, had encouraged me so in my writing, didn't live long enough to see my first book published. She was living in Florida in 1975 when she got sick and we brought her to Baltimore to a hospital and then to a nursing home until she died of a brain tumor that summer, just months before I learned that my first book had been accepted. Years afterward I wrote a book called *Julie's Daughter* about Slug October, the main character of *Evy-Ivy-Over,* now seventeen, who is reunited with her mother Julie, and how the two of them help to care for a dying neighbor, Harper Tegges. I found, as I got into the book, that I was drawing on the experience of my mother's sickness and death, the way I had

The Rodowskys in 1993

drawn on so many other parts of my life to use in my writing, maybe so I could better come to terms with them.

With my mother's illness the doctors, the nurses, even the family conspired to keep her from finding out how sick she really was. But times and attitudes changed and by the time I wrote *Julie's Daughter* I think I wanted a chance to do it over, to do it right this time. Here is how Julie describes a visit to Harper Tegges shortly after her surgery:

I almost didn't go back to the hospital the next day. But the more I tried not to go, the more I thought about Harper . . . and Dr. Reinecke leaning over the side of the bed and mouthing platitudes at her. Anyway, when we got there she was awake and staring at the clock.

"They said you had a good night," I said.

Harper made a face, wincing at the effort. "I think that means I didn't make any trouble, though I considered it."

"How about the pain?"

"Bad."

"Slug's here with me," I said, stepping back.

And Harper raised her right hand inches off the bed and let it drop again. She tried to move her head, then stopped, clutching the top sheet in her hand.

"The tumor—the thing in my head—it was malignant, wasn't it?" she said.

"What did Dr. Reinecke tell you?" I asked, playing for time.

"Dr.—Who's —"

"The neurosurgeon. The one who operated on you," I said.

"Oh, him." Harper unclenched her fingers, but the wad of sheet stayed crumpled there.

The clock on the wall rasped and jerked forward.

"It's what he *didn't* say," Harper said. "But it was, wasn't it?"

Through the glass partition I looked out at the nurses' station, at the monitors and machines and dials and buttons.

"It *was,* wasn't it?" said Harper again, her fingers opening and closing on the bed beside her.

"Yes. Yes, it is," I said slipping my finger into her claw-like grasp. "But there's always the chance that something—that someone—." I just couldn't knock all the props out from under her.

I wanted to turn away from Harper's face and the emotions that played themselves out across it, made all the more grotesque by the swath of bandage that bound her head and dipped onto her forehead. But Harper still had hold of my finger, pulling me forward so that I had to plant my legs against the bed to keep from losing my balance.

"Well that's good," said Harper, her voice suddenly strong. "They found it—and operated. Now I can get on with my life—work to be—". . . .

Harper let go of my finger, but it was a long time before I was able to pull away, watching, instead, as it went from white to angry red to white again.

"Now that that's over," said Harper as I straightened up, resting my hands on the side of the bed, cooling my finger on the metal, "I want to get in touch with my gallery, the people who take care of my affairs, as soon as I get into a room with a telephone. There was talk of a retrospective. I have to let them know."

I saw the glossy look in Harper's eyes and the way her fingers still worried the sheet as she said fretfully, "There are people I have to call. There are—"

NO, something screamed inside my head. You're not listening to me. I said *is not was.* The tumor in your head *is* malignant. It's cancer and they're talking about custodial care and you're talking about a show . . .

Through the years one question I've often been asked, especially when people find out that I have six children, is, "Do you write about your children? Are they your protagonists?" The answer to both questions is "No." Though I've often used incidental bits of family life in my novels (the yellow throw-up bucket; the dirty handprints that the brother in *P.S. Write Soon* left over the top of the doors every time he jumped up—just as Gregory always did; the Spanish chicken cooking in the crockpot) I've never presumed to get *inside* my children's heads, to know how they think. I have to confess here that my main characters are made up of bits and pieces of myself. Either the way I am or, more likely, I guess, the way I'd like to be. After all, who wouldn't like to be as gritty as Henley (*H, My Name Is Henley*), or as perceptive as Mudge (*The Gathering Room*)? Who wouldn't like to get around the way Drew does (*Keeping Time*) or be convinced, like Sydney, that she is really the daughter of one of the world-famous Boomerangs (*Sydney, Herself*)?

If I've been careful not to infringe on my children's privacy, through the years I've made free use of the family dogs. In book after book they keep turning up. Golden retrievers, who were really our wonderful Sandy in disguise, appeared in both *P.S. Write Soon* and *A Summer's Worth of Shame*. At the time I was working on *The Gathering Room* we had a large and rambunctious puppy, half black Lab and half German shepherd, who kept tearing through the house, chewing everything in sight while I was trying to work. The only way I could deal with him was to change his name from Homewood to Thanatos and write him into the story, making him a totally *silent* dog.

Two of our dogs, Sandy, a golden retriever, and Mimi, a poodle and schnauzer mix, claimed a whole book for their own, starring as themselves in *Dog Days.*

In this book Rosie Riggs lives with her mother, father, little sister, and her dog Mimi, about whom she says, " . . . mostly she just sleeps and snorts and scratches and hardly notices things she's supposed to notice. And she never does anything splendiferous." When the children's author Dawn O'Day moves in next door, bringing her dog Sandy, the protagonist of a whole series of adventure books, Rosie is sure that Sandy will be a "super dog" indeed. She eventually learns that most of Sandy's magic comes from Dawn O'Day's imagination but that Sandy is wonderful and lovable and loyal in his own right. As all of our dogs have been. And it's

Colby Rodowsky's children and grandchildren, 1994

probably just a matter of time before our young Dalmatian Pongo (he came with the name already firmly attached) turns up in more than the walk-on part he has in *Remembering Mog*.

Family summers in Ocean City, Maryland, have also found their way into several of my books. When the children were young we bought a *small* house back on the bay at 12th Street—the same house, the same town where I set *A Summer's Worth of Shame*. In the book I described the activity on the bay, the comings of the powerboats, the slap of water against the bulkhead, the cry of the gulls. Thad St. Clair wanders the same streets we all wandered, passing the library and the municipal tennis courts, the crab houses, the string of motels. His little sister Muppy sits on a piling at the end of the pier, swinging her legs, her hair blowing in the breeze, just as my children sat on that same piling through the years.

And when Thad sets out to find a summer job, how could I have him do anything but what my son Gregory did for *his* first summer job, be a spook in a spook house up on the boardwalk. But since I didn't *really* know how Gregory felt inside that haunted house, I could only imagine how *I* would have felt.

> Inside the House of Terror it was hot and smelled of sweat and bubble gum and suntan lotion. The dark oozed and pressed down around him, lightened only by the eerie green exit light at the end of the tunnel and the murky grayness of the fake windows streaked with cobwebs. Thad sank down on the stool inside the cage and loosened the neck of the black cape. His own clothes felt damp and sticky underneath, and he took a deep sniff of one armpit. He peeled the rubber mask off his head, turning it inside out and feeling the holes that were nose and fangs and hideous bulging eyes. He waved the mask up and down in the darkness trying to dry it, and wiped his own face with the backs of his hands. He could feel his hair in sweaty, scraggled clumps sticking out around his head.

In another book, *Lucy Peale*, I used the same Ocean City setting, describing the boardwalk that ran the length of the town as Lucy sees it for the first time.

> They stood at the top of the ramp, caught in the wind and the swirl of people and the rumble of the boardwalk train. From

somewhere out in front came the pounding of the surf, and overhead, kites swooped and danced against the darkened sky. Lights from the shops and rides and shooting galleries blazed out over the boardwalk and the air smelled of the sea and of cotton candy.

As the years went by we were, if anything, busier than we had been before. Larry became a judge on the Maryland Court of Appeals, a job he considers his avocation as well as his vocation—so much so that none of us can bear the thought of his ever having to retire. I continued to write, agonizingly slowly at times, but somehow the books inched their way along and now manage to fill a satisfying section of the top shelf of the bookcase in my den. The children grew up, went to work, and moved away, sometimes moving back and then away again. Laurie married Andres, and then, seemingly in the blink of an eye, Alice married Jimmy, Sarah—Til, Emily—Jay, and Gregory—Julie. And Kate, the youngest, is engaged to Steven.

And suddenly the house was empty. Larry and I noticed it first with the orange juice. The pitcher we had made for breakfast one day was still there the next, and the next, and the one after that. There were towels in the closet, and the buttons on the car radio were set for the stations we had selected.

Over time we learned to set the timer on the VCR ourselves, and to deal with a loose wire on the stereo, and that it was up to us to play ball with the dog. We found that it was hardly worth running the dishwasher for two people and that a pan of lasagna turned green around the edges before we had a chance to eat it all. The phone didn't ring as often, but the music we heard in the house was of our choosing. We brought thick books home from the library and planned and went on vacations. We made lists of things to do: a lecture, a concert, a trip to Washington to the National Gallery. And if there was time left over we planned to clean the cellar—but haven't yet.

The children haven't gone very far, living stretched out, as it were, up and down Route I-95 from Philadelphia to northern Virginia. They visit often and now there are grandchildren, ten at present count, to make our lives richer. We get together for holidays and sometimes at the beach in the summer. We go to their houses for christenings and birthday parties, for soccer games or just for a visit. There are twenty-four of us when we are all together, and when everybody comes here, for Christmas or Easter dinner, we line the children up at the dining room table while the rest of us balance plates on our knees and try to hear one another over the din.

And through it all I keep on writing, never as much or as well as I would like, but I keep at it. Why? Well, because I can't imagine *not* writing. And, like the large extended family I am finally a part of, it defines me: It's who I am; it's what I do.

But also because I look on whatever ability to write I have as a kind of gift, and my responsibility to that gift is to use it as well, as faithfully as I can. And so I take the words that have been given to me—words that I must sometimes fight for, and struggle for, through occasional sleepless nights and many cups of tea, days spent filing my nails and straightening my desk. And with these words I weave my stories—hesitantly, tentatively, always sure that when a book or a story is finished I'll never think of another one. But they are woven with joy, and much love.

BIBLIOGRAPHY

FOR CHILDREN

Fiction:

Dog Days, illustrated by Kathleen Collins Howell, Farrar, Straus, 1990.

Jenny and the Old Great-Aunts, illustrated by Barbara Roman, Bradbury, 1992.

FOR MIDDLE-GRADE READERS

Fiction:

What about Me?, F. Watts, 1976.

P. S. Write Soon, F. Watts, 1978.

Evy-Ivy-Over, F. Watts, 1978.

A Summer's Worth of Shame, F. Watts, 1978.

The Gathering Room, F. Watts, 1981.

H, My Name Is Henley, F. Watts, 1982.

Keeping Time, Farrar, Straus, 1983.

Fitchett's Folly, Farrar, Straus, 1987.

FOR YOUNG ADULTS

Fiction:

Julie's Daughter, Farrar, Straus, 1985.

Sydney, Herself, Farrar, Straus, 1989.

Lucy Peale, Farrar, Straus, 1992.

Hannah in Between, Farrar, Straus, 1994.

Sydney, Invincible, Farrar, Straus, 1995.

Remembering Mog, Farrar, Straus, 1996.

J.otto Seibold

1960-

"J.otto Seibold draws all of the time. It's his job. He's a professional. He draws on a computer, which makes him sort of like a scientist. But he doesn't wake up until noon, which makes him like an artist."

Vivian Walsh, 1994

I spend my days drawing bugs, dogs, and the Monkey. Let's start with my formative years to see how this could have happened to a grown man.

I grew up in a small California town called Martinez, an hour east of San Francisco. Martinez is dominated by two things: oil refineries and the noted naturalist John Muir. A modern oxymoron of municipal pulls. The town was built on the old Muir Orchard. Actually, it was his wife's property. John Muir was always off, more at home in Yosemite or walking to Alaska or something outdoorsy like that. You can still make out the orchard grid of trees from the air. Houses interrupt their lines, but otherwise the trees are doing a good job of staying in their rows. This meant everyone in our neighborhood got an apricot tree in their yard.

John Muir would not have liked the refineries. About once a year, one would catch on fire. It would light up the nighttime sky and, if it hadn't burned out by the next morning, its smoke would block the sun and make the day dark. Super-unnatural. More often you would wake up to find the town had been blanketed with a mysterious white ash, or black sticky substance. It would cover everyone's car and everyone's house, and if someone was lucky enough to have a swingset outside, it would be on that too.

The road I grew up on was short and dead-ended. It dead-ended for one of the best reasons you might have a street dead-end for: a train trestle. We spent a lot of time playing beneath the trestle (in the mud) and loved to watch as trains sped in one direction or the other.

J.otto Seibold, Vivian Walsh, and Thea, 1994

There were no sidewalks on my block, just grass or dirt all the way to the road. The suburban ranch-style houses were all just one story high. One family took the ranch-style label seriously and had a horse live with them inside their house.

Creativity showed its beautiful face in unusual ways in my neighborhood. Around the corner at "Little Johnnie's," his mom decorated the family room as a John Wayne shrine. Big pictures of the movie star the Duke, or "Big Johnnie," hung on every wall. Another house had a grotto motif interior, with big fishing nets and glass balls. Our next-door neighbor made elaborate Christmas decorations out of the green plastic baskets strawberries come in and Styrofoam egg cartons. She made a Noah's

Ark and a tiny train traveling somewhere with wagons full of animals. Mothers were into crafts. Our house, the home of a German from Germany, my father, was decorated with beer steins, Bavarian figurines, and accordions. All possibly slight influences on my drawing style.

Definite strong factors that developed my drawing style:

1. Drawing Hot Rods
2. Legos
3. Japanese cartoons: watching *Ultraman* and *Speed Racer* on TV.

My brother Joe and I would spend hours each day building elaborate cityscapes. We used Legos, erector sets, or just sticks and stones in the mud. My brother now works as an engineer. Our infrastructures were superstructures, solid and well thought-out. Our villages had bridges and alternative routes. Long hours of effort and concentration never deterred us from finishing our day's work with an explosion or igniting our own little play refinery fire.

My parents were divorced and we lived with my father. Most nights he worked late at his machine shop. This is what gave us so much time to fool around building our make-believe towns. Around six each night he would telephone to talk us through heating up a TV dinner. Otherwise we were under our own supervision.

I got my first taste of artistic accolades in first grade. My drawing of a red-winged black bird was entered in our town's John Muir Art Contest. It won first place. I was surprised and encouraged. I spent more time working on my drawings, but didn't let my artwork get in the way of my baseball and basketball practice. The hippie kids were the overt artists at my school. I think the cheerleaders formed a committee to pester me to make banners for their games, but otherwise I was able to lead a normal life.

People often ask me which art school I attended. I didn't go to any. I never had much luck, or interest, learning at school. While I was attending my refinery town's high school it was rated third from the bottom for the entire state of California. Fear, cars, and illegal pills had a stronger presence than anything academic. The biggest impression any teacher made on me at Alhambra High was an English teacher. One day he showed up late for class dressed all in red. He had even painted his face red. Midway through the period his efforts to convince students he was the devil were interrupted by the police. He was taken away. Word was he had been committed to an insane asylum, but that was probably just gleeful student talk.

There were not many role models for us young Martinezians. Besides the illustrious John Muir, our town's one other name of renown was Joe DiMaggio, the baseball great also remembered for marrying (and divorcing) Marilyn Monroe or as the spokesman for Mr. Coffee.

In high school I took drafting classes. After graduation, I decided I'd had enough of school, it was time to go to work. I got drafting jobs with my neighbors, the refineries, and other nearby giant corporate places. If Chevron had a drafting backlog, they would call me and a handful of others. We would work nights after the regular employees had gone home. The atmosphere at these chemical corporate giants could get pretty surreal. Before I was pointed to a chair or handed a pencil, I might be instructed on how to use the emergency eye-wash rinse station. Dow Chemical had bikes to get around its huge industrial complex. While riding you had to wear a hard hat that was equipped with a protective plastic bag. If an alarm went off, you scooped up air in the bag, pulled it over your head, and rode out of there. The alarm warned of a chlorine leak that would paralyze your lungs upon contact.

J.otto at age three

242

I floated from corporation to corporation, secure that I was good enough to always get a job but not wanting to be considered staff. I did end up freelancing on and off at the Clorox Corporation for a number of years at their Design and Research Laboratory, where they test and retest all their products and invent brilliant new things. They had a huge technology budget that gave me access to the most sophisticated computers of that time. Clorox tried to keep a corporate atmosphere but they also understood you have to give people creative freedom if you want them to make great leaps in the fields of cleansers, salad dressing, barbeque lighter fluid, or kitty litter. These were Clorox's main products while I worked there.

I designed a wall of washing machines to test cleansers. Fabrics could be treated (washed) after they'd been soiled by a very special machine that made identical stains. One day I made sketches of a giant Clorox bleach fountain, always pouring. I was told Clorox actually went ahead and built it as the corporate art fronting some big new building.

My favorite project was the new kitty litter testing lab. The scientists had to make sure odors were contained. I was told to draw up the plans for a number of kitty litter closets. To each closet's door I added a smaller head-sized door, and then within that, for a more subtle sniff, a third door, just big enough for a nose. People from the community were brought in as test groups. Their job was to smell and rate the escaping kitty litter odors. The kitty litter lab people told me the nose-sized doors were especially appreciated during those sessions.

The Clorox people did build the fountain and nose-sized doors, and they also kept me busy, like the cheerleaders at school. I made lots of cards and banners for promotions, birthdays, or if someone had a new baby. They paid me a ton of money—or at least it seemed like it to someone who had been a newspaper delivery boy just a few years prior. But I was just finishing up my teen years. I had a lot of new interests outside of the corporate world. For instance, the drummer had just quit from my brother's band. They didn't really know any other drummers, so I learned how to play. The band used a pretty simple beat during my first few weeks. The group was called Love Circus.

Love Circus became the house band at one of the grittiest clubs in San Francisco, the Sound of Music. Not too many other bands were willing to drive out there and chance having all of their equipment stolen. So we could play whenever we wanted to, which was usually once a week. All of our friends were on the guest list. It was a weekly party where we could be as loud and messy as we wanted to. It was loose—our rhythms were not slaves to the fashions of the day at our little punk hideaway. We could play anything and then, when we looked out at our audience (our friends), they'd all blow kisses and give us the thumbs-up signal. It was pretty encouraging. And so we got pretty good. We were blessed with Mr. Tom Sumner as our front man; he was something of an entertainer. Before we knew it, really good musicians were asking if they could jam with us . . . and be in our band. Amazing. One guy in the band wanted to be a rock star, so he booked gigs, got us interviewed on the radio, and things like that. Our proudest moment was when the seminal band Flipper named us as their favorite band.

While working on and off for Clorox and playing in a band, I tried classes at three different colleges. My favorite classes were lectures on architecture at U.C. Berkeley. I decided I would study to be an architect. It was the early eighties, during the postmodern boom in buildings. Architects were superstars. Exciting new buildings were going up everywhere. My infatuation with the field was ruined by complicated math equations. The math classes were getting me down. Spending evenings with my big trig textbook didn't feel right. I decided that if I ever got to design the theme park-type conceptual buildings I liked to draw, I'd hire an engineer to do the math.

Some friends of mine were leaving town for a three-month trip through Asia. Two weeks before they left I decided to go too. They drove me out to the airport clinic so I could get all the vaccinations, pills, etc., I needed to go there. It's a funny feeling getting a weak dose of all these diseases shot into you. Just the idea of a wee dose of malaria mixed with a little yellow fever and typhoid makes me tipsy.

Traveling through Asia was the big handshake of culture everyone should be so lucky to have. We saw things we could never have imagined. Through Burma, Thailand, and Nepal, the richness of the arts and the kindness of the people was a wonderful experience. As a 6"4' hairy white man I stood out in the remote Asian villages. I was very much the outsider. The foreignness of it all gave me a better sense of who I was. How lucky I was to have the opportunities that are rare in this world but available to most young Americans.

Not long after I got back, I found out about a previously inconceivable way of making money: illustrating. I was looking for a good seat at the movies when my friend pointed out someone he knew and said, "See that guy? He draws pictures for a living." After the movie I went home and started looking more critically at the illustrations in the newspaper and magazines. Before that I hadn't noticed the human effort behind the illustrations. I must have thought there was a machine somewhere that spit them out. I made some calls to Clorox and got the job of designing and illustrating that year's company Christmas calendar.

In 1988, a good friend of mine, Vivian Walsh, had invited me to travel to Spain with her. She wanted to rent a house there for a couple of months. She'd been working two jobs in Washington, D.C., for the last year, and was ready for a change. She saw herself arranging wildflowers and writing. She also wanted to be out of the country during the Olympics since a bum knee had ruined her once-promising stab at being an ice-skating contender. I decided to go with her. I would draw and build myself a portfolio of illustrations.

We started our trip in Germany, where Vivian had been visiting her grandmother. We decided it would be a shame to head for Spain without spending a few days in Munich. Our first night there we met a talkative beer-drinking girl who was studying to be a clown: "There is no better feeling than pulling on the oversized shoes and gluing on the red nose." She was a puzzle to us. But somehow, she convinced us we had to change our plans and head for Turkey. Destination Spain got pushed back by our travels through Germany, Austria, Italy, back to Austria, Yugoslavia, Greece, Turkey, and back to Greece . . . and then, finally, an airplane ride from Athens to Madrid.

On the trip I put in one intensive drawing session. It was in the beautiful ancient port city of Dubrovnik (which since then has been a victim of the violent dissolution of what was Yugoslavia). One night Vivian and I wanted to see a famed Soviet violinist perform. The concert cost more than we had in the local currency. It was late and all of the currency exchange windows were shut. I set up my draw-

ing pad at the town's busiest fountain. Working in a manner that must be the equivalent of midterm crunch at art school, I offered to sketch portraits for Yugoslavian cash. A crowd gathered while I made the customary likenesses of renowned celebrities. My portrait of Gavin McLeod (from his "Love Boat" days rather than his "Mary Taylor Moore" era) was an impressive solid hit on the head. I had a big crowd, and a loud crowd, but no sitters. Finally I challenged the loudest heckler to a draw-off. He was to draw my portrait as I drew his. The man was all words. I easily emerged as the victorious drawer and was accepted by the townspeople as their personal portraitist.

An hour later I was able to pay my way and treat Vivian to the concert. It was one of the most emotionally powerful concerts I've ever seen. The strength of the music was amazing from a solo violinist. Part of the beauty was the setting of the carved marble cortile of the Rector's Palace.

By the time Vivian and I chose the Celtic coast of Spain as the perfect place to rent a house, we were exhausted by our travels and had spent all of our money. I got back to San Francisco with only three decent drawings for a portfolio but very much in love with Vivian Walsh. First things first. Back home I quickly built up my portfolio and got my first job, which luckily led to more and more work until I was, yes, a Commercial Artist.

Initially I made my illustrations by cutting shapes from colored paper and then gluing them together. Then the nice people at Adobe Software invited me to spend a weekend at their compound to learn how to use their Adobe Illustrator software.

Ah . . . the digital revolution. It saved me from my artistic handicap at the time, mixing paints. I used to watch in horror as all my colors got messed up and became too brown or too grey. I got modern and outfitted myself with a big Macintosh computer. On the computer, I worked in a process that was similar to gluing together pieces of colored paper. Now I plotted color shapes on the screen and then applied them next to, or on top of, each other. My computer experience at Clorox and my background in drafting made creating illustrations on the computer a natural step for me.

Almost every day I had a deadline. A new picture for a glossy, a tabloid, for *Newsweek*,

"In Burma with a monk who decorated his room with old batteries," 1986

Money magazine, or some legal journal. I was making a picture a day to fit someone else's story. It was a great deal of a drill that taught me to think quickly and let my style reveal itself. I honed my craft.

I made my first music video for the band They Might Be Giants. The video was for their single "Istanbul, not Constantinople." John Flansburgh, one of the two Giants, came up with the idea of using two different illustrators and two different types of animation for the video. I drew up story boards for traditional cell animation. The other half was made by Mark Mareck. He did stop-motion animation by moving and filming paper maché puppets.

I didn't have any experience in animation. I'm not sure if I conveyed that to Flansburgh at the time, though he was supportive of doing something different anyway. The budget was tiny. I got my first lesson in the often sorry clash of "commercial" and "creative." I was ambitious to make something spectacular while the production house had the obstacle of pay-

ing its bills. They were running a business. All their best animators were working on a big-budget commercial for an insurance company. The resources and talent for the Giants project were, if I remember right, a how-to guide, a rusty old pencil, and some pieces of plastic. Maybe also a few guys to draw the hundreds of pieces of cell art we would need to film and make the animation. I spent my nights doctoring and redoing what others had done that day.

The video won a surprising number of awards. Silver medals from film societies I had never heard of began to arrive, special delivery. The video became a regular on the MTV animation showcase *Liquid Television*. It was also shown in movie theatres around the world as part of the annual *Tournée of Animation*. A friend of mine saw it on a black and white TV in Hungary.

While I was finishing the video, a friend, the illustrator Phillipe Weisbecker, called to say he knew of an apartment available. It was nice, did we want it? The thing was, it was on the other side of the U.S. in New York City. Vivian and I (recently married) were very happy in San Francisco. It didn't take long for us to make up our minds. I think we asked Phillipe, "How nice is it?" before agreeing to take the place. What a smooth deal. Each time we had visited New York we'd mumbled something about moving there. Someone had heard us and set us up good.

In New York it seemed every other person I met—at parties, walking the dog, eyewitnessing taxi accidents—was an art director. New York is a great place, and they need a lot of people to draw pictures for all of their magazines. Even when I had my Do Not Disturb sign up, opportunity knocked. Most art directors would let me do whatever I wanted. My favorite art directors would even say the words, "Do whatever you want, J.otto." That's when I enjoy illustrating the most and the pictures look their best.

In New York our group of friends started a regular slide show party. People were always going on trips and got in the habit of taking slides wherever they went. I'd always enjoyed taking photos. I really enjoy filling the rectangle. When I illustrate, I draw something over and over until I am happy with the sketch. Then I redraw it all over again on the computer. With a camera I like to go for the quick shot. I would even push it, taking pictures from a car, or of a passing truck—the thrill of the temporal quality. I enjoy trusting in intuitive sense and luck. Our slide shows got better and better. A gallery in Brooklyn, Four Walls, invited us to show our slides to larger audiences there. It was a similar situation as when I was in the band. A fun, relaxed, shared creativity that led to better work.

I was ready to work on my own projects. One evening, airborne, flying over the Arctic Ocean, Vivian came up with an idea for a children's picture book. It was based on our real-life experience. Our pampered New York City lapdog was traveling with us, but unfortunately he had to ride below, in the luggage compartment. We were worried that our dog, practically still a puppy, might not be pleased to be riding in the bottom of the plane like a common suitcase. This was, after all, a dog with a first and last name, Dexter Lunch. Dexter to some, and Mr. Lunch to others. In New York he went with us to shops and restaurants. When company came to visit, Mr. Lunch would entertain them by playing the piano . . . with his nose. He understood full sentences, especially if they contained the words "ball" or "park."

We compared Dexter Lunch to the other New Yorkers we were meeting. Everyone in New York is caught up with their career, so we decided if Dexter had a career it would be in the field of bird-chasing. At the park when he stalked a bird you could practically hear his concentration. By some unknown formula, he would calculate just the right instant to strike and then take off. For someone with five-inch legs his speed was very impressive. Even the pigeons seemed surprised by his ability to pounce. He was good, he was like a professional.

That became the story for our first children's book, *Mr. Lunch Takes a Plane Ride.* A professional bird-chasing dog is invited to demonstrate his bird-chasing skills on television. This means he gets to take his first plane ride to get to the TV studio. Vivian and I wrote it together. If we ever got stumped as to what to write we'd call our dog into the study. It's also true that a lot of this first book had to do with what I thought I could draw the best at the time: airplanes, birds, and TV cameras.

A friend of ours, Lane Smith, suggested we show our book in progress to his publisher at Viking. Viking Children's Books was our first choice for publishers. Besides the talented Lane

Smith and Jon Scieszka, they published books by Maira Kalman, and later Richard McGuire, Steven Guarnaccia, and Michael Bartalos. These books stand out in the children's section of a bookstore. They don't look or read like most children's books. Viking was taking chances and putting out books that have original voices. They're fresh, something kids are good at identifying and like. Regina Hayes, President of Viking Children's Books, was giving the artists more control over what they wrote and drew, and even the design of their picture books.

At one point I felt like I was making an endless amount of illustrations that were all thrown away, literally, with the evening paper at the end of the day. Making books is much more rewarding. My ego thanks me. It's a lovely industry to be part of—which might explain why there are 4,000 new children's books published each year, and only a hundred or two are successful enough to be available in the stores a year later. The rest are boiled and recycled into newspapers or something like that. I enjoy making these books. It's very nice to spend Saturdays in bookstores answering children's questions about my drawings. The questions are often very specific, such as: Which bird is friends with whom? What kind of flowers did the pink bug, Penelope, plant around her house? They are columbine, fuchsias, and of course wildflowers. The most common question is, "Does Mr. Lunch ever catch a bird?" We don't make that clear as a tension-building

"J.otto's finger with Mr. Lunch"

device . . . but the answer is no. He and the birds understand they're just in it for the chase.

Our first child was born just before I finished the illustrations for *Mr. Lunch Takes a Plane Ride.* The child to be was the inspiration for long hours and detailed illustrations. Her arrival was perfect timing for our new career. Thea introduced us to a lot of other kids. We grew a big library of picture books. I can never get over how much children love to look at picture books. The books are in step with how the brain wants to grow. Children are so eager to learn as much as they can from the images and stories.

It is amazing how quickly a child learns to identify different animals. You'd think it would be a hurdle that kids see animals drawn so differently. For instance, a cat might be drawn realistically or in the cat shorthand of a circle with two pointy ears on top. Kids pick this up right away. In no time children can distinguish between a tabby, tiger, panther, lion, mountain lion, etc. . . .

One of our daughter's first favorite books was *Madeline,* also published by Viking. The drawings by illustrator Ludwig Bemelmans are loose and gestural, kind of messy and beautiful. They are sophisticated to my eye, but at the same time a favorite of one-and-a-half-year-olds around the world. I am endlessly impressed by Bemelmans getting a year's free lodging at the best hotel in New York City, the Carlyle, in exchange for painting pictures on the walls of their bar. I am available for that job.

Another favorite book of my daughter's was *Good Dog Carl,* by Alexandra Day. The illustrations are much more realistic, but Alexandra Day often draws only half of her dog, Carl, leaving his head and shoulders unconnected to a stomach, etc. . . . The last illustration in the book is a detailed painting of a woman and Carl; for some reason the toes on one of the woman's feet are left undone. This really troubled our daughter. "Where is the rest of the mommy's foot?" It's the end of the book and the end of the lady is missing. Bemelman's loose style allows him to leave off toes, and even feet, and no one questions it. But in Alexandra Day's illustration the absent toes stand out because the rest of the picture is so tight, with every detail thought out. It doesn't seem natural to leave the toes unfinished . . . maybe the deadline for the book snuck up on Alexandra Day before she could finish the last page. We

The author with Thea, 1993

illustrators are working under stiff time constraints.

Vivian and I decided to make a second book. It was difficult to make the time around our daughter's nonstop requests to read one more book to her. But what could be a stronger inducement?

Our second book is titled, *Mr. Lunch Borrows a Canoe.* I'm not sure why we put our leading man, Lunch, into a boat. That may have been inspired by a weekend we spent visiting some friends up the Hudson River. Not only did we get to escape a steamy and stinky humid weekend in New York City, our dogs were invited as well. We had a second dog by then. A weekend invite including dogs was very kind because Mr. Lunch and our second dog, Olive, are Jack Russell terriers, a breed known for its manic energy. Of course, like all manics they are intelligent but somewhat crazy.

As soon as we got out of the car Olive made it clear by her actions she would have the hide of our hosts' black cat. The cat was larger then Olive and had a sixth toe on each front paw. After listening to a few hours of barking, the cat made a move on Olive. Luckily, it only took one hiss to reveal Olive to be a dog of jello. No one was hurt. To give the cat a rest, and save Olive from further embarrassment, we headed for a nearby lake.

One guy, an outdoorsman from Brooklyn, came equipped with an attaché case. Inside, neatly packaged, was a deflated inflatable canoe. He blew it up, put Vivian and me in, and gave us a push toward the center of the lake. Now poor Dexter Lunch must have thought we were sneaking off, emigrating to another land, after all the animal fuss Olive had made earlier in the day.

Not much of a swimmer, he dove in, caught up with us, and started scratching, trying to climb into the very poppable boat. It was tricky getting a frantic twenty-pound dog into a craft known for tipping over. Once rescued, and united with his masters, Mr. Lunch took his place at the helm of the boat, serious, stiff, scared. He never took his eye off the sometimes close, and sometimes not, shore. Mr. Lunch is such a city dog. I think that's why I liked the idea of a dog getting put into a canoe by an overly generous elephant. Trying to remain in control while actually scared of nature, then waking up in a city where everyone is at home in a boat, our favorite city, Venice.

It was smart of us to set *Mr. Lunch Borrows a Canoe,* in our favorite city. The book had just hit the stores when the telephone rang and a charming Italian man said, "Giotto, you must let me fly your family to Venice for a big show, Ciao." My work was part of an exhibit of American Illustrators, "New Pop," that was shown in an old gondola factory in Venice. When the show curator, Giorgio Camuffo, saw my book, with the pictures of Venice, he decided to print them on T-shirts and make posters to plaster all over town.

I spent a lovely week in Venice with Vivian and our daughter, Thea. Our first night there the evening sky began to grumble with hours of warning of a storm to come. When it seemed that there were only minutes left until everything would be soaked, we took cover at a lovely cafe right next to Teatro la Fenice, Venice's lovely opera house. We thought we would watch the storm safe under an umbrella enjoying our cappuccinos, Thea charmed by the funny waiters who kept bringing her cookies.

The waiters knew better. The first drop was their cue to send everyone inside. It was as if high-powered hoses were emptying the canals to dose the square. Then the lightning hit; people yelled with fear. One streak as thick as a tree truck bounced off the piazza floor. Halfway through the storm the whole city went dark.

The rain stopped and everything was quiet. We had no idea how to get back to our hotel; we had no map, and it was pitch black. We headed out. Venice is usually always full of lost tourists. On this night we didn't run into one other person, but we did learn that on every other corner you can find an arrow pointing the way to San Marco or to the Accademia. We made our way through the narrow walkways and then waited for lightning to hit to light up an arrow and send us in the right direction. The lightning also gave us a glimpse of where we were. We might have been right in front of a white marble lion, a boat on a canal, or below a balcony. It was lovely.

Around midnight we made it to the Piazza San Marco, and were well rewarded for our efforts. A fancy café had a generator with a little bit of light. Their band, which usually played restrained background music, was loud and happy. Everyone was excited, talking to each other, dancing and singing. A beautifully dressed old lady asked if she could dance with our daughter. She took Thea's hand and danced her through the Palladian archways. Next she succeeded in having the band slow its tempo so everyone could watch the beautiful seventy-year-old dance with the beautiful two-year-old whom she had just met. Meanwhile the lightning became more and more distant. When it struck it made the golden mosaics on the face of the church light up. The gold glass reflected brilliantly. Then the lights came on. A waiter insisted on warming some milk for Thea. Everyone said good night. Vivian said, "Let's move here."

Internationally, I was also getting a lot of telephone calls from Tokyo. Vivian and I started working on an animated program for Saturday morning TV, a cartoon for Japan called "Monkey Business." Our hero, Space Monkey, was sent into space in a rocket ship! He was the first astro-chimp, but our saga caught up with him years later as a middle-aged monkey running a manufacturing interest. The monkey has a run-in with a pink bug, Penelope. The monkey was to represent industry and the bug, nature; our story was the conflict between the two.

Our animation was part of a variety show of computer animated shorts. It was put together by a couple of Japanese disk jockeys. The show was fast and flashy. It was called *Ugo Ugo Llugho,* which roughly translates into Go-Go Dancer, sideways.

It was a project full of mystery. We had a problem communicating art direction, in that our calls or faxes were only rarely responded to. Fully understanding that we had slim control over what would be the finished cartoon, we gave the project the green light, eager to see whatever might be made. Each week we'd put our show's storyboards, with all of the careful animation directions, into an envelope, seal it, and mail it across the sea. At the end of a few months we were sent a tape. We were surprised at first. Apparently our careful instructions were taken only as suggestions—even the sequencing had been changed. Favorite parts, crucial to the monkey's tale, had been omitted! A narrator told a very dramatic-sounding story in Japanese. The animation was the most remedial effort ever seen. It was so crude . . . you had to love it. It was an interesting collaboration.

The "Monkey Business" show evolved into *Monkey Business,* the book. A favorite sequence in the cartoon is when a bug's cute little house gets destroyed by a large bird who unknowingly steps on it. For television I drew in the big action, a lot of smoke, and a young girl screaming, "NO!" This was the one part of the cartoon I wanted to use in the picture book. The pink bug, Penelope, tells how the bird smashed her house. To illustrate that, I filled a grid with a series of small images on one page, showing the action, like stills from animation.

While I was working on *Monkey Business,* Vivian was pregnant with our second child. To commemorate that I drew in a very pregnant woman, accurate to Vivian's size, crossing the street near the Monkey Business Headquarters. Considerately, I drew her comfortable shoes. I had to draw the Headquarters a second time near the end of the book. By the time I got to that picture, Vivian and I had our second baby, Amelia, so I drew the woman in again, but this time she was walking in the other direction with two children: her new baby and holding the hand of another small girl. That would be our elder daughter, in the guise of one of her favorite book characters, Madeline.

Before having kids I loved New York City. With two beautiful babies the city became a danger zone. When three stoplights near our apartment were knocked over in one month by traffic accidents, it just wasn't funny like it used to be. Also, I was getting tired of opening the safe each month, filling up the wheelbarrow with rubies and gold bars and wheeling it over to our landlord's office. Tiny NYC apartments cost too much. I knew we needed to start saving for when our girls wanted to go to space camp, or for some other new type of parental expense. We moved back to San Francisco. (Mr. Lunch's second plane ride.)

As a San Franciscan the top item on my new resident shopping list was a car. I was looking for a vintage Citroen. I test-drove a few beauties but they were in such need of mechanical pampering I couldn't bring myself to purchase any. Instead I drew a Citroen in the book, *Monkey Business.* It is the fine fancy French car driven by the man Quincy.

We keep it low-key, but to be accurate *Monkey Business* is set in the future, maybe five years ahead of its actual creation date. Our next Space Monkey book dares to edge a little nearer to the sci-fi genre. It will contain my first monster. That would be Glüp, my entry in the big mascot contest for the Expo 2000 in Hanover, Germany. His head looks somewhat like a protective smoke mask or a cute pink nuclear reactor—maybe not cute enough for the Expo 2000 jury. I had sent him over with this note, "Gut Gluck Glüp!" But Glüp was not the Expo's winner. He was returned, available for mascot duty elsewhere. I decided he fits in nicely with the Space Monkey characters.

Space Monkey has been to space. Glüp is from Space. He is the space monster that will propel Space Monkey to take leave of his corporate arena for space. Once again the monkey will leave earth's atmosphere, but this time instead of space program history he will be making a visit to the genre of sci-fi. Glüp also has a lot in common with the bug Penelope. They are both pink, they like flowers, and they like the products churned out by Monkey Business Headquarters. My big hope for Glüp is that someday he will exist as a huge neoprene suit, to be worn by a hired professional. The person inside the suit will greet the kids, the readers of Glüp, as Glüp. From inside, watching carefully through a smartly-hidden screen, a college student will say, "Hello, children. I am Glüp."

It was after our third Mr. Lunch book that we began to boldly refer to these books as the Action Adventure Series. Despite Mr. Lunch's strong cerebral side he is always running around and stirring up trouble. Mindful of his place, goals, and friends, Mr. Lunch somehow always becomes the center of unexpected adventure. I guess that's why there are these books about him. In *Free Lunch,* for instance, Mr. Lunch is minding his own business when an evil elephant picks him out as an enemy. The angry elephant decides that Mr. Lunch has ruined his plan to sell bad birdseeds (dust and rocks) to the birds. So he has Mr. Lunch arrested on a trumped-up charge of leash law infringement. With the help of a bird and a good elephant Mr. Lunch is able to escape. Yes, he becomes a free Lunch.

In each of the Mr. Lunch books we like to introduce one new bird by name. In *Mr. Lunch Takes a Plane Ride,* it's Ambrose, the red bird who volunteers to be chased on television. He travels with Mr. Lunch on the airplane. In *Mr. Lunch Borrows a Canoe,* it's Falconé, a Venitian pigeon who so admires the bird-chasing skills of Mr. Lunch he asks to return home with him to serve as an intern. This is advantageous for the dog because Falconé is part homing pigeon and is able to navigate the boat ride back to the bird-chasing office.

In *Free Lunch,* Ambrose gets a big part, Falconé can be spotted in the big birdseed harvest scene, and the book's new bird is Gunhild, a country bird who lives surrounded by sumptuous seed trees. A careful reader will notice in the front of *Free Lunch* that the book is dedicated to Ned and Gunild. Those are the Walshes, Vivian's parents. Her mother, Gunild, who has spent a lifetime correcting the pronunciation of her name, is much appreciated as the inspiration for the funny new bird name.

Another bird plays a small part but has so far made it into every book. It even jumps the gap to the Space Monkey books. That would be the tall yellow bird. His biggest part is when he steps on the Penelope's bug house in *Monkey Business.* Mr. Lunch also has a run-in with this bird. He takes its picture from the borrowed canoe. The photograph Mr. Lunch took is hanging in the bird-chasing office. Some day this tall yellow bird may have to take command of his own picture book to tell his story. That is how our stories develop. Vivian and I spend a lot of time together, as a husband and wife will do, and start talking about different characters until they take on a personality and claim their own story.

We are working on a new story about our second dog, Olive. She's proven herself to be faithful, our best friend, and all that kind of good dog stuff. She's paid her dues while watching Mr. Lunch get all the fame and fan mail. Her book is a Christmas story called *Olive, the Other Reindeer.* She gets to work for Santa Claus, but just for one crucial night.

Vivian and I have built a Web site on the Internet (http://www.jotto.com) where the different characters from our books interact. Here we have the luxury of space and can write all we want about the different characters. In a picture book you want to get your story across with as few words as possible, so we are always trying to pare our story down and edit ourselves. We also get mail from readers. We got in the routine of starting each day with a café latté and e-mail from Mr. Lunch's or Space Monkey's pen pals. It's a nice way to start your day. There are a lot of clever kids out there writing entertaining letters. We quickly noticed that children were identifying with Penelope, the bug, and Ambrose, the red bird—the small characters. On the Internet we are able to develop our characters and set up fun games for people to fool around with.

I like it when people write to ask what Mr. Lunch and Space Monkey think of each other. Might they work together? Here's a couple of letters sent to Space Monkey, with his replies that were e-mailed back to the senders:

> Dear Space Monkey,
> My son, Mitchell, wants to know how you liked space. Should he think about becoming an astronaut? He also wants to tell you he liked the book.
> Dad wants to know if I should encourage a future Space Boy.
> Space Monkey replies:
> Tell your son Mitchell space is a lot like mountain climbing—only higher. You have to wear protective clothing, there are great views, but there are no stores nearby.
> I think one of the best ways to decide if you want to be an astronaut is to employ the lunar birthday theme. Equip each child's head with a protective goldfish bowl. Cover the lawn with slices of Swiss cheese. Then hand out specimen collection kits for the big search-and-find contest. Speak only in moon words, such as: affirmative, roger, and AWOL.
> Your friendly monkey friend,
> Space

Dear Space Monkey,

Just a note to say hi, and I love your books. I was wondering if Space Monkey or Mr. Lunch has ever been to Jupiter, where I hear gravity is pretty tricky. If you could stand there (which of course you can't, since it's all just swirling dust and gas), but if you could, you would weigh three times as much. So you'd be kind o' slow there.

Also, did you know that the government sent gold records into space with images of earth recorded in the grooves? Stuff like the theory of relativity, airports, and a man eating grapes, plus some music. All on records that aliens could find.

Space Monkey replies:
Madam,

Jupiter is not in my travel plans. It would be far too disruptive for my banana digestive system. I am considering a trip to Alaska though. I understand the majesty of the scenery can make you feel wonderfully small (at least three times smaller).

Yes, we know about the earthling data sent to space. My own track came right after Flip Wilson's "Here comes the judge . . ."
Yours truly,
Space Monkey

Children's books are taking over my working hours, but I do still illustrate articles in newspapers or magazines. Unlike most illustrators, I don't have stacks of oil paintings or piles of watercolors. Since I work on the computer my artwork is in the form of digital information. I see it on my computer screen and then mail it out on a computer disk or modem it right to an art director. There are no originals to hang on the wall.

I see my illustrations printed when a job is finished, in my morning *New York Times,* when ordering from the children's menu at the Café Florian in Venice, or on a shopping bag at the Japanese department store, Loft. I take these printed images and cut them up to reassemble as a collage. In my collages I like to experiment and play with the images and compositions more than I would normally.

Hopefully I will arrange my collage so that the ripped up pieces of whichever illustrations were on my desk hold together as one new picture. I want to re-create an image that is not scared of disorder—arranging things in an unconventional manner but working to attract the eye. When I make collages I try to work on a different level, trusting an intuitive sense

"The whole family," 1995: (from left) Thea, Amelia, J.otto, Vivian

to create something interesting, but at the same time mindful that I need to control the viewer's eye. I want to build channels of movement that will encourage someone to look more closely at the picture.

I like simple, clear compositions such as the illustrations in a children's picture book where you are trying to tell a story. Collage lets me create something different. Sometimes an art director makes me add their bosses' ideas, or worse, I have to write in some silly ad copy. These are the jobs that are the most satisfying to pull apart and make into something new. I am reclaiming and reassociating the pictures I have made as an illustrator. The collaging of my own printed work acts as a balance to the images' original context; that is, created on the computer, produced under a deadline, and with an art director's topic. The ability to free associate the threads of the narratives that I subconsciously add to all my illustration work allows me to relate the elements of my "private life" to those of my "professional life." Or, hopefully, they just add up to one artistic life.

BIBLIOGRAPHY

FOR CHILDREN

Books written, with Vivian Walsh, and illustrated:

Mr. Lunch Takes a Plane Ride, Viking, 1993.

Mr. Lunch Borrows a Canoe, Viking, 1994.

Monkey Business, Viking, 1995.

Free Lunch, Viking, 1996.

Also creator of television programs and music videos and contributor of illustrations to international newspapers and periodicals.

William Jay Smith

1918-

When I was a small boy and woke up in the morning, I would gaze towards the window where my mother had drawn the shade the night before. We were very poor and the shade was an old faded dark green one that we had had for some time. Through it came pricks and points and lines of light scattered unevenly up and down, making, together with the rips and tears in the canvas fabric, a series of odd designs. As I lay there, I tried to shape these points and lines of light into patterns resembling animals and plants. It was like looking up at the sky, but this sky belonged only to me, and in it I could create my own world.

While I was designing these visual patterns, I was also making patterns of sound like those I had heard in nursery rhymes that had such a pleasing effect on the ear when I said them over and over to myself:

> Hey diddle, diddle,
> The cat and the fiddle,
> The cow jumped over the moon.

I would make up my own patterns, my own rhymes from words I had heard or thought I had heard or words that I had never heard but thought I should have heard, words that I was inventing and that made sense only to me. I loved to listen to what grown-ups were saying, especially if they were telling stories, but often what they said made no sense at all. They were always talking about "taking things *for granted*," which I understood as taking them *for granite*—a strange thing to do,

I thought, with so much of the world—to turn it into hard stone instead of allowing it to sing and dance as it should and as it certainly did in those patterns of sound I was repeating to myself and which were, of course, the beginnings of poetry.

I was a great listener: I loved to listen to my parents. They were both Southerners and never stopped talking. I have sometimes said

William Jay Smith at the time of the publication of his Collected Poems, 1939–1989, *in 1990*

that I had to become a writer in order to get a word in. Both my mother and father were accomplished storytellers in the Southern tradition, and I loved to listen to the lilt of their language as it flowed out in their stories. I listened when my father told of his father, who had run off from the farm in Louisiana at the age of fourteen to join the Confederate Army as a fife player, how he had come back after the Civil War and been made Postmaster of the town but never spoke of the war. I listened when my mother told of her father, a big ruddy blue-eyed six-footer, who went off from time to time to Oklahoma to buy up cattle and drive them back to Arkansas. Once when he returned with a herd, a steer took out after him and the children watched from the porch of his store as men rushed out to rope the steer and save his life. I listened when she told of her grandmother, a tall woman with high cheekbones, a long face, and straight black hair combed back into a knot, who used to drive about in her own buggy. At Sunday School and church I also listened to passages of the King James version of the Bible, the rhythm of which held me fascinated.

In grade school I was fortunate to have teachers who gave us poetry to memorize, and in high school I had one teacher in particular, enamored of poetry, who began each morning by reading a poem. She didn't tell us the name of the poet she was reading but I discovered later that it was Robert Herrick, one of the great lyric poets of the English language. As soon as I heard poetry of this quality—simple, direct, and rhythmical—I began to write poems myself. When I was fourteen one of my teachers who wrote verse urged me to send some poems to a little magazine to which she contributed, *Versecraft,* published in Atlanta. "Observatory," which was printed there, contrasted the vast serene heavens with the tight, restricted human world below, and concluded:

> Let them squeeze my soul with walls
> And tear my heart with iron bars;
> But do not let them take the hole,
> Oh God, through which I see the stars.

I continued to submit poems to national magazines, and at seventeen, when I was a freshman in college, I had a poem accepted by the *American Mercury.* I have been writing and publishing poetry ever since. I had published two collections of poetry by the early 1950s before I thought of writing for children. My decision to do so came about when I listened one day to my son David.

Poetry, especially children's poetry, always begins with the particular; and, like that of most poets who have written for children, my interest began with a particular child on a special day. When David was four years old, I was sitting in the living room of our New York Greenwich Village apartment. We had rented the apartment furnished (with massive, dark Span-

ish furniture) from a man who, in the course of his long years in Spain, had collected, along with the furniture, objects that looked like instruments of torture; most of these we had stored away in closets, but the room was still rather somber (with something of a fairy-tale atmosphere about it) save for the light that poured in from a bay window overlooking a garden in back.

I was working with a pad on my lap when David, as four-year-olds will, came parading up and down the room reciting to the rhythm of his step:

> A Jack-in-the-Box
> Fell in the coffee
> And hurt himself.

At first I paid no attention and went on with my work, but he also went on, coming down hard on every syllable again and again. I can't remember whether or not I actually wrote the phrase down, but it certainly stayed with me. It stayed until that night when I lay awake—in a huge, dark, brocaded four-poster bed that made me feel a child again myself. I made up the poem:

> A Jack-in-the-Box
> On the pantry shelf
> Fell in the coffee
> And hurt himself.
> Nobody looked
> To see what had happened:
> There by the steaming
> Hot urn he lay;
> So they picked him up
> with the silverware,
> And carried him off
> On the breakfast tray.

The next morning I said the poem to David, and he was delighted with it—it was his. And indeed it was; all I had done was to complete what he had begun. What happens in the poem is what happens in the world of the four-year-old—for no reason and with no result—just as it happens at the circus, which is the child's dream of action realized. He asked me to repeat it to him several times, and then he turned to other things that interested him, and I went back to working on what seemed more serious poems. A night or two later, when we were entertaining friends, someone told a story and everyone burst out laughing. David, who had come out of his room, poked his head from behind one of the large armchairs and said, "It's laughing time!" and everybody naturally laughed all the harder. The next day I thought again about the jack-in-the-box and about laughing time. When one is four, there is a time for everything: a time for eating, a time for playing, a time for sleeping; why shouldn't there be a time for laughing as well? And so I began at once, in a kind of frenzy, to write the poems which have subsequently appeared in *Laughing Time.* It seemed rather as if the poems wrote themselves—they flowed out as I listened and watched. When I held David up to the mirror, I said:

> I look in the mirror, and what do I see?
> A little of you, and a lot of me!

And again he took these to be his lines, and they were. For the next few weeks I listened to my son and watched his every movement. I had, of course, watched and listened before, but now I was like a painter with his model: there was no line, no bone structure, no shadow that I did not wish to explore. I wanted to get inside him, to see things as he was seeing them—and as I could remember having seen them once myself; I wanted to give back to him the delight that he had given me, and in such a way that he would not even realize he was being given anything. And so I worked on as if all my life and training as a writer had been meant only for this moment.

When I finished the manuscript a few weeks later I took it to my agent who handled the prose that I had been writing but who did not ordinarily deal with poetry. I thought that he might in this case make an exception, but he returned the manuscript with a note saying that he could remember nothing of his early childhood and hence had no way of knowing whether this was good or bad; he suggested that I get in touch with an agent who dealt with children's literature. This I did, and her response was very discouraging indeed. She herself thought that the book was delightful, but she said that even if it were written by Robert Louis Stevenson, Walter de la Mare, or A. A. Milne, she would still be unable to place it for there was just no market whatever for children's verse. (Fortunately the situation today has improved somewhat but at the time very little poetry for children was being published.) I decided to try

the poems with magazine editors, and here I began to have some success. *Ladies' Home Journal* took one and the editor expressed regret that there was not space for more; *Harper's Bazaar* accepted another. I sent the entire collection to the *Atlantic Monthly* and heard nothing for months. Finally Seymour Lawrence, then the assistant editor, wrote and asked me to be patient: the Atlantic Monthly Press was considering it for book publication. There it was at last accepted and appeared in 1955. I was told later that although the poems had been tried out in several schools and had met with considerable success, the editors were still reluc-

Father, Jay Smith, in his Navy Bandsman uniform before his marriage

255

tant to risk publication. Then apparently the treasurer of Little, Brown, which controlled the Atlantic Monthly Press, an old bachelor who was never concerned with children's books, read it with great enthusiasm and gave the go-ahead signal.

I am happy to say that now after forty years, the book, combined with several other subsequent publications under the title *Laughing Time: Collected Nonsense,* is still in print. One of the most popular poems in the books has been

The Toaster

A silver-scaled Dragon with jaws flaming red
Sits at my elbow and toasts my bread.
I hand him fat slices, and then, one by one,
He hands them back when he sees they are
   done.

This poem over the years has had a great variety of fascinating illustrations when it has appeared in anthologies and textbooks, but my favorite of them all is one sent to me by a young boy who copied out the poem and beside it drew a fierce yellow dragon standing with flame pouring from his jaws while he holds in one claw a real piece of toast, which the young boy had carefully pasted in place. I framed his illustration and it hangs above my desk.

I was born in Winnfield, a town in north central Louisiana, which my father's family helped to found. At the age of three, I left it to accompany my father and mother to Jefferson Barracks, Missouri, just south of St. Louis. It was there on the edge of the Mississippi, as the son of a corporal in the Sixth Infantry, that I grew up. Because my father was a clarinetist in the band, he was not transferred regularly, and so, unlike other children who grew up in the army, I do not have a patchwork of memories of various posts scattered across the country and around the world, but a single vision of the twenty years spent in and around a particular one. Jefferson Barracks, on bluffs overlooking the river, was then a post of major importance. Founded in 1826, it became the Army's first permanent base west of the Mississippi. The woods on the reservation were a child's paradise; we knew every inch of these acres: here we followed the fern-lined muddy streams to our swimming holes, fished for crawfish with strips of bacon fat, and on the banks built our tree houses and lean-tos of sassafras

Mother, Georgia Ella Campster, at age sixteen

in air blue with bluebells and heavy with the perfume of sweet william. On the edge of sink-holes and limestone caverns we gathered bittersweet, hazelnuts, and persimmons in the fall and made our way to the Old Rock Spring (later called Sylvan Springs) to spend hours lying and drinking the clear water, watching the waterbugs dart across the surface of the sandy pool. No one had told us that this was where Jefferson Barracks had actually begun when Captain Stephen Watts Kearny had set up his camp and built the first log houses in 1826. It was the discovery of this spring that assured him that there would be an adequate water supply for a military post. No doubt even before Captain Kearny the Indians had found this a treasured, and even a sacred, place. In finding our way to it, we were turning instinctively to the most ancient part of the reservation.

We were quartered beside the woods in old cantonment buildings that had served as barracks during World War I. They had once been neat and symmetrical, but now appeared worn away as if their white paint had been attacked by blight; along the buildings was a strange assortment of screened-in porches, all somewhat askew, many enclosed in morning-glory vines in the summer. In their asymmetry and with the thick growth of summer vegetation, they resembled barges blown there in a hurricane, abandoned and overgrown. I never thought of these quarters as being ugly and dilapidated, as they certainly were, because as children we spent so much of our time in the woods. And then we had canvas-covered World War I Liberty trucks that took us to and from school in South St. Louis. It seemed in every way a perfect life, and it would have been but for the problems that my father created for himself and for his family. In the 1920s and '30s gambling was a way of life on Army posts and my father was a compulsive gambler. Every monthly payday he would join his fellow soldiers in poker games; sometimes he would bring home hundreds of dollars but more often he would return home without a cent. To make ends meet my mother began sewing for the officers' wives. The two sounds that haunted my boyhood were those of my father's clarinet as he practiced and the hum of my mother's sewing machine as she fashioned beautiful dresses. In spite of the monthly anxiety, all went well until shortly before I entered high school, when we were notified that the old buildings we occupied were to be torn down and that we would have to move off the post. When we moved to a building right next to the north gate, my father proposed that we enter what he called the "Bootleg Business." His idea was to make some home brew and invite his fellow Bandsmen to share it with him and thus make a small profit that would take care of our increased rent and give us an easy and comfortable place to live in. My mother was not exactly enchanted by the plan, especially since she did not drink herself, but she was quite aware that during Prohibition there were bootleg joints all over St. Louis County and that most of them were frequented by my father, who was a heavy drinker as well as a gambler. So my father began making home brew and my brother and I were given the job of bottling it. For the big gatherings that took place on paydays and weekends my mother cooked huge meals—baked ham, fried chicken, and turkey, with cornbread and her own hot rolls. It became clear very soon that home brew and food were not bringing

in much money, especially since my father extended credit to most of his customers. My father then decided to deal in hard liquor. He poured a five gallon can of pure alcohol into an oak barrel that rested in a frame on the shelf of the closet in the middle room upstairs, which was the bedroom that my brother and I shared. My father would cut the alcohol in half, adding five gallons of water to five gallons of alcohol. The charcoal-lined interior of the oak barrel would color the alcohol in due time and then the whiskey, put into pint and half-pint bottles, would be ready for sale.

I began to think of the entire business as not only extremely distasteful but also dangerously unlawful. Now that we sold hard liquor as well as home brew, a steady stream of men would dart in and out, especially on payday, just to pick up a bottle—right under the nose of the guard at the gate. Our house was so close to the gate that from the windows of the front bedroom I could gaze down through the branches of the oak tree in our front yard right onto the gate. Whenever a car drew up and parked in front of the house or across the street for any length of time, I would hold my breath: this was surely a private detective who was waiting for the police to arrive to arrest us.

My anxiety about the "Bootleg Business" was made all the greater by a tragic experience I had had not long before we moved off the post. On a hot July afternoon when I was ten, I stole off with two of my playmates, Evelyn and Nancy Langley, aged eight and nine, to smoke cigarettes in a cornfield on the edge of the woods. On a warm day no place was more inviting than a cornfield, its cool rows unfolding like the pleats of a fan and leading to secret passages and rooms. The edges of the corn had already begun to turn brown in the heat, and I was aware, after some experience with campfires in the woods, that it was not the safest place to be lighting a match. When we had found an open area around the corn, I cleared away a circle as if for a fire, and around it we sat like Indians for a council meeting. I explained to my companions that we should put out our matches and cigarettes in the cleared patch and not toss them near the cornstalks. And so we solemnly lit a cigarette and passed it around, the smoke making us dizzy and sick with the first puff, but no one daring to admit it. When the cigarette came to Evelyn Langley, she put it to her lips, let some ash fall on her dress, and the material, as light and flimsy as cornsilk, immediately caught fire. She screamed, leapt to her feet and ran as fast as she could, the flame rising around her, and the cornfield flying behind her like a cape. We were right at her heels. When she emerged from the field, our next-door neighbor Mrs. O'Hara, who had heard her scream, rushed forward, an Army blanket flying behind her, like a grotesque attendant at the birth of some corn goddess. She swept the screaming girl up in her blanket, a crowd gathered within minutes in the wail of the ambulance, and I was sobbing by the roadside.

Over the next few months while Evelyn was in the hospital undergoing skin grafts, I noticed a complete change in the attitude of everyone on the post toward me. While previously I had been popular and welcome wherever I went, I was now shunned and avoided. What had happened, I discovered later, was that a few days after the accident an article had appeared on the front page of the St. Louis *Star-Times* which was totally false; the only thing that the reporter had managed to get right was my name. He said that I had found a match and struck it behind Evelyn's back with the intention of scaring her. My parents had hidden the article from me and I had discovered it much later when looking for something in one of my mother's dresser drawers. Evelyn recovered completely, but the lie had been prominently printed and believed, and nothing could be done about it. I had learned something about the power of the written word.

My anxiety at the time was soon alleviated by the appearance in my life of Mrs. Nettie Bradbury, the widow of a doctor at the local Veterans Hospital, who had studied at the University of Chicago, and who came to enroll students at Jefferson Barracks in classes in expression and dramatics. I became Mrs. Bradbury's star pupil and she set out with determination to train my voice and prepare me for a career in the theatre. For dramatic exercises she introduced me to great poetry, to which I took an immediate liking. Soon, in the upstairs room where whiskey was being readied in the oak barrel of my closet, I stood for hours reciting passages from Shakespeare which she had carefully marked to indicate the inflections of the voice, the pauses, and the stresses:

If music be the food of love, play on;
Give me excess of it, that, surfeiting,
The appetite may sicken, and so die.
That strain again! it had a dying fall:
O, it came o'er my ear like the sweet sound,
That breathes upon a bank of violets,
Stealing and giving odor!

                              Twelfth Night, I.i.1

I was soon drunk not on the alcoholic vapors that I was breathing in but on poetry. I had fallen in love totally, blissfully, and eternally with language. And before long I was writing poems of my own that I recited with equal fervor. At Mrs. Bradbury's request, I memorized a tract on the evils of alcohol and delivered it so forcefully in a citywide contest that it won for me the Women's Christian Temperance Union's silver medal for oratory. My victory, of which my father was totally unaware, did nothing to curtail his heavy drinking, which continued unabated and kept him a corporal right up to his retirement after twenty-seven years

The poet at age four, Pine Bluff, Arkansas

of Army service. The last three years he spent at Schofield Barracks, Hawaii, where he was when the Japanese attacked and where I joined him when I reported for active duty at Pearl Harbor in June 1942 as an ensign in the Naval Reserve.

The end of Prohibition brought an end to our bootlegging about the time that I completed high school and entered Washington University in St. Louis on a scholarship established by Gerard Swope, President of General Electric. General Walter Short, the commanding officer at Jefferson Barracks who was later in charge in Hawaii when the Japanese attacked, had written a letter of recommendation that had impressed the selection committee.

Jefferson Barracks was deactivated not long after World War II and the northern section of it is now a park administered by St. Louis County, which has established a museum in one of the old ordnance depots overlooking the river. On a visit there recently, I found the house, the center of our "Bootleg Business," still inhabited but covered with huge panels of fire-engine-red aluminum siding. The trees around it had been cut down and the back yard leveled; the grape arbor, the shrubs, the flowers had all disappeared. The white limestone gates to Jefferson Barracks with their black cannon balls, without the guardhouse or any buildings beside them, looked like the abandoned section of a stage set, especially now that Broadway is no longer a thoroughfare and little traffic comes this way. I stood for a while next to the gates gazing at the house and marveled how it was that within its bleak walls, under the most unpromising circumstances, I had discovered poetry and the power of language and how it was that here, more than sixty years ago, my career as a writer had really begun.

At the time of my anxiety about our bootlegging, I began to have a special concern, exaggerated no doubt by Mrs. Bradbury's thrusting me constantly before the public, about my appearance. I realized that I had only the faintest of eyebrows and that my eyelids folded up rather than back over my eyeballs as they did for everyone else. My eyes, I became convinced, gave me the Oriental look that prompted some of the toughs on the school playground to call me "Chink" or "China-boy." The normal pimply face of the adolescent is hard enough to cope with, but I found that I not only had

pimples but virtually no beard. Bits of fuzz grew only on my chin and my upper lip, with no sign that my beard would ever grow on the sides of my face. There was no one to turn to for help because I was not even sure what kind of help I needed: I became more and more withdrawn and found true friends only in books. It was in books also that I found what I felt was the answer to my problem. I read that American Indians of all tribes had very light beards and hairless bodies. What hair grew on their faces they extracted with clam shells. I thought of the only real Indians that I had seen—Big Ike and Little Ike, both of whom served with my father in the Barracks Band and came frequently to our house. They both had light beards, and although their complexions were darker than mine, still I looked more like them than like the other people around me. I decided that I *was* an Indian.

Throughout my boyhood I had identified with the Indians, not the Plains Indians of the films, who very early on seemed to me absolutely phony, but the Indians of the woods and of the settled villages who greeted the early explorers; not the Indians of the wild war whoops and the tomahawks, but the Indians of the stealthy movement through the forest. I had discovered their arrowheads in the caves on the post, and I identified with them on my walks through the woods when I constructed my lean-tos of sassafras beside the muddy creeks, or when I moved on the balls of my feet over the underbrush, listening carefully for the slightest sound, the darting movement of a snake or the sudden thundering of a covey of quail:

> Like brightness buried by one's sullen mood
> The quail lie hidden in the threadbare wood.
> A voice, a step, a swift sun-thrust of feather
> And earth and air once more come properly
>   together.

Early on Jefferson Barracks had become the focal point for forays against the Indians. Lt. Jefferson Davis had escorted Black Hawk, the famous Sac (Sauk) and Fox Chief, together with his son Naopope (the Prophet), to Jefferson Barracks after his defeat and capture in 1832 near Bad Axe River. Black Hawk praised the courtesy shown them by Davis, whom he described as "a good and young chief in whose conduct I am much pleased." When George Catlin came to the Barracks to paint portraits of Black Hawk and his son, Naopope raised his ball and chains above his head and exclaimed, "Paint me thus and show 'the Great Father.'" When Catlin painted Black Hawk, he was dressed, in Catlin's words, "in a plain suit of buckskin, with strings of wampum in his ears and on his neck." In his hand he held his medicine bag "which was the skin of a black hawk, from which he had taken his name, and the tail of which made him a fan, which he was almost constantly using." The limestone ordnance depot where Black Hawk had been imprisoned was near our house at the Barracks north gate and I visited it often.

About this time my cousin Clara Louise came to live with us for a year. She looked exactly like my Aunt Lucinda; although not quite so plump, she had the same high cheekbones, black eyes, and straight black hair. I became convinced that it was in them, and in my mother's brother who had similar features, as it was in me, that the traits of our Indian ancestors, whoever they may have been, showed themselves.

It was not until much later that I discovered that we did indeed have Choctaw blood. My cousin William Carroll Tabor, a member of the House of Representatives in the First Oklahoma legislature of 1903, put in a claim to the Dawes Commission stating that his great-grandmother Rebecca Tubbs Williams was the daughter of Chief Moshulatubbee, the head of the Choctaw nation at the time of the removal from Mississippi to Oklahoma. That claim was denied but it was always understood in my mother's family that her grandmother Catherine Williams, about whom she had often spoken to me, was definitely a Mississippi Choctaw.

I have been asked what influence, if any, this modest measure of Choctaw blood may have had on my work. I like to think that the still center from which I believe my poetry springs has much in common with the reverential attitude of the Native American towards the elements, the sensory and spiritual connection between earth and sky that makes for that magical instinctive balance that permits the Mohawk to walk with perfect equilibrium on the edges of skyscrapers at great heights. And I would like to think that the visual element in my work may owe something to my Choctaw heritage. When I started to do my typewriter poems—concrete poems composed on the typewriter—someone pointed out that these typewritten patterns and inscriptions resembled the petroglyphs that Native Americans left on the stone walls of caverns throughout the country as a record of the world with which they were in close touch and to which they paid constant tribute.

Whatever heritage it may have brought me, the discovery at the time gave me new strength to face the limited—and limiting—aspects of military life: I found it reassuring that while I had been brought up on an Army garrison founded as an outpost in the Indian Wars, I had forebears on the outside and in the enemy's camp.

Washington University opened up a whole new world to which I responded with great enthusiasm. Because my work in French was quite advanced, I was immediately placed in an upper class taught in French by Professor Albert Salvan. As an assignment early in the semester we were given a list of topics suggested by Alain-Fournier's novel *Le Grand Meaulnes* (*The Wanderer*), which we were reading and which I thoroughly enjoyed. The topic I chose to write about was "Silence." I thought about it for a while without putting a word down on paper, and then just as I was about to start writing, some friends came by and lured me off to the picture show at Jefferson Barracks. We walked to and from the Post Theater over the road from the North Gate where the streetcar track once ran. I can't remember which film we saw, but all its bright images behind us, we plunged on our return into the woods and were soon surrounded by the mysterious night sounds to which over the years I had become accustomed. The darkness around us seemed unending and the stars above us appeared as close as they must have to those early explorers who made their way down the Mississippi. I thought of the words of Pascal that I had read somewhere: "The eternal silence of those infinite spaces frightens me."

It was late when we got home, but still under the spell of the vast silence of the night through which I had walked, I quickly put down my thoughts on "Silence." When the papers were returned a few days later, I noticed that mine was not among those that Professor Salvan distributed. The next moment I realized that he was holding it in his hand and reading it to the class. At the end of his reading he pronounced my composition of great merit and worthy of a talented French writer, all the more extraordinary to have come from a young American student. His reception took my breath away: I had always dreamt of being a writer, but to have my writing in another language meet with such approval was unexpected and overwhelming. He took my essay to Professor Harcourt Brown, who had just come to Washington University as head of the French department and Professor Brown soon called me to his office. He gave me permission to take other advanced courses and persuaded me then and there to major in French, a decision that I never regretted because doing so gave me a background that I would never have had if I had majored in English.

In one of the advanced courses in which I enrolled I made the acquaintance of Clark Mills McBurney, a graduate student in French who had published poems in national magazines. At the same time I met Thomas Lanier Williams, who, after some years at the University of Missouri and a job at the International Shoe Com-

pany in St. Louis where his father was a sales manager, had come to Washington University as a special student. Tom Williams, who later became the playwright Tennessee Williams, was writing poetry as well as plays and had won several local prizes. He and Clark and I organized a chapter of the College Poetry Society and began to publish poems in *College Verse,* the national magazine published by the Society. The three of us met regularly at Tom's house near the university to discuss our poems and we learned a great deal from these discussions, during which we were extremely severe with one another. Tom was the shyest, quietest person I had ever met. His stony-faced silence often put people off: he appeared disdainful of what was going on around him, never joining in the quick give-and-take of a conversation but rather listening carefully and taking it all in. He would sit quietly in a gathering for long periods of time until suddenly, like a volcano erupting, he would burst out with a high cackle and then with resounding and uncontrollable laughter. Those who knew him well found this trait delightful but to others it seemed rude and disconcerting. He was certainly quick and ready with words when we discussed our poetry.

For both Tom and me, Clark, who had already published widely as Clark Mills and was familiar with the work of Eliot, Auden, Spender and other modern poets, was an inspiring mentor. When I was away on a job in Michigan the following summer, Clark and Tom organized what they called the Literary Factory in Clark's basement and they both worked regularly there on poetry and plays. The Mummers, a St. Louis theatrical group, produced one of Tom's plays, *Candles to the Sun,* in 1937, but he continued to write poetry. The following year when Clark was in Paris on a fellowship, he and I formed what we called the St. Louis Poets Workshop, and continued to send our poems out to national magazines, undisturbed by the frequent rejection slips that we received.

Tom went off to complete his degree at the University of Iowa and during the summer of my junior year, with money saved from odd jobs, I went off to France to study for three months at the Institut de Touraine in Tours. This brief exposure to the best French as well as to the company of students from all over Europe had a profound effect on me. I found

Smith at age fifteen in front of his father's tent at the Century of Progress Exposition, Chicago, 1933

my intellectual background sadly inferior to that of my European colleagues and I returned with a determination to make up for it. I continued advanced courses in French and took as well courses in English, Italian, and Spanish literature. I stayed on at the university, teaching courses in first and second year French while working for my master's. Just after receiving it, I enlisted in the Naval Reserve. In January 1942, following the Japanese attack on Pearl Harbor, I spent four months at Northwestern University in Chicago in the V-7 Naval Officers Training program. In June when I received my commission as an ensign, I had two poems accepted by *Poetry* magazine, the office of which was around the corner from Abbot Hall, where I had undergone my naval training. I was invited by George Dillon, the editor, to read my poems at a gathering at the magazine office and I kept in touch with the magazine, which continued to publish my work during my four years of active duty.

I reported first at Pearl Harbor and then a few months later was transferred to Palmyra Island, a thousand miles southwest of Honolulu. There I spent ten months as personnel officer of the airbase and could have stayed even longer had I not been reminded by a yeoman who worked with me that Naval officers were requested to report their language ability each year to Washington. This I did and some months later received orders transferring me to Casablanca in North Africa, where I arrived shortly after the American landings in 1943. In January 1944 I replaced a British liaison officer on board the aviso colonial *La Grandière*. The ship had been built as a patrol vessel or gunboat for use in the French colonies. Three hundred fifty feet in length, it had five-inch guns and was quite elegantly fitted out. The French Admiralty requested that this ship be sent to join the American fleet in the South Pacific, and so, with a liaison party, a radioman and two signalmen who were French-speaking New Englanders, to help me to decode messages, I was the first American naval officer to be placed on a French ship, and it became my home for the next year-and-a-half.

When I first went on board, the officers who had fought against us Americans at Casablanca and were admirers of Admiral Darlan and General Pétain were not very pleased to have me join them. They treated me very coldly—properly, but coldly. This, of course, was

easy enough to do because when they resorted to using French Navy slang, I couldn't understand a word they said. I was fluent in French but the slang was incomprehensible, as it would have been to any ordinary Frenchman. As time went by, I was not only accepted but was warmly received by officers and crew, as were the men in my liaison party.

We crossed the north Atlantic in January in terrible weather at a very dangerous time. It took us twenty-one days. We were one of the transports of a convoy of some thirty ships, and because we had little speed we were towards the back. When we were several days out and I had just crawled into my bunk at dawn, one of the French sailors rushed into my cabin to tell me with great urgency that the captain wanted me at once on the bridge. I pulled on my pants as I struggled as quickly as possible up through the dark. Once on the bridge, I was handed by the captain a message that had just been flashed from one of the cargo vessels in the convoy. It read: MATE, ARE YOU A NEW KIND OF SHIP OR WHAT? The captain wanted to know what he should reply and was unhappy when I told him to ignore this silly inquiry, which was in dangerous violation of the rules of the convoy, especially coming as it did at dawn. The captain could simply not understand how any message could go unanswered and called me a total incompetent in no uncertain terms. But when later that morning the signalmaster of the ship sent an apology, the captain decided that I wasn't quite as stupid as I had seemed.

After being refitted in Norfolk, we made our way through the Panama Canal and stopped first at the Marquesas Islands, where no French ship had been for a very long time. I was able to spend one day on the island of Nuku Hiva and to travel by horseback up the mountain over the ruins of ancient Polynesian temples and to gaze out on the valley that Herman Melville describes in *Typee*. Another day on the island of Hiva Oa, where Gauguin spent his last years, I visited his grave and met several of his Polynesian descendants. The *La Grandière* then sailed on to Tahiti, to Nouméa in New Caledonia and Espiritu Santo in the New Hebrides (Vanuatu). For some months we were the station ship at Espiritu Santo and made a tour of the other islands in the group, then on to Guadalcanal, Tulagi, Manus, and Funafuti, usually escorting cargo ships along the way.

With his father, Corporal Jay Smith,
at Schofield Barracks, Hawaii, June, 1942

Duty on *La Grandière* was far from perilous: on a number of occasions we pursued what proved to be nonexistent Japanese submarines but we never saw any real action. All the same, I had two very narrow escapes: the difference, in one instance, of a few hours, in the other, of a few seconds, and I would not be here to tell my story. We had been tied up for several days next to an ammunition ship at Guadalcanal when suddenly and unexpectedly we received orders in the middle of the night to depart to escort a cargo ship. We sailed at dawn and a few hours later the ammunition ship blew up, and with it, the entire dock. Another time, in Espiritu Santo, the officers of an American training submarine, whom I had met ashore, invited me to accompany them on one of their regular runs. I was standing with the captain in the conning tower of the submarine when he spotted a plane from an incoming American carrier headed down on us. Within seconds he had the submarine, which the pilot had mistaken for a Japanese one, deep under-

water. Although it shook like a battered cocktail shaker from the impact of the bombs, it managed to struggle back to port. This was my first, and only, venture on a submarine.

My shipboard duty left me much free time, which I devoted to writing and translating. I sent out poems from various ports of call, and a number were accepted by the *New Republic, Poetry,* and by Oscar Williams for his anthology *The War Poets;* I also translated some of the poems of Louis Aragon. I left the ship in Panama in 1945 when it returned to France, and I decided to take advantage of my experience with the French as opening up the possibility for further language study. I volunteered for duty at the Navy Language School in Boulder, Colorado, where I ended my Naval career with intensive study of Russian, which was to serve me much later as a translator of Russian poetry on my many visits to Russia.

In the year 1947 everything that I had been working toward for some time seemed to come together. I had spent a year at Columbia University as a graduate student in English and comparative literature while at the same time teaching classes in beginning and intermediate English and French. I had applied for a Rhodes scholarship from Missouri. The age limit for applicants for the scholarships had been extended so that veterans might apply. In the spring I went out for interviews in St. Louis and in Iowa and I was one of those chosen to enter Oxford in the fall. At the same time my friends Claude Fredericks and Milton Saul, who had founded the Banyan Press in New York, came to ask if I had a book of poems ready for publication. I quickly put together what I thought were my best twenty-one poems and just as they were completing the printing of the book, which I had called simply *Poems,* a letter was forwarded to me by the editors of the little magazine *Furioso,* which had printed a poem of mine entitled "Cupidon." The letter from poet Marianne Moore stated that she considered this poem "a permanence, a rare felicity." Marianne Moore gave us permission to quote her and although the book had no dust jacket a special band with her statement was made to wrap around each copy. The result was that she really launched my poetic career: her recommendation meant that the book was reviewed by the *New York Times* and other important newspapers and magazines, which was very unusual for a first book by an unknown poet published by a new and unknown press. Then just three days before leaving for Oxford I married the poet Barbara Howes. We had met in New York when she accepted a poem of mine for *Chimera,* the literary quarterly that she edited. The rules for Rhodes scholars had been changed, and for the first time, because of the dislocation of the war years, members of our class were allowed to be married. I arrived in Oxford as a married man and a published poet. Stephen Spender, whom I had met on his first trip to New York, had accepted a poem of mine for publication in *Horizon,* which he edited in London with Cyril Connolly. We had introductions to some of the leading poets, among them the Welsh poet Dylan Thomas, who was then living near Oxford. We used to see him and his wife Caitlin regularly along with other Oxford friends such as Enid Starkie, a lecturer in French, the historian A. L. Rowse, and Lord David Cecil. Living in Oxford at the time was not easy; food was still rationed and heating was difficult. But I was delighted to have the opportunity to meet such talented writers and scholars. I went on writing poetry, but rather than stay on at Oxford to complete my doctorate, we left at the end of the year to take up residence in Florence, where we had gone to visit friends. Florence at the time was like Paris after World War I: it attracted a great number of American artists and writers. Living was inexpensive and we were able to rent a villa on the outskirts of the city while I studied Italian language and literature at the university. We stayed for two years and our elder son David was born there. We returned to America to settle in Pownal, Vermont, in a farmhouse that Barbara, who had attended Bennington College nearby, had purchased before our marriage. I then began teaching part-time at Williams College, just over the border in Massachusetts. But Italy drew us back again and we spent a second two-year period in Florence from 1955 to 1957. On this second visit I accompanied my son David to the zoo in Rome, and it was there that I started to write the poems that eventually made up *Boy Blue's Book of Beasts.* In Florence we got to know the art critic Bernard Berenson and went often to see him at the villa I Tatti; we also visited the writer Harold Acton, at La Pietra. Among the well-known American writers who came through Florence while we were there

The author reading from Laughing Time *to sons Gregory and David, Florence, Italy, 1957*

was Eudora Welty, who became a lifelong friend.

Pownal, Vermont, is a town of some 1500 people, and the farmhouse we occupied looked out on one of Vermont's most beautiful valleys. I grew to love the countryside and the quiet was ideal for my writing and translating. In the late 1950s several of the townspeople came to ask me if I would agree to run for the office of selectman since I taught only one or two days at Williams and had much free time. I was flattered that the people thought well enough of me to ask me to help manage the town. I agreed to run, and since I felt that I needed to know the townspeople better I got in our four-wheel-drive jeep and made the rounds of the houses on the backcountry roads. I lost the election by forty votes, and right afterwards the same townspeople came to me to say that the result had been unusually good for someone who was little known in town, and now they asked if I would be willing to run for town representative. That position would require only a few days residence in Montpelier, and the legislative session lasted usually only a few months. I agreed to run and was nominated by both the Democratic and Republican parties. But a complication arose when I was asked my views on pari-mutuel betting. A referendum on this issue had been placed on the ballot and if the vote carried, Pownal was due to have the first racetrack in the state. Once I examined the issue, I had to come out and say that I thought a racetrack, while it might bring temporary tax relief, would in the end be a disaster for our beautiful valley. When I made my views public, the nature of the election changed completely. I discovered that the backers of the track who came from cities like Providence, Rhode Island, were incensed by my opposition. They telephoned— often in the middle of the night—threatening to burn our house down. My wife and I decided to fight back and I again made the rounds of the back roads, calling on people and explaining my views. As a result, although pari-mutuel betting was voted in and Pownal did indeed have the first and only racetrack in Vermont (which after losing money over the years was turned into a dog track and then finally completely abandoned), I was elected town representative by some forty votes.

The 1961 session of the Vermont legislature turned out to be the longest in the state's history because the question of its reapportionment had come before the Supreme Court of the United States. The Vermont House of Representatives was cited as one instance where eleven percent of the population could control the vote—a far cry from the democratic ideal of one man, one vote. When the Supreme Court ruled against Vermont, our legislature was called back into session to begin reapportioning itself.

My experience in the Vermont House of Representatives was time-consuming but fascinating and I ended up writing an account of it that appeared in *Harper's.* As a Democratic member, I joined a group of eleven Young Turks, as we were called, of both parties who set out to work for what we considered sound legislation, particularly to protect the environment. We also set out to change the Republican *status quo* and to help elect my seatmate Philip Hoff of Burlington as the first Democratic governor in 109 years. During our long session, we had many important matters to consider but on one bill we were all united: this was to make the Morgan horse the official state animal. Various other animals had first been proposed—the porcupine, the goat, the catamount, the cow. (The cow was always prominent in Vermont and milk is recognized as the official state beverage; for many years there were more cows than people.) Since I had been elected Official Poet and represented the town that was to have the first racetrack, I was asked to comment on the bill and on this occasion I read:

A Minor Ode to the Morgan Horse

I may not incline
To the porcupine,
And I may be averse
To what is much worse:
The bear
That is rare,
The goat
That's remote,
The sheep, from which year after year
   you must remove the coat,
The catamount
That does not amount to that amount,
The cow
That somehow
We, as a human minority, cannot allow;
And although, as one of the Democratic
   minority, I should, alas,
Far prefer the jackass,
I must—until a state animal can choose
   its own state—
Not hesitate
To vote, of course
For the Morgan horse.

My Ode was taken up by the press and reprinted in newspapers around the country, but somewhere along the line the final two lines got dropped off. I had a note from friends in Colorado inquiring whether or not Vermont politics had begun to affect me mentally since it did seem strange to write an ode to an animal without even an indirect reference to it.

I had much wonderful support during my heated campaign for office but none that pleased me more than that of one of Vermont's most revered citizens, Robert Frost. Although at the time he came regularly to Amherst College, Frost had not been to Williams College in thirty-five years. The Williams lecture committee asked me to invite him, and when I did, to everyone's astonishment, he agreed to come. I told him the morning after his reading that he had drawn the largest audience in the history of the college.

"More than for Mrs. Roosevelt?" he asked.

"More than for Mrs. Roosevelt," I replied.

At the start of his reading, he led me out on the platform and said, "Vote for this man, he is a good poet."

I didn't tell him that this endorsement, which, of course, I valued highly, would have little effect because few Pownal residents had crossed the border to hear it.

The morning after the reading, he kindly came out to Pownal to visit Barbara Howes and me. When he discovered that Barbara was also a published poet, he frowned and commented that it was dangerous to have two poets under the same roof. I didn't pay attention to his comment at the time since Barbara and I had always admired each other's work, as we still do; but in the end problems did indeed arise and our marriage ended in divorce. One of the unfortunate results of the breakup was that I had to abandon Vermont. But I have returned for frequent reunions with my fellow legislators.

The poet with Robert Frost in Pownal, Vermont, 1961

It is difficult, if not impossible, to speak of the events of my life without referring also to the poems that have accompanied, or overshadowed, them. The writing of poetry, as Walter de la Mare pointed out, is the most curious of human activities, and the poet must always be ready for the poem to arrive, whether it wells up from the deepest layers of sense or bubbles out from the upper levels of nonsense.

I used to go hunting mushrooms in Vermont, and gradually I came to know one particular place where morels, those rarest and most delicious of mushrooms, were to be found. It was not far from the house at a bend of the road under large maple trees. They would spring up overnight each year at the same time, at the end of May after a night of rain. I had gathered them for several years when finally one day, having brought them back to the house I sat down, when they had been cooked and eaten as they had been so many times before, and wrote off in about twenty minutes a poem, "Morels," that I had not consciously planned to write. I knew after it was written, however, that it was one I had lived with for a long

time, although it spoke only of the events of that one afternoon and had seemed to spring up as quickly as the morels themselves.

Other poems, sometimes much shorter, have not sprung up so quickly but have taken many years to write; one such is

American Primitive

Look at him there in his stovepipe hat,
His high-top shoes, and his handsome collar;
Only my Daddy could look like that,
And I love my Daddy like he loves his Dollar.

The screen door bangs, and it sounds so funny—
There he is in a shower of gold;
His pockets are stuffed with folding money,
His lips are blue, and his hands feel cold.

He hangs in the hall by his black cravat,
The ladies faint, and the children holler:
Only my Daddy could look like that,
And I love my Daddy like he loves his Dollar.

A poet friend remarked to me once that this was one of my poems that he most admired and that it must have been a delight to write it right off, as I so clearly had done. It was indeed a delight to write it right off—as it now stands—after working on it at odd moments for a period of five years. I cannot recall how many versions I put down during this period, most of them discarded. I knew exactly where I wanted to get to; the problem was getting there, and getting there with directness and *élan*—and without fuss. I had in mind a Mississippi River guitar tune—absolutely mechanical in its rhythm—an out-and-out child's innocent unadorned view of horror—horror with the resonant twang of strings to it. In its original version, the poem was very much longer. There were a good many little ballad bits, of which this is an example:

> I fear the feel of frozen steel,
>   I fear the scarlet dagger;
> But more than these I fear the eel,
>   I fear the carpetbagger.

I had indeed the vision of the carpetbagger who had gone into the South after the Civil War and made his money in some suspect manner; and with the sunlight and the screen door I wished to suggest the large, open, airy Southern house that I remembered from childhood. The most difficult line for me to get in the poem was the one that now seems the simplest, and it is the turning point:

> He hangs in the hall by his black cravat.

Poetry is all in verbs, in verbs and nouns, and it seems to me it is all here in the verb "hangs." I have frequently been asked to discuss this poem with grade-school children, and, although it may appear a macabre choice on the part of the teacher, I have discovered that children respond to it without hesitation. They understand that a child is speaking and that the father has hanged himself for some reason involving money. College students, on the other hand, have often found this piece bewildering; they have lost the down-to-earth metaphorical approach of childhood and cannot follow the simple words to their unexpected conclusion. I think that I scarcely need add that although "American Primitive" is a bitter poem in the tradition of Edwin Arlington Robinson's "Richard Cory," it is certainly not intended as my sole view of the American scene.

Poems do not always come quickly to mind, nor do they always spring up in the same place or in the same form. I took my younger son Gregory, then ten years old, deep-sea fishing off Long Beach, California. I am a poor fisherman, although I love "messing about in boats." I certainly did not in this particular instance relish the thought of this trip with some sixty-odd tourists on board a ship "eighty-five feet long, twenty-three foot beam, twin diesels, twin stacks painted red, white, and blue." But I knew from the moment we went

> Through gray streets, at 10:00 P.M., down
>   to Pierpont Landing, Long Beach,
>   where, in the window of a shop offer-
>   ing every type of fishing gear,
>
> Are displayed fish carved from driftwood by
>   the natives of Bali, each representing in
>   true colors and exact dimensions a fish
>   found on their reefs,
>
> Colors derived from bark and root (each fish,
>   when completed, is bartered for rice;
>   no money is involved) . . .

that somewhere on this trip a poem lay waiting to be written. Perhaps for this reason I began at once, while my son looked around the shop on the pier, to write down in detail the description of the fish in the window. It was not until we got back that I realized that the poem I thought might grow out of this display was really the journey itself and all that had happened on it, all that we had seen and done, from beginning to end. It was not a story really; there was no story to tell: sixty-five people on a regular fishing trip 135 miles off the coast of southern California had caught 125 albacore. My son and I were among them; he had caught one, and I, none. It had all been a bloody business, the albacore coming up half-eaten by sharks, and then, on the way back, we had come close to a pod of whales. But in sorting it all out afterwards I knew that it was a narrative that I had to put down just as I saw it, one whose whole meaning would gradually become clear to me—and I hope to my reader—during the three years that it took me to record "Fishing for Albacore."

Poetry for me should be continually expanding within its frame. Humor is itself a form of expansion; laughter, as Max Beerbohm said, is "but a joyous surrender." I have been drawn to light verse because of a firm belief that humor is one of America's greatest and most enduring characteristics. Children's poetry, with its wide use of stanza forms and the range of its nonsense, has been for me a liberating influence, giving me a chance to explore in a light vein themes that I have developed and expanded in adult work.

There is, I am told, a Poets' Competition in Barcelona. After the poems have been read aloud, the judges award the prizes in a most unusual fashion. The author of the third best poem receives a rose made of silver, the author of the second best, a rose made of gold, and the author of the best—the most enduring and most original—a real rose. One might think of these awards as a metaphor for the making of poems. What is given the poet— that phrase, that image, that scrap that circles around for months in his head, that God-given inspiration—is of silver. The second stage, that of composition and revision, when the poet must work constantly over every syllable, never at the same time losing sight of the whole, and when

anything earned seems more precious than anything received—that stage is of gold. The third and final stage when the poem is released and belongs to the reader and to the world, if the poet has succeeded and has been true to his vision, that final stage is the *natural* one, when the finished work may take its place; organically whole, beside the great work of life itself.

On September 3, 1966, in Paris I married Sonja Haussmann, whom I had met the previous Christmas when she had come to Wesleyan University to visit friends of hers and mine. Of an old Strasbourg family, she is an experienced translator from German and English and has translated into French a selection of my poems in a volume titled *L'Arbre du voyageur.* We later collaborated on a translation of the novel *The Madman and the Medusa* by the Congolese novelist Tchicaya U Tam'Si. We spent a year at Williams College, where I was Poet in Residence, and then the following year went to Hollins College, Virginia, where I had previously been Writer in Residence and where I accepted a permanent post as Professor of English. But no sooner had we arrived in Virginia than I was named Consultant in Poetry to the Library of Congress in Washington, a post now called Poet Laureate, and which I occupied from 1968 to 1970. I returned after that time to Hollins College, where I remained until my retirement from teaching in 1980—with two years away in the mid-1970s when I served as Chairman of the Writing Division of the School of the Arts at Columbia University in New York.

Because of my interest in poetry for children, Virginia Haviland, head of the Children's Book Section of the Library of Congress, and I collaborated on a bibliography of poetry for children. In the fall of 1969 I organized a Children's Poetry Festival to which I invited the Irish poet Padraic Colum, William Cole, the anthologist, and Louise Bogan, the poetry critic of the *New Yorker,* with whom I had compiled the anthology *The Golden Journey: Poems for Young People.* "We had a *packed* audience," Louise Bogan wrote later to a friend, "with P. Colum pulling long poems out of his eighty-nine-year-old memory. Fantastic!" Under a grant from the National Endowment for the Arts I made a program of my children's poetry with television station WETA in Washington, which

Examining the printing of Typewriter Town *with son Gregory, Bennington, Vermont, 1960*

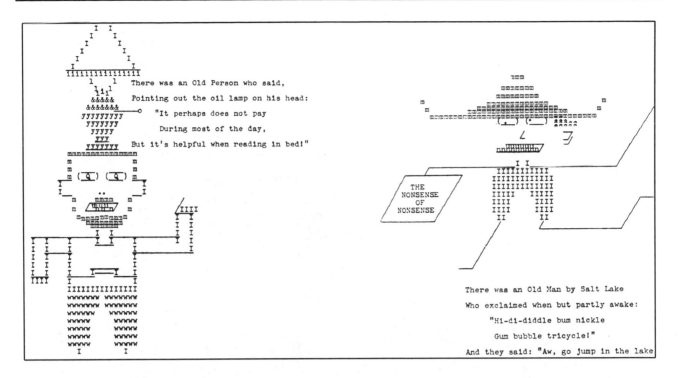

There was an Old Person who said,

Pointing out the oil lamp on his head:

"It perhaps does not pay

During most of the day,

But it's helpful when reading in bed!"

There was an Old Man by Salt Lake

Who exclaimed when but partly awake:

"Hi-di-diddle bum nickle

Gum bubble tricycle!"

And they said: "Aw, go jump in the lake

Limericks from Typewriter Town, *written and illustrated by Smith, 1960*

took its title from one of my recently published children's books, *Mr. Smith and Other Nonsense.* The film, illustrated with drawings especially executed, had its first showing on Christmas Day, 1969, and a few months later won a National Educational Television Award.

During my two years in Washington, I traveled more widely than any of the previous Consultants. In May 1969 I left with Sonja for a six-week lecture-and-reading tour of Japan, Korea, Singapore, and Indonesia under the American Specialists Program. I met more poets on this trip it seemed at times than there are images of the Lord Buddha, and each one of them presented me with a volume of his works. In turn, I handed out mimeographed copies of the poems I read, some of my own, some by representative poets who had come into prominence since 1945, poets such as Roethke, Wilbur, and Bishop, poems in which I felt the language would not be too difficult to follow. One of the high points of the tour was meeting in Tokyo Yukio Mishima, who invited us to a performance of his play *Madame de Sade* and to dinner afterwards. Another memorable occasion, when we had a few days off the tour, was a visit to the famous temple of

Angkor Wat in Cambodia, which is surely one of the world's great monuments.

A year later I went alone on a much longer trip, the first of many to Eastern Europe. I was the first American writer in three years to be sent to the Soviet Union and the first one ever to visit the Academic City in Novosibirsk, Siberia, where I read and lectured at the Institute of Nuclear Physics and at an American educational exhibit that had been mounted there. I had already met the poet Andrei Voznesensky in the United States and had begun translating his poetry. I was happy to see him again on his home ground at Peredelkino on the outskirts of Moscow, where I also met the poet Yevgeny Yevtushenko. On this first visit to Moscow I also met the well-known children's poet Boris Zakhoder, the translator of *Alice in Wonderland* and *Winnie the Pooh.* Zakhoder is a witty roly-poly character like one right out of *Alice* and I spent many hours with him and his charming wife in their dacha in Kamarovka, near Moscow. He immediately began to translate my children's poems, which he had handsomely illustrated and published in editions of hundreds of thousands of copies. He also arranged for me to read my poems with him on the radio

Smith with wife Sonja beside Lake Baikal, Siberia, April, 1981

and television so that I found when I returned to the Soviet Union years later that my work was widely known. My name looks strange in Cyrillic script: *CMUT,* but Zakhoder arranged for it to appear far and wide.

My wife and I returned several times to the Soviet Union as guests of the Writers Union, which arranged for us to travel to Kiev and Georgia. I went as a Fulbright lecturer at Moscow State University for four months in January 1981. There was so little color in the world around us during this Russian winter that, gazing from the windows of our university rooms high in the Lenin Hills toward the distant gray outlines of the city, I sometimes wondered if I had become color-blind or was seeing the world suddenly as dogs apparently see it: in black and white. Black iron railings everywhere stood out sharply against the mounds of snow; the fir trees in the park around the university rose like so many dark-coated sentinels along the way, their branches snow-tipped arms extended to block the path. There were only two or three heavy snowfalls and it was often warm

enough for the snow to start to melt. The resultant slush would then freeze into brownish-gray fringes along the snow drifts lining the black streets. The water from the snow that had melted on the walks before the subway became treacherous glare ice, its black surface resembling an old mirror that sparkled but gave back no image. The paths across vacant lots were so many strands of black thread winding crookedly through a dirty white tufted fabric.

In spite of the bleak landscape, this was an incredibly rewarding and fascinating visit. We were there at the height of the Afghan War and all cultural exchange between the Soviet Union and the United States had ceased. But since I was already known to many writers in the Writers Union, regular readings were arranged for me and thousands of people of all ages came to hear me. To understand the reception I had at this time, one must realize the important position that a poet occupies in Russian society. He or she is revered in a way that is extraordinary. Poetry is popular with vast segments of the population and was especially so during the Communist regime, when poets were able to say things couched metaphorically that prose writers would never have been able to get away with. I was treated everywhere like a rock star. If I told a taxi driver that I was a poet from America, he would take me all over Moscow free of charge. I gave a lecture every Wednesday at the School of Journalism in downtown Moscow not far from Red Square. At first my students were a select few from the advanced students of English at the university, but gradually word of my lectures made the rounds of other institutes and some of the most interesting students appeared from their faculties. I spoke each week about an American poet who had come into prominence since World War II. At the American Embassy I copied out poems which were avidly read, studied, and passed around. Each week after my lecture Sonja and I would leave to visit another part of the Soviet Union. One of the most interesting trips was to Siberia. In Irkutsk I spoke at a television station to a large gathering of students and there was a long question period afterwards. We visited Lake Baikal, the deepest lake

on earth and one of the wonders of the world, and then went on to Novosibirsk, where I was welcomed back by students and professors familiar with my work and also that of other American poets. Apparently my poems are still popular in Novosibirsk because just last year Kathryn Crosby (Mrs. Bing Crosby), who had been there playing in Chekhov's *The Sea Gull*, told me, on her return, that a musical based on my children's poems was playing to packed houses at the Red Torch Theatre there. She kindly brought me a cassette of some of the songs. It was wonderful to feel that I had given pleasure to people so far away and in a most inhospitable place. On our return to Moscow, I gave other readings with poets Voznesensky, Yevtushenko, Bella Akhmadulina, Ionna Morits, all of whom translated poems of mine that were collected in a volume edited by Andrei Voznesensky and entitled *What Train Will Come?* My last visit to Moscow was in 1990 when I joined some seventy-five other writers from all over the world whom Voznesensky had arranged to invite to celebrate the centenary of his mentor Boris Pasternak.

With students at a television studio in Irkutsk, Siberia, April, 1981

In 1970 when I left the Soviet Union I continued on to visit Poland, Romania, and finally Hungary. In the latter I made connections with some Hungarian poets that would last for many years. In Budapest Dr. László Kéry, Secretary of the Hungarian PEN Club, and Miklós Vajda, editor of *The New Hungarian Quarterly,* asked me if I would be willing to return with my wife, all expenses paid, to assist in the translation of Hungarian poetry. I protested that I knew no Hungarian and that I was too busy to study it. They said that that didn't matter. For far too long, they said, Hungarian poetry, which is the country's major literary genre, had been translated into English by people who knew both languages but who were not poets. Now they wanted to enlist the help of British and American poets, even though they knew no Hungarian, so that the resulting translations would be poetry. I knew instinctively that they were right. The translation of poetry is fundamentally impossible. Poetry must be translated by poets; they have a way of understanding one another whatever the difficulties of language.

Translation by more than one person is fraught with difficulty. If, as has been said, a camel is a horse designed by a committee, the joint translation can often also produce strange results. Writing is a lonely art, and in the end the poet-translator must work in isolation to recreate the translated poem with the same undivided attention that he gives to the creation of his own poetry. But the isolated end process is preceded by consultation with the informant, and here joint translation efforts so often flounder. The informant must not only know both languages perfectly but he must have a special grasp of poetry in both languages and a strong feeling for poetry in general. Ideally he should, like the translator, know a third or even a fourth language so that the equivalents of the words of the poem in question may be weighed precisely and measured from more than one angle. The Hungarian informants with whom I have worked have all met these requirements superbly, and in my collaboration with them over a period of years I have been rewarded with insights into Hungarian poetry and into the nature and poetic qualities of the Hungarian language.

In April 1970, on my return to Washington, I was host to eight foreign poets for an International Poetry Festival. The participants and their translators were: Jorge Carrera Andrade, from Ecuador (translator John Malcolm Brinnin); Nicanor Parra, from Chile (translator, Miller Williams), Yehuda Amichai, from Israel; Francis Ponge, from France (translators, Donald Finkel and Serge Gavronsky); Philippe Thoby-Marcelin, from Haiti; Vasko Popa, from Yugoslavia; Zulfikar Ghose, from Pakistan, reading in English; and Shuntaro Tanikawa, from Japan (translator, Harold P. Wright). Two venerable former Consultants also participated. Allen Tate delivered a lecture on the influence of permissiveness on creativity and the poet's need for rules and boundaries. "We are now in an age of great translations," he said. "I think this is indisputable but . . . good translations are never obsolete. George Chapman's rhymed decasyllable translation of the *Odyssey* is as good as it was in 1615, and I submit that Robert Fitzgerald's free blank verse translation is as good as Chapman's. Do we need both? I think we do. . . ." On Wednesday morning, Louis Untermeyer led a panel discussion on the difficulties of transmitting the magic of poetry in translation. The audience included poets, teachers, and editors from all over the country. On Wednesday afternoon, a tour of the White House and tea with Mrs. Nixon were the feature; and

With children's poet Boris Zakhoder at Kamarovka, near Moscow, 1981

the First Lady's staff had consulted the Poetry Office about a suitable gift for the visitors. I suggested copies of a facsimile edition of *Leaves of Grass* that had been published by the New York Public Library, at thirty dollars each. The White House considered this outlay excessive, and decided to present copies of Elizabeth Bishop's collected poems, newly published and prominently reviewed. The publishers contributed eight copies, which Mrs. Nixon autographed and handed to the visitors as she greeted them, lined up alphabetically in a receiving line. Some of the poets weren't aware they were meeting Mrs. Nixon and supposed she was Elizabeth Bishop. Fortunately, there were no gaffes. The press in attendance suggested that someone come up with a poem. Untermeyer, ever resourceful, offered an impromptu "Ode to the Miniskirt":

> I think that I shall never see
> A poem as lovely as a knee.

To which I added:

> And if the miniskirt should fall
> I may not see a knee at all.

It was a successful festival, in spite of a bit of political embarrassment for one participant when a photograph of him shaking hands with Mrs. Nixon was published in his country.

I now live in the small town of Cummington, Massachusetts, in the Berkshires. Our house, the Bryant Cottage, on a mountainside overlooking a beautiful valley, was once part of the William Cullen Bryant homestead, the birthplace of the poet. It served as the medical office of the poet's father and it is said that in a drawer of this office the poet at the age of seventeen placed a copy of his famous poem "Thanatopsis." The house was detached from the homestead in the middle of the last century and moved to another part of the mountain. Mrs. William Vaughn Moody, the wife of the Chicago poet, bought it in 1910 and moved it yet again. She restored it and organized a writers colony here in the twenties and thirties. Many well-known poets—Robert Frost, Edwin Arlington Robinson, Padraic Colum, and Rabindrinath Tagore—came here to read their poems in a log cabin in the woods nearby which is today in ruins. When I view it on my walks, it calls up a rich poetic past, about which I knew nothing when I bought the house in 1966. My stepson Marc has de-

signed our addition to the house and Sonja, with her exquisite taste, has decorated it. Many poets have come to visit and enjoy Sonja's inimitable French cooking, among them Andrei Voznesensky and Bella Akhmadulina from Russia, and Thorkild Bjørnvig from Denmark. Marc, who is Superintendent of Buildings and Grounds at the YMCA camp in Becket, Massachusetts, lives just down the hill from us with his wife Deborah and their two children Marissa and Alexandre, for whom several of my recent books have been written. My son Gregory, a talented sculptor who works in welded steel, lives nearby in Vermont. I am always fascinated to see his work as it develops in a medium so different from mine. I see my son David, for whom I wrote *Laughing Time,* in New York whenever I go there.

I'd like to conclude with a poem that might better have served as an introduction. It is a self-portrait based on the famous self-portrait of Edward Lear, the laureate of nonsense, which begins:

> How pleasant to know Mr. Lear!
> Who has written such volumes of stuff!

T. S. Eliot wrote his version, which begins:

> How unpleasant to meet Mr. Eliot!
> With his features of clerical cut.

My poem is humorous but it has a tragic edge to it, as does Edward Lear's, and I have incorporated in it a line of Lear's:

> He weeps by the side of the ocean.

It may indeed have been that one line that started me off for I was staying at the time at Le Lavandou in the south of France in a house looking out on the Mediterranean. Returning one afternoon from a walk on the beach below, I sat down at my desk, and, as rarely happens, the poem came pouring out almost exactly as it is. It came so readily I think because I had always wanted to write something that made a playful use of my name. Smith is the most common proper name in English and one that is easily recognized abroad. Perhaps because the name lends itself to humor, the poem has been translated into several languages. I read it often to school children and when I

The author reading his poems at the Hungarian PEN Club, Budapest, 1981

do, I ask them to try writing their own self-portraits. Although the task is not as easy as it looks, they sometimes come up with quite amazing results. *Roussette* is the French name for a flying fox or fox-bat found in the South Pacific. Because *roussettes* feed only on fruit their flesh is tasty, as I discovered when I ate them in the New Hebrides during World War II, thinking that I was eating rabbit or chicken and horrified to discover that I had been feeding on bats.

Mr. Smith

How rewarding to know Mr. Smith,
  Whose writings at random appear!
Some think him a joy to be with
  While others do not, it is clear.

His eyes are somewhat Oriental,
  His fingers are notably long;
His disposition is gentle,
  He will jump at the sound of a gong.

His chin is quite smooth and uncleft,
  His face is clean-shaven and bright,
His right arm looks much like his left,
  His left leg it goes with his right.

He has friends in the arts and the sciences;
  He knows only one talent scout;
He can cope with most kitchen appliances,
  But in general prefers dining out.

When young he collected matchboxes,
  He now collects notebooks and hats;
He has eaten *roussettes* (flying foxes),
  Which are really the next thing to bats!

He has never set foot on Majorca,
  He has been to Tahiti twice,
But will seldom, no veteran walker,
  Take two steps when one will suffice.

He abhors motorbikes and boiled cabbage;
  Zippers he just tolerates;
He is wholly indifferent to cribbage,
  And cuts a poor figure on skates.

He weeps by the side of the ocean,
  And goes back the way that he came;
He calls out his name with emotion—
  It returns to him always the same.

It returns on the wind and he hears it
  While the waves make a rustle around;
The dark settles down, and he fears it,
  He fears its thin, crickety sound.

He thinks more and more as time passes,
  Rarely opens a volume on myth.
Until mourned by the tall prairie grasses,
  How rewarding to know Mr. Smith!

BIBLIOGRAPHY

FOR CHILDREN

Poetry:

Laughing Time, illustrated by Juliet Kepes, Little, Brown/Atlantic Monthly Press, 1955, Faber, 1956.

Boy Blue's Book of Beasts, illustrated by Juliet Kepes, Little, Brown, 1957.

Puptents and Pebbles: A Nonsense ABC, illustrated by Juliet Kepes, Little, Brown, 1959, Faber, 1960.

(Self-illustrated) *Typewriter Town,* Dutton, 1960.

What Did I See?, illustrated by Don Almquist, Crowell Collier, 1962.

My Little Book of Big and Little (Little Dimity, Big Gumbo, Big and Little), illustrated by Don Bolognese, Rutledge, 3 vols., 1963.

Ho for a Hat!, illustrated by Ivan Chermayeff, Little, Brown, 1964, revised edition illustrated by Lynn Munsinger, 1989.

If I Had a Boat, illustrated by Don Bolognese, Macmillan, 1966, World's Work, 1967.

Mr. Smith and Other Nonsense, illustrated by Don Bolognese, Delacorte, 1968.

Around My Room and Other Poems, illustrated by Don Madden, Lancelot Press, 1969.

Laughing Time and Other Poems, illustrated by Don Madden, Lancelot Press, 1969.

Grandmother Ostrich and Other Poems, illustrated by Don Madden, Lancelot Press, 1969.

Laughing Time: Nonsense Poems, illustrated by Fernando Krahn, Delacorte, 1980.

The Key, illustrated by Erik Blegvad, Children's Book Council, 1982.

Birds and Beasts, illustrated by Jacques Hnizdovsky, Godine, 1990.

Laughing Time: Collected Nonsense, illustrated by Fernando Krahn, Farrar, Straus, 1990.

Big and Little, illustrated by Don Bolognese, Boyds Mill Press, 1992.

Editor:

(With Louise Bogan) *The Golden Journey: Poems for Young People,* illustrated by Fritz Kredel, Reilly & Lee, 1965, Evans, 1967, revised edition, Contemporary Books, 1990.

Poems from France, illustrated by Roger Duvoisin, Crowell, 1967.

Poems from Italy, illustrated by Elaine Raphael, Crowell, 1972.

A Green Place: Modern Poems, illustrated by Jacques Hnizdovsky, Delacorte, 1982.

(With Carol Ra) *Behind the King's Kitchen: A Roster of Rhyming Riddles,* illustrated by Jacques Hnizdovsky, Boyds Mills Press, 1992.

Translator:

Elsa Beskow, *Children of the Forest,* illustrated by Beskow, Delacorte, 1970.

Lennart Hellsing, *The Pirate Book,* illustrated by Poul Ströyer, Delacorte, and Benn, 1972.

(With Max Hayward) Kornei Chukovsky, *The Telephone,* illustrated by Blair Lent, Delacorte, 1977.

Federico García Lorca, *Songs of Childhood,* illustrated by John DePol, Stone House Press, 1994.

FOR ADULTS

Poetry:

Poems, Banyan Press, 1947.

Celebration at Dark, Hamish Hamilton, and Farrar, Straus, 1950.

Snow, Schlosser Paper Corp., 1953.

The Stork: A Poem Announcing the Safe Arrival of Gregory Smith, Caliban Press, 1954.

Typewriter Birds, Caliban Press, 1954.

The Old Man on the Isthmus, privately printed, 1957.

The Bead Curtain: Calligrams, privately printed, 1957.

Poems 1947–1957, Little, Brown, 1957.

Two Poems, Mason Hill Press, 1959.

A Minor Ode to the Morgan Horse, privately printed, 1961.

Prince Souvanna Phouma: An Exchange Between Richard Wilbur and William Jay Smith, Chapel Press, 1963.

Morels, privately printed, 1964.

Quail in Autumn, privately printed, 1965.

A Clutch of Clerihews, privately printed, 1966.

The Tin Can and Other Poems, Delacorte, 1966.

Winter Morning, privately printed, 1967.

Imaginary Dialogues, privately printed, 1968.

Hull Bay, St. Thomas, privately printed, 1970.

New and Selected Poems, Delacorte Press, 1970.

A Rose for Katherine Anne Porter, Albondocani Press, 1970.

At Delphi: For Allen Tate on His Seventy-Fifth Birthday, 19 November 1974, Chapel Press, 1974.

Venice in the Fog, Unicorn Press, 1975.

Song for a Country Wedding, privately printed, 1976.

(With Richard Wilbur) *Verses on the Times,* Gutenberg Press, 1978.

Journey to the Dead Sea: A Poem, Abattoir, 1979.

The Tall Poets, Palaemon Press, 1979.

Mr. Smith, Delacorte, 1980.

The Traveler's Tree: New and Selected Poems, Persea, 1980, Carcanet, 1981.

Oxford Doggerel, privately printed, 1983.

Collected Translations: Italian, French, Spanish, Portuguese, New Rivers Press, 1985.

The Tin Can, Stone House Press, 1988.

Journey to the Interior, Stone House Press, 1988.

Plain Talk: Epigrams, Epitaphs, Satires, Nonsense, Occasional, Concrete and Quotidian Poems, Center for Book Arts, 1988.

Collected Poems, 1939–1989, Scribner, 1990.

The Cyclist, Stone House Press, 1995.

Also author of Christmas card poems with Barbara Howes, all privately printed: *Lachrymae Christi and In the Old Country,* 1948; *Poems: The Homecoming and The Piazza,* 1949; and *Two French Poems: The Roses of Saadi and Five Minute Watercolor,* 1950.

Plays:

The Straw Market (comedy), music by the author, produced in Washington, DC, 1965, Hollins College, VA, 1966, New York, 1969.

Army Brat: A Dramatic Narrative for Three Voices (based on Smith's *Army Brat: A Memoir*), produced in New York City, 1980.

Editor:

(And translator) *Selected Writings of Jules Laforgue,* Grove Press, 1956.

Herrick, New York, Dell, 1962.

Witter Bynner, *Light Verse and Satires,* Farrar, Straus, and Faber, 1978.

(With Emanuel Brasil) *Brazilian Poetry 1950–1980,* Wesleyan University Press, 1983, Harper, 1984.

(With J. S. Holmes) *Dutch Interior: Post-War Poetry of the Netherlands and Flanders,* Columbia University Press, 1984.

(With Dana Gioia) *Poems from Italy,* New Rivers Press, 1985.

(With F. D. Reeve) *An Arrow in the Wall: Selected Poetry and Prose of Andrei Voznesensky,* Holt, and Secker & Warburg, 1987.

Nina Cassian, *Life Sentence: Selected Poems,* Norton, Anvil Press, 1990.

Translator:

Romualdo Romano, *Scirroco,* Farrar, Straus, 1951.

Valery Larbaud, *Poems of a Multimillionaire,* Bonaccio & Saul, 1955.

Two Plays by Charles Bertin: Christopher Columbus and Don Juan, University of Minnesota Press, 1970.

Szabolcs Várady, *Chairs above the Danube,* privately printed, 1976.

Andrei Voznesensky, *Saga,* privately printed, 1977.

(With Leif Sjöberg) Artur Lundkvist, *Agadir,* International Poetry Forum, 1979.

(With Ingvar Schousboe) Thorkild Bjørnvig, *The Pact: My Friendship with Isak Dinesen,* Louisiana State University Press, 1983, Souvenir Press, 1984.

Jules Laforgue, *Moral Tales,* New Directions, 1985, Picador, 1987.

(With Leif Sjöberg) Henry Martinson, *Wild Bouquet: Nature Poems,* Bookmark Press, 1985.

(With Edwin Morgan and others) Sandor Weöres, *Eternal Moment: Selected Poems,* New Rivers Press, and Anvil Press, 1988.

(With Sonja Haussmann Smith) Tchicaya U Tam'Si, *The Madman and the Medusa,* University Press of Virginia, 1989.

(With others) *Window on the Black Sea: Bulgarian Poetry in Translation,* 2nd edition, Carnegie-Mellon University Press, 1992.

Christopher Columbus, illustrated by John DePol, Stone House Press, 1992.

Other:

The Spectra Hoax (criticism), Wesleyan University Press, 1961.

The Skies of Venice, Andre Emmerich Gallery, 1961.

(With Virginia Haviland) *Children and Poetry: A Selective, Annotated Bibliography,* Library of Congress, 1969, revised edition, 1979.

Louise Bogan: A Woman's Words, Library of Congress, 1972.

The Streaks of the Tulip: Selected Criticism, Delacorte Press, 1972.

Green, Washington University Libraries, 1980.

Army Brat: A Memoir, Persea, 1980, Penguin, 1982, Story Line Press, 1991.

Cumulative Index

CUMULATIVE INDEX

The names of essayists who appear in the series are in boldface type. Subject references are followed by volume and page number(s). When a subject reference appears in more than one essay, names of the essayists are also provided.

INDEX

INDEX